Michael Twaddle
Eastbourne, 2007

THE OPENING OF THE NILE BASIN

Kirchner

Morlang

Comboni

Knoblecher

Kaciual

Logwit

Beltrame

THE OPENING
OF THE
NILE
BASIN

Writings by Members of the
Catholic Mission to Central Africa
on the Geography and Ethnography
of the Sudan
1842 - 1881

EDITED BY

ELIAS TONIOLO

AND

RICHARD HILL

BARNES & NOBLE
BOOKS
10 East 53d St., New York 10022
(a division of Harper & Row Publishers, Inc.)

Published in the U.S.A. 1975 by
HARPER & ROW PUBLISHERS, INC.
BARNES & NOBLE IMPORT DIVISION

© C. Hurst & Co. (Publishers) Ltd., London, 1974

ISBN 0-06-496933-9

Printed in Great Britain

CONTENTS

		page
Preface		v
Introduction: the Historical Background		1

KHARTOUM

I. Khartoum, Description of a Changing City
Khartoum in 1843 *by Luigi Montuori* — 31
Khartoum in 1853 *by Giovanni Beltrame* — 35
Khartoum in 1858 *by Alessandro Dal Bosco* — 38
Khartoum in 1881 *by Bartolomeo Rolleri* — 41

THE WHITE NILE

II. The Official Journal of the Missionary Expedition in 1849-1850 *by Ignaz Knoblecher* — 47

III. A Report on the Voyage of 1849-1850 *by E. Pedemonte* — 55

IV. *Angelo Vinco*, first Christian to live among the Bari. His Journeys 1851-1852 — 74

V. The White Nile, its People and its Source, the State of European Knowledge in 1851 *by L.G. Massaia* — 106

VI. The Journeys of *Franz Morlang* East and West of Gondokoro in 1859 — 109

VII. On the White Nile from Khartoum to Gondokoro 1850-1860 *by G. Beltrame* — 129

VIII. The White Nile Valley and its Inhabitants *by A. Kaufmann* — 140

IX. A Dinka Priest Writing on his own People *by Daniel Deng Farim Sorur* — 196

THE BLUE NILE

X. Khartoum to the Gold Workings of Fāzūghlī, 1851 *by L.G. Massaia* — 207

XI. Up the Blue Nile Valley from Sinnār to Banī Shanqūl and Back, 1854-1855 *by Giovanni Beltrame* — 219

XII. From Khartoum to al-Qallābāt and Fāzūghlī, 1876-7 *by G. Martini* — 249

NUBIA

		page
XIII.	Nubia in 1861 *by Giovanni Beltrame*	261

THE NUBA MOUNTAINS

| XIV. | In the Nuba Mountains, 1873 *by S. Carcereri* | 283 |
| XV. | People and Government in the Nuba Mountains *by G. Martini* | 293 |

THE DESERT ROADS

XVI.	Kurusku to Khartoum, 1851 *by L.G. Massaia*	303
XVII.	Sawākin to Berber, 1876 *by S. Carcereri*	313
Index		321

MAPS

	facing page
The White Nile, 1860	47
North-Eastern Sudan, 1842-1881	207
Kurdufān and Gebel Nuba	283

PREFACE

These writings, chosen to illustrate the contribution of the members of the Catholic Mission to Central Africa to the geography and ethnography of the Sudan, are only a small part of the total literary output of the missionaries during the first half-century of their contact with the Sudanese people. Except in passing, these contributions do not include examples of the missionaries' important work in Sudanese linguistics. Nor do they bear directly on religion, or on the foundation of a Christian community in the Sudan which has been a joint work shared by several Christian bodies of which the Catholics, in point of time and numbers, are the senior partners. We have stopped short at 1881 because by that year most of the major blanks on the map of the Nile basin had been filled and ethnography was passing from a pioneering to a more sophisticated stage, and the new science of anthropology, in which the missionaries were to take a significant part, was born. The reader who wishes to explore further into these fields should consult the bibliography of the mission, *Bibliografia di studi africani delle Missioni dell'Africa Centrale* (Verona, 1948), compiled by Fr. Stefano Santandrea, a fundamental work of reference which deserves a new edition.

To call these missionary writers amateurs is not to denigrate them, for they anticipated the professionals on the Upper Nile. It would be wrong to dismiss their writings as the leisure-hour diversions of clerics whose real interests lay elsewhere. Their journeys and their studies of peoples and languages were essential equipment for their apostolate. In the course of their missionary travels Ignaz Knoblecher and Angelo Vinco got nearer to the source of the White Nile than any other Europeans thirteen years before Speke and Grant, coming from the South, announced that they had uncovered — at least for the world outside Africa what Kenyans and Ugandans knew already — the secret of the Nile's springs. In much of their geographical and ethnographical work, and in their studies in African languages, they were forerunners. Their role was exploratory and preliminary; others who followed them built upon their intellectual foundations.

Unlike the two British explorers, the missionaries were not engaged primarily in geographical discovery. Because of their poverty they were woefully short of scientific apparatus; Knoblecher, by talent and temperament an explorer, apologised for the deficiency of his observations, limited as they were by the primitive equipment at his hand. The money given to the missionaries by the Christian communities in Europe and America was for the founding of missions and schools, not for geographical exploration. If Knoblecher, Vinco and Morlang, to name only three, had received some of the massive aid later given to Sir Samuel Baker and H.M. Stanley, and if they could conveniently have forgotten their vocation, they might well have been the first Europeans to reach the source of the White Nile.

What is remarkable about the missionaries is their continuing enthusiasm for the sciences in the face of poverty, discouragement, discomfort, fever and death. They were nearly all young men. Intellectually they were extremely tough. In the tradition of Knoblecher, a founder of the mission, Bishop Comboni, shared with the juniors his own interest in exploration. He drew up for his researches a list of African explorers and writers on Africa, including many whom he had himself known,[1] a document recalling Sir Harry Johnston's later 'roll of fame of those who started on the Nile quest in modern days', printed at the end of his book *The Nile Quest* (London, 1905). When news of the lonely death of the explorer Giovanni Miani beyond the Nile-Congo watershed in December 1872 at last reached Khartoum, the Bishop composed and signed this entry in the parish register of the Khartoum Mission — a generous epitaph to a difficult, if brave, man from one who was himself to die from the exhaustion of travel:

Giovanni Miani
A scientific explorer
Venetian-born
A celebrated, most daring Knight
of the Order of Saints Maurice and Lazarus
who, two years ago, set out from Khartoum
and travelling by way of Abu Kuka penetrated
the interior traversing the Niam-Niam tribes
to reach the province of Monbuttu
Arrived at the settlement of Gurgur
at the 3rd degree of North Latitude he
was attacked by fever and
deprived of all human help

[1] *Archivio Comboniano*, Roma, X, 1972, 1-2, pp. 40-1.

he died without the light of the Cross
We at Khartoum have been informed that he died
in December 1872 [2]

The price which the missionaries paid in human lives was high.
At a time before the true cause of malaria was understood and tropical
medicine itself was in its early infancy, we should however be cautious
in blaming the missionaries for their neglect of medical precautions.
Bishop Comboni, as we shall see, was only too acutely aware of the
problem of health in the tropics. In proportion to their numbers the
European merchants on the White Nile suffered almost as much in
death and disablement. And it is as well to remember that the
missionaries had their own order of priorities in which care for their
own physical welfare was decidedly second.

The missionaries spoke and wrote German or Italian, the native
languages of most of them. Some were masters of both tongues. A
few — Franz Morlang among them — came from deep Alpine valleys
with ancient memories where they learnt Ladin in the cradle and
German later, at school. Several, like Mgr. Knoblecher and Bartolomäus
Mozgan, were Slovenes who added a Slav language to their repertory.
In their hands the Latin of the parish registers courageously coped
with African proper names. As each missionary author and writer used
his own national or personal system of spelling Arabic and African
words, we have tried to adopt a rough consistency of transliteration in
preparing these texts for publication. For Arabic place-names we have
used the only modern gazetteer to have full regard for Arabic spellings:
*Sudan, Official Standard Names approved by the United States Board
of Geographic Names* (Gazetteer No. 69, Washington, D.C., 1962).

Words rapidly change their meanings and their nuances. A word
used correctly and spontaneously in 1853 could by the 1970s have

[2] A pallid reflection of the Bishop's original Latin:
EXPLORATOR SCIENTIFICVS
VENETIIS NATVS
CELEBERRIMVS AVDACISSIMVSQVE
EQVES STI. MAVRITII ET LAZARI DOMINVS
QVI JAM A DVOBVS ANNIS CHARTVMIO PROFECTVS
PER ABV KVKA IN INTERIORIS PLAGAS INGREDIENS
PER NIAMNIAM TRIBVS
PERTRANSIENS IN MONBVTV PROVINCIAM PERVENERAT
IN ZARIBA GVRGVR AD TERTIVM GRADVM LATITVDINIS
SEPTENTRIONALIS FEBRI CORREPTVS
NECNON HVMANIS DESTITVTVS AVXILIIS...
SINE LVCE ET SINE CRVCE DIEM SVPREMVM OBIIT
DE CVJVS MORTE IN MENSE DECEMBRIS 1872
CERTIORES CHARTVMII FACTI SVMVS

become a pejorative. The missionaries wrote to inform their contemporaries and used language appropriate to their time; they did not write to flatter us with euphemisms. They could not have known, for example, that the Italian word *selvaggio* (English, savage) would one day become a term which no educated or sensitive person would like to use to describe a Southern Sudanese, nor could they have foretold that, in English at least, the rational, precise term, native, for one born and bred in a place, would become unfashionable through misuse. So too their use of negro (German *Neger*) which the missionaries employed comprehensively to describe any dark-skinned African, has not survived the researches of modern ethnologists who teach us that the racial mosaic in Africa cannot be confined by so restrictive a term. Consequently in our preparation of these narratives we have generally, though not invariably, replaced these dated words by currently acceptable equivalents.

We are deeply in the debt of many friends for their help in lessening the deficiencies of our editing. In particular we thank the following for their guidance in matters of tribal customs and nomenclature: Natale Akolawin, Trinity College, Oxford, for the Shilluk, Akolda M. Tier, Jesus College, Cambridge, and Alier R. Makol, University of Hamburg, for the Dinka and their ramifications, and Dunstan Wai, himself the editor of *The Southern Sudan and the Problem of National Integration* (London, 1973), for the Bari and their neighbours. We are grateful to Professor J.R. Gray for reading our typescript and making valuable suggestions for its improvement, and Dr. G.E. Wickens of the Royal Botanic Gardens, Kew, for bringing some order into the botanical names abounding in our text.

THE HISTORICAL BACKGROUND

Men's work cannot be separated from their lives. As the travels and studies of the missionaries were inseparable from their duties we introduce these selected examples of their writings by a brief history of the Catholic Mission to Central Africa.

A Vincentian Contribution

In May 1842 Fr. Luigi Montuori, a refugee from religious persecution in Ethiopia, arrived in Khartoum. Here he opened the first Catholic church and the first Catholic school in the city. He obtained from the Turco-Egyptian government of the Sudan, through the good offices of Blondeel van Cuelebroeck, Consul General of the newly-created Kingdom of the Belgians, with whom he had travelled from Ethiopia, a plot of land for a Christian cemetery. The cheerful narrative of Montuori's doings in Khartoum forms the first part of Chapter I below.

But the odds against this lone pioneer were overwhelming. Though the Governor-General, Ahmad Pasha abū Adhān, was helpful, he received little encouragement and much hostility from the Christians in Khartoum whose commercial activities may well have caused them to view the presence of a Christian missionary with some embarrassment. The arrival of a second Vincentian priest, Fr. G. Serao, from Italy, failed to save the mission. Montuori abandoned Khartoum in September 1845 and Serao followed him. Clearly the founding of a mission in Khartoum was beyond the strength of two unsupported refugee priests.

Foundation of the Apostolic Vicariate of Central Africa

The abandonment was however only temporary. A decree of Pope Gregory XVI of 3 April 1846 established the Apostolic Vicariate of Central Africa. The objects of the 'Mission to Central Africa', thus formally approved, were: the conversion of the Africans to Christianity, the bringing of assistance to the Christians who were in the Sudan as

1

traders and officials, and the suppression of the slave trade. The boundaries allotted to the Vicariate were: Egypt, Tripolitania and Algeria to the north and north-west; the Red Sea and Abyssinia to the east; the Mountains of the Moon to the south; the Two Guineas and the Sahara to the West.

Fr. Maximilian Ryllo, S.J., a Pole, already a missionary in Syria, was appointed head of the first missionary expedition. His companions were Bishop Annetto Casolani, a Maltese who had been elected Vicar-Apostolic because he was the first to conceive the founding of the mission but later resigned the leadership in favour of Ryllo; Fr. Emanuele Pedemonte, S.J., Dr. Ignaz Knoblecher, a Slovene, and Fr. Angelo Vinco, an Italian from Verona, completed the party. Muhammad 'Alī Pasha, the Ottoman Viceroy of Egypt, facilitated the coming of the missionaries to his dominions. In the spring of 1847 the missionary party assembled at Alexandria. Salīm Qapūdān whom Muhammad 'Alī had entrusted with the command of three voyages in 1839-42 up the White Nile in an endeavour to discover its source gave valuable, if somewhat unscientific, advice on the country ahead. More precise data were brought back by a French engineer, J.P. d'Arnaud Bey, who had served on two of Salīm's voyages.

Fr. Ryllo was granted an audience by the Viceroy and his son, Ibrāhīm Pasha who, some years before, during the Egyptian occupation of Syria, had put a price on the Jesuit's head for having encouraged the Christians of Mount Lebanon to resist oppression. Fr. Ryllo had a competent command of Arabic, and he soon won the respect of Muhammad 'Alī, who gave him letters of recommendation to the governors and chiefs of the Egyptian-occupied Sudan. About Christmas 1847 the expedition reached Dongola by *dhahabīya*, then crossed the Bayuda desert by camel. On 11 February 1848, Fr. Ryllo and his companions entered Khartoum.

The Khartoum Mission estimated that the city contained 15,000 inhabitants, most of whom were slaves. [1] The missionaries were first the guests of al-Sharīf Hasan, a local Muslim merchant, then they settled under tents along the bank of the Blue Nile. Life was not ideal. Their health and financial condition soon became serious, almost tragic. 'Our expedition resembles a hospital', wrote Knoblecher in 1850, 'and our means are exhausted'.

[1] These were for the most part domestic servants rather than chattel slaves of the American plantations type (*See* 'Abbās Ibrāhīm Muhammad 'Alī, *The British, the Slave Trade and Slavery in the Sudan, 1820-1881*, Khartoum, 1972, p. 13.

Yet Khartoum was chosen as the base of the future mission. No other place seemed so suitable for the missionaries to secure communications with the centre of Africa, to draw up projects concerning the method of their apostolic work, to learn and transcribe the language of the more important tribes and to study their customs. al-Sharīf Hasan gave valuable help to the missionaries. He bought a property for them situated within the town limits on the bank of the Blue Nile, west of the Governor-General's residence. Though the Mission has long since moved to other sites, a section of the east wall of what were possibly the schoolrooms still stands near the junction of Malik avenue and Jamīʻ avenue. Part of the mission building, constructed in 1853-6, was incorporated by the Condominium government in what was until recently the city District Commissioner's office.

On 17 June 1848, Fr. Ryllo, Pro-Vicar, died of fever and dysentery. He ceded his power as Pro-Vicar to Dr. Knoblecher. Mgr. Casolani also was in bad health; he was repatriated with Fr. Vinco, who was sent to Europe to seek financial help. A Veronese priest, Nicola Mazza, promised him help with missionary personnel. On the feast of Pentecost the first church of the mission was opened in Khartoum. A school for African children bought in the slave market was also instituted.

The political revolutions which swept through Europe in 1848-9 bore heavily on the newly-founded mission. At Rome where there was street fighting culminating in a full-scale siege, the Sacred College of Propaganda declared that it was no longer in a position to help the missionaries and gave them leave to abandon the mission. Financial help failed almost completely. It was a grim prospect which faced the tiny group living anxiously on the Blue Nile bank at Khartoum. Johann Dichtl was right when he wrote in his story of those days that, without Knoblecher at the head, the mission to Central Africa would not have existed after 1848.

The missionaries held on. Being both energetic and poor they transformed the land round their house into an orchard and garden for feeding the mission school pupils and themselves. The orchard flourished and over the years became a noteworthy feature of the capital and a series of visitors, like George Melly of Liverpool, relished its yield and recorded in their journals the baskets of figs, bananas, pomegranates and cream-fruit [1] from the Mission garden. [2] The tide was turning. The European community which had rebuffed Montuori now experienced

---

[1] i.e., custard apple, Arabic *qishta* (*Annona reticulata*).

[2] G. Melly, *Khartoum and the Blue and White Niles*, 1951, II, p. 91.

somewhat of a change of heart. Reinforcements at last came from Rome when Mgr. Casolani obtained from the General of the Jesuits two priests, Fr. Gaetano Zara and Fr. Giuseppe Repetti and a lay brother. Half way through 1849, when the need was still extreme, help arrived from Ljubljana, the native city of several Slovene missionaries in the Sudan.

Reading, writing, arithmetic, music and handwork were taught in the school. In 1850 the British trader, John Petherick, wrote of the Khartoum Mission:

> The only stone edifice is that occupied by the Roman Catholic Mission for the intended conversion of the negroes.... It is handsomely constructed and contains a neat church and school-room. The former is attended during Divine Service by members of the institution and the Europeans. The school is for the education of the negro children, who have been principally supplied from negro families on the White Nile. A few of the Europeans, and Copts, who have families, availed themselves of this establishment for their children's education. Situated about five hundred yards from the river, the space between it and the stream is laid out in a fine garden containing delicious fruit trees and luxuriant shrubberies.

Melly added: 'We examined their pretty little chapel and their school with equal interest.

'The latter consisted of about twenty boys in various costumes and of almost as many hues. Many of them are children of the European residents. Some can speak a little French and Italian, and nearly all can read and write.' The German geographer Carl Ritter wrote that the Catholic Mission intended to establish in Khartoum a day and a boarding school for boys of different negro tribes. In addition to the usual subjects they would be taught agriculture and handicrafts. After their training they would return to their tribes and become the instructors of their own people. [3] On this last point Bishop Comboni, in a report written twenty years later, stated: 'In 1848 the missionaries bought in the slave market many youths who looked intelligent.... They started to teach them the simplest things that would be useful to them in their country, among their tribesmen, whom they would have to lead to security.' On the other hand Dr. Knoblecher and his com-

[3] C. Ritter, 'Dr. Ignaz Knoblechers Reise auf dem weissen Flusse', *Monatsberichte d. Berliner Ges. für d. Orient'*, IX, 1852.

panions were disciples of their own pupils, as they endeavoured to learn the language of the different tribes; they also collected all the facts that could make known their character, habits and customs.

The Creation of Missions on the White Nile

Soon after the return of Don Angelo Vinco from Europe Knoblecher, not without difficulty, obtained permission from Khālid Pasha Khusrū, then Governor-General, to accompany the annual trading expedition up the White Nile in order to study the possibility of founding mission stations on the upper reaches of the river.

It must be explained here that the government objected to trading voyages on the White Nile by individual merchants, whether European or Turkish or Northern Sudanese, beyond the effective limits of Turco-Egyptian rule which at that time extended to about 150 miles upstream of Khartoum. Government not only insisted that the merchants should fit out a combined fleet, for which government provided an armed escort at the merchants' expense, but claimed a percentage of the trading profits on the return of the expedition to Khartoum.

Leaving Fr. Zara to look after the Mission in Khartoum Knoblecher accompanied by Vinco and Pedemonte sailed with the trading expedition on 13 November 1849. Selections from Knoblecher's and Pedemonte's reports on the voyage appear in Chapters II and III below. As their narratives abundantly prove, their forced association with the merchants and government officials frustrated them at every turn.

On 7 March 1850 the missionaries were back in Khartoum. Everything necessary for founding a mission station up-river was lacking: personnel, equipment and money. Knoblecher decided to return to Europe and seek help for his Mission. He founded in Vienna, with the assistance of Mgr. A. Agarian, a society, Der Marien-Verein zur Beförderung der katholischen Mission in Central Africa, for the purpose of collecting subscriptions for the mission. The young Emperor Franz Joseph received the Pro-Vicar kindly and helped him financially. The Emperor also took the mission under his protection and obtained from the Porte a *firman* which granted the mission to Central Africa the rights and privileges which Catholic missions enjoyed throughout the provinces of the Ottoman Empire.

In 1851 the Austrian government opened a vice-consulate in Khartoum, the first European Power to do so. The new vice-consul was instructed among his various duties to protect the interests of the mission. With less than his usual tact the Imperial and Royal Consul

General in Alexandria appointed a Protestant to the post. Consul Constantin Reitz was an energetic but sick man who was for long absent from his duties. On his death in 1853 he was succeeded by the naturalist and future Arctic explorer, Theodor von Heuglin, who in turn handed over the vice-consulate to Josef Natterer. The last of the protecting vice-consuls, Martin Ludwig Hansal, formerly Mgr. Knoblecher's secretary and a devout Christian, was appointed in 1862. Reitz and Natterer died of fever in the Sudan, Hansal was killed in the Mahdist rising; only von Heuglin left the Sudan alive.

These vice-consuls, whose salaries were small, were permitted to engage in private trade and by this fact embarrassed rather than assisted the mission. For the taint of indulging directly or indirectly in the slave traffic then hung over the entire merchant community on the Upper Nile.

With financial means now assured, Fr. Knoblecher went to Rome to report to Pope Pius IX. The death of Ryllo, the decrease in the revenue of Propaganda Fide owing to the political turmoil of 1848-9, as well as other causes, including a pessimistic report on the mission by Mgr. (afterwards Cardinal) Massaia, who had passed through Khartoum in 1851 on his way to Ethiopia, had contributed to persuade the Pope to sign a decree abolishing the Vicariate of Central Africa. On 10 August 1851, the Pope listened for over an hour to the missionary who pleaded for his mission.

The Pope, convinced by Fr. Knoblecher's pleading, revoked the decree and the mission was entrusted to Knoblecher as Pro-Vicar-Apostolic. At the end of August, Mgr. Knoblecher left for Africa. He brought with him funds and a group of Slovene missionaries: Frs. B. Mozgan, M. Dovjak, O. Trabant, J. Kocijancic, M. Milharcic and some laymen who were skilled craftsmen. In Cairo Knoblecher met with difficulties from the new Viceroy, 'Abbās Pasha, who would not at first recognise the *firman* from Constantinople, though finally he recognised it. From past experience of wood-hulled sailing craft on the White River, the Pro-Vicar bought an iron *dhahabīya*, 'for a moderate price' from Khayr al-Din Pasha, [4] and christened it *Stella Matutina*.

The party reached Khartoum in two groups: one by the Nubian desert, the other, led by Fr. Kocijancic, making the voyage by river over the cataracts on the Nile flood, a hazardous venture. Meanwhile, on 12 January 1851 Fr. Vinco had left Khartoum for the Bari country in a boat belonging to the Savoyard trader, Antoine Brun-Rollet. The

---

[4] Director of transport and dockyards, Egypt.

circumstances surrounding his journey were peculiar and for a lesser man would have been frustrating. The mission at that time had no money to hire him a boat or pay his passage up-river, so he accepted Brun-Rollet's offer of a free passage on one of his boats in return for helping to collect ivory. Mgr. Massaia, Vicar-Apostolic for the Galla, who was passing through Khartoum at the time, felt bound to criticise this arrangement but was unstinting in his praise of Vinco whom he likened to St. Francis Xavier. [5]

On 13 December 1852 Mgr. Knoblecher with Frs. Dovjak, Trabant and Mozgan sailed up the White Nile as far as Illibari where they arrived on 3 January of the New Year in what was for a sailing ship a remarkably quick voyage. Four days later Knoblecher went to Gondokoro and bought a piece of land from Chief Lutweri for a gourd-full of beads *kulya ti Bari*, according to the Bari custom. Several chiefs spoke on that occasion. The theme of their speeches was: 'The Stranger must buy a field for himself and his friends; he may grow trees on it and instruct our children; and because the Strangers have nothing in common with the robbers and murderers from foreign lands, the chiefs bind themselves to ensure that no one damages their possessions.' Anton Kaufmann who arrived at Gondokoro in 1857 and whose description of the Bari appears in Chapter 8 below recorded that Mgr. Knoblecher made an average fix of the latitude of Gondokoro at 4° . 54′ . 42″ N. a fair approximation to the Sudan Surveys figure of 4° . 54′ N, obtained with modern apparatus. According to Kaufmann 'the site is one of the best in the White Nile area. It enjoys a fairly healthy climate. It lacks, however, wood for fuel and for building, and the soil is sandy and unsuitable for agriculture.' Fr. Vinco died of fever on 22 January 1853, in the arms of Mgr. Knoblecher. Vinco had lived hard for almost two years at Libo among the Bari. He was the first missionary to die in the front line. The French consul and traveller, G. Lejean, wrote of him in 1860: 'A. Vinco was the perfect type of the Christian missionary in the Sudan ... he was adventurous, brave, gay and an excellent shot; he was greatly esteemed by the Bari, whose language he spoke.' His narrative of his travels in and beyond the Bari country and his relations with the people will be found in Chapter IV.

Mgr. Knoblecher planned soon to build a home for the missionaries, a school and a church; but skilled workers were wanting. 'All the technical knowledge acquired during leisure hours in college days was of great

[5] Ministère des affaires étrangères, Paris, Correspondance commerciale, Alexandrie, vol. 34, Massaia to consul-general A. Le Moyne, 12 Nov. 1851.

use to the missionaries. At one time they handled the trowel, at another the saw or the square; one would equip himself with an axe, another with a hammer, a third with a hoe, others with pick or spade . . . and the people watched and laughed.' Thus the work being started, Mgr. Knoblecher returned to Khartoum accompanied by Nyigilò. *

Knoblecher found the Khartoum mission flourishing. 'The Khartoum mission presents a picture of active life. Fr. Milharcic who has a gift for managing children, is in charge of the boys' school. Its forty pupils keep their master very busy. In our workshop we work from morning to night and make all the furniture necessary for the house.' In September 1853, Mgr. Knoblecher was in Alexandria to make purchases and await the arrival of new missionaries. These were six, including M.L. Hansal, teacher, printer and musician, from Vienna. On his way back, at Korosko, Mgr. Knoblecher was overtaken by two Italian missionaries, Frs. A. Castagnaro and G. Beltrame, who were coming to arrange for a possible mission to be entrusted to the Mazza Institute of Verona. The combined party sailed back to Khartoum from Berber. When they disembarked at Khartoum on 29 December 1853, they found Fr. Kocijancic dying. On 6 February 1854 Fr. Castagnaro died of dysentery in Khartoum.

Mgr. Knoblecher with a priest, Fr. I. Kohl, left for Gondokoro which they reached on 4 April. Here they learnt of the death of Martin Dovjak on 22 January and of Otto Trabant on 15 March. In the meantime a third priest, Bartolomäus Mozgan, had gone to establish a mission among the Cic Dinka near Abū Kūka between Shambe and Bor which he called Heilige Kreuz, Holy Cross, a spot which is known to this day and shown on modern maps in its Arabic form Kanīsa, from the Greek *ekklesia,* a church. Anton Kaufmann, a missionary from Holy Cross, describes the station in Chapter VIII.

At the same time an incident occurred in Gondokoro which threatened to undermine the work of the missionaries who, one after the other, were dying in the field. The missionaries frequently reported to Khartoum cases of oppression which called for justice from the Turkish government. European merchants were often accessories to these injustices. Among the forty boats that reached Gondokoro in 1854 were three belonging to the Sardinian Vice-Consul in Khartoum,

---

* Although Knoblecher with other missionaries and the traders considered that Nyigilò was an important chief, they were seriously misled in this opinion. Nyigilò was merely the brother of a rain chief, a ritual expert whose political authority was at least uncertain (R. Gray, *A History of the Southern Sudan, 1839-1889,* London, 1961, p. 43.

A. Vaudey. He intended to attack the Bari, but Mgr. Knoblecher dissuaded him from his mad design. On the evening of 5 April, one of Vaudey's boats anchored between the *Stella Matutina* and the mission garden. Its presence seemed to compromise the mission, causing the Bari to think that the mission was a party to the threatened attack.

Vaudey attributed all his misfortunes to the missionaries', wrote Mgr. Comboni. Two shots were fired from Vaudey's boat at the natives on the river bank, while firing also started up from Vaudey's other boats anchored near Libo. War drums were furiously beaten, while the Bari, howling terribly, hurled spears and shot arrows. Mgr. Knoblecher ordered the crew of the *Stella Matutina* not to fire. It was a bloody fight. The negroes carried their wounded to the missionaries. Vaudey himself fell dead pierced by a spear. His two nephews, Jules and Ambroise Poncet, barely escaped death. [6] Several chiefs, impressed by the peaceful attitude of the missionaries, came to Knoblecher after the fight to ask the missionaries to settle among them.

So Knoblecher went to the cataracts south of Garbo, Cumlo and Tokiman. But on 12 June Fr. Ignaz Kohl, after assisting a sick person, died a victim of his apostolic zeal. Knoblecher was compelled to return to Khartoum. He entrusted the Gondokoro mission to the old chief Lutweri now that there were no more missionaries to staff it. In Khartoum a rumour, as foolish as it was malicious, circulated that Mgr. Knoblecher had been eaten by the natives. While journeying on the Nile he visited all the boats he met en route to set free any slaves he found, availing himself of the powers given him by the Government. European as well as Arab merchants implicated in the trade bore him no good will.

The Khartoum Mission Building constructed

The construction of the big mission building in Khartoum was started in 1853. An Italian mason, Pietro Agati, who worked with the missssionaries, was the first since ancient times, to introduce into the Sudan the art of burning bricks. He found clay first at Omdurman then later at Soba. Over a thousand boatloads of stone and bricks were carried for the new construction. This work cost the missionaries much effort

---

[6] Vaudey's people attributed the fracas to the firing of a salute from Vaudey's own boats in honour of Knoblecher which caused accidental injury on the river bank.

and money; but the chief difficulty was the absence of lime which, only after several trials, was discovered along the Blue Nile. By the autumn of 1856 the fine brick and stone building was 104 metres long, only a third of the size of the structure planned. By 1859 the cost of the building had exceeded 500,000 francs. The local school flourished; mathematics, singing and drawing were included in the school cirriculum.

The trade school attracted the attention of Khartoum and its visitors. Many of its pupils afterwards found employment in the government workshops. On 28 October 1854, a fresh contingent of missionaries arrived; three priests and five lay brothers, among them a skilled foreman, Leonhard Koch. Mgr. Knoblecher left for Gondokoro with Fr. A. Ueberbacher and a lay brother. On 15th April they moored alongside the Bari mission among a cheering crowd. Travelling with the Pro-Vicar was the famous Nyigilò, the Bari notable who brought back a graphic account of the magnificence of the Turks at Khartoum where he had been on a visit. But there was famine among the Bari. Mgr. Knoblecher had with him two boats loaded with *durra*; the whole was distributed. Over forty poor were given shelter at the mission.

During his leisure Mgr. Knoblecher, a scholar by temperament with a natural bent for acquiring languages, translated prayers and hymns into Bari. There was a Bari boy named Logwit, who later helped Prof. J.C. Mitterrutzner of Brixen (Bressanone) in the transcription of the Bari language. Mitterrutzner gave the mission to Central Africa, financial and linguistic help as well as precious personnel. He prepared grammars and dictionaries in Dinka and Bari, [7] and translated catechisms into those tongues. Fr. Ueberbacher remained alone at Gondokoro, where he applied himself to the study of the Bari language, translated long extracts from the Gospels and the Epistles of St. Paul, wrote a brief Bible history, and composed various hymns in Bari.

In the annual Report of the Viennese missionary journal, *Marien-Verein* for 1855 we read 'The number of the school boys is now twenty-eight. Two of them have already gone to Malta with Mgr. Casolani; one has left for Holy Cross with Fr. Mozgan; seven are learning arts and crafts; four are preparing for higher studies; the other attend the school with several day-boys. Father Pro-Vicar thinks it would be good

---

[7] *Die Dinka-Sprache in Central Afrika,* Brixen, 1866; *Die Sprache der Bari,* 1867, of which Col. R.C.R. Owen published an unacknowledged version for English-speaking readers, entitled *Bari Grammar and Vocabulary,* London, 1908. F. Morlang contributed an appendix entitled *Kleines Vocabular der Sprache der Nyang-Bara,* which he compiled in 1859. The vocabulary is in fact of Moru words.

to send our best pupils to Europe for education . . . but in any case they will be sent in pairs so that they will not forget their native language or feel homesick.' The teacher M. Hansal writes: 'The final examination in August gave me much satisfaction. It was gratifying to see these little boys neatly dressed and disciplined. They could answer freely in Arabic (which was not their mother tongue) questions about many things which were unknown even to their chiefs. They could read the Arabic and Roman alphabets, write in Arabic and Italian, and do arithmetical exercises on the blackboard. At the end of their examination the pupils sang beautiful songs with much precision.'

Beltrame on the Blue Nile

Meanwhile Fr. G. Beltrame in Khartoum collected information about the places and languages of the peoples on the Blue Nile as far as Fāzūghlī. With the consent of the Pro-Vicar he undertook a journey among the tribes south-west of the Blue Nile in the southern Gezira. At Sinnār he was the guest of Dr. Alfred Peney, chief medical officer of health of the Sudan. From here he went to Karkūj and al-Rusayris. There he took three camels and three donkeys, and travelled as far as Banī Shanqūl. Beltrame was the third European to get so far, the first was J. Russegger, the second P. Trémaux. On 5 April 1855, Beltrame was back in Khartoum. In 1869 he wrote: 'The journey to Banī Shanqūl, despite much hardship and discomfort, did not attain my object.' Communications were almost impossible between those tribes and Khartoum. Interesting geographical, linguistic and ethnographical notes assembled in Chapter XI below were, however, a fruitful result of that journey. Fr. Beltrame asked Dr. Knoblecher for a mission among the Dinka of the White Nile, which was granted. At the end of 1855 he returned to Europe to seek helpers.

Steadfast in Adversity

In 1856 more missionaries arrived for Mgr. Knoblecher, but some fell ill on the journey out. Fr. M. Wurnitsch died at Kuruskū. Frs. F. Morlang and L. Pircher reached Holy Cross, but the latter died a short time after. Morlang went on to Gondokoro. A year later Fr. A. Kaufmann arrived at Gondokoro and Fr. J. Lanz at Holy Cross. Lanz studied the Dinka language.

The news of so many deaths among the missionaries resulted in the Marien-Verein reducing its help. So Knoblecher, wasted by fever,

decided to return to Europe to confer with Propaganda Fide, and at the
same time regain his health. At Aswan he met a Veronese party, headed
by the returning Fr. Beltrame. With Beltrame were Frs. F. Oliboni,
A. Melotto, D. Comboni, A. Dal Bosco, and a layman, I. Zilli.
Mgr. Knoblecher said to Fr. Beltrame: 'I recommend to you the
Verona mission, of which you are taking charge. Orders have already
been given that you and your companions will be welcome at Holy
Cross. You will stay there for some time to explore the country, record
the customs of the inhabitants, and study their language. You will then
choose a suitable site to found your mission ... I do not know whether
we shall ever meet again. I am worn out. I feel that I shall soon die.'
His presentiment was true. Exhausted and ill, Knoblecher died at
Naples on 13 April 1858. He was only thirty-eight.

Knoblecher's valuable manuscripts on botany, geography and
geology were given to the College of Propaganda in Rome, while his
studies of the Bari and Dinka were deposited in the Imperial (now the
National) Library of Vienna. James Hamilton in *Sinai, the Hedjaz and
Soudan* (1857) wrote:

> One of the most interesting establishments in the Sudan is the
> Mission ... respectable both for its object and the character of
> the men who compose it.... It is in the hands of volunteers,
> headed by Dr. I. Knoblecher, a young man of great enterprise,
> who is known to all students of African geography and has carried
> his *peaceful investigation* of the While Nile to a point beyond that
> reached by the warlike expeditions of Mohammed Ali.

> The Mission is entirely supported by funds furnished from
> Austria: its object being the establishment of Stations amongst
> the idolaters of the While Nile, and the redemption and education
> of black slave boys brought down from the interior.... Artificers
> of various kinds, the pioneers of civilisation and religion, are
> attached to the house so that the pupils may learn and carry back
> to their countrymen many useful arts. The Superior makes yearly
> journeys of inspection up the While Nile, where three Stations have
> been established, and if, as I have every reason to believe, his
> patience and discretion equal his zeal and that of his fellow-
> labourers, they cannot fail in time to overcome the immense
> difficulties which surround their undertaking.

> Both among Turks and Arabs, Abuna Suleiman, as Dr.
> Knoblecher is called, enjoys the highest consideration; far and
> near I heard him spoken of with respect.... This is already a great

success, alone worth the large sums which the Mission has cost, for it helps the breaking down of colour and religious prejudice, older than history or tradition, if not as old as nature itself. Many of the missionaries have already fallen victim to the climate and perhaps also the excessive austerity of their lives, but they have not died in vain. Those who had been long enough in the country to be known, have left a memory venerated by all even by the pagans, and the funeral chant of one who died last year at his Station up the river, Don A. Vinco, a gentleman of Verona, is still sung in their assemblies, as it was composed by the Africans themselves.

The American diplomat and traveller, Bayard Taylor, in his *Life and Lanscapes* (1854), confirmed the judgement of Hamilton when he wrote from Khartoum:

I was sorry to part with Vicar Knoblecher and his brethren. Those self-sacrificing men have willingly devoted themselves to a life — if life it can be called, for it is little better than a living death — in the remotest heart of Africa.... They are men of the purest character and animated by the best intentions. Abuna Suleiman, as Dr. Knoblecher is called, is already widely known and esteemed throughout Soudan.

Taylor describes Dr. Knoblecher as a small man, slight and rather delicately built.... His complexion was fair, his eyes a grayish blue and his beard ... a very decided auburn. His face was one of those which wins not only kindness but confidence from all. His dress consisted of a white turban and a flowing robe of dark purple cloth.

'He is a man of culture, conversant with several languages and possesses a wide scientific knowledge which will make his explorations valuable to the world.' Even a free-thinker like Count Luigi Pennazzi, a traveller to Khartoum on the eve of the Mahdist revolt, admitted the success of the missionaries in raising the condition of the people and in hardening public opinion against the slave trade.

The Verona expedition under the leadership of Fr. M. Kirchner reached Holy Cross on 14 February 1858, welcomed by Fr. J. Lanz, who was mourning the death of Fr. Mozgan on 24 January. Fr. Kirchner proceeded to Gondokoro and returned with the news that Fr. Ueberbacher had died on 22 February. At Holy Cross he found Fr. Oliboni dead.

On his death-bed Oliboni bade them take courage: 'Even though only one of you should remain, let not his confidence fail, nor let him withdraw.' The Italian missionaries built new dwellings because, wrote Comboni, 'the five of us had been installed in one small hut, which had until then lodged the cows'. All applied themselves to the study of the Dinka language. A Dinka grammar, dialogues, a dictionary of about 2000 words and an elementary textbook of religion of over 300 pages were compiled. 'The whole was the fruit of the common labour of Lanz, Melotto, Beltrame and myself', wrote Mgr. Comboni, who continued: 'We have explored the country of the Dinka, where we have investigated their habits, customs and beliefs. In a short time these regions will yield to Christianity, if the ministry can be continued. The foot of the trees are our pulpit, which is always surrounded by chiefs and naked Africans armed with spears. They listen to God's word with great eagerness.'

At the cost of much labour to the untiring Lanz and the other missionaries they built a church twenty-two metres long and twelve high. It had a straw roof thatched in the native fashion. On 3 August 1859, Fr. P. Viehweider died at Gondokoro, where he had been only a few months. Fr. F. Morlang then explored the country west of the Nile, visited the Nyangwara and journeyed beyond Yei, the first European to visit this region. A translation from his narrative is reprinted in Chapter VI below. [8]

Morlang collected a small vocabulary of 150 words which he believed to be Nyangwara but were in fact Moru. The following year he and the German explorer, Wilhelm von Harnier, sailed up the Nile as far as the Bedden rapids. Shortly afterwards von Harnier, having returned to Holy Cross, was killed by a buffalo in a hunt and was buried in the mission cemetery.

Fr. Kirchner returned to Khartoum, where he found the Pro-Vicar Fr. Josef Gostner dead at the age of thirty-six. When the Prefect of Propaganda, Cardinal Barnabò, [9] heard of all these deaths (twenty-two between 1851 and 1858, and several missionaries repatriated for reasons of health, and to crown all, the death of Gostner, whose appointment as head of the mission they had contemplated confirming), he wrote: 'After so many sacrifices we shall have to give up this mission.' Prof. Mitterutzner, the scholar of the Dinka and Bari languages, pleaded so hard for the unfortunate mission that he saved it. He also drew attention to the fact that two Sudanese pupils studying in the College of Propa-

---

[8] For a critical edition of Morlang's diary, 1855-63, in an Italian version, edited by a group of Comboni missionaries, and published in 1973 by Editrice Nigrizia, Verona, see p. 109.

[9] Alessandro Barnabò (1807-74) of Foligno, cardinal from 1856.

ganda had proved their worth by being at the top of their class in talent, piety and judgement.

Fr. Matthias Kirchner was appointed to succeed the late Pro-Vicar. He accepted the difficult task with reluctance. He went to Rome to confer with Cardinal Barnabò, and it was agreed to establish stations where the missionaries could acclimatise themselves and rest. al-Shallāl was chosen as such an acclimatisation centre. The Viceroy, Muhammad Saʿīd Pasha, was prepared to present them with the island of Philae, provided that its ruins were to remain the property of the Government. [10]

Mgr. Kirchner, however, preferred fifteen acres of land nearby in al-Shallāl with the possibility of cultivating a large garden there. In 1859 Kirchner returned to Africa, bringing with him five missionaries among whom was Fr. Johann Reinthaler, a Franciscan from Styria. The Verona missionaries, continually ill with fever, decided to abandon Holy Cross, 'a mission too unhealthy and, moreover, too close to the trading stations'. In the evening of 15 January 1859, Beltrame, Melotto and Comboni, left Holy Cross. On their return voyage they sailed a long way up the Sobat river to look for a possible new site, but found none. On 22 February Beltrame and Melotto again landed to look for a suitable place among the Dinka. Finally they chose a site for a new station on the Tarciam channel near the village of Meigik among the Abialang Dinka.

On 4 April they arrived in Khartoum, where Fr. Melotto died on 26 May. Four days previously the chief carpenter lay brother, G. Kleinheinz, had also died, Comboni returned to Italy with the Ferrarese trader, Angelo Castelbolognese, who related to him his various travels to the Bahr al-Ghazāl. Mgr. Kirchner ordered Beltrame to sail up the White Nile again 'to recall the missionaries, to take with them such of the black pupils as prudence would suggest, and to withdraw all furniture that could be of any use in the new house at Shellal.' As soon as Beltrame reached Holy Cross he ordered everything to be got ready for the evacuation. He and Lanz then went on to Gondokoro, where Morlang was alone.

The three missionaries departed with heavy hearts. It was sad to see the Bari crowds rush into the house to carry off everything they could. The Cic Dinka at Holy Cross, on the other hand, wept over the departure of the missionaries. 'If you abandon us, who will defend us from the Danagla armed men, when they come to take away our children?

[10] Public Record Office, London, F.O. 84-1120, Consul General Sir R.G. Colquhoun to Lord John Russell, 8 June 1860.

You have helped our poor and cared for our sick; who will console and cure us?'

The missionaries arrived in Khartoum on 29 March 1860. There the pious and zealous Fr. J. Lanz died a few days later. No new missionaries came. Mgr. Kirchner, in a fit of depression, wrote in June 1861: 'The situation of the mission is such that I feel obliged in all conscience to make a last bid for support by calling on a religious order to which I can entrust it, otherwise it will have to be abandoned to save strength, resources and personnel.'

So he went to Europe to confer with Propaganda Fide and other interested bodies. Morlang and Kaufmann went to al-Shallāl. There they remained from June 1860, until February 1862. Beltrame employed much of his time in linguistic and anthropological study of the local Beja and visited their villages.

The Franciscan Contribution

On 4 September 1861, Propaganda Fide entrusted the Vicariate to the Franciscan Order headed by Fr. J. Reinthaler from the province of Styria. Reinthaler left Trieste with five fathers and twenty-eight lay brothers and reached the station at al-Shellāl in January, 1862. He and some of the missionaries proceeded further over the Nubian desert as far as Khartoum, where he left some of the party, while with the rest he sailed up the White Nile. Falling ill in the Shilluk country, he had to return to Khartoum, while his missionaries went on to Holy Cross.

It was at this time that the Franciscans opened a mission station at Kaka amongst the Shilluk. In March, 1862, another caravan of Franciscans consisting of eight priests, two seminarists and fifteen lay brothers reached al-Shallāl. Several Franciscans fell victim to their lack of foresight in not taking proper safeguards against a climate so different from their own. On 10 April 1862, Fr. Reinthaler died of fever at Berber. Twenty-two missionaries had died since January of that year, including a group at Kaka. The few survivors, appalled by so many deaths and persecuted by the slave-dealers, decided to go home. Propaganda Fide temporarily entrusted the direction of the Sudan mission to the Vicar Apostolic of Egypt. The mission stations on the White Nile, as well as that of al-Shallāl, were closed, and only two Franciscans, Fr. F. Pfeifer and a lay brother, remained in Khartoum.

The Annals of the Propagation of the Faith recorded that 'each mission station of the Vicariate is marked by several graves, and more tombs mark the road from al-Shallāl to Gondokoro. The day will come when life will arise from these graves.' In February 1863 we find Fr. Morlang with two missionaries on a visit to Gondokoro. Fr. Morlang had returned from al-Shallāl to Holy Cross in December 1860 and with some Franciscan fathers lived there until March 1863. To the end the merchants continued to be an unmitigated nuisance to the missionaries, as to their Dinka flock, for they encroached on church land and stole children and cattle from the Dinka. The French trader J.A. Vayssière and others were pursued in the consular courts in Cairo in 1858 but without effect, and in October 1861 Fr. Morlang had to administer a strong reminder to the brothers Poncet.

J.H. Speke, the discoverer of the source of the White Nile, informs us of his meeting with Fr. Morlang and his companions at Gondokoro. He pays tribute to the missionaries fallen in these lands: 'The missionaries never had occasion to complain of these Africans, and to this day they would doubtless have been kindly inclined towards Europeans, had the White Nile traders not brought the devil amongst them. . . . The shell of the brick church at Gondokoro and the cross on the top of a native-built hut in Kich, are all that will remain to bear testimony to these Christian exertions to improve the condition of these heathens.' [11]

Sir Samuel Baker also speaks of Holy Cross and Gondokoro. On 23 January 1863, he was at Holy Cross: 'The mission station consists of about twenty grass huts on a patch of dry ground close to the river. The church is a small hut neatly arranged.' Fr. Morlang was very discouraged. 'He had worked with much zeal for many years, but the natives were utterly impractical people, lying and deceitful to a superlative degree. The more they receive the more they desire. . . . It is a pitiable sight to witness the self-sacrifice that many noble men have made in these frightful countries without any good result.'

Baker, however, benefited from the faithful service of two mission products, boys whose names he spelt Richarn and Saat, the latter 'a boy that would do no evil'. Of the Gondokoro mission station Baker wrote in his diary: 'There remain to this day the ruins of the brick establishment and church and a derelict garden; groves of citron and lime trees still exist, the only signs that an attempt at civilisation had been made.' Sir Samuel asks himself the reason for the failure of so much work: 'What curse lies so heavily upon Africa and bows her down beneath all other nations? It is the infernal traffic in slaves — a trade so hideous that the heart of every slave and owner becomes

[11] *Journal of the Discovery of the Source of the Nile*, London, 1863, pp. 604-6. Speke somewhat credulously added an unverified story which a trader had told him that the missionaries undermined their health by idleness (p. 600).

deformed and shrinks like a withered limb incapable of action'. [12]

So much for the men who had been on the Nile and wrote of what they saw. But there was another, different kind of literature. By the end of our survey it had become impossible to discuss Nile exploration without some reference to the part played by missionaries. An example of the new popular travel literature, using the new technique of photographs for illustration, was Robert Brown's sumptuously illustrated *Story of Africa and its Explorers,* in which the author, writing on the fruits of 'the Austrian Mission on the Nile', states: 'It is certain that when an Egyptian Station was established at Gondokoro, many of the Bari became partially civilised and learned sufficient Arabic to find employment about the military stations, as interpreters, translators and inspectors. [13] From that curious character, P.V. Zucchinetti, for some time a member of the Mission to Central Africa, we learn that the Governor's modest residence at Gondokoro in Emin Pasha's time was built from bricks taken from the ruins of the Catholic mission there. [14] The only mission still active in the Sudan was at Khartoum, which Baker found 'swarming with little African boys from the various White Nile tribes'. Fr. Pfeifer stayed in Khartoum for nine years, when he was succeeded by Frs. D. Stadel-Meyer and H. Schlatter.

At the end of a long historical report on the Vicariate of Central Africa written in French in 1867 and often quoted in this Introduction, Mgr. Comboni asked firstly: what were the results achieved by the various missionaries from 1846 to 1867? Secondly: why had the Franciscan Order not obtained the results that had been expected from its activities?

As to the first question, the mission to Central Africa had succeeded in reaching the 4th parallel of north latitude and had placed on the map a large region previously unknown. It had made important contributions to the study of the customs and languages of those parts. It had gained for its missionaries the love of the native people. As to the second question, the missionaries, though full of the best intentions and actuated by the highest ideals, lacked experience of tropical conditions.

Daniele Comboni

Comboni was present at Holy Cross when the dying Oliboni uttered his last injunction: 'Even though only one of you should remain, let not his confidence fail, nor let him withdraw.' In obedience to this command

---

[12] *The Albert N'Yanza,* London, 1866, II, pp. 310-311.
[13] *The Story of Africa and its Explorers,* London, 1892-5, II, pp. 111-12.
[14] *Souvenirs de mon séjour chez Emin Pacha,* Le Caire, 1899, p. 14.

the future bishop dedicated all his energy and talent for the next twenty-two years to missionary work in the Sudan. In 1864 he published his *Piano per la rigenerazione dell'Africa,* a plan for the renaissance of Africa, in a pamphlet reprinted in several languages. This was a project to regenerate Africa *through* Africa. In brief the proposal was to establish institutions, possibly round the African coast, where the mild climate would suit Europeans as well as Africans and where African boys and girls would be taught the secular arts and be prepared for missionary work in the interior of the continent. The scheme is interesting as providing an early example of 'indirect administration' in the missionary sphere; it is perhaps not an overstatement that its ideal inspired subsequent developments in the political administration of tropical Africa. Today Comboni's plan is being carried out in its broad lines by the institution of an African hierarchy, with African clergy, sisters and helpers. *

In 1865 Comboni, accompanied by Fr. L. da Casoria, founder of the Institute for African Negroes in Naples, reached al-Shallāl. Three Africans were with them: two lay brothers, Lodovico and Giovanni, and Fr. Bonaventura from Khartoum, who had been baptized by Knoblecher in 1851 in the Khartoum mission, and afterwards educated in Verona and Naples. A division of the vast Vicariate was mooted, but was not felt to be timely. The new house at al-Shallāl was maintained for eight more months, but was then closed for lack of funds.

In 1867 Comboni opened in Old Cairo two institutes for Africans of both sexes. In the same year he had opened an institute for men in Verona with the same object, entrusting its direction to Fr. A. Dal Bosco, his companion in the Sudan in 1857. He also opened an institute for sisters in Verona. Comboni now had his own personnel, trained in the two institutes which he himself had founded, instead of having to rely on missionaries recruited here and there as previously. He founded the Association of the Good Shepherd to provide funds.

France, England, Ireland, Spain, Austria, Germany, Poland, Russia, Hungary and Italy saw Comboni begging from rich and poor. Between January and May 1871, he wrote 1347 letters. He assured the direction of the two institutes in Cairo by obtaining the help of two Camillian Fathers and some Sisters of the Apparition of St. Joseph. By that year eighteen African girls out of fifty-four in the Cairo institute were ready to return to the Sudan. On 15 August 1871, Comboni was ready to send

* Bishop D. Comboni's Outline study on the *"Discoveries in Africa"* shows his keen intellectual interest in research in African Explorations. Cf. "Quadro storico delle scoperte africane", Verona, 1880.

the Camillian fathers S. Carcereri and G. Franceschini and two lay brothers, P. Bartoli and D. Polinari, to explore Kurdufān.

Missions founded in Kurdufān and Berber

Comboni gave as a reason for abandoning the White Nile in favour of Kurdufān: 'During the first period of the Vicariate the Africans of the White Nile were found to have been corrupted by the traders. . . . I therefore thought it best to avail myself of the inland routes and establish a mission between the While Nile and the Niger. It seemed to me that these inland regions were in less danger of corruption.'

Comboni's party left Cairo on 26 October 1871, and reached Khartoum on 20 December. By permission of the Holy See and the Vicar Apostolic of Egypt the missionaries set out for al-Ubayyid via Sinnār and Tura al-Khadra. On their way they drew a useful map giving the positions of villages and wells. Carcereri's report emphasised his preference for the choice of al-Ubayyid as a mission centre for the Africans.

The Fathers therefore took up their residence there. By a decree of 26 May 1872, Propaganda charged the Institute for African Missions of Verona with the direction of the Mission to Central Africa, and elected Comboni as Pro-Vicar Apostolic. On 18 September Mgr. Comboni, four priests, three laymen and three African girls left Trieste for Africa. In Cairo his party grew to twenty-one persons. They reached Khartoum on 4 May 1873. Fr. Carcereri had already returned to al-Ubayyid and taken over the Khartoum mission from the Franciscan D. Stadel-Meyer. Now Mgr. Comboni took formal possession. In his sermon on the following Sunday he formulated his programme. His words revealed the man: 'I make my own cause the cause of each of you, and my happiest day will be that on which I may lay down my life for you.'

On 19 June 1873, Comboni and various other missionaries arrived at al-Ubayyid. Among the company was a Benedictine priest, Dom Pio Giuseppe Hadrian, O.S.B. Dom Pio was a Sudanese born in the region of Sinnār; at four years of age he was carried off into slavery and sold and resold in Nubia. Rescued in Cairo by an Italian priest he was afterwards educated at the Benedictine monastery of Subiaco near Rome. Unfortunately affected by tuberculosis he was advised to go back to his home with Mgr. Comboni. But on 10 July this first priest from Central Africa died. After conferring with Sa'īd Aghā the Nuba chief of Dilling — they spelt it Delen in those days — Comboni wished to visit the Nuba mountains, but administrative business kept him at al-Ubayyid and he sent the two Camillians, Carcereri and Franceschini, accompanied by the layman A. Wischnewski. The last was an experienced and courageous man, who had been in the mission since 1856, and was greatly trusted by Comboni.

They left on 13 October 1873, and reached Dilling passing through the ungovernable Baqqāra[15] tribes. On their way they made a map of a part of the Nuba mountains hitherto unmapped,[16] and wrote a report contained in Chapter XIV, giving geographical and ethnographical details. They were enthusiastic about the sincere and intelligent character of the people.

On 17 November Comboni and Carcereri returned to Khartoum, where the growing number of pupils demanded the enlargement of the school buildings. On 9 June 1874, the sisters moved to the new brick building, in area 61 by 5.5 metres, built on the same style as the older part of the block. It is a tribute to the quality of the structure that, ten years later, during the siege of Khartoum, General Gordon borrowed it for use as a power magazine, as it was the best and safest building in the town.

In October 1874, Comboni opened a mission at Berber, a centre for caravans to and from Egypt and the Red Sea coast. Its direction was entrusted to the Camillian fathers. The institute for missionary sisters which he had founded in Verona on 12 January 1872, was growing steadily and was firmly established by 1874, when Comboni called the sisters 'Le Pie Madri della Nigrizia', the Good Mothers of Negroland.

Early in 1875 eighteen missionaries — fathers and sisters — reached Khartoum. Among them was Fr. L. Bonomi, later Comboni's deputy and for three years a prisoner of the Mahdi. Bonomi and another priest went to al-Ubayyid and Dilling where they opened a mission station, and were cordially welcomed by the Kojur Kakum, Comboni's friend. The missionaries started learning the local Nuba language and compiled a grammar vocabulary — helped by Comboni, who had joined them in September with two sisters. As the Nuba had refused to pay taxes, the governor of Kurdufān who had his residence at al-Ubayyid, sent an expedition against them, and Comboni and his missionaries were advised to withdraw. Being men of peace they therefore left everything in the custody of Kojur Kakum and withdrew temporarily at al-Ubayyid.

[15] Collective name for the Arabic-speaking cattle-owning tribes who range from the White Nile Valley westward to Dār Fūr.
[16] *Cordofan e Gebel Nuba secondo i viaggi nel 1871-72-73 di P. Stan. Carcereri* [etc.], Verona (Lito-Gelino), 1874; *Carte du Kordofan et du pays des Noubas,* Paris, Missions Catholiques, 1874; 'La nuova carta di Dar o Gebel Nuba', Verona, *Nigrizia, 1883-5, passim.*

In any case most of the missionaries, weakened by fever, needed a change. At al-Ubayyid the new guests were of great help: the boys' school was given a vital impulse; the buildings were improved and a well was dug. By 1876 the missionaries were surrounded by a nucleus of Christian families. Fr. P. Rosignoli gives us a description of the church at al-Ubayyid: 'It was a very beautiful church: it measured thirty by ten by fifteen metres and the windows were of stained glass. The Christians of the town contributed £E. 654 towards the cost and the Africans of the Mission, led by their teachers, gave their work free. The Mission was well equipped for the instruction of skilled workers: there were a hundred and fifty apprentices, a dispensary, library, sewing machines and all sorts of tools.'

Having at heart not only the evangelization of the people but also their material welfare, the missionaries decided to found an agricultural station, a project which would promote social stability and economic security. They opened this station at Mulbas (Malbes), 11 miles south-east of al-Ubayyid. Homesteads were built, one for each family. Five years after its foundation the Mulbas colony numbered about thirty families in an area of 30,000 square metres. The need of a similar agricultural establishment was felt also in Khartoum. Comboni started negotiations with the government to acquire a piece of land close to the town, but the attempt failed. Permission to reopen the Dilling mission was likewise delayed by the Khartoum government, but Colonel Gordon, appointed governor-general in February 1877, gave the necessary authorisation. In October the missionaries reopened the mission to the great rejoicing of the Nuba people.

Martini's Journey to the Ethiopian Border

In Chapter XII below is the narrative of Fr. G. Martini's journey. On 21 September 1876, he set out up the Blue Nile with the object of founding a mission station somewhere between the Sudan and Shoa. The prospective site was in the neighbourhood of al-Qadārif, a suitable region, as the new station was intended to be of an agricultural character. [17]

The Camillian Fathers abandoned the Berber house on 22 February 1877, and on his return from the Ethiopian border, Martini was ordered to occupy it. At the beginning of 1879 the Sisters of the Apparition of

---

[17] The Condominium government established a farm for mechanized agriculture near the prospective site.

St. Joseph also left the Mission, but by this time Comboni received an invitation from Sawākin to start a school and church there. It was not possible to open them until 1885, when Sawākin had become the base for an Anglo-Egyptian military campaign against the Mahdists. In 1876 Mgr. Comboni was back in Europe with a young Dinka of the Bahr al-Ghazāl, Daniel Sorur, who later became a priest whose notes on his fellow-tribesmen appear in Chapter IX below. On 8 July 1877 the Pro-Vicar was appointed Vicar-Apostolic and consecrated Bishop.

Licurgo Santoni, an Italian postal official in the Egyptian service, in the course of a tour of inspection in the Sudan in 1877-8, visited the Khartoum Mission. He wrote:

> When I arrived in Khartoum in January 1878 the missionaries were busy with the education of many African boys. . . . Domestic science was taught to the girls. When you consider that in those countries women are looked upon as worthless objects, useful only for bearing children, it is easy to imagine how pleased the parents were when they saw their daughters learning to cook, embroider and sew. The boys were taught, according to their aptitudes, carpentry, black-smithing, tailoring and shoe-making by experts specially brought from Italy. . . . 200 day-girls and nearly 300 boys attended the school. Besides these, eighty negro girls and some hundred boys were fed, clothed and educated till they grew up, entirely at the expense of the mission. . . .[18]

The superintendent of the government arsenal, an engineer, Lorenzo Spada, gave instruction in mechanics to those who showed ability and these could then find employment in the government dockyard.

Famine, Flood and Pestilence

Bishop Comboni returned to the Sudan with a party of fourteen missionaries — priests, lay brothers and the first sisters from his Institute in Verona. On 12 April 1878 they arrived in Khartoum. On the way, at Aswan, Comboni received the first inkling that a disaster had befallen the Sudan. Colonel Gordon, whom he met there, expressed his anxiety. The year before there had been a frightful famine owing to lack of rain. The Mission stations were overcrowded with hungry and thirsty people, especially at al-Ubayyid. 'I myself', Comboni wrote later,

[18] *Alto Egitto e Nubia* . . . *(1863-1898)*, Roma, 1905, pp. 371-2.

'witnessed the extreme poverty of very many localities where whole villages reduced by famine lived on grass, wild seeds and even on the dung of animals. It is impossible to put into words the great privations endured by the missionaries and sisters.'

At the end of July 1878 heavy rain began to fall, and the Nile overflowed, threatening Khartoum. Temporary embankments were built to save the Mission garden. In October, after the flood had subsided, pools were left that produced myriads of mosquitoes. Malaria spread and 1878 came to be known as 'the mosquito year'.

Gordon, the Governor-General, wrote: 'The whole town is sick this year.... This country is a pest house, the people have been dying like flies.' The Italian explorer, P. Matteucci, wrote from Ethiopia in January, 1879: 'I write and weep. One year has elapsed; out of all the missionaries in Khartoum and of those who came while I was about to leave [Khartoum] for Europe, only Mgr. Comboni survives. . . . He withstands the struggle, but in his twenty years of Africa spent in striving against so many arduous difficulties Comboni has lost his robust vigour.... It was last year that the Sudan was afflicted by a fearful famine ... the Mission exhausted its provisions to relieve so many miseries.'

Yet this did not divert Comboni from planning for the future. Matteucci mentions Comboni's project for an agricultural station at al-Qadārif and another for the creation of a mission station on the Equatorial lakes, a project which, if realised, Matteucci considers, would have been the most important of Comboni's achievements. Gordon had once sent his colleague, Romolo Gessi, to the Vicar-Apostolic with a message: 'Tell Mgr. Comboni that his expedition to the Equatorial lakes will be sent at government expense; he needs provide only food.' The expedition was to have started in the autumn of that year. Gordon had requested Comboni to send the sisters to staff the government hospital at Fashoda. But how could it be done? Fr. Martini recorded that ten missionaries had recently died in Khartoum alone. Comboni wrote: 'We have consumed the provisions we had, and spent all our money, to feed the numerous institutions we had at Berber, Khartoum, El Obeid, Jebel Nuba.... We also helped the Muslims who were in extreme need ... but now we are compelled to close the door to so many unfortunate people, who come to beg for bread.' Physically exhausted, he returned to Italy in May, 1879 in order to obtain fresh financial aid.

The following year, in December, he left for the Sudan with a good company of missionaries among whom was Fr. J. Ohrwalder. They reached Khartoum on 28 January 1881, where Gessi Pasha, formerly

Governor of the Bahr al-Ghazāl, worn out by his privations and campaigns, lay desperately ill in the mission, attended by the sisters. Two years earlier Gessi had invited Comboni to found a Mission in the Bahr al-Ghazāl and had promised official help. Comboni had planned to establish this mission in 1882.

On 8 March 1881, unaware of the impending tragedy, a group of missionaries with thirty camels left Khartoum for al-Ubayyid. A few days later they were followed by Mgr. Comboni and Rudolf von Slatin Bey, the new Governor of Dār Fūr. On 24 June Bishop Comboni, Frs. J. Bonomi, L. Henriot, V.P. Marzano and the layman G. Regnotto, left Dilling to explore Ghulfān. They prepared an accurate and valuable map.[19] Comboni was particularly requested to report on the slave trade in that region. The Governor-General, Muhammad Raūf Pasha, Gordon's successor, had written to him from Khartoum on 10 May 1881: 'Monseigneur . . . you may have already reached Jebel Nuba. I beg you to examine the country and its administration carefully, that we may take necessary measures for the welfare of those people. The question of slavery in particular must be the object of close study. Being on the spot, you will be able to examine the problems and propose suitable remedies. You will receive from me the strongest support in the execution of H.H. the Khedive's orders.'

Death of Bishop Comboni

But Comboni's strength was on the point of breaking down owing to fever, sleeplessness and the death of so many of his missionaries. There were six missionary deaths in September alone. On his return to Khartoum in the last stages of exhaustion, Daniele Comboni died in the evening of 10 October 1881. The people of Khartoum of every race mourned the dead bishop, but grief was greatest among the slaves and the poor. Comboni's voice had everywhere denounced the physical and moral miseries of the slaves. He had the courage to write: 'The whole world has been told that the slave trade is suppressed. That is false . . . the abolition of the slave trade in Central Africa is a dead letter, for the slaves constitute the principal revenue of the Sudan Government and the merchants.'

[19] Bishop Comboni's fellow-missionaries prepared a map of his journeys in the Nuba Mountains: *Schizzo dei Monti di Nuba (Africa Centrale) dell'itinerario di Monsignor Comboni compilato dai Missionari del Vicariato Apostolico di Chartum*, 1° luglio 1881, Milano (Lit. Lebrun Boldetti), 1881. Both this and Carcereri's map (note 16 above) were much cited by contemporary geographers of Africa.

Bishop Comboni was a true friend of Gordon. When in 1878 there were rumours in Cairo that Gordon had encouraged slavery, Comboni replied:

I maintain that it is really a marvel that Gordon has, single-handed, by sheer force of will-power, succeeded in striking a blow at the slave trade and slavery.

It is an undeniable fact that today there are no longer to be seen on the Kordofan, Fashoda and Dongola routes those immense crowds of slaves that I saw twenty years ago.... The story that the Government has, with Gordon's consent, sent people to the Bahr al-Ghazāl to capture ten thousand slaves there, is absolute nonsense. Such stories are concocted by people who, not being able to drive their trade without being dropped on by the government, and being prevented from making money as they used to do from the sale of slaves, now seek to discredit Gordon. But truth must triumph. Gordon Pasha is the greatest foe of slavery.

M. Grancelli, a biographer of Comboni, writes of him: 'Strong, bold and fearless in all enterprises, he never shrank from obstacles which others would have thought insurmountable.... Comboni always and everywhere suffered toil and fatigue gladly for the people of the Sudan with courage and a spirit of self-sacrifice.'

We conclude this appreciation by citing Count Pennazzi's book, *Dal Po ai Due Nili* (1882): 'The Khartoum Mission has counted and still counts among its members fine men who have contributed to the progress of science. Today Comboni ... does not fall short of his predecessors, whose names I recall with pleasure since they have removed, as best they could, the dishonour into which a blackguardly rabble has brought the European name. It will be enough to mention Knoblecher, Kirchner, Dovjak, Morlang, Kaufmann, Beltrame and Dal Bosco, who all contributed to overthrow a trade which was the negation of honour and humanity.'

Mahdism and the Missions

Bishop Comboni died during the first stages of the revolution of the religious and political leader Muhammad Ahmad al-Mahdī. On 29 June 1881 he proclaimed his Mahdihood and as a consequence rose in arms against the Turco-Egyptian government of the Sudan. While Comboni was dying the Mahdī and his followers were heading for the Nuba mountains, where the revolutionary movement attracted thousands of disaffected tribesmen. Here they annihilated two armies sent against them and debouching on the plains of Kurdufān laid siege to the capital, al-Ubayyid which they captured. In November 1883 they obliterated an Egyptian relieving force commanded by General W. Hicks. In the course of the campaign the Mahdists overran the Mission stations at al-Ubayyid and Dilling and the farming settlement at Mulbas.

It was a tragic story. As late as 12 March 1882 Emin (Muhammad al-Amīn) Pasha, Governor of the Equatorial Province, had written to Fr. Henriot proposing the re-founding of the Mission in the Southern Sudan. 'If you come soon I will pay your fare and maintenance for one year. I will help you in every way to build the Mission'. But on 15 September of that year the Mahdists occupied the Dilling Mission and Frs. Bonomi and Ohrwalder, Sisters Andreis, Caprini and Pesavento with the Lay Brothers Mariani and Regnotto, were captured. At the al-Ubayyid Frs. Losi and Rosignoli, Sisters Chincarini, Corsi, Grigolini, Quasce and Venturini, and Brother Locatelli, were captured. At the Mission training farm at Mulbas neglect and destruction followed the tide of war. The captives endured hardship and suffering. Sister Eulalia Pesavento died on 28 October, Brother Mariani on 31 October and Sister Andreis on 7 November, while the survivors, according to a contemporary account, were 'hovering between life and death, lying helplessly side by side'. On 28 December Fr. Giovanni Losi, the acting Superior of the whole Mission, died of dysentery during the siege of al-Ubayyid. The captives from Dilling were joined by the surviving missionaries from al-Ubayyid, 'more dead than alive' and suffering from scurvy. The massacre of Hicks's army ended the last hope of freedom for the missionaries in Kurdufān. The Mahdist armies were everywhere victorious and every day they became a greater threat to Khartoum and its communcations with Egypt.

By formal order of Mgr. Francesco Sogaro the Vicar-Apostolic, the staff of the Khartoum Mission withdrew over the desert road first to al-Shallāl, then to Cairo, leaving one lay brother, Domenico Polinari, as caretaker in Khartoum. He died in Mahdist hands in Omdurman in 1890. After Fr. Bonomi's escape in June 1885 Fr. Josef Ohrwalder, 'Abūna Yūsuf', became the Father of all Christian captives in Omdurman. On the night of 29 November 1891 he, with Sisters C. Chincarini and Venturini, escaped to Egypt followed in October 1894 by Fr. Paolo Rosignoli.

In November 1885, Fr. Henriot and Fr. Specke opened a missionary station in Sawākin. Very soon the boys' school had forty-five pupils, and the number continually increased with a strong Muslim representation. The school plays especially attracted the townspeople. In 1893 a fine church was built, but with the abandonment of Sawākin as the main port of the Sudan after 1906, church and school were closed as new and larger buildings were opened at Port Sudan. In 1891 Fr. Henriot founded a mission station at Tokar but on account of the insecurity of the place it had to be abandoned the following year.

In September, 1898, the Mahdist military power was broken on the battlefield of Omdurman. In October 1899, Fr. Ohrwalder, accompanied by Fr. L. Banholzer, re-entered Omdurman, 'greeted enthusiastically by all his friends'. Thence onwards begins the development which we witness today. As not unworthy sons of over a century of suffering and achievement, the missionaries of our time work to realise the dreams of those stout-hearted pioneers, Knoblecher and Comboni. [20]

With a touch of prophecy Fr. Johann Dichtl, writing of the desolation of the Mahdist wars, ends his book *Der Sudan* (Graz, 1884) with these words: 'May God soon give peace to the people of the Sudan . . . may He give them His blessing, that out of the present stress may come good fortune . . . and that the State and the Church may equally complete their mission for the civilization of the Sudan.'

---

[20] On 12 December 1974 Pope Paul VI set up an independent Ecclesiastical Hierarchy for the Southern Sudan. The former Bishop of Wau, Mgr. Ireneo Dud (a Jur), was elected Archbishop of Juba (Equatoria); Mgr. Pio Yukwan Deng (a Shilluk), Bishop of Malakal (Upper Nile); Mgr. Joseph Gasi (a Zande), Bishop of Tombora (Equatoria West), and Mgr. Gabriel Zubeir Wako (a Ndogo), Bishop of Wau (Bahr al-Ghazāl).

KHARTOUM

CHAPTER I

KHARTOUM, DESCRIPTIONS OF A CHANGING CITY

Khartoum in 1843, by Luigi Montuori

The following is a translation of a letter in Italian from Khartoum, dated 23 September 1843, and addressed to Mgr. Spaccapietra[1] in Naples. The writer was Fr. Luigi Montuori (1798-1857), a Vincentian father who went to Ethiopia in 1839 but left owing to religious persecution in 1842 when he came to the Sudan and set up the first Catholic church and school in Khartoum, a city founded sixteen years previously by the Governor General 'Alī Khūrshīd Pasha. The original letter is in the possession of the parish priest of Priano (Salerno), by whose courtesy this translation has been made.

On 23 March 1842 I left Gondar for Sinnār in the company of the Belgian consul general and many others who attached themselves to our party.

After six days of perilous journeying, we drew clear of Abyssinian territory and entered that of Sinnār, belonging to the Egyptian government. We stopped for food at the village of al-Matamma, the first village under Egyptian dominion and consequently, the first where law and order rule. A few days before I arrived, the chief of the village and a leading personality had been killed for having, according to the people, acted unjustly. [2] Leaving al-Matamma we made our way towards al-Qallābāt an arid, waterless locality stretching almost as far as al-Qadārif, where the *kāshif* or provincial chief, a Turk, resided, and he warmly welcomed us. From al-Qadārif we crossed the Ghiseldinet desert

---

[1] Vincenzo Spaccapietra (1801-78), of Francavilla al Mare, Chieti, a brother-Vincentian, afterwards archbishop of Smyrna. See *Ricordi della vita di Mons. Vincenzo Spaccapietra, arcivescovo di Smirne,* by his nephew, L. Spaccapietra (Napoli, 1885).

[2] The chief of the Takārīr (Westerners) settled in the locality was then Ibrāhīm al-Qandalāwī who died later.

(mountain of the monkeys) [3] and frequently came across heaps of bones
and skeletons and the corpses of people recently killed by lions.

We thus arrived at Gala [? Buwayda al-Qal'a], a poor village but
not without interest where the *qa'im maqām* [4] or governor resides. In
addition to beef, mutton and camel meat, ostrich flesh and guinea-fowl
were being sold on the market here very cheaply. As the surroundings
of Gala were considered to be dangerous because of the number of
lions, we were forced to continue our journey about noon, when the
sun was at its height, in order to avoid encountering them. After we
had been on our way for about half-an-hour we began to hear frightening
roars coming from several directions, not more than 40 or 50 feet away.
Bones and skulls lay everywhere, while sandals and clothes had been
torn to shreds and then scattered in all directions by the wind. This
appalling sight frightened not only the members of our caravan but also
the camels and mules. In particular, my mule was so frightened that it
no longer heeded the bridle, and bucked violently until I was thrown
heavily to the ground, severely injuring my face. I lay there stunned
for some time suffering greatly from the wounds. Then I was bandaged
as well as possible under the circumstances; the blood that covered me
was wiped away, I was helped on to my mule and the journey continued
until we reached Abū Harāz, a large village on the banks of the Nile,
on the road from al-Qallābāt. At Abū Harāz, we decided to continue
on our way in a small Arab boat, and after eight days of pleasant
travelling, interrupted only by the interference of thousands of crocodiles
encountered along the way, we finally arrived at Khartoum, the capital
of the Sudan and of the whole of Sinnār, the territory of the renowned
Muhammed 'Alī, Viceroy of Egypt.

The site on which the city of Khartoum stands is a pleasant one.
It would be hard indeed to find a better position for this city, as it
stands at the confluence of the White and Blue Niles. Here the turbid
waters of the White Nile, coming perhaps from the famous and much-
renowned Niger, [5] and the clear crystal waters of the Blue Nile coming
from Abyssinia, converge, change their names and give birth to the

---

[3] Unidentified locality. The party took the northern (dry season) route from
al-Qadārif to the Blue Nile. For 'Mountain of the Monkeys' (? Jabal Qurūd)
see p. 253n.

[4] *Qa'im maqām kaymakam*, in this sense an assistant to the *kāshif* (district
officer).

[5] An illustration of the diversity of views on the location of the source of the
White Nile until Speke and Grant in 1863 announced their discovery of the
true source twenty years after this letter was written.

Nile proper. This river presents an enchanting sight as it winds its way through the vast desert plains enriching and fertilising Egypt. From this description it will be clear that Khartoum is built on an isthmus which is shortly to be turned into an island, as the Pasha has ordered a canal to be cut between the White and Blue Niles. [6]

The city has nearly 13,000 inhabitants. With the exception of 200 Copts, a few Catholics, Turks and Algerians, these are Arabs from the neighbouring provinces. The city itself sprawls in all directions, and has wide but irregular roads as is customary with the Muslims. A machine called *sāqiya* for lifting water from the river is used daily to provide the numerous gardens with water. In addition, the city has large open spaces full of stones and dirt. There is a good bazaar and a beautiful mosque, the only two buildings made from fired bricks taken from the ruins of the ancient city of Soba, about half-an-hour's distance away. The rest of the houses, including that of the Pasha, are made from sun-dried mud bricks. To prevent these from crumbling under the heavy rains, the outer walls are plastered each year with cow-dung which has been soaked in water for four or five days. There is also a military hospital, a printing press which issues government bulletins and maps, and a medical storehouse.

I have already purchased a small house, with a nice garden in the best part of the city, surrounded by Government storehouses, and away from the disturbance of neighbours. I purchased this house from a certain Selim, a sea captain. [7] The house itself is unpretentious but well-built and comfortable, and stands on flat ground. The garden is very large, and a few days ago I had it sown with all kinds of seeds, including lettuce, cauliflower, horse-radish, parsley and turnips. In the garden there are already thirteen pomegranate trees, three fig trees and one lemon tree, as well as a little arbour. I will shortly be planting more trees. There is also a small pond from which I can water the garden. The surroundings of the house are both pleasant and varied. The wide, clear waters of the Blue Nile, looking like a sea, are always dotted with ships and within easy reach of my house, thus conveniently enabling me to procure food supplies from the town. The banks of the Blue Nile are noted for their beautiful vegetation, the abundance of good fish and many birds of various species especially large ones, such as pelicans,

---

[6] The canal was never built though its construction was contemplated by the Condominium government, not for defence but to make possible the planting of a green belt south of the city.

[7] He may well have been the *binbāshī* Salīm Qapūdān, commander of three voyages of exploration up the White Nile in 1839-42 to endeavour to find its source. He would now be returning to his post in the Egyptian naval dockyard.

ibis, phoenix and royal cranes. In the far distance, beyond the plain, on the right bank of the river, mountains can be seen, which seem, early in the morning or at sunset, to be huge blueish pyramids.

The rainy season is almost over, and better weather is expected soon. I will then authorise the building of five small rooms, and an elegantly designed church, dedicated to Our Lady, Help of Christians. The fired bricks from the ancient ruins of Soba will be very useful, especially in the building of the church, although I am only forced reluctantly, by necessity to utilise them. In the meantime, I am having the nearby plains excavated so as not to demolish any ancient ruins.

I am already known as the *Qassīs al-Kāthūlīkī*. I have blessed the wedding of a Greek lady, Catherina Vaissière,[8] to Ibrāhīm Khayr, a Syrian. The ceremony was conducted with all possible splendour, attended by a crowd of people, together with numerous officials and Muslim men and women who earnestly begged me to allow them to attend a Catholic marriage ceremony, with which they were impressed. Not knowing what to play, the Egyptian band struck up the *Marseillaise* and the *March of Sultan Selīm*. One must be satisfied with anything here! The building operations will start at the beginning of next month, while in the meantime I have obtained a piece of land 400 feet square from Hamed Pasha[9] with the intention of making a Christian cemetery.

I am thinking, furthermore, of opening a small college for the Galla of Suazal, Dar-Berta, the Shilluk and other pagan countries, newly discovered along the White Nile by the expeditions ordered by the Viceroy of Egypt, Muhammad 'Alī. Thus, from all aspects, this Mission in Sennar may be considered as a headquarters and centre of communications.

In no other part of Nubia is there such disorder and corruption as here. Women are publicly bartered and hired out as prostitutes, the owners being paid a certain sum per month. Young girls between the ages of thirteen and fifteen are completely naked except for small strips of cloth covering the thighs.

When I was in Abyssinia, I dressed according to the Abyssinian fashion, in trousers, shirt, a band of white cotton round the waist and a cloth round the shoulders, while the feet and head were bare. Now I follow the custom here: an open caftan fastened at the sides, white in colour with a pattern of small red flowers. Over this I wear a long sky-

---

[8] Widow of Joseph-François-Marie Vaissière (1786-1841), a French merchant who died in Khartoum.

[9] The writer evidently means Ahmad Pasha Abū Adhān, the governor general.

blue wide-sleeved coat, reaching the ankle. On my head I wear a *tarbūsh* or red fez, from which hangs a tassel of blue silk, and on my feet a pair of Morocco leather shoes, of Turkish style. When officiating or visiting, I change the tarbūsh for a white turban. The Catholics and Copts call me their *Qassīs al-Kāthūlīkī* and the Muslims the *Papas Franco*.

Khartoum in 1853, by Giovanni Beltrame

Father Giovanni Beltrame (1824-1906) was a north Italian, born at Valeggio sul Mincio near Verona, then in Austrian territory. He came to the Sudan in 1853 and travelled as far as Benī Shanqūl. In 1857 he returned as leader of a missionary expedition sent out by the Mazza Institute of Verona. For a year he was one of the priests of the Holy Cross Mission among the Dinka on the White Nile. His travel narratives attracted a wide reading public in Europe, for Beltrame possessed all the journalists' appreciation of light and shade in the situations which he described. He is chiefly remembered however for his linguistic studies; he shares with Josef Lanz the honour of being the first to compile a manuscript grammar of the Dinka language, afterwards published as a 'Grammatica della lingua Denca', in the Bulletin of the Italian Geographical Society, Florence, 1869. Beltrame collaborated closely with Professor Johann Mitterrutzner of Brixen (Bressanone), the author of grammars of Dinka and Bari, who dedicated the Dinka Grammar to our missionary. The passage which follows is a translation from Beltrame's book Il Senaar e lo Sciangallah, 2 vol., Verona, 1879, I, pp. 51-66.

The city of Khartoum was rebuilt on a slightly different site to the previous one. Nearly all the houses, some of which have two floors, are built from sun-dried mud-bricks. The Governor's palace stands out conspiciously among the buildings. It rises on the banks of the Blue Nile and is constructed of fired bricks; on one side it faces the river, while on the other it overlooks a large square.

Europeans, using stone from the hills of Omdurman, have also started to build a village on the left bank of the Nile about two kilometres from Khartoum. The Catholic Mission was the first to set the example. This Mission was founded by the Pro-Vicar Ryllo, of Polish nationality, together with the two missionaries Dr. Ignaz Knoblecher, who succeeded Mgr. Ryllo, and the Italian Fr. Angelo Vinco of the Istituto Mazza. The latter was my colleague and friend, and was the first to press along the Nile to a point beyond Gondokoro, where he died.

The first stone of this spacious mission building of tasteful design was laid in January 1854, when I was in Khartoum. At first the workers were Italians from Tuscany, but they were followed by bricklayers from the Tyrol. These belonged to the Mission, and their work was directed by the president, Fr. Josef Gostner, who had studied drawing, and ably directed the building operations.

The building was finished in July 1856, and the new quarters offered two main advantages: the health of the missionaries was now better cared for — they had previously been very uncomfortable especially during the rainy season — and the inhabitants of the town profited from the experience. Every day they would come along to see how the building was progressing and already more than fifty Sudanese have learnt how to use the trowel and build walls.

The city of Khartoum greatly resembles all the other cities of Egypt and Nubia, as for example Asyūt, Qinā, Dunqulā and Berber. The streets are long and quite straight. There is a large mosque and a fair-sized bazaar, consisting of three or four streets covered with a roof of straw and branches of trees, which is situated almost in the centre of the city. Small shops follow one after another without interruption along these dusty roads. A kind of platform made of earth, about two feet high, enables the buyer to approach the merchants who remain in their shops, which are similar to small hide-outs.

The merchant sits in oriental fashion, with part of his goods heaped before him, and part behind him, arranged in tiers. There is everything to be had; over here are clothes, over there red berets (*tarbūsh*) and socks. On one side drugs and ointments are sold, on the other long pipes (*chibuk*), [10] tobacco, etc. Now and again, one comes across a shop selling food and drink, and everywhere the air is filled with aromatic smells. The owner of the shop will not press you to buy and may not even look at you, he will continue running the beads of a rosary through his fingers, murmuring prayers and yawning now and again. Only when an object is touched or picked up will he draw back slightly from the spot where he is sitting to make room for you, and motion you to sit down,

[10] Modern Turkish *çubuk*. This and many other Turkish words introduced by the Turkish-speaking conquerors have since dropped out of the Sudanese Arabic vocabulary.

accompanying the gesture with the word *itfaddal* 'be seated'. He will immediately offer you a *chibuk,* then he will have coffee brought to you. You can remain there thus seated for a quarter, or even half an hour, but he will not say a word; you must be the first to break the silence and ask him 'how much does this cost'? 'So much', he replies; if you were to offer less he would merely shake his head, and if you were to raise your price a little, he would hand over the article without further ado, take the money and bid you farewell, and that would be all.

The business of the bazaar begins and ends with daylight; as soon as evening comes, everyone shuts his shop and goes home. Here no one works or has dealings by candlelight.

As regards the general characteristics and customs of the people of Khartoum, I must refrain from commenting because the population here consists of at least seven distinct groups, whose customs are quite different. The city of Khartoum is too young, and the merging of the customs of one class with another has not yet had time to take place, so that each of these different classes bears the stamp of its native race.

The first group consists of the Europeans, about forty or fifty in number, and most of them are traders, plying between the White Nile — or Khartoum — and Cairo. This number remains fairly constant. If anyone falls victim to the unhealthy climate of the town, he is replaced by another, who generally comes from Cairo or Alexandria.

The second group is that of the Turks. They too are few in number and are either employed by the government, or have been banished from their towns by the Viceroy of Egypt.

The third group is made up of Arab traders, more numerous than the Europeans and Turks, and nearly all coming from Upper Egypt. They trade principally in Sinnār, Sawākin, Fāzūghlī, Kurdufān and Dār Fūr.

The fourth group is made up of a very limited number of Copts who, as throughout the whole of the East, are clerks by profession.

The fifth group is made up of the *fuqaha* [11] (priests), who earn their living by teaching children, inventing talismans to which they attribute wonderful powers, and sometimes dabbling in trade. The school in Khartoum is held four times a day: from four o'clock in the morning until sunrise, from eight until half-past nine, from one till three in the afternoon, and finally from sunset until eight o'clock in the evening. The pupils pay their teachers ten *para* (cents) per week, while in addition, they are obliged to make him presents on each of the two greatest

---

[11] Singular *faqīh,* in popular Sudanese parlance *fekī,* a teacher of Islam.

feast days of the year. The greater part of these *fuqaha* claim to be able to cure the most serious illnesses by writing a few lines from the Koran on a piece of paper which, when rolled, is handed to the invalid, who must keep it tied above his elbow or attached to his hair.

The sixth group include Egyptian artisans, who are mostly coffee-house keepers, bakers, shoe repairers, painters and armourers.

The seventh group, which is the most numerous, is a mixture of Dongolese, *jallāba* (travelling merchants), and negro ex-soldiers. Two-thirds of the latter are employed, either as soldiers or boatmen, in the expeditions along the White Nile carried out by the ivory or slave merchants. At the moment, they are being paid 45 piastres a month.

The five last mentioned groups of inhabitants have little or no idea of human dignity and self-respect. If opposed, they react very feebly. Sometimes they may retaliate like sheep but are convinced that it is useless to fight. Thus, during the period of conscription they show great reluctance to join the armed forces; a few are killed, and the rest, without any further opposition, are taken down the Nile on government boats, followed for several miles by weeping women and children.

There are many amusements, dances and songs in Khartoum by day and night. It must be said that such amusements give spontaneous joy to all classes, but despite this the common feeling of citizenship is missing; it may be true that each loves his own house and his district, but nevertheless they recognise no country.

Khartoum in 1858, by Alessandro Dal Bosco

This letter, dated Khartoum, 27 October 1858, of which the original manuscript is in the Archivio Mazza, Verona, conveys the first impressions of a young priest, a former student, to his Superior, Don Nicola Mazza, founder and first head of the Mazza Institutes of Verona. The writer was born in 1830 at Breonio near Verona and came to the Sudan as a member of the Mazza Institute missionary group in 1857, staying in Khartoum as procurator of the Mission there. He was later appointed the first director of the newly-founded Comboni Institute at Verona where he died in 1868.

Khartoum was founded some thirty-six years ago by the conquering Muhammad 'Alī, when he subjected these as far as Fāzūghlī on the Blue

Nile to his dominion. Before that date, there was no vestige of a town, except for a few rough fishermen's huts. From the time of Muhammad 'Alī some small houses began to rise and, little by little, they formed a large village called Khartoum.

Khartoum is situated between the two rivers, the White and Blue Nile, and actually stands on the latter, being only a short distance from the confluence of the two rivers which forms the Nile proper. Its geographical position is 15°45″ N. and 30°15″ E. The equinoxes occur in May and August.

Although I described Khartoum as a town, it cannot be compared with any European town. I called it so merely on account of its size, but its aspect is ugly and unsightly and, were it in Europe, not worthy of a glance, consisting only of hovels and mud huts. There is neither order nor symmetry, the roads are full of potholes, the blind alleys have to be traversed many times before they become clearly known, and to the uninitiated are like a labyrinth. The roads, in fact, are not like those of Europe, passing through the town from one side to the other, but almost all of them lead to this or that house, which is enclosed by a wall, making it impossible to find a way round.

The houses, ugly and unsightly in appearance, are made of mud and sun-dried bricks. They have low roofs, also made of mud and matting, which are held up by joists. Sometimes the roofs and corners of the walls collapse blocking the road. They crumble especially during the rainy season owing to their poor construction and, if the rain falls with its usual intensity during the night, the occupant of some such miserable house sits with trembling heart fearing to see his hovel reduced to a heap of mud at any moment. He will also have to think of finding refuge from the water which is coming through a hole in the roof and, by flooding the house, forcing him to abandon it.

The only building differing from the others, on account of its size and appearance, is that of the *dīwān* [12] where the ministers of justice and religion reside.

It was left to the Catholic Mission for Central Africa to provide a solid and symmetrical building among the huts of Khartoum — a building of stone and mortar in the European fashion, unique in the entire Sudan and Sinnār, and vast regions of the White Nile; a building which has been, and will be, the wonder of thousands of Africans. To give you an idea of it: the mission house is built on an east-to-west axis, measuring 314 feet in length, and some 30 feet in width, including

---

[12] A Persian word meaning in this context the government.

the verandah. It has seven very wide rooms, which serve as living quarters, dormitories, school and stores. In addition, there are the kitchen and dining room, and two rooms serving as a church, which forms a wing on the east side of the building extending northwards. Khartoum is strategically placed between two rivers, which are like gateways leading to the interior, both to the people along the White Nile, and those of the Blue Nile, as far as Ethiopia and the Galla.

One cannot but praise the genius of the man who founded the city and who foresaw the importance of its position. On the other hand, there is a drawback, for when the river rises, the town is flooded. This is because Khartoum is below the level of the Blue Nile. As the water has no outlet by which it can drain off, it remains in the hollows formed by the uneven ground, and stagnates; gradually, it dries up, giving off an unbearable stench of mud and refuse, increased by the decomposing bodies of dead animals and other waste which is to be found along any stretch of road. When will the day dawn when this city will be properly run, giving it the beauty and lustre to match its important position?

Apart from the river, the surroundings of the town have more the appearance of a desert than anything else. On the south-easterly and south-westerly sides, there is a vast plain, which except in the rainy season, cannot boast of a single flower or blade of grass; it is barren and desolate. All is sand and arid soil, often whirled into blinding storms by the wind.

On the other side, along the Blue Nile, is a large stretch of land, cultivated as a garden and, because of its nearness to water, vegetables and plants grow easily, offering a welcome relief to the eye of the passer-by. On the banks of the river, one can see pleasant fruit trees all the year round: lemons, custard apples, pomegranates, oranges and other treees. The date palm stands majestically over all, raising its crowned head with the glory of its leaves, now hanging like the dishevelled tresses of a weeping woman, now lifted and straight like a king wearing his diadem.

The climate of Khartoum is commonly acknowledged to be unhealthy, owing to the fact, already mentioned, that the town is low-lying. Although present all the year round, the malignant evaporations are increased during the rainy season by the stagnant water, and much sickness is caused. During that time, which lasts three months, fatigue, lack of appetite, drowsiness and heaviness of the head, oppression of the stomach, sleepless nights, gloomy days, are the melancholy and usual effects of the unhealthiness of the atmosphere. Few are immune, even among the natives, but these painful inconveniences are as nothing to those that follow — burning fevers, acute illness, dysenteries and the like which bring sudden death.

Khartoum in 1881, by Bartolomeo Rolleri

This is a translation of an article which Fr. Rolleri (1839-1902) wrote in the periodical Annali del Buon Pastore, *1881, No. 26, pp. 20-25; No. 28, pp. 33-8. The writer was born at Pione di Bardi in the province of Parma and died at Piacenza. He was in Kurdufān in 1869 and was afterwards Procurator in Cairo. Later in life he became Superior of the missionary Society called the Scalabrini after its founder, Giovanni Battista Scalabrini, Bishop of Piacenza (1839-1903).*

Khartoum is situated between the White and Blue Nile, at the very point where they meet and form the Great Nile, but the whole of the city is on the Blue Nile. It takes its name from its position because in Arabic, Khartoum means the trunk of an elephant, the strip of land it stands on being this shape. It is very difficult to give an accurate estimate of the number of inhabitants in towns in these parts, because of a lack of statistics. However, it is estimated that Khartoum has between 50,000 and 60,000 inhabitants. The city is built essentially in Arab style, and the houses, with few exceptions, are of mud. Each year, a short time before the rains are due, the outer walls are smeared with cow-dung to prevent the rain-water from seeping through to the inside. As soon as the rains have stopped, however, and the burning sun once more shines, an overpowering stench emanates which, together with the mist from the many marshes and the lack of cleanliness, makes the air so unhealthy that there are many cases of fever, often fatal.

The best houses are the Governor's, the Mission, and those of a few European and Syrian traders and some of the wealthier people. They are all built in the Arab style, with a single storey. For some time past fired bricks of quite good quality, have been cheaply produced, and this is the reason why there are several solidly built dwellings in the city. Rough bricks are also made, that is, bricks dried in the heat of the sun, which are cheaper by half than the fired type. These rough bricks are quite useful because they are used on the inside of buildings, while the others are used for the outside. Both interior and exterior are plastered with lime, and the resulting houses are quite strong and of good appearance. Thus it can be seen that progress is being made and that in time Khartoum may become another Cairo, with a new modern part and the old part traditionally Arab. One might ask: why such expense? why such fine houses in a place said to be so unhealthy, when a healthier climate is readily available elsewhere? I will try to give a satisfactory answer as to how a good climate could be made possible. This strip of land which stretches out towards the centre of the country soon becomes a desert. However, after the rains, grass grows and flourishes everywhere. The city itself is built on this desert and, with the exception of a few riverside gardens watered by the Nile and the area taken up by the houses, there is nothing but dust everywhere; there is not the least sign of a road, but only sand and dust. Worse still, when anyone intends to build and has no earth available for the construction of his ground floor, and wishes to protect his house from being flooded by the rain-water, he takes the quantity of earth he requires from the nearest available spot. Hence, there are holes and ditches everywhere which, during the rains, fill up with water which stagnates and produces the fatal miasma [18] I have already mentioned. During the rainy season, one is forced to wade through water nearly everywhere. The patient donkey is admirably suited to overcome this difficulty but not without everyone becoming plastered in mud. The Sudanese have no idea of carriages or carts. Only the Mission and a European trader possess these.

Let us suppose then that the local government intends to do all within its power to make Khartoum a healthy city. I think it can well be done along the lines followed in Cairo, where, formerly there were many low-lying parts. Some still exist and are so deep that, despite their having been filled in, it is impossible to reach rock-bottom when laying foundations of new buildings. Our houses there were at least three metres below the city level, and it was at great expense that we had our entire enclosure raised, so as to avoid being flooded during the rising of the river. Outside the walls we were surrounded by a large lake of water. It was certainly not a very healthy state of affairs, but it was quite a different matter to the position here, where the water collects and stagnates. There, at least, when the level of the Nile fell, all the excess water was drained off into the river.

So, let us assume that Khartoum is raised so that the superflous water drains off into the river; that everyone is made to realize the

---

[18] Although quinine from the cinchona bark was much used as a febrifuge, malaria was still commonly attributed to *mal'aria,* foul air.

necessity for cleanliness; assume that roads and squares are built, and that these are flanked by rows of trees; assume that the banks of the river are cleared of infection; that plantations are sown; that large public gardens are set up; and that all these works are well maintained and the entire city is supplied with water by means of a huge steam pump — then I am certain that Khartoum would become a very close second to Cairo in beauty and healthy climate.

At the present time, the building of houses is not expensive. The greatest expense incurred is for the wood necessary for doors, windows, beams, etc., which must be imported from Europe. In general, the local wood is warped and thorny, and suitable only for firewood, but for these poor people, who are content with the bare necessities, this wood has its uses. It is true that there are large woods with beautiful tall trees, some of which are ebony, but they are far off, and there are no means of transport; moreover, nobody bothers about them. The natives do not need them, and the Europeans enjoy a more lucrative trade than they could from them. To cut down the costs, even in solidly constructed buildings, this local wood is used quite successfully, provided the main beam is a good one. As this twisted and thorny local wood is of inadequate thickness, strips of it are pressed one against the other, and then covered by a well-stretched kind of netting made from strong date-rope. Mats are then placed over these, and all is finally covered with lime, earth, etc. Thus they do without planks and boards which are extremely expensive.

Apart from some European buildings here and there, glass is not used in the windows. In the mission house, there is glass only in the church and in one or two rooms. It is already something for the other window openings to be covered by pieces of cloth. . . . There are a few earthernware vessels in which food is cooked, and which also serve other purposes; bowls are made out of gourds; there are a few agricultural implements, and a few mats and 'anqarībs. [14] Everything is made locally. This is all that can be found in the houses and single rooms of the Africans. It is well for them that outside the rainy season, the weather is good, and they make use of their huts only to protect their poor and scanty belongings — as they live and sleep in the open, sometimes even on the roofs of their houses.

The inhabitants of Khartoum are made up of two races, Arab and African. I believe that the Africans are the more numerous. The wealthy

---

[14] 'Anqarīb, a bed made of wooden legs and a frame strung with criss-crossed leather thongs or cords.

Arabs go about fully dressed, and even more so their women, who also keep their faces covered, leaving only two slits through which to see.

On the other hand the Africans of both sexes have only a thin cotton cloth around their waist with which they cover their bodies leaving their legs bare. They wear such apparel only when the weather is either fresh or damp, and when they are not working. They never cover themselves in the burning rays of the sun; they remain exposed with the greatest indifference and are not harmed in any way. Around the neck or on the arms they wear charms and amulets, while occasionally one of them can be seen wearing sandals. Some have their teeth sharpened, while others have a few of their teeth extracted so as to be able to pronounce better the language of their respective tribes. The women have many bracelets on their arms and ankles and even on their lips, and round their necks they wear necklaces of pierced coins. Sometimes, instead of the cotton cloth, they tie a simple band of leather round the waist, from which hang thin strips of leather about a span wide. Although their hair is frizzy, fine and short like that of the men, they know how to arrange it and make it look very presentable. The young boys and girls go about entirely naked until they are about thirteen years old.

The Arabs, and especially the women, paint their nails with a yellowish colour extracted from the henna plant, while they blacken their eyelashes with antimony. Tattooing is also practised, the markings being chiefly on the face. They sit and sleep on the bare earth or on a mat; those who can afford it have an 'anqarīb on which to lie. They do not sit in the way we do, but cross their legs beneath them.

The customs of the Africans who are taken in, educated and supported by the Mission are respected as far as decency allows. They are fed on local food, and around a large pot containing their share, they enjoy themselves immensely, plunging their hands into the pot, taking what they like, and lying all over the courtyard without even thinking of going indoors. For some time there will be difficulty in getting them accustomed to our way of eating, i.e. with spoons and forks, and our food. Once they have become used to it, however, they will not easily slip back to their former habits. This is one of the main reason why they should not be taken to Europe to be educated. If the far-sighted plan of our Mgr. Comboni is to be realized, of re-creating Africa through Africa, the young Africans of both sexes must necessarily be educated and taught in African institutes.

THE WHITE NILE

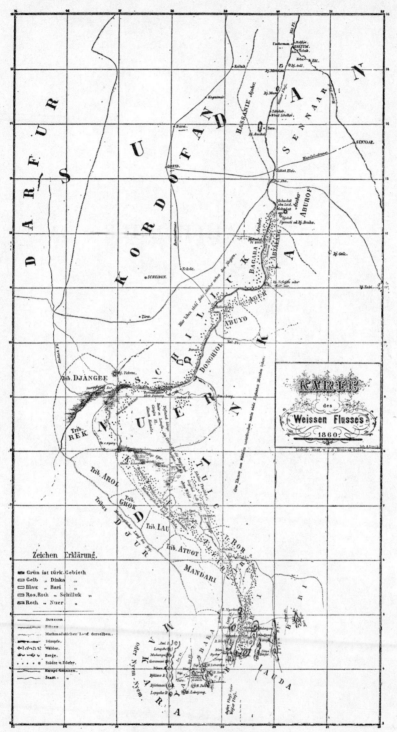

The White Nile, 1860

CHAPTER II

THE OFFICIAL JOURNAL OF THE MISSIONARY EXPEDITION IN 1849-1850

by Ignaz Knoblecher

Monsignor Ignaz Knoblecher (1819-58), one of the principal founders of the Mission to Central Africa, belonged to a generation nurtured in the supra-national, multi-racial culture of the old Austrian Empire. Though born a Slovene, by name Ignacij Knoblehar, he used for convenience the Germanized form of his name. He was a highly intelligent, urbane man with a flair for languages, an indefatigable curiosity in the sciences, particularly in geography, and a great love of Africa. Several national biographical dictionaries contain extensive lives of him.[1] And he was a young man, barely thirty years old, when with two companions, Frs. Pedemonte and Vinco, he set out on this, the first of his five voyages to the Upper Nile.

The original manuscript of his journal is preserved in the Austrian National Library in Vienna (codex 14152) together with other papers of his (codex 14151). Knoblecher did not claim to have made any resounding geographical discoveries. Ever since 1839-40, when an armed flotilla sent by Muhammad 'Alī Pasha, the Ottoman Viceroy of Egypt, made its first voyage beyond the southernmost limits of Turco-Egyptian occupation, the course of much of the White Nile was known to Khartoum merchants and their ships' crews. Knoblecher was the first to bring back a detailed, systematic, reliable description of the river and of the people living on its banks; that alone was a considerable achievement. For in 1849-50 the world's knowledge of the course of the upper river was vague and its knowledge of its source was nil. It was still possible to assert without incurring ridicule from geographical

---

[1] Notably *Allgemeine Deutsche Biographie*, 1905, XVI, p. 308; *Slovenski Biografski Leksikon*, 1925, I, pp. 472-5; *Osterreichisches Biographisches Lexikon*, Vienna, III, pp. 442-3.

societies in Europe and America that the White Nile rose in the far west, in the Chad basin or in southern Dār Fūr, or, following another geographical school, in the south-western highlands of Ethiopia. Knoblecher's findings reinforced the thinking of a third school of geographical speculation which postulated a source somewhere south of Gondokoro. Thirteen years would pass before the discoveries of Speke and Grant would vindicate the theory of the third school.

This journal was published in German and Serbo-Croat at Ljubljana in 1851 (2nd German impression, 1852) and elsewhere in German, but never in English. [2] *World geographical interest in the document grew as controversy over the location of the White Nile's source intensified and the journal was much discussed in geographical periodicals. One critic in* Petermann's Mittheilungen *was unhappy with Knoblecher's method of recording the course of the river. The Times Vienna correspondent reported an interview with 'the Pope's Vicar-General in Central Africa' who mentioned that he was equipped with sextant, thermometer, and* Griffin's Practical Navigation *but regretfully admitted that he could not afford a chronometer.* [3] *All were impressed by the scientific value of Knoblecher's contribution.*

As Knoblecher's journal is scarcely easy reading since it is not written as a flowing narrative as is Fr. Pedemonte's journal in Chapter III, we have cited only two short passages from it while printing Pedemonte's narrative in full.

JOURNAL OF THE VOYAGE ON THE WHITE RIVER — CENTRAL AFRICA

Tuesday 13 November 1849: 2.0 p.m. Set off, using oars. 2.30. Entered the White River. Sails up. 4.0. Stopped.

Wednesday 14 November: 11.30. Cast off. 6.30. Stopped on the right bank. For the first time one can see the Southern Cross on the horizon.

Wednesday 14 November: We slept in the ship until the early hours. It tossed about all night on the mighty swell of the river stirred up by

[2] See Santandrea, *Bibliografia*, pp. 11-13.
[3] *The Times*, 15 February 1851.

the high wind. The morning was chilly: we had to shield ourselves with our coats against the biting north wind. The ship which we had left behind yesterday at Khartoum caught us up at about ten in the morning. 'Alī Efendī came aboard straight away and apologized for having been unable to leave yesterday as he had been called to the *dīvān* to make over Ibrāhīm Pasha's available ships to an important stranger who wanted sixteen *dhahabīyas* for Berber.

As soon as the last ship had arrived there was a roll of drums to summon the scattered soldiers and sailors. Ahmad Efendī, who alone had accompanied us aboard, hastened to disembark. He embraced us all warmly and we asked him to take our farewell greetings to all our friends and relations in Khartoum.

In a moment all the sails were spread and the little flotilla of seven ships sailed off in line down the heaving river. Our ship, a light sailer, was soon to the fore and the Imperial Eagle of Austria raced ahead of the Turkish Crescent so speedily that we soon lost sight of them.[4] We stopped at sundown on the right bank in a mimosa wood and spent the night by ourselves on the deserted shore. The silence was broken only by the cries of the storks resting opposite.

Thursday 15 November: 6.45. Set off with the middle and back sails. 9.45. Under full sail. 12.30. Stopped on the right bank and sailed off again immediately; dense woods all over the eastern shore. Herds of horned animals were drinking at the water's edge. Profusion of mimosa and creepers. 1.30. Landed at Wad Shalā'ī.

Thursday 15 November: This morning from the ship we could see the ships of the expedition far behind us. After sunrise they got going and we sailed off at the speed of the favourable north wind which is still strong though not so much so as yesterday. All along, the right bank was higher than the left and except for a few stretches was covered with dense mimosa woods. From the ground — sand-covered alluvium — colossal creepers come up and twist themselves round the trunks of the thorn trees. A very few portions of land where the trees had been felled were cultivated, but at this season of the year there is a lack of arable land on the shores of the great river, though they are massively cultivated when the river returns to its rightful bed.

---

[4] Each owner or charterer of a small sailing vessel on the Nile was permitted to hoist the national flag of his choice, a practice followed by tourists well into the twentieth century. Knoblecher, the senior missionary, would appropriately fly his national flag.

On the western side the shore slopes down; the meadowland seems planted with trees.

At half past one p.m. we stopped at Wad Shalāʿī where the ships which had got left behind arrived after a couple of hours. Wad Shalāʿī is the dockyard where the ships that sail on the Blue River, the White River and the combined Nile to Berber are built. These ships are much heavier than those built in Egypt, for they are made of hard *sunt* wood brought from the more southerly region of the Shilluk. As one of the arriving ships passed alongside ours, I heard two voices calling me by the name I was given in the Sudan, Abūna Sulaymān, and as soon as the ship had landed two dear little white boys came rushing towards me in the cabin and asked me for medals of Our Blessed Lady. They were two children of Christian origin and it was a most pleasant surprise for me in this frontier zone between Islam and Heathenism to be asked for Christian mementos. May the Lord swiftly grant the grace of His salvation to these unhappy lands.

Friday 16 November: The night was calm and pleasant and I wanted to take a closer look at the geographical layout of Wad Shalāʿī. The first large star to come over the Meridian was Fomalhaut in the Southern Fish. As soon as we had finished supper I took my little sextant and my astronomer's horizon that I made in a lead box out of melted pitch and plunged into cold water to get a really straight line, but just as I set up my observation the star passed over the Meridian and I waited late into the night for Achernar which was already shining on the horizon. The observation seemed to me to be fairly precise but I wanted to try another with Canopus and asked one of my black attendants to wake me when that unusually bright star was high in the sky. He did wake me, but a good two hours before the star came near the Meridian. I went back to the cabin and woke myself up a few minutes before the proper time, so as to be able to make the observation.

Saturday 17 November: 6 o'clock. Cast off. To the south one can see the mountains of Tura. First monkeys, with dull grey fur and black faces, about the size of a child, among the trees on the right bank.

Before the mountains of Tura the river-bed spreads out to the west to an incalculable distance, the shore in that direction is remarkably low lying and treeless and the horizon reminds one of the sea. 12.00. Stopped near the left bank. 3.0. The rest of the ships arrived. The two Arab ships brought the news that the Shilluk had approached them in forty boats, hoping to steal their cattle, etc. The sailors' commandant has ordered the ships to come closer together in readiness for an attack.

Report of the Return Journey

Thursday 17 January, 1850: At half past ten we prepared the return journey. At eleven Leghe, the king of Tokiman, took leave of me and disembarked.

17 January: We left the ship before dawn and Alī Aghā escorted me to Logwek hill. As mist had yesterday blurred the view of the distant mountains to the south-east and west I wanted to improve on my map. The western mountains were clearer than they were yesterday but to the south the horizon was not as sharp as one would have wished. I made what improvements I could. We went down to the ships through the hilly landscape of gneiss and quartz and soon after set off on the return journey. We fired a salvo of three cannon shots as a farewell signal to the good natives, the sailors seized their oars and intoned their rowing song.

Friday 18 January: Arrived at Gondokoro at seven in the morning. Three cannon shots for our arrival. Fr. Pedemonte says he intends to settle in the land of King Shobek and to prepare the ground there. The people are beginning to fear that their land will be taken from them. Shobek, who shared this fear, disliked the idea of the missionaries settling there. Nyigilò on the other hand wanted to have them and promised to give them his house in Feriyat at the birthplace of his mother. This pleased us. Our Turkish escort, who have probably been conferring secretly with the chieftains....

Saturday 19 January: Notes. Sailed from Gondokoro at 6.p.m. In the morning we waited while the sailyard of one of the ships was being mended. I talked with five Bari who had come to visit Nyigilò. At half past ten we were ready to go, the ships set sail, Nyigilò came up to me and asked me for a few glass beads and a little basket to put them in. I gave them to him and imagined that he would go to another ship. But I heard that 'Alī Efendī had been blaming him for aiding the settling of the missionaries and persuading him that his kingdom was going to be taken from him. We told him to go home from here and not to come to the ships any more.

Region of the Shir

20 January: Left Nyago. Landed at Gori. Nyigilò promised to come with me to Feriyat, and told me the whole story of that evening we had sent him home, while the Turks tried to persuade us that the blacks are not to be trusted. Fr. Pedemonte and Don Angelo became so enraged at this that they resolved to stay behind in the region of the Shir, even should force be used to stop them.

As soon as we arrived at Gori I had the French and Austrian flags put out in case the Turks tried to attack us on account of the settling. Don Angelo went by land to Ferijat, Fr. Pedemonte went to the village of Gori to see about a house with his smith whom we had met on the journey out. He found him at once, told him his plan, and he and the other villagers were willing to have the missionaries settle there. We were beginning to unpack the things and carry them ashore when the Turks sent an interpreter to the village to intimidate the people, as they had done previously with Nyigilò and Shobek [Subek]. At once the villagers assembled under the trees and screamed for us to take the things back to the ship and move on. We complied but I went back to them and asked them what they were afraid of since the missionaries had their own food and would protect their herds against enemies and so on: In the end they were almost sorry that they had listened to our enemies.

After this setback we travelled to Feriyat. In the evening I went to see the chieftain of the village. He was lying on a skin rug outside his hut, suffering from a spear wound in his mouth. There were a number of men crouching round him. He held out his hand to me. I sat down beside him and in an instant a throng had gathered in a most orderly way. I told the chieftain of the plan of my two missionaries and expounded the advantages that the mission settlement would afford the people. They were pleased with my speech and as night had fallen we agreed to settle the matter in the morning.

21 January: Early in the morning the chieftain, whose name is Lokushek [Lokusek], came to the ship and presented me with an iron bell to hang round the necks of my cows, as he explained in the manner of the land. I was not quite happy that he should come to the ship, although the Turks assured me that they were not trying to turn anyone against our plan. So I bade him return home where I would shortly join him with my two missionaries. He left me my present and set off home.

I went straight to the village to the chieftain's house, but found only his household and glimpsed him in the distance hastening away as he saw me coming. Don Angelo went after him, handed him the pipe and persuaded him to come back. He did so somewhat under compulsion. I wondered at the change in him since yesterday evening, and suspected that the Turks were yet again involved in this. I asked him candidly what had made him so change his mind since yesterday evening. He replied with equal candour that he was afraid of me, for during the night Gumberi the interpreter had come and warned him to beware of us, telling him that we were cannibals and incendiaries. At the same time he asked me for a few glass beads, which I gave him, and then he hastened away with his son. I could no longer restrain myself from confronting the Turks with this web of intrigue. I bade them sit down in the shade of a big tree and I sent for Gumberi to account for his night-time expedition and his calumnies. He denied everything, even though the villagers accused him and marvelled at his effrontery in denying it. Muhammad Aghā and the other interpreters backed him up with spirit. They affirmed that the military watch had not seen Gumberi or anyone else leaving the camp. These asseverations only strengthened my suspicion and I let the meeting break up since the chieftain and his son, to whom the interpreter's calumnies had been addressed, were not present and the other villagers, who were present, had only heard them from the chieftain. We left at once.

22 January: Today the whole web of lies was exposed. Khālid Pasha [5] had ordered 'Alī Aghā and Muhammad Aghā to keep us under observation for the whole of the journey and to bring us all to Khartoum together. In the performance of this duty Muhammad Aghā resorted to the brutal means of calling us cannibals, etc.

23 January: We had hardly been going a couple of hours today when Alī Efendi, who had stayed on the right bank, called to us that Nyigilò and his followers had arrived. We turned that way at once and I waited for Nyigilò himself to come aboard. I did not have to wait long. He appeared with a troubled face and held out his hand and we understood each other although neither could speak at first. He told me that when he wanted to come aboard our ship in Gondokoro he had been chased away by the Turks, but he hoped that the two missionaries had remained in Feriyat and he was making his way there when he heard instead from the natives of our proposals to them, and that the Turks had sent an interpreter who had terrified the simple Bari by telling them that we were cannibals, incendiaries and sorcerers with the power to withhold the rain and wither the grass. He told the people that this was quite untrue and had been coming after us non-stop for two days to catch us up and take back the two missionaries no matter what the Turks might say. I assured him of the esteem in which I held him and his,

[5] Khālid Pasha Khusrū, Governor-General (*hukumdār*) of the Sudan.

gave him a present which I had long had ready for him, praised him for his diligence and promised to plead with our Kaiser for everything that would be of benefit to him and his good underlings. He was grieved that I did not entrust my two companions to him, but the reason why I did not was that I wanted first to settle the question of the freedom and independence of the Mission from our sworn enemies the Turks. The king placed total confidence in what I said. I gave him a last fare-well and we sailed on.

When we got to the Aliab country I noticed that the natives were much shyer of us than they had been on the outward journey. The sailors explained to me that former expeditions had stolen boys and girls on their return journey and taken them in slavery to Khartoum. That was why, as one of the ships drew near the villages and houses on the opposite shore, women, girls, boys and cattle were running away inland for safety. They need not have feared that fate this year as my presence would have hindered the Turks in any such undertakings, and I myself had made a point of setting free various boys who had been captured.

28 January: Today the rear ship of our expedition was greeted with clods of earth and arrows from the natives. Muhammad Aghā and a soldier fired two guns behind them and claimed to have shot two negroes. But natives who came to us later told us that no one had been hurt and that the assailants had moved off from the shore at the mere sound of gunfire.

29 January: The chieftain of Angwen, whom we met on our outward journey, has quite recovered from his head wound. On our journey we had met few Cic face to face but now we came across a number of shepherd encampments of theirs along the shore, such as we had met among the Aliab. . . .

CHAPTER III

A REPORT ON THE VOYAGE OF 1849-50

by E. Pedemonte

Fr. Emanuele Pedemonte (1792-1867) was the right man to accompany Knoblecher up the White Nile if, as was said, this tough Jesuit had served as an officer in the Napoleonic armies in the last days of the Empire. He would thus have been trained in mapping and possibly also in the use of surveying instruments. A Genoese by origin and a subject of the Kingdom of the Two Sicilies, he entered the Society of Jesus in 1818 and was no longer young when he and a brother-Jesuit, Fr. Gaetano Zara, came to the Sudan with Mgr. Ryllo, rector of the College of Propaganda Fide, in 1848. A contemporary wrote of him as a handsome man with a patriarchal beard. He died in Naples.

His report in manuscript, Viaggio sul Fiume Bianco del Vicario Generale dell'Africa Centrale Mon. Ignaz Knoblecher, *which he sent to his superiors in Rome, was a labour indeed. As he was exceedingly fatigued by the journey he dictated it to his younger companion, Fr. Zara, who took it down. The original is in the Curia Generalizia dei Padri Gesuiti in Rome.*

... The easiest way of reaching the Southern countries is along the White Nile, which joins the Blue Nile at Khartoum to form the great Nile. The regularity of the winds, which for six months blow from the north and six months from the south, coupled with the seasonal increase and decrease of the waters, is the reason why the river is used for this purpose in the month of November only. During this month, there is a steady stream of merchant boats leaving Khartoum on their way to purchase ivory and other goods.

In October 1849, the missionary Fr. Angelo Vinco returned to Khartoum from Italy. Despite the shortage of resources and missionaries, the Pro-Vicar decided to take part in the expedition,[1] but not having a boat he hired one, although the price was extravagantly high. He informed the Pasha (three of whose boats were taking part in the expedition) of his plan, and requested him to ask his people not to molest him during the trip. Khālid Pasha, a distinguished politician and shrewd merchant, after making fair promises raised a number of difficulties, and a meeting was called to which all the Europeans in the pay of the Khartoum government were summoned. The Governor claimed that the Pro-Vicar should refrain from buying ivory as for several years the monopoly had been taken over by the governors of the Province. To the Pro-Vicar this would have been tantamount to giving up the trip altogether, as it was the only way in which he could raise the money to pay for the boat. After several discussions the Pro-Vicar finally carried his point by producing a further letter from the Austrian consulate giving notification of the abolition of all monopolies above the Aswan cataract, as stipulated between the Sublime Porte and the European Powers.

Having overcome this obstacle, the Pro-Vicar handed over the mission house and young orphans of Khartoum to the care of Fr. Gaetano Zara, S.J. He left on 13 November with Fr. Angelo Vinco and Fr. Emanuele Pedemonte, S.J.

Upstream on the White Nile, the territory of the Pasha of Egypt is left behind on the left bank at about 13° 20′ and at about 12° 10′ N. on the right bank. Then for about two and a half degrees the left bank belongs to Baqqāra Arabs, and the right bank for about three degrees to Africans called Dinka. The islands between these banks, however, belong to other Africans called Shilluk.

As the Baqqāra Arabs and the Dinka are shepherds they were at this time of the year pasturing their herds in the interior of the country, where they find water left behind by the earlier rains. Not only were the banks deserted but the Shilluk islands were also — and until 28 November we made our way without seeing a living person — with the exception of some fleeing or frightened Africans. The reason for such terror is that these poor people live in fear of the Turks, and are aften ill-treated during these annual expeditions.

One day, the boats moored at one of the Shilluk islands and the Pro-Vicar set off for the interior, accompanied by boatmen from his

---

[1] The reference here is to the annual trading expedition protected by government troops at the traders' expense. The missionary party was compelled to join it as the authorities in Khartoum would not have permitted the missionaries to sail alone.

and other boats. They came across an entirely deserted village — the fires were still alight but the inhabitants had fled in terror.

In addition to the islands between the Dinka and Baqqāra, the Shilluk also occupy the left bank from the boundary of the Baqqāra to the lake which receives the tributary of the White Nile from the west. It is said that they inhabit 7.000 villages, and from the stream can be seen many of these villages, which are often large and very close to each other. Although the people are wild, they are nevertheless quite good agricultural workers and shepherds, and more adaptable than others to culture and civilization. Nowhere else along the river did we come across such fertile and extensive fields as those of the Shilluk. They grow beans, sesame, maize, and principally *durra,* which can be described as Africa's principal food. Bread is made from *durra,* but it can be used in other ways, and in particular, when fermented, the people make their *marīsa* from it. *Marīsa* is a kind of beer which would be intoxicating if taken in quantity. *Durra* is almost unknown in Europe. The *tukuls,* or huts, of the Shilluk are high and well constructed.

Like other Africans, the men go naked all their lives, but the women and girls are almost completely covered in skins. Their heads are kept uncovered and their hair is completely shaven. The men, on the other hand, pay some attention to their short and woolly hair. We did not learn much about the religion of these people, as we did not understand their language, but we discovered that in each village a certain tree was held in esteem. Around such trees the villagers would build a clay wall, on which were hung amulets and charms. Their dead are buried in the ground, while nearly all the other tribes along the river throw their dead into the water after tying them to a small bundle of dried canes.

28 November, we had the first opportunity of dealing with the Shilluk. We moored our boats on the left bank. At first we saw only a small number of them, but then a crowd approached us, all armed with spears. They halted on the other side of a marsh. The dragoman [2] of the boats then went out to them to barter for the exchange of a few oxen for cloth, which he offered them. The exchange was agreed upon, and the natives suddenly ran off in all directions, and in the twinkling of an eye they were back with the oxen. In general they are very fast runners, and they run like gazelles.

As soon as the oxen had been handed over, they seemed to pluck up courage and, together with the dragoman, crossed the marsh towards

---

[2] In this sense an interpreter speaking both Arabic and Shilluk (from the Arabic *tarjumān*).

our boats, and remained with us amicably until the signal for our departure was given.

On the following day we halted at Wau, [3] a large village also belonging to the Shilluk. Here, however, the inhabitants were neither diffident nor frightened. In fact, while on the previous day it was only the strong, young armed men who had ventured out to trade with us, both men and women of all ages came out to try and sell us their goods. However, we only bought meat, poultry and a few vegetables. There are many elephants in these parts, and the Shilluk hunt them for the ivory. This is not sold, however, but must be handed over to the chief, who then sells it to the merchants of the interior, keeping the profit for himself.

On 4 December, after having visited many other villages and bartered supplies, we came to the end of the Shilluk territory. Here the banks are covered with tall grass, [4] very thick, and even extending into the river itself, thus making it impossible to approach the banks. This grass grows the whole of the way along the banks, between g° 26' and 6° 50' N., that is, the southern limit of the Shilluk country, the whole of the Nuer, and half of the Cic. The grass flourishes in abundance and is often half as tall again as a man. On looking at it one would say it was delicate and quite smooth, but when one of the missionaries picked a piece to examine it at close quarters, he was sharply stung. On looking at his hand he found the palm covered with small thorns.

These banks, which seem to be deserted, are nevertheless inhabited by people called Nuer, but their dwelling places are some distance away from the river, dotted here and there and separate from each other; there are no village groups. During the first expeditions, the soldiers of the Pasha bought ivory from these tribesmen, but as the Arabs murdered some of them, they no longer dare to go near them with their boats. They speak the same language as the Shilluk, and this language is common to the Cic, Aliab and Bari. [5]

On 10 December, we left the Nuer territory and entered that of the Cic. It would appear that these people rely for their food entirely on fishing. Their villages are small and their huts miserable. Because of their occupation the stench along the banks is almost unbearable.

---

[3] Not to be confused with Wau on the river Jur, capital of the Bahr al-Ghazāl province.

[4] Particularly papyrus, and a plant often called by its Arabic name *umm sūf*.

[5] The writer was one of the first Europeans to investigate the linguistic affinities of the Nilotic peoples. Fr. Pedemonte was however misinformed on the Bari language which is distinct from the Dinka/Shilluk language group.

When we approached, the people fled from the villages; men and women scrambled into their fishing-vessels and immediately disappeared behind the tall grass. Those who did not find room in the boats, ran off as fast as they could into the bush.

The cause of their terror is the barbarous way in which the Turks abduct boys and girls, keeping them under conditions of slavery, and then selling them as such at Khartoum. Despite this, a little way further on, the people came out to meet the boats to trade their ivory. We noticed how few inhabitants there were, especially in the first villages we came across. On seeking the reason for this, we discovered that a *kojur*, a kind of witch doctor, had been going around these parts, forbidding the people to approach the boats with their ivory, and threatening them with certain death if he were not obeyed; this applied also to any of them venturing to talk to the Turks.

On learning this, and hearing that the *kojur* was not very far distant from where they were, those in charge of the boats debated whether or not they should seize the *kojur*, either by trick or violence — all were in favour of seizing him, except the Pro-Vicar, whose opinion was asked. By virtue of his office, he was naturally opposed to bloodshed, and he saw that if the *kojur* were seized, bitter revenge would be taken. After all, in view of the past abductions and cruelty on the part of the Turks among these tribes, it did not seem to be such a crime but rather a precautionary measure, for a person of authority among them like the *kojur* to warn them to steer clear of danger which might have had serious consequences for them. Those in charge of the boats agreed with the opinion expressed by the Pro-Vicar. We continued on our way, and on the 13th we stopped at a village where the inhabitants had not all taken the *kojur's* threats seriously, and here we were able to buy some ivory, but very little. This scarcity persisted until we reached the village of Angwen.

The residence of the chief of the Cic is situated in this village, and here our party was warmly welcomed. This was not only because the father of the present chief had always maintained good relations with the expeditions sent there each year by the government but because after the death of his father, the present chief was himself set up in his father's place by a similar expedition two years before. The chief of this expedition was a European, who, wanting to give these people some idea of the power of the civilized countries, and seeing that the chief had been killed in battle, decided that it would be a good thing for the son to succeed his father as chief. With this end in view, as many of the inhabitants as possible were mustered and the election of the son as chief was announced to the sound of rifle and cannon fire and the proclamation of a long list of punishments that would fall on anybody refusing to accept him as chief. These punishments included, among other things the prevention of fishing and the hunting of animals, and confiscation of pasturing grounds. This scene greatly impressed these simple people and stimulated the *amour-propre* of the newly-elected chief. The latter lives like his subjects, except that he is deeply respected and his dignity distinguishes him from the others.

After the warmest of welcomes, he expressed his gratitude by procuring some ivory for our party, and he himself took part in the bartering. To no-one was he so deferential and almost affectionate as to the oldest missionary. Perhaps the spectacles that the latter was wearing, coupled with his long almost-white beard, caught the fancy of the chief. Each time he came across him he would follow him and take him by the hand, but they could not converse because neither of them knew the other's language. Even when the missionary stepped into the boat he was followed by the chief, and we judged this to be an opportune moment to speak to him. The Pro-Vicar was called and immediately sent for a dragoman interpreter. In the meantime, the chief repeatedly kissed the palm of the right hand of the Pro-Vicar and the other two missionaries with great respect. From the conversation that ensued after the dragoman had arrived, we learnt the reason for this extra-ordinary demonstration of reverence and affection, especially towards the elder of the missionaries. It was because the latter had been taken for a very solemn and distinguished magician. Instead of leaving us in the traditional style of the natives, that is by asking for some presents, he asked for some effective tailsman to make four of his dearest wishes come true. In the first place, he wished for numerous children; secondly, he wished for the death of the people who had killed his father and injured him (he had, in fact, a long open wound on his head which he had received three months earlier from a spear, and which gave off an unbearable smell); thirdly, he wished to emerge victorious from any battle with his enemies, and fourthly, he wished his wound would heal.

The first thoughts of the missionaries turned to the last of his requests, which the chief, however, thought the least important of his four wishes. The wound was washed and cleaned and covered with plaster. Enough plaster was given to the chief so that he could change the dressing every few days. Without referring to this incident again later, I will say that when the missionaries visited him on their return journey, they had the satisfaction of knowing that the wound had completely healed. However, as this wish was not so important to him as the other three, he hardly thanked the missionaries for it.

As soon as his head had been dressed, the chief pressed for the other three wishes. The missionaries had some difficulty in answering him because of the limited intelligence of both the chief and the dragoman. Suddenly it occurred to the Pro-Vicar to give him a medal of the Blessed Virgin, and the chief allowed this to be tied around his neck. He appeared quite satisfied, and asked whether, in case of need, the medal would speak to him. The Pro-Vicar answered that it would help him in his needs. On the return journey we found that the chief was no longer wearing the long wide garment we had previously seen on him, but that he still wore the medal around his neck.

This chief accompanied us to the end of the Cic territory, and through his good offices we obtained more ivory than in any of the other villages. However, compared with previous years the amount of ivory was small, because the words of the *kojur*, as described above, resulted in the abandonment of elephant-hunting by the people.

On 25 December the convoy reached a point between the Aliab on the left bank and the Bari on the right, and the missionaries solemnized as best they could the Nativity of our Lord. Two flags were flown from the masts, the French flag belonged to the boat, while the Austrian was the national flag of the Pro-Vicar. In the morning and evening the small cannon on board was fired, while a few rockets were let off during the night. The other boats joined in the ceremony and flew their own flags.

The Aliab and the Bari are more sociable than the preceding tribes. They live in large villages and have numerous cattle, principally oxen; their character is happy and care-free. These people, too, feared abduction and hid their boys and girls. Ivory was to be had here in the same quantities as in previous years, as these people had not been threatened with any danger in offering it.

On the 27th we reached 5° 16′ 44″ N., at which point the Nile is divided into two wide branches by an indeterminate number of islands. The northern part of the largest of these islands is held by the Aliab. To the south these occupy the north-western part, and the Cic the south-south-eastern part.

Generally, the convoy splits up into two groups at this point. This year it was decided to do the same, and three boats were allocated to the western branch of the river, and four, including the missionaries' boat, to the eastern branch.

As sunset was approaching, the entire party decided to spend the night at one of the Aliab villages on the left bank, precisely where the two branches of the river meet. However, as soon as the inhabitants of the villages became aware of this, they showed their discontent by waving the boats away. The boat leaders decided to leave the inhabitants in peace, and wishing to be left in peace themselves, three of the boats were moored on the left bank and four on the right, as had previously been planned. The following day, it became clear why the natives had not desired our presence, for a little further along the remains of a burnt-out village were seen. This village had been set on fire by the Turks during one of their previous expeditions.

Before leaving the Aliab and Bor territories, where the dialects of the Dinka language end, the boats take on native dragomans who know the language of the Shir, Northern Mandari and the Bari, and a little Arabic. The Pro-Vicar had brought with him from Khartoum a young man from the Bari country who had a fair knowledge of Arabic and proved to be of great help to the missionaries.

On the last day of the year, the convoy entered the Shir country, and here the scene was different again. The people came out in their crowds to meet the boats for a good part of the way. On reaching the boats, women of all ages, boys and girls, followed them from the bank, singing '*Mata, da do-to; Mata, da do-to*' with such a tuneful melody as could hardly have been expected from these simple people, and beating time with the palms of their hands. They greet their chief in this way, and it means: 'Sultan, keep well', 'Sultan, keep well'.

This singing was interrupted only to scramble for handfuls of small beads that were thrown from the boats, but as soon as these had been picked up they would hurry back to rejoin them and follow them for the same distance they had covered in coming to meet them. The great friendliness of these people and the neighbouring Bari is due to the fact that the Turks did not leave the usual wake of cruelty and abduction behind them.

On mooring, we found their villages and their great cattle enclosures full of life. Everywhere were men and women of all ages. The Pro-Vicar, wishing to leave some token behind him, distributed a few beads to the somewhat reluctant boys and girls, who were led up to him by their parents.

That day, the river level in the channels that intersect these islands was so low that some anxiety was felt as to whether the party could continue its voyage. From the first day the convoy had been split up, the boats that had been allocated to the eastern branch of the river had tried to reach the right bank by navigating the two channels leading to it (this had always been done on previous expeditions), but as soon as the first boat set out, a rifle shot made it known that it was impossible to proceed.

Fortunately, the inhabitants of this area were numerous, and unlike the people met earlier along the route, were not afflicted by the brutality of the Turks, otherwise the boats would certainly have had to turn back. Almost at every yard the boats kept running aground. The crews were often in the water, digging their feet into the bed of the river, straining their backs against the sides of the boats, and at a shout heaving forward a little.

At the same time hundreds of Africans, tugging at an enormous tow rope, were pulling the first boat slowly forward. This slow, laborious task was repeated again and again until the boat had been freed from the river bed. We felt that we ought to reward these kind, helpful people for their efforts, but this proved the hardest part of the whole operation. As soon as they saw that the craft was afloat, they dropped the tow rope, whooped with joy and crowded round the boat's sides. Trinkets were handed out to them, but such was the confusion, jostling and scrambling with outstretched hands that most of them were lost in the water. Thus a better way had to be found of distributing the presents which was done by throwing the trinkets from the mast of the boat into the water at a point where it was very shallow. What a sight to remember — a disorderly mass rushing towards the spot where the trinkets had fallen, groping and scooping up mud in their efforts to find them and, once found, putting them into their mouths, for want of other containers. This frenzied search went on for two or three hours until, gradually, the Africans dispersed. The first boat then helped the second along, and the second the third and so on, until all were floating normally.

On 1 January, the New Year greeted us with a sudden storm of rain, lightning and thunder, unusual at this time of year as there was still more than a month to go before the start of the rainy season. Next day another storm threatened, but this fortunately did not break.

On 2 January, the Niercanyi ([Nyarkanyi] Lado mountain became visible in the distance to the south-west. This mountain is in the Bari territory not far from the river, and the Bari obtain iron ore from it. This was the first mountain which the party came across after leaving the one marked on maps as Tefafan, commonly called the Mountain of the Dinka, on the right bank of the river at about 10° 35′ N. [6]

Among the Shir, it was observed that that not only were they

[6] Now shown on Sudan maps as Jabal Ahmad Aghā or Jabal Bibba'n.

shepherds, but they were also farmers, in which they were only slightly inferior to the Shilluk. At this time of the year, there were fields of sesame and beans and an abundance of *durra*. The people have few vegetables, but they gave the party some cucumbers, which were most welcome, especially in view of the prolonged shortage of fresh vegetables.

On 7 January the boats finally drew clear of the islands with their tortuous navigation, and rejoined the three other boats which had arrived the previous night. This was the boundary between the Shir and the Bari. Once, these two tribes recognised a single chief, who was the father of the two brothers who now divide the Bari people. Apparently, they live in great harmony.

When the above-mentioned chief died, the Shir did not recognise either of the two brothers, and are now living in groups; that is, each village district has its own chief (*muga*). Because of this fragmentation, there are frequent disagreements and brawls among them, and especially between those on the opposite river banks. The party was witness to one of these confrontations, when some of the natives from the opposite bank came to the market.

On 9 January Nyigilò, the younger of the two brothers, came to meet the boats. He was greeted by cannon and rifle fire from all the boats. He was dressed in a red garment given to him by a previous expedition, but which was now faded. He was accordingly reclothed with trousers, a white tunic and a red coat.

While he was with the boats, Nyigilò never once changed his attire, but we were told that as soon as we were gone, he would go about naked like all the rest of his people. He never left the boats for a single moment, eating and sleeping on the mission boat. He was busy trading ivory throughout the day; during the year he had gathered together as much ivory as he could, so that, despite the refusal of the Cic to sell, the present expedition obtained more ivory after all than the preceding one.

Nyigilò was tall, keen in both eye and mind, and extremely active. It was said that during a battle he would majestically lead the others, like the king of the jungle. His people love and respect him, and this love and respect, coupled with his personal qualities, are the only things that distinguish him from the rest. He lives in a simple hut like the rest of his people, works with his own hands, and carries his own stool with him. It is the distinctive custom of this tribe for the chief to make use of a small stool to sit on, when necessary. These stools are made from the trunks of trees, roughly cut into shape with spears, and sometimes studded with small glass beads.

On the 11th, Nyigilò was joined by several of his wives, daughters and sons, each of whom was carrying a basket on the head filled with cooking utensils and toilet articles. Some of the older women had a red skin hanging from the waist down to the knee. The others and the daughters all wore a narrow leather belt, from which hung an apron of woven string and iron rings. Some also had a thick fringe of small chains made from minute strips of leather. This hangs from behind and is almost as bushy as a horse's tail, reaching down almost to the back of the knee. This is the only dress that these queens and princesses wear. They adorn themselves with trinket necklaces, iron bracelets and rings, sometimes so heavy as to cover their skins with sores but they nevertheless continue to wear them.

On the same day Shoba [Subek], Nyigilò's elder brother, came to meet the boats accompanied by a troop of his women. He was as affable as his brother, but was neither as active nor nearly as courageous. This may lead to the country being again divided and reduced.

Of all the Africans to be found along the river banks up to this point, the Bari are the most intelligent. Without spending too much time on this subject, I will touch only upon their skill with iron. Among the mountains that are dotted here and there on their territory are rich iron mines discovered by one of the forefathers of the two chiefs. The skill of these people is enhanced by their lack of tools; it is as though their great ingenuity has scorned their use. They have no bellows, but instead use two round vases of baked clay with convex bottoms. A tube protrudes from one side at the bottom of the vase. The mouth is covered with a soft skin, which is tied to the vase with a string, and almost covers the vessel down to its base. A hole is pierced in the middle of the skin, and a rod inserted — this does not close the hole but lets air into the vase. A circular piece of hard leather, larger than the hole pierced in the soft skin, is then attached to the top of the rod. The circular piece is close to the soft skin and acts as a valve in these primitive bellows. Now let us see how it works.

A small circular-shaped ditch is dug in the shade of a tree. On one side of the ditch a cutting is made, which is bridged with ordinary pressed clay at the point where the cutting meets the edge of the ditch. Very close to the clay bridge, the two tubes of the above-mentioned vessels are placed into the cutting, and the worker's apprentice plunges the bellow-rods up and down with a rapid motion. When raised, the circular leather fixed at the top of the rod opens the hole pierced in the skin, and when lowered closes it. This has the effect of pushing the air drawn in by the upward motion, through the tube and on to the fire under the clay bridge. These bellows do not achieve the same results as those used in Europe, but nevertheless produce a stronger and more continuous stream of air than our hand bellows. To increase the intensity of the fire, they do not spray it with water as we do, but they sprinkle it with a certain kind of fine earth. Once the iron has become red-hot, they have no tongs to pick it up, so they use a newly-broken branch from the nearby tree, and break it to the length they require. They have no anvil, so they use a large and very hard flat stone. They have no hammer, but use hard stones to give their work the first rough shape, and then finish it off with an iron roller, smoothed at one end. Vice, pliers, shears, files, wire-drawers, drills — the natives have not the slightest inkling of any of these tools. It is hard to believe that with such a small range of primitive tools these natives produce thousands of different articles, providing not only the other tribes with them, but also the Arab shepherds and camel-men. The implements made are used in agriculture and fishing.

The vanity of both men and women is flattered with ornaments for the head, ears, neck, waist, arms, thighs and legs. Thus the iron must be shaped to all sizes. Their chief skill, however, lies in the manufacture of their arms, and it is difficult to believe, on seeing their arrows and spears in the museums of Europe, that they could have been so well finished, without the use of files and hammers. If any of our leading craftsmen were supplied only with the primitive tools of these Bari iron workers, they would have great difficulty in equalling the quality of their work.

The Bari are the most courteous of all the native people living on the river banks, and the missionaries discovered that the eulogies paid to them by the French traveller, Dr. Arnaud, [7] and others who had previously visited them, were in no way exaggerated. Therefore, the moment was thought opportune for the Pro-Vicar and his companions to put into effect the plan, drawn up in Khartoum, and kept secret till now, by which, as soon as the missionaries felt that their lives were in no danger among these people, Fr. Vinco and Fr. Pedemonte should remain there. For the moment, however, Fr. Vinco was to study the geographical nature of the country, whilst Fr. Pedemonte, well supplied with seeds, was to apply himself to agriculture and produce many new products from the soil.

[7] Joseph Pons d'Arnaud Bey (1812-84), a French engineer employed by the Egyptian government. He accompanied the second and third voyages by a government flotilla commanded by Salīm Qapūdān to attempt the discovery of the source of the Nile, 1840-2.

The plan for the two missionaries was put before Nyigilò and Shoba and the commanders of the boats; it could not be kept from the latter because of their long-standing friendship with Nyigilò. The two brothers expressed great joy, and each hoped to have the missionaries with them. The leaders of the boats, however, did all they could to dissuade the missionaries; for no other motive, they said, but that their lives would be in danger among the Africans.

On the morning of the 14th, the boats were at a point 4'. 50° N., not very far from the spot where other expeditions normally halted, because of the report that there was a cataract a short distance away, which would hinder progress. This time, however, it was decided to push on as far as possible, at least, as near the cataract as possible. However, the river, at this point, widened like a lake; various attempts were made to navigate it, but the surprising shallowness of the water made it impossible for the loaded boats to continue. It was then decided to unload three of the boats, among them that of the Pro-Vicar, and continue the trip with them. Shortly after noon the boats had been emptied, and left, accompanied by Nyigilò. Fr. Pedemonte was left here to choose the most propitious spot on which to establish himself.

Pedemonte immediately made inquiries about the dwelling-place of Nyigilò, and although it was distant from the river, he wanted to visit it first, to ascertain whether it was possible to accept Nyigilò's offer that the missionaries should live with him. Shoba answered that Nyigilò lived at Belinian [Bilinyang], a place near the mountains, which could be seen to the east. It was not so far away from the river as to make it impossible to return to the boat before nightfall. Pedemonte immediately left, accompanied by several members of Nyigilò's family on their way back to their huts. They walked, as neither these nor other Africans had ever heard of mounts. The worst part was trying to keep up with them, as they were striding forward so swiftly, and it was useless to ask them to slow down because having done so they would immediately have stridden off again at an impossible speed. It is true that they consoled him somewhat when they pointed to a few huts, which appeared in the distance, and which Pedemonte thought to be the dwelling place of Nyigilò; but once the huts were reached, they still had to go on further because they were not Nyigilò's. They had already drawn so close that each tree was distinctly visible on the neighbouring mountain. but still there was no sign of Nyigilò's home. Turning his head, Pedemonte saw that the sun was about to set, and that there was just sufficient daylight left for him to return to the boat. In addition, he had already summed up the position as being unfavourable, because being at the foot of the mountain the heat would have been unbearable. To this must be added the poor quality of the water that was drawn from the wells there; a few sips were sufficient to upset his stomach for two days. He decided to settle on the bank of the river, and two members of the Nyigilò family were kind enough to accompany him on the journey back.

As I said, the three empty boats set off, and after having precariously crossed the stretch of water which had previously hindered their progress, they were now sailing smoothly, and the night was spent at the usual stopping place of previous expeditions. The next morning they again set sail and towards midnight they were approaching the cataract, which as yet had never been crossed by an expedition. Dr. Arnaud had been forced to stop here, despite his great desire to go further on.

At this point the river again widens enormously, and because of the inclination of the river bed the water flows very rapidly, dotted here and there with projecting rocks. It was imperative for someone to find a spot where the water was deep enough to keep the boats floating, and the Pro-Vicar's *ra'īs*, [8] as was usual in difficult circumstances, took charge of this risky enterprise; it succeeded without any setback, and the two other boats followed in his wake.

His courage, skill and bravery deserves to be recorded as this was the first time this formidable rapid had been navigated. In further praise it must also be recorded that the water was never as shallow as in that year. His name is Sulaymān Abū Zayd, from Wādī al-Kanūz in Nubia, where some of the finest steersmen come from. May this brief remembrance serve in place of the monument which would surely have been erected in his honour, had he belonged to a European nation, where men of genius undertake great enterprises and are rewarded by the honour of their achievements.

After this stretch of water had been left behind, the boats forged ahead for a few miles, when suddenly the river appeared to be blocked across its width by sandbanks; but on closer inspection it was found that there was sufficient depth of water for the boats to pass through the banks; and the boats just slipped through, with their bows turned to the left. On emerging into the open from this narrow cutting, the boats went on for another four miles without incident, and then several rocks were seen jutting out here and there in the river. However, it was not difficult or dangerous to navigate these.

There was still some daylight left and induced by the beauty of this thickly populated spot, the boats moored at the village of Tokiman

[8] Arabic, in this sense a pilot.

[Tokimang]; as soon as the boats had touched ground, the people crowded around, attracted by the novelty. This was the first time they had seen bearded white men clothed from head to foot. No less wonder was expressed at the boats with their wide sails, which carried them so easily through the water, although heavily loaded. Nothing, however, filled them with such astonishment as the sound of an accordion which the Pro-Vicar had with him. They attentively followed the movements of the hands and fingers, and they would have liked to know how such pleasing and measured sounds were possible. A chief of one of the villages was so enraptured that he told the Pro-Vicar that he would give him his village if he remained there. These were the first Africans on the voyage who gave evidence of their inclination towards music, which is so common among the American negroes. Their compatriots below the cataract had derived a certain amount of pleasure from the music, while Nyigilò and Shoba had been highly delighted, but the rest of the people had shown complete indifference.

This accordion later made a welcome gift for Nyigilò. On the following day, 16 January, the boats left on time and after two hours they reached Logwek on the left bank of the river. This village takes its name from a small isolated hill situated to the west, about a thousand feet along the bank, at 4° 10′ N. The Pro-Vicar expressed his intention of climbing the hill in order to study the lie of the land, and he was accompanied by several of the Africans. From the top he could see the heights and depressions of the land beneath him. There were isolated houses everywhere, and small villages, especially near the river. There were trees growing all about, but not close enough together to form woods.

In the distance to the south-west, Kego and Kidi could be made out. These are two mountains, one near the other, which mark the border of the Bari territory. The river, which according to the people, passes by these mountains, appeared to be running parallel to them and then first curving to the east and then northwards until it reached the hill. Not far away, towards the east, stands Mount Kerek [Kereki], where large quantities of iron ore are obtained. Behind this, further and further away in the distance there are other mountains, inhabited by the Yangwara, who are the enemies of the Bari. To the north, quite a long distance away, there rises the above-named Nièrcany. To the east there is a group of mountains, the tallest and most extensive of which is Belinyan. Iron ore is to be obtained from all of them, but the quantities vary. Behind this group are the summits of the Lagwaya [Logwaya] chain, inhabited by the Beri, and bordering with the Bari and the Galla.

To the south, almost indistinguishable in the distance, there is a long stretch of high ground, but the Bari did not know to whom it belonged. Although the commander of the boats had previously decided to press on towards the source, and although this would have been possible in view of the height of the water, they decided to turn back because of the difficulties on the return journey. Therefore, on the morning of 17 January, they started to go downstream and on the following day rejoined the other four boats.

The first thought of the missionaries was to unload their equipment, by Nyigilò and Shoba had changed their ideas. Shoba told them openly that he did not wish them to stay with him, while Nyigilò said he no longer wanted them at Belinyan (where he had previously invited them) but instead, said they should set themselves up at the village of Berigia, where his mother's house was situated. This change of attitude seemed very strange to the Pro-Vicar and his companions, but they obeyed his wishes without protest.

Therefore, on 18 January, all the boats prepared to go downstream to Berigia. It seemed strange to the missionaries that Nyigilò did not accompany them but instead came to the boats and said that he would be going on to the village overland, and that he would be awaiting them on their arrival. In everybody's mind there arose the suspicion of a possible Turkish plot. This suspicion was increased on the way downstream, as no one reported having seen Nyigilò.

After two days the boats were at Gheri [Geri], a village on the right bank a mile above Berigia, and here they moored, awaiting word from Nyigilò. But nothing was heard of him, and it was then assumed as certain that such a change was due to the commanders on the boat, and that it was at their instigation that Nyigilò had made his false appointment. This duplicity was the more repugnant to the missionaries, as what had pleased them most was the simplicity of Nyigilò and his people. Convinced of this, the missionaries decided to stay in the hope of overcoming opposition. Therefore, Fr. Vinco went on foot to Berigia to see whether Nyigilò had sent word regarding them and if not, whether the chief of the village would agree to their establishing themselves there.

Since the death of the last chief, no successor had yet been chosen in Gheri, but during his first visit there Pedemonte had made the acquaintance of a very obliging blacksmith, from whom all the above information on the working of iron was obtained. He went in search of the blacksmith, and when he was found, led him to the boat, showed him all his instruments and explained their use, and then told him that it was his intention to remain with him and that they could use the tools together, like good companions. The man appeared both astonished and pleased at the sight of the tools, and on hearing of the missionary's plan, stepped off the boat with him, and told the news to everyone he met. Shortly they came to his workshop under a tree, around which was a great crowd of Bari showing their pleasure at having the two missionaries with them. Then Fr. Pedemonte returned to the boat, and at the same time Fr. Vinco arrived. He had not heard from Nyigilò, nor had he been able to find the chief of the village to discuss the proposed stay. The people there, although they gave evidence of their willingness to have them, were unable to decide owing to the absence of the chief. However, the missionary left a servant there, with orders to inform him as soon as the chief arrived.

In the meantime, the Pro-Vicar and the missionaries thought it wise to take advantage of the friendly disposition of the people in Gheri. The boat was moored near a tree, and the unloading of the goods and baggage began, thus assuring them of the necessary provisions until the next expedition.

Meanwhile, an old chief from a nearby village, seated on a stool and surrounded by a large crowd, was watching the unloading, which was nearly completed, when one of the commanders of the boats approached, followed by a dragoman. The commander of the boat took the chief by the hand and led him to one side. Fr. Pedemonte, who saw this, immediately left the goods he was guarding and ran after them to see what was afoot, as he already understood something of the language, having learnt it from his Bari servant. However, he was not able to hear anything, for as soon as he reached them, they broke up. The chief, touching the missionary, looked interrogatively at the dragoman as if to say: 'Is this the man?'

Two minutes went by; then that great circle of murmuring Africans broke up into one confused mass, and one of them boldly stepped up to the missionary and waved him back to the boat. While the missionary was trying to quieten him down, two others came up and followed the example of the first. The missionary anxiously glanced round for his blacksmith acquaintance, but already with one voice, the natives were shouting 'to the boat, to the boat!' '*to kibo, to kibo!*'. The missionary then saw that any further attempt to placate them was useless. He advised the Pro-Vicar, and everything was immediately reloaded into the boat.

While this was going on, the Pro-Vicar went under the tree and asked the people why they feared his companions. As no one answered, he went on to speak of the advantages they would gain by having him among them. They listened to him silently and attentively, and their faces reflected a mixture of fear and sorrow. As soon as the loading operations were completed the boats moved off from Gheri. Two hours before dusk, when the boats halted, they found a delegation of about ten Bari from Gheri, who expressed their sorrow at having ordered the missionaries to leave and now invited them to return. Among them was the friendly blacksmith. The people said that the dragoman had intimated to the chief that the white men who wanted to remain with them were two evil sorcerers who would have stopped the rains on their soil, thus depriving them of their *durra* for food and drink, and their pastures. The dragoman also told the chief that, as soon as the food became scarce in his country, the missionaries would feed on the flesh of their children. How easy it is to persuade these credulous Africans.

However, the missionaries did not comply with their wishes, but decided to stop at Berigia. Towards evening the chief arrived, and the Pro-Vicar went to see him at his hut. Near the door, on a hard, smooth pavement, the chief was seated on his stool. He had summoned all the inhabitants of the village to be present at the conference. A great circle was formed, with some of the natives seated on stools and some squatting. Behind this circle was a confused mass of boys and girls and women of all ages. The Pro-Vicar also sat down on a stool, and outlined his plan; that his two companions wanted to remain among them. The chief and all his people agreed and promised that in two days time huts for the missionaries would be ready. That night the missionaries slept in peace, in the knowledge that the commanders of the boats would not ruin their agreement with the natives, as it was a rule on such expeditions that no negotiations could take place during the night, and everyone is ordered back to the boats after sunset. Sentries, more vigilant than those of armies on the battlefronts in Europe, are posted all round the boats, keeping a sharp look-out throughout the night. It was barely daylight when the chief of the Berigia was seen approaching the boat. He stepped on to the bank and presented the Pro-Vicar with a roughly-made iron bell, saying to him: "Hang this on your oldest cow." The Pro-Vicar accepted it and reciprocated with another present, and asked him why he had not waited for him the evening before in the village as agreed. The Pro-Vicar then returned to the boat for something, but when he returned the chief was no longer on the bank. Astonished, he went to the village and arriving at the chief's hut he found it also deserted. The two missionaries who were accompanying the Pro-Vicar set off in search of the chief, and after a prolonged search he was found by Fr. Vinco, who had great difficulty in persuading him to come to the Pro-Vicar. He came accompanied by a few men and women. It was not possible to get an explanation, but he made a demand for beads. These were given to him. After being interrogated at length, he finally explained that he was afraid of the two white men remaining on his territory. He said that during the night, a dragoman had visited him and had assured him and his people that the two white men were evil magicians who would have stopped the rains on their soil, depriving them of their harvest and pasturing grounds, and that when food was short the white men would have eaten the flesh of their sons. In fact, it was a repetition of the calumny that had occurred in the other village. All the people confirmed this and gave the name of the dragoman. It was the same man who had spread the slander at Gheri. The Pro-Vicar saw that the chief had been influenced by the dragoman. Sadly, he and his missionaries decided that it was impossible to establish themselves among these people on this trip. On the same day, 21 January, they left for Khartoum. . . .

On the way back, one of the commanders of the boats, who did not belong to the Pasha of Khartoum, admitted to Fr. Vinco that the Pasha had secretly ordered that the three Europeans should be brought back to Khartoum at all costs. . . . The return journey was completely without incident, except for difficulty with shallow waters here and there, and the boats moored at Khartoum on 7 March 1850.

CHAPTER IV

ANGELO VINCO, FIRST CHRISTIAN TO LIVE AMONG THE BARI. HIS JOURNEYS, 1851-1852

Like several of the writers whose work we have reproduced Don Angelo Vinco (1819-53) came from the Veneto, for he was born at Cerro Veronese not far from Verona. After theological training at the Mazza Institute in Verona he studied Arabic in Venice and Rome and came to the Sudan with the first missionary party in 1847 under the leadership of Mgr. Ryllo.

Don Angelo (as he was universally called) made two journeys up the White Nile: the first in 1849-50 as a colleague of Pro-Vicar Knoblecher and Fr. Pedemonte, a journey already described in Chapters II and III above; the second in 1850-1 which he narrates in the present chapter. His lively narrative is incomplete for he died among the Bari people shortly after writing this first report.[1]

The various printed editions of his manuscript are listed in Sant-andrea, Bibliografia, *p. 13. The first printed version appeared in* Annali della Società di Maria per le missioni cattoliche, *Verona, anno 2, II, Monza, 1853, pp. 3-48, though at the end of the fascicle the date is printed 27 May 1857 as the date of publication. A separate printing was made at Trento, 1853. We have used as a basis an English translation by Fr. F. Sembiante of the annotated edition by R. Almagià published in* Annali Lateranensi, *Roma, IV, 1940, pp. 300-28 and reproduced in* Don Angelo Vinco, *by E. Crestani, Verona, 1941, pp. 74-134. The fate of the original manuscript is not known to us.*

Towards the end of 1849 together with some missionaries I left Khartoum and made for the White Nile. I will not dwell at length on the expedition and the countries and tribes between Khartoum and the Bari tribe,

---

[1] For an account of the presumed place of his death see 'Sul presunto ritrovamento della tomba del . . . Vinco', *Boll. r. soc. geogr. ital.* 1934, pp. 195-9.

because much has already been said about them by others. I am going
to concentrate rather on those areas nearer to the Equator, and relate
what I was able to learn during my fourteen months' stay there.

Since our first expedition it had become evident to us that we would
have to return to those distant countries as quickly as possible, in order
to set up a mission station there. Such an enterprise really required
many more of us, but as there was no one available, I was actually the
only one to set out again during the following year. I left Khartoum on
12 January 1851 and made my way up the White Nile with two boats.
The White Nile is the western branch of the two rivers which form the
Nile proper. Having passed the Shilluk and Dinka tribes, I reached
the Nuer country, where I saw some of the natives staring at the boats
from the banks. I immediately requested the captain of my boat to put
me ashore, as I felt that I must pause in my voyage and speak to them.
The captain was greatly alarmed and did all he could to prevent me
carrying out my plan. 'Are you aware', he kept on saying, 'that the Nuer
are very wicked people, and that five years ago they murdered many
members of an Egyptian government expedition?' He added other
stories of this kind, but seeing that my mind was firmly made up, he
finally agreed and our boat nosed its way into the bank, where we landed.

As soon as the natives saw the boat approach, they made off like
a group of gazelles, despite the fact that my interpreter was shouting at
the top of his voice in an effort to recall them. I immediately seized a
handful of red and white beads called 'pigeon-eggs' and scattered them
among the fleeing Nuer, while my interpreter unceasingly invited them
to come back, and assured them that we were good people, and had
nothing in common with the men in the Turkish boats. After some
time a few of the people ventured cautiously towards my boat. I enquired
about their chief, and he was immediately sent for. He then appeared
surrounded by a multitude of his followers, whom he ordered to lay
down their weapons whilst they were still some distance away from us.
The chief's name was Kan; he was tall, well-built, handsome, and had
long hair falling down his back. I chatted with him for two hours and
when he was quite convinced that he had nothing to fear from us, he
thanked me very much and had a ram brought to me. I then presented
him with some glass necklaces, and he was so pleased that before leaving
he said to me: 'I will consider you a traitor, if you do not pay me
another visit on your return, provided, of course, that you are not
accompanied by Turks, with whom I want no dealings'. Finally, he
imparted what I took to be a blessing on me, using a vessel filled with
ox-urine and water, into which the more distinguished of those present

spat, while I was forced to do the same. The chief then wished me a very pleasant journey and bade me farewell.

It filled me with great joy to think that I had been received with such great kindness because, in view of the warnings I had previously received, I had really expected trouble. I felt increasingly encouraged to carry out what I had undertaken, despite the fact that I was alone and with scarcely any means of defence in case of attack. I had refused to join a government expedition,[2] as I was certain that the Turks would have once more upset all my plans, as they had done on a previous expedition. I continued my voyage and made my way towards another tribe called Cic, where I was warmly welcomed by their two chiefs, one of whom is called Tusicvien. The latter invited me to stay with him and presented me with an ox, as on a previous occasion I had cured him of a septic spear-wound which he had received in battle. . . . More remarkable still was the fact that Tusicvien was still wearing the medal of the Blessed Virgin round his neck. This medal had been given to him during our first journey. I gave a few beads as a gift to the two chiefs and then pressed on towards the Aliab and the Shir, when an unforeseen event occurred. As it had always been my intention to settle among the Bari, I had been making a study of their language since my first journey. As the language was difficult and I had not studied it well, I had secured the services of a Bari interpreter, who had accompanied us on a previous expedition. No sooner had we reached the Shir than I discovered one night that my bag had been opened, most of the beads had disappeared and the interpreter had vanished. I was thus left alone in the midst of these wild tribes, without a working knowledge of their language and unable to converse with them. I cannot express the anguish I felt. I could see myself being forced to turn back and, what was more important to me, I would have been unable to remain among the Bari, even if I were to succeed in reaching them. However, I trusted myself to God, and without further meditation I gave orders to set sail, and the voyage continued. As the Shir have the same language as the Bari, I began to make myself understood a little, partly with the limited vocabulary at my command, and partly with the help of signs, but, nevertheless, the thought of my difficult position grieved me.

On 24 February 1851 I arrived safely at Margiu, a large Bari village lying on both banks of the river, between 4° and 5° N. As soon as I landed, I asked the whereabouts of their chief Nyigilò, whose acquaintance I had made during the first expedition. In answer, I was

---

[2] I.e., the annual trading expedition.

told that Nyigilò had asked the members of the Egyptian expedition
which had preceded me, whether I would be returning this year. He
had been told that I would not be coming back, and that, indeed, I had
already left Khartoum on my way back to my native country. Later,
Nyigilò told me that this news had saddened him. Having lost all hope
of seeing us again, Nyigilò had gone off to Lotuka to exchange the few
beads given to him by the above expedition, for oxen, rams and other
things. Thus he was absent when I arrived.

I gave two Bari some valuable beads, and sent them to fetch him.
I instructed them to tell him that Fr. Angelo, whose acquaintance he
had made the year before, had returned this year, despite some delay,
and requested him to settle his affairs as quickly as possible, and to
return to Mariū where he was eagerly awaiting him. In the meantime
I was content to lodge with another chief, Jubek by name, whom I had
also met the previous year. This chief has one of the most difficult
and dangerous jobs among the Bari, for he has either to make rainfall
or die, according to the wishes of the people. He is called *Matat-lo-
kodu,* or rain-chief. Like his predecessors, he has to give the impression
that the sky is an open book to him, that he is able to produce clouds
and to make rain fall or stop, according to his commands. He receives
numerous heads of cattle from the tribe in payment, otherwise, according to what he tells them, their fields would be scorched by the burning
rays of the sun. These poor credulous people believe him. Woe to him,
however, if a drought persists. In such a case, the natives all gather in
his hut, and after intoxicating themselves with many gourds of *yawa*
(in Arabic, *marīsa*) tear his stomach open with a spear, because, according to them, the rain he has been maliciously hiding will now have a
chance to pour out. I remained eight or ten days with this chief,
awaiting Nyigilò's return. During this time, I cultivated his friendship
by making him daily gifts of beads, and continually bought *yawa*, milk,
sesame, and many other things I could find for him and his family,
especially when I became aware of the supreme authority he wielded
among the people. In addition, I presented him with a suit of clothes,
and I had the satisfaction of knowing that he was very pleased, and
was presenting me in a favourable light amongst the people.

At last, Nyigilò arrived with a very large following. I immediately
made by way to the river bank, embraced him, greeted him, and led
him to my boat. While I was chatting with him, a messenger arrived
from Jubek, and addressed me in the following manner: 'As Nyigilò
has arrived, and because, having been to Khartoum, he is the white men's
favourite, Jubek has instructed me to tell you that he is leaving. If you

have anything to tell him, do so at once'. I immediately understood that Jubek was behaving in this way through jealousy. Anyhow, I sent him some beads and let him depart. I therefore remained with Nyigilò for two or three days, but I did not have an opportunity of discussing my affairs with him, because he said he was very tired from the journey he had just made — and I believed him, because the only means of travel is by foot in these regions. I realised that he was still well disposed towards us, although the Turks had tried to poison his mind with a lot of wicked stories about us. The Turks had told the people here that, if we remained among them, their animals would die, the rains would stop, the vegetation would wither and perish, and what was more terrible, many of the people would die.

Nyigilò took me to see his aged mother, so that I could give her some beads, which I willingly did. In addition, I presented Nyigilò with all sorts of things I had with me. I gave him a good Arab dress, many beads, two brass bells, a mirror, and other trinkets, which pleased him very much. This was proved by the fact that, in addition to the two oxen he had presented to the crew of the boat, he forced me to accept four beautiful elephant-tusks. Judging the moment to be opportune, I laid my plans before him, and told him that I would have liked to remain at least one year among them. He answered that as far as he was concerned, he would be pleased, but added that he was afraid, if he gave me permission to stay, that the people, who were ignorant and full of prejudice, would kill us both if any of the Turkish predictions materialized. I then suggested that I should be allowed to go to Belinyan for two or three weeks. Belinyan is inland, at the foot of a very long range of mountains, on the right bank, and about six hours from Margiū. Nyigilò had his residence there. My proposal was willingly accepted, and I explained the position to the captains of the boats, saying that I wished to go to Belinyan to explore the mountains, and especially to visit the iron mines. The crews were unanimous in saying that they would not remain one single day, as if I died, they too would surely perish with their boats. I assured them that I would speak to the chiefs about this point, but it was in vain. I then enquired whether any of the servants would accompany me, but they, too, refused. Though sad and dispirited to see myself deserted by everybody, I decided to go on alone with Nyigilò, and leave the future to Divine Providence.

Early in the morning, on 4 March 1851, I left for Belinyan. I was the first to venture so far from the river. After pressing on for about two hours, to my surprise, I was overtaken by four of my people, who, after long discussions with the rest of the crew, had decided to accompany me. I felt very relieved and we continued on our way in company. We were in the midst of a vast plain, studded with tamarind, rubber and other trees. From time to time we came across small villages, and one can say that Belinyan and Margiù are really one large village. About halfway, we broke our journey and paused awhile with a village chief called Lochidi [Lokidi]. He was a man of about fifty-five years of age, and we found him lying in a hut on some ox-hides. As soon as he saw us, he immediately had gourds of *marīsa* brought to us, and invited us to rest awhile. Being thirsty after that long trek under the scorching sun, I greatly enjoyed the cooling drink. I presented the chief with some beads and we immediately resumed our journey. We reached Belinyan at 3 p.m. At the request of Nyigilò we fired some shots, to the great amusement of the population. When we arrived at Nyigilò's house, part of it was allotted to us. In addition, Nyigilò had mats and skins brought to us to lie on, while I was given a small chair with four legs cut from a single piece of wood. Earthen pots to hold water and *marīsa* were also brought in and then we were left alone. I felt very tired and decided to lie down for a while, but any rest was out of question, as a huge crowd soon gathered eagerly waiting for a glimpse of the newly-arrived white man. They jostled and pushed one another in an attempt to greet me first. Some seized my hands and held them high, some danced before me, whilst others shouted '*ta doto komonit*' — 'I greet you, new traveller'. Some laughed at my colour and others, noticing my beard, went so far as to call me '*agueron*', 'man-eater'. For the whole of that day and most of the night, I had to endure these irksome visits, without being allowed to close an eye. At last, overcome by exhaustion, I fell asleep and the people slowly went away.

Very early the following morning, the visits started all over again, and I had to exchange greetings and compliments without showing any signs of impatience. On the previous day the natives had all come empty-handed, but now they all brought something, and I received *marīsa*, milk, honey, roasted sesame, meat, and so on. In short, they were competing against each other, offering me the best they had. That occasion cost me many beads, because I realised that they were only offering these goods with the aim of receiving something in exchange.

On the third day, it was my turn to visit the leading personalities of the village, who had previously come to me, and whom I knew by sight. First, I went to see Jubek (mentioned earlier on), then to a certain Ton-on [Tongun], to Doka and others. With kind words and gifts I tried to gain their favour, and was quite successful, as I was now able to express myself reasonably well in their language. In the meantime, the news of my arrival spread like wildfire to all the surrounding villages. Many of the inhabitants came to see me, and in a short time I had the opportunity of meeting the chiefs of Gedian, Uagnan, Lacer, Mogri, Godian, Duerū and other places, and I endeavoured to gain the confidence of them all. [3] I remained there for about twenty days, doing my utmost to lay the foundations of my plan, that is, to find out whether it would be possible for me to stay among them.

With great patience, my plan succeeded. The chiefs who knew me sent me many gifts and I was therefore never without *marīsa*, meat or milk. As things were thus arranged, I sent one of my servants to Feriscia, [4] where the captains and crews of my boats had retreated after my departure, thinking themselves to be safer there than at Margiù. I ordered them to return to Margiù immediately, as I had decided to stay among the Bari for a year. They immediately set sail, and three days later they were at Margiù; I went to the boats to fetch my things, and to give the necessary instructions for the return of the boats to Khartoum. On leaving Belinyan, I was accompanied by Nyigilò and by four of my servants from Berber who, seeing that things were turning out smoothly, had made up their minds not to leave me. Many Bari accompanied us, which proved to be very convenient as otherwise we would never have been able to carry back all my things. When my people had arrived at Margiù, they already knew of the success of my stay at Belinyan, and they no longer pressed me to return with them to Khartoum, but with one voice all exclaimed 'Rabbunā yastūr, Rabbunā yastūr, Rabbunā yasa'il', or 'May God smooth out all your difficulties. God help you.' In a short while, all my luggage and trunks were put ashore, and, after wishing me good luck, they set sail for Khartoum.

I must confess that, at this moment, I was assailed by many varied thoughts as to my future, but trusting implicitly in God, I succeeded in regaining my tranquillity. First of all, I made arrangements to have all my belongings transferred to Belinyan. I divided the goods into two parts and distributed the loads according to the carrying power of the porters, as everything in these parts is carried on the head. To encourage

[3] In reply to questions put to him by A.T. d'Abbadie (1810-97) traveller in Ethiopia, Vinco informed him that the Bari nation was divided into two sub-tribes, the Labot and the Lokes. The Labot included the Fegelu, Fekisha and Shir, while the Lokes included the Makedo, Muruli, Lugufi, Liefara, Gnianke, Dueru, Godian, Belinian [Bilinyang], Uagwan, Palkar, Mogri, Magiri, Karijik and Marjiok. The paramount chief, an old man named Pitah, lived at Cenderu [Shindurru].

[4] Fekisha in the preceding note. A. Peney's map (*Bull. soc. géogr. de Paris*, sér. 5, V, 1863, gives Fekiscia, north of Gondokoro.

them, I gave them some beads, and, supervised by two of my servants, the first half of my belongings was taken away. I remained behind on the river bank, guarding the other half. After two days, the porters returned, and I gave them some more beads, which I had prudently kept back with me, as I realised only too well that money is a wicked companion, especially when travelling among the Africans whose desire for it is unlimited. As soon as the load was distributed, we started the journey back together. While passing through the various villages, I was afraid of being attacked, as all the inhabitants looked at me suspiciously, and ran away from me as if I were a wild beast. I then realised that my safety was not as yet assured, but I took courage and continued on my way.

I had already gone part of the way, when I came across some young women drawing water from a well. As I was extremely thirsty, I approached them and, in their language, asked them to give some to drink, in return for some beads. No sooner had I uttered these words than they stared at me, and hurriedly made off with their pots towards their huts. My companions and I shouted after them, begging them to stop, assuring them that we would not harm them, but it was all in vain, and the only result of our shouting, was that we were thirstier than ever. Parched, I rested from time to time under the shade of trees on the way, and we continued the rest of the journey in this way.

As soon as we arrived at Belinyan, I went straight to a hut which had previously been allotted to me, and where two of my servants were awaiting me. The first thing I did was to arrange all my belongings so as to prevent the people from stealing them. Nyigilò, accompanied by other chiefs and a long retinue of tribesmen, then called to see me, bringing several drinks to refresh me. Towards evening, I was brought a gourd filled with a mixture of boiled *durra* and beans, seasoned with a little sesame. This dish is known as *dilong* and while the Bari find it delicious, I certainly did not. I was then given a mat and skin to rest on during the night, and one by one the people returned to their huts.

Thus, in a few words, I have told the story of how I, the first European, succeeded in entering the Bari country and living amongst them. My next thought was to concentrate on mastering their language, and to learn all about their customs, so as not to make a false step, because all my future depended on the impression I created during the early part of my stay. Although complimented and insulted in turn, especially by those callers who came to see me from afar, this state of affairs did not last long, and slowly the people became accustomed to my face and dropped all uncomplimentary remarks. Moreover I was beginning to be held in higher esteem; they spoke well of me on all occasions, treated me with greater respect and consulted me in their public and private affairs. They went so far as to call me *Giuoc* [Juoc], the name of one of their gods, who, according to them, lives in heaven.

Generally speaking, the rains were abundant this year, and the crops and fodder for the cattle were in plentiful supply. There was only one period of eight or nine days, when the sky remained clear and there was no rain, whilst the *durra*, which is their staple food, began to droop and wither. The natives went to see Jubek, the rain-chief, and bluntly told him that if he did not produce rain within three days, they would kill him. Moreover, the next day all the headmen of the country met at Jubek's house, and I too was invited. I thought it wise to accept the invitation, especially as it had been unanimous, and went along, accompanied by Nyigilò and one of my servants. We entered a large hut, where all the chiefs had already gathered; I greeted them with the customary '*Ta dotore*', and sat down on a small chair, intently watching the developments. Several oxen were led in, one of which had been given as a present to one of their priests, who are called *bonit* in their language. The rest of the oxen were slaughtered and all the people, men and women, indiscriminately tore at the flesh, whilst the chiefs, Jubek and the *bonit* discussed the problem of rain. A bell-shaped vessel filled with water was brought in; Jubek repeatedly washed a green stone in the water, while the other chiefs spat into the vessel. After this ceremony was over, I was assured that rain would fall on that very day. I got up and holding a forked stick in my hand as is customary with their speakers I addressed them in the following manner:

'Bari, as you have been so good as to receive me among you, and honoured me with the invitation to be present at one of your tribe's most sacred ceremonies, grant me leave to speak freely to you. I do not intend to offend anybody, but I simply wish to bring forth the naked truth, as it is for this very reason that I have been placed among you by Heaven.

The God, who created me and you, also created the sun, the moon, the stars, your cattle, trees and rivers. The same God makes the grass and seeds grow — in other words, the same God who from nothing created everything in heaven and on earth. Although this great God is, as yet, not known to you, and, therefore, not honoured and served by you, He nevertheless loves you and helps you in a thousand different ways. This is the God who makes the rains fall, thus preventing your fields from being scorched; He keeps you in good health; He multiplies your cattle; He gives you the strength to overcome your enemies; in short His love for you is greater than that of any father or mother for the sweetest and most cherished son. Hence, if you wish the rains to fall on your fields, you must desist from the quarrels and wars, which rage continuously among you, and must stop killing your fellow-creatures. You must refrain from theft and robbery, and must not give way to wantonness, in other words, you must not do to others, what you would not have them do unto you'. [5]

The people were astonished at the unexpected tenor of this speech, the like of which they had never heard before. Despite this, everybody, including the chiefs, the people and Jubek himself, warmly applauded me, saying that my reasoning was sound and that what I had said must indeed be true. My speech was particularly welcomed by the people, who above all admired me for having thus spoken before Jubek himself, as each year they had to hand over many oxen to him, in his capacity as rain-maker. After a while, I again stood up and announced my intention of leaving them (this is an indispensible form of etiquette among the Bari). With one voice, they answered '*anabut*', 'it is good', and I returned to my hut.

Not very long afterwards, a chief (Doka, by name) approached me, sobbing in a most disconcerting manner, and I asked him what was the matter. 'We are lost', he answered. 'We have just heard that the Laude [Loudo] chief has joined forces with the Liria chief and the three Lokoyo chiefs, and that they are on the point of waging war against us. What can we do to save ourselves from such powerful enemies? We cannot do anything to avoid this calamity.' So saying, he turned his eyes towards his own children and exclaimed, 'Behold, the victims', and then pointing to his wives and cattle, 'the booty'. In the meantime, he kept sobbing and weeping, whilst I did what I could to quieten him a little, consoling and promising to do all in my power to settle this affair.

After a little while he calmed down, putting his trust in my words. I was not aware until then that wars were so frequent among these

---

[5] The reporting in direct speech of lengthy and elaborate conversations was a literary convention of the time but often misunderstood by modern readers ignorant of literary history. The reader is not expected to accept the literal meaning of each recorded word but rather the general sense of the passage. We may safely assume that neither Don Angelo's knowledge of the Bari language, nor the Bari vocabulary itself, would have sufficed to represent accurately the abstract concepts here recorded.

African tribes. I immediately sought for messengers to be sent to the chiefs of the Laude and Liria tribes, but all refused to undertake such a task, for fear of death on the road. I say 'on the road', for when a man has set foot in the village he is safe from attack, because the immunity of inhabited localities forbids any man to attack another, even though he may be a stranger. I was told, however, that there were two privileged classes of people who could go to and fro unmolested at any time, even in wartime, namely, smiths and women. The former are untouched because of their public work, while as regards the weaker sex it is generally held to be a base and shameful thing to take revenge on a woman, no matter what the reason. I therefore sent three messengers to the chiefs with presents, consisting of beads, a suit of clothes, a mirror, and other small objects which I knew would be most acceptable to them.

I also asked my envoys to repeat the following to the chiefs: 'Fr. Angelo, the white man, of whom you may have heard, asks you to accept these small gifts and at the same time to lay down your arms and not wage war, but live in peace. He also promises to come and see you himself, and after having heard the grievances on both sides, will do all in his power to restore peace and give due satisfaction to all.'

The messengers went off and I impatiently awaited the outcome of the negotiations. After six days they returned, each carrying an extremely large elephant tusk. They told me that on the whole they had been given a good reception; two of the chiefs had, at first, apparently refused the presents but later agreed to accept them, 'and thus peace was concluded', added the messengers cheerfully. Moreover, I was told that these chiefs sent me their greetings and that they wished to see me as quickly as possible, and would I, in the meantime, accept these small presents as a token of their esteem and friendship. I cannot do justice to the happiness I felt at this successful outcome, and I thanked God for having listened to my prayers and for having softened those bitter hearts.

As soon as the leading personalities of Belinyan heard the good news, they immediately ordered a great feast to be held to which all the people were invited, including myself. At the feast, I heard myself being described as 'liberator' or 'father' and my name was hailed by all for having preserved them from such imminent danger without fighting or bloodshed.

From that time onwards I was greatly esteemed throughout the whole country. Everything I did was well done and all prejudices against me were forgotten. Although things were going so smoothly, there were also some dangerous moments. One day, when hunting in the forest, a tribe unfriendly to the Bari heard the report of my gun, and mis-understood it for a sign that the Bari had induced me to wage war on them. Although I tried my best to pacify them, I was not successful in convincing them of their mistake, whilst the chief of the tribe swore that he would cut off my head with his spear, and would not rest until he had done so. Thus my servants and I took it in turns to keep watch for a month, and at least once I would have fallen a victim to that sworn enemy of mine had not God protected me.

Together with other assassins, this enemy chief came one night and hid in the plantation near my hut. Concealed by the tall *durra*, they took up positions on both sides of a narrow path, awaiting the opportunity to kill us. Nyigilò, I and a third man actually passed so close to them that they could easily have speared us, but as they admitted later, their courage and strength failed them at the critical moment. From that day on, I had little to fear from them, and I began thinking of visiting the Beri,[6] a neighbouring tribe of the Bari.

I had already tried to penetrate into their country many times before, but my efforts had failed, because of the many and serious prejudices the Beri entertain against white men, and especially because of the fierce war that was raging between the two tribes. When I succeeded in re-establishing peace among them mutual communications were restored between the two tribes, and they also exchanged goods. The Beri traded principally in tobacco, ivory, giraffes' hair, tame bulls and the hides of wild bulls; while the Bari have iron, salt and beads, which they obtain from the various expeditions. Although I ardently wished to visit the Beri and other tribes, I did not do so until the three chiefs of the Beri sent over thirty men to take me to them. I thought that this would be an excellent opportunity, and accordingly I went with them.

I therefore left on 24 June 1851, accompanied by Nyigilò and many of his people, together with the Beri envoys, among whom were three of the country's most distinguished personalities. One of the people carried a small bag of beads on his head, another carried my clothes, a third, some millet bread, everybody in fact carried some-thing. We headed eastwards. The grass in the forest was very tall, and we were obliged to follow the elephant tracks, despite the fact that it meant a longer way round. The sun was scorching, and I felt very

[6] The Beir/Böri/Beri who live to the east of the Bari.

thirsty. We had brought no water with us because the people had assured us that we would find many pools of rain-water on the way. However, we were doomed to disappointment, because the elephants and other wild beasts had already drunk what little was available, and now not a drop could be found. My thirst was becoming greater and greater, so our companions brought me a kind of lemon and very small wild-grapes, which grew in these areas. Although somewhat refreshed by these fruits, the sun was so hot, that I was soon being tortured by a greater thirst than before, and I would certainly have died had not God come to my aid.

Towards four o'clock in the afternoon, the usually clear sky was suddenly broken by small clouds, rapidly appearing from the southeast, and before long there was a heavy downpour. The rain water collected among the cracks and cavities formed by the stones, and we were thus able to quench our thirst and continue our journey until we reached a well of brackish water. The route we had followed had been due east of Belinyan, and it had taken us through so many thick thorns that my clothes were torn to shreds, and in the evening I had to change my garments in order not to appear half-naked like my guides. But, whilst waiting to change my clothes I had to tie the tattered garments I was wearing with cords made from grass so as to prevent them falling to pieces. Utterly exhausted and scratched in a hundred places by the thorns I lay down to rest on the soft grass near the well. In the meantime, firewood was being collected, with which to light the fires which would keep off the wild animals at night. A patch of dried grass was set on fire, thus clearing a space where we would pass the night. This gave me the opportunity of witnessing a scene the like of which I had never seen before. The wind was blowing from the west, and in a few minutes a terrific fire was raging, with the flames shooting so high towards the sky that the clouds themselves seemed to be alight. As the flames enveloped enormous tree-stumps and patches of grass that were not quite dry, there was a tremendous crackling noise, and coupled with this din was the frightful roaring of the wild animals. The fire lasted for more than four days.

Before leaving Belinyan, I had acquired a big ox, with the intention of providing us with food, but later in the evening I was told that the animal had escaped and that my men had not succeeded in recapturing it. Thus I had to be content with a little bread toasted in the fire. I then tried to snatch a few hours' sleep, but, though dead-tired, I was constantly getting up to see if the fires were still alight, because the carelessness of both the natives and the Berbers was well known to me. Early the following morning, 25 June, we continued on our journey.

This time, we struck south-east. Towards noon we found ourselves facing a very high mountain, called Lirya, and left it to our right. I paused a little to refresh myself and rest under the shade of a tamarind tree, when another misfortune occurred. I was told by one of the guides that a member of our party was missing. We waited a few hours to see if he would appear, and fired a few signal shots, but in vain — the unfortunate man was not seen again. Saddened by the loss of one of our companions, we pursued our way through a vast treeless plain, covered by a luxurious growth of grass taller than two men. Scattered here and there, we saw groups of elephants, giraffes, gazelles and wild cattle. We continued until sunset and then halted, both to protect ourselves from the wild animals and because rain was imminent. The sky was black with rain clouds, heavy peals of thunder reverberated across the stillness, whilst the flashes of lightning warned us of the approaching downpour. Indeed, this was not long in coming and sheets of rain immediately extinguished all our fires, and I had to make use of a lamp to scare the wild beasts, which are very numerous there. Fortunately, we were able to seek the shelter of a tree, but even then we were not completely protected. We were all drenched to the skin and impatiently waiting for the dawn. Although my clothes were literally soaked, I was so exhausted that I managed to doze a little, and somewhat restored my flagging strength.

At the first flush of dawn on 26 June, we resumed our journey eastwards. It would be difficult to describe the additional hardships imposed on us by the recent rains. I need only say that I had to remove my shoes, carry them in my hands, and walk barefoot like the Africans. At about 11 o'clock, we approached four high mountains, two of which were called Corola, and the other two Icuda. They told me that three years ago these mountains had all been inhabited, but that the inhabitants had been forced to leave because of the continual assaults by enemy tribes, and were now living partly in the Lirya chief's and partly in the Laude chief's territories. As usual, we halted at sunset to eat and rest.

On 27 June, we again set off in a south-easterly direction. I still felt extremely tired; my feet were swollen, lacerated by thorns, and bruised by the hidden tree-stumps, whilst the swaying grass was continually blinding me and yet, despite these discomforts, my heart began to fill with great joy, when, from a tree-top, I could just make out the Lopeit mountains to the south-east, and the smaller Beri mountains to the east. At about 11 o'clock, we arrived at the Sobat river, [7] called Chol by the natives. The river itself is very wide, but its width is mostly covered by a luxuriant growth of grass. I removed my clothes and clad only in my shirt I began to wade across. In some parts the water was so deep that it reached my neck, but the grass helped me to keep my balance, otherwise I would surely have been drowned. When I reached the middle of the river, I found that there was no more grass to which I could cling, and, moreover, there was a strong current. As I was unable to swim, and as there were no boats available, I was in a quandary as to what I could do. I asked for my belongings to be passed across to me, and tying them together with two empty gourds, I placed them under my chest. Then, assisted by one of my servants, an expert swimmer, I was able to reach the opposite bank in safety.

Shortly afterwards, I had the pleasure of meeting the three chiefs of the tribe, Wari, Masherbon, and Guara-Kolmion. They had heard of my impending arrival and had come to receive me at the river, accompanied by a multitude of people dancing and playing their various musical instruments. Many had brought gourds, filled with *marīsa*, meat and fish, whilst some had even come along with tobacco. Having somewhat appeased our hunger, we headed for the village. On arriving there, I was immediately lodged in Wari's hut. The chief then appeared with two lambs, led them round me three times, and then handed them over to my servants to be killed. In the meantime, I was invited to sit down upon two hides, one of ox and another of lion, and there I remained — the object of their unceasing admiration. Filled with wonder, people were flocking from all parts to catch a glimpse of the newly-arrived white man.

Here, too, I was forced to endure these aggravating visits, similar to those at Belinyan. The natives cast themselves on their knees in front of me, dragged themselves towards me, lifted my arms in greeting, and then dragged themselves back, making room for others.

When these visits were over, I was allotted a large hut, half-way up the mountain-side, where the air was very pure, and from where an extensive panorama unfolded itself before me. The hut was situated on an excellent site, and considering the country and the people, I was treated extremely well. In the early mornings, the daughters of one or the other of the chiefs would bring me a decorated gourd filled with hot water, so that I could wash my hands and face. I was also supplied

---

[7] Probably the perennial river Kinyeti which discharges into the swamps to the north. Not to be confused with the Sobat, an eastward tributary of the Nile.

with a smaller gourd, also filled with hot water, with which I could rinse my mouth. A wooden dish bearing cooked fish would then be brought in for my breakfast, whilst a gourd of *marīsa* (called *quen*) served as a drink. These same young girls also brought me my lunch and supper, which usually consisted of *marīsa*, plentiful meat, and a porridge made from *durra* flour, and seasoned with butter, which is in plentiful supply among the Beri.

The customs of this tribe are almost identical with those of the Bari, but there are a few outstanding differences. For example, the Beri grow beards, let their hair grow long, and arrange it in tresses, whilst the Bari are the sworn enemies of any form of hair. The older men wear sheep-skins, but the younger go about naked, except for a tiara-shaped cap, made from hair. These caps are adorned with billowing ostrich-feathers and strings of beads and shells, giving them a striking appearance, which is enhanced by a broad strip of the same material hanging down in the form of a tail from the back of the cap to the heels. Girls and women cover themselves with sheep or gazelle skins. This mode of dressing is also prevalent among the Bor, Aliab and Cic tribes, who, originally, must have formed one large people. This may also be assumed from the similarity of their language, which also includes the Nuer, Shilluk and Dinka.

During my fifteen-day stay among the Beri, I was visited by many chiefs from different tribes, coming from far and near. Although most of their languages and customs were different, they were all full of wonder and respect, and all invited me to go and stay with them. These visits proved particularly useful to me and I was able to discover many interesting things.

One day, accompanied by Wari and many others, I made my way to the mountain-top, and from there I was able to admire the immense view that opened out before my eyes. The summit of the mountain on which we stood was dotted with huts, whilst the foot of the mountain was itself encircled by an unbroken ring of dwelling-places, which gave it the appearance of a large arena. Casting my eyes slowly around, I was confronted by vast green plains set among the mountains. Turning towards the east, I was able to see the mountains of Galla, called Juba, about two days distant from the Beri. One of the most terrible and warlike tribes — the Karakra [8] — lives in the vicinity of these mountains. The Karakra are the sworn enemies of the Beri and wage war against them nearly every year. They are well-equipped and have long spears

---

[8] Karoko, the name of the Didinga people of the Murle group.

and large shields, which protect most of the body. As far as I know, this is the only tribe that uses camels and asses to ride on — while no mounts of any description can be found among the other tribes. They wear lamb-skins and adorn themselves with beads and other fancy trinkets like the rest of the tribes, but in addition they have a large copper disc on their foreheads. To the north-east, at a distance equivalent to a four days' journey, are the Galla mountains. To the north of the Beri, five day's walk away, is the large Nyagi tribe. Before the Egyptian government opened the traffic lane along the White Nile, most of the tribes from the eastern Sudan used to trade with the Nyagi, bartering their goods for beads. These beads are taken to Khartoum merchants, /who then sell them on the Fāzūghlī or Fadasi mountains. The beads slowly find their way to the Nyagi and so to every part of this portion of Central Africa. The beads are called *dinyagi* by the natives, and are either white, blue or red. There is one particular kind, much in demand in Ethiopia, silver-white, with a large hole like an ear-ring, which is chiefly used as a pendant ear-ring.

To the south-east of the Beri, about half a day's walk away, there is a very high range of mountains, stretching from west to east, terminating in the Galla country. These mountains are inhabited by the Lopeit tribes, whose customs are similar to those of the Beri, the only difference being the language. One day's distance to the south of the Lopeit, there is a small mountain inhabited by the Lutuche tribe, also unfriendly to the Beri. Finally, to the west, about one and a half day's away, there are two towering mountain ranges, stretching in parallel lines from south to west; these are the mountains of Liria, Naire, Laude (Loudo), Ofirika, Imogu, Chiaciari (Chahari), Fere, Omeo, Kilio, Obao, (Obbo), Fidian and finally that very distant and high mountain, Imatong, [9] which takes its name from its inhabitants. This last is well-known because of the fine quality of the tobacco grown there, and each year many tribes make a special journey there to purchase this commodity. About four years ago the Liria tribe also used to call there to buy tobacco but, on one of their trips, they casually gave some *durra* grain to a young boy, who subsequently died. In revenge, the Imadon natives killed all the Liria people they could find, and since then this tribe has never been allowed to go there.

The Imatong mountain, is about ten days' walk to the south of the Beri, and it has three rivers flowing from it. The first, called the Sobat, is the largest. This river flows from the south to the north-west and

---

[9] The Imatong range of which Mt. Kinyeti (10,456 ft.) is the highest in the Sudan.

joins the White Nile at 11° North. The second is known as the Attondi, flows from south to north, reaches a point half an hour's distance from the Beri mountains, runs through the Nyagi, winds its way through the Galla country, and joins the Blue Nile on the Fāzūghlī and Fadasi side. The third river, which is also the smallest, is the Pupuni, and this flows from north to south, but I have not been able to discover where it ends.

All these tribes, which I had the pleasure of getting to know or visit personally, are indeed fierce and primitive, but most of them are well-disposed towards civilization and will gladly receive missionaries who without thought of danger or personal safety, are willing to come and teach them.

Towards the middle of September, I decided to return to Belinyan. During my stay, I had explored and visited several tribes, but I was being continually attacked by bouts of fever, which never gave me more than four or five days' respite, and morever, I was exhausted by my continuous journeys and the bad food. I presented the three Beri chiefs with the usual gifts, and requested them to supply me with a guide and escort. They said that they would be willing to do this, but begged me to postpone my departure for a few more days, so as to give myself a chance of getting a little stronger. Nyigilò and all the other Bari who had accompanied me had left me on the day that I began visiting the other tribes. Thus I was abandoned by all except my servants and, what was more, I did not wish to stay on any longer as I heard that a battle with the Karakra was imminent and I did not wish to be associated with it in any way. According to the Beri, the clash was indeed inevitable and preparations in the form of public dancing were already under way. They repeatedly begged me to wait until the arrival of the enemy and aid them in their defence, but to this I replied that very important business required my immediate attention at Belinyan and could not therefore delay my departure any further.

When they saw that I was determined to leave, I was given an escort of twenty-five men, and set off immediately. The sky was extremely overcast, and thunder and lightning followed each other in rapid succession and then the rains came pouring down. Although it poured throughout the day, I did not pause until I arrived at the Sobat. By then it was night, and we lay down to rest. Still feverish, and soaked to the skin by my day-long exposure to the rain, I was obliged to lie on the bare ground and pass the night in my sodden clothes. In the morning, a strong bout of fever made it impossible for me to carry on and I had to remain where I was with all my escort. There I was, shivering with fever and sadly contemplating my unhappy position. The way ahead was long and tortuous, there were no villages on the way, the distance had to be covered on foot — and I was not even able to stand. Assailed by these distressing thoughts, I raised my eyes to Heaven and placed myself entirely in God's hands, recommending my soul, if the time had come for it to pass to Him.

After a few hours, the fever abated a little and we were able to resume our journey. The roads were almost impassable, owing to the huge ruts caused by the elephants, and being weak and so unsteady on my feet I often fell into them along the way.

On the whole I had been cordially welcomed by the chiefs of the tribes I met along my journey, yet the journey itself was not without its dangers, and on one particular occasion I would surely have been murdered had it not been for the grace of God.

The powerful Lirya tribe were very displeased when they heard that I was going to the Beri, without first calling on them, and many lay in wait for me at the only watering-place along this route. Thinking that my way would no doubt pass by this place they gathered at night with their spears and poisoned arrows, waiting to kill me. By Divine Grace, however, I reached the watering-place before dusk and pushed straight on after having stopped only to fill our gourds with water, despite my guides' advice to the contrary. The night was inky-black, and although the Lirya people were creeping stealthily through the tall grass, their movements betrayed them. Several guinea fowl, called *jidād al-wādī* by the Arabs, which were roosting on a tree, were roused by the noise and flew away in great panic. This caused such a frightful pandemonium among the enemy themselves that they shrieked and hurled spears at one another, killing six of their number and wounding many more, as I was later informed by other Lirya people. My food supplies were running low and I had little water left, so that I was obliged to make quicker progress despite my failing health.

At last I reached Belinyan, where I greeted Nyigilò, but uttered no word of reproach at his having abandoned me in those distant parts among strangers. I unsteadily made my way to my hut and fell down on the four joined boxes that had always constituted my bed, hoping to rest a little after my strenuous journey. But this was not to be; once more the Bari renewed their visits and kept coming for three or four days without a break. They kept on asking me if I had had a good journey, and were amazed that I had borne such hardships and faced such dangers. They kept up their praises, spoke of my courage, and I soon realised that they were doing so in the hope of receiving more beads, so I did not send any of them away empty-handed. Jubek himself, the rain-chief whom I mentioned above, called on me the day after my arrival to pay his respects. He asked whether I had been pleased with the reception given to me by the various chiefs and eventually enquired whether such great hospitality also existed between white chiefs, on similar occasions. I replied that this was so, in a greater degree, among the white chiefs, whilst they had many more comforts than the African chiefs, who had almost nothing. 'How many wives has one of chiefs?' he asked. 'Only one', I replied. On hearing this, he burst out laughing and said, 'Why then do you boast of the greatness and wealth of your white chiefs when, in reality, they cannot afford to keep more than one wife?' 'Our chiefs only have one wife', I retorted, 'not because they cannot afford to keep more, indeed, if this were the reason they could keep thousands, but because there is a divine law which forbids them to do so.'

I took this opportunity of speaking to him about the creation of the world and man, as well as about the ten comandments and the future life.

I remained at Belinyan for several days, firstly to recuperate, and secondly because the torrential rains had swollen the streams so much that it was impossible to ford them. I therefore contented myself with organising a few short excursions to the neighbouring villages, such as Godian, Duka, Gnanchi, Carigie, and in addition I made my way to the tops of the surrounding mountains to examine the soil, but above all to visit the iron mines and see how the natives worked them.

Iron here is nearly always extracted from huge stones which contain a very high percentage of this metal. However, the local people do not know how to take full advantage as they have neither hammer nor other equipment necessary for this kind of work. They simply break the stones with a short iron rod, which in other words, means that the result of their labour does not justify the effort. Once the stones are broken and crushed, the iron is separated by means of a great fire which burns in small ditches. The iron itself is of excellent quality, especially for cutting instruments, as it contains a high proportion of steel. After this preliminary operation the metal is worked in a very simple fashion. In the place of bellows they use two round earthenware pots, dried in the sun, with a hole at the bottom. Two tubes of the same material are attached and these pass air into a third tube which joins the first two together its open end being placed near the burning charcoal in the ditch. A skin is attached to the upper parts of the pots, but it is purposely left loose and a small hole is perforated in the middle, where there is a kind of valve. A piece of wood is fastened perpendicularly to this valve and by the means of this wood the skin is raised and lowered. A large stone is used instead of an anvil whilst a smaller one takes the place of a hammer, with which they shape the iron. Sometimes, they even use the short iron rod I mentioned above. When hot the iron is handled by a forked piece of wood but as this often burns away, they have to replace it with another. Although the smiths are generally considered to be the lowest class among the tribe and are, more or less, considered as slaves, yet, there are none so rich as they, as iron in this country is a source of wealth second only to beads. They marry only their own class because no one else would deign to be related to them.

Ever since I had decided to remain among the Bari I had also made up my mind to try and discover the source of the White Nile, and to this end I left nothing undone. I continually questioned the Bari and the people who were on friendly terms with them about this. However, I concentrated chiefly on the merchants because, as I realised, booty was the only prize powerful enough to lure the others on a journey into the interior. The information I received on this question came from so many varied sources that I no longer entertained any doubt as to its authenticity. Previously, when I had journeyed among the Beri I noticed that nearly all the natives wore shells as ornaments whilst many were adorned with copper bracelets, and I asked the chiefs how they had come into possession of these trinkets. They were unanimous in saying that they had been received from the Cioko, [10] a tribe about twelve days' walking distance to the south-east of Belinian, and that the chief of this tribe was called Aurelin. In addition, they told me that they visited the Cioko every year buying these objects in exchange for oxen, beads and other commodities. Questioning them further, I asked where the Cioko obtained similar goods, and the reply was, that they were obtained from the Quenda [11] tribe situated on the right of the river at about four days distance to the south-west of the Cioko. The Quenda, they said, visited the Cioko every year when the *durra* was ripe (about August) and exchanged shells and bracelets for ivory. They come by small boats as far as Madi and then travel overland until they reach the Cioko tribe. I learnt that the Quenda chief was called Kerabombi.

This information profoundly interested me and urged me to probe deeper into this important question. I therefore, dispatched two expert

[10] Unidentified (?Acholi).

[11] Unidentified (?Ganda). Don Angelo may have intended the Buganda though if so, he or his informers underestimated the distance which separated them from the Bari.

Beri travellers, one called Lailon, the other Abugi, giving them a large quantity of beads and other presents which they were to hand over to the Cioko and Quenda chiefs. I also urged these travellers to try and return with at least two natives from each of these tribes. They departed and returned only after two months. They were accompanied only by two Cioko because, as they said, the Quenda would on no account venture into a land which was completely unknown to them. However, both Kerabombi and Aurelin sent me their greetings, thanked me for the presents I had sent them, and said they would be very pleased to see me. The two Cioko natives remained with me for three days, during which time I continuously questioned them regarding the possible source of the White Nile. They were able to confirm the information I had already received elsewhere but they gave me the additional information that the Quenda carried the ivory, purchased from the Cioko, as far as Mua, which is two days' distance to the south of Quenda. Here, there are white men, [12] who have boats similar to those of the Turks, who are engaged in purchasing ivory in exchange for shells, blue beads and bracelets. These white men are circumcised, like the Turks who come up the Nile, and, like them, touch the ground with their heads when praying; speak the same language, and dress in the same manner. I asked them if they knew where these white Moslems came from, and they answered that they had heard it said that they came from a large salt water river, which then joined another large fresh water river, stretching as far as Mua. They also added that this river flows into the Bari river (referring to the White Nile) between the Madi and Quenda tribe. I further questioned them as to the source of the White Nile and they replied that this came from the Kombriat Mountains, [13] about four days distance to the south-east of Quenda.

I was very anxious to visit these tribes and discover the source of this river, and it would have been possible for me to have joined company with those four brave men, who were ready to take me anywhere, having made up my mind to undertake this journey. But the continuous bouts of fever, which had been troubling me for some time, forced me to postpone my departure. Thus I reluctantly had to let them go but with the promise that as soon as I was a little better I would do my utmost to make that journey with them. The rainy season was not yet over and there were heavy downpours every day, changing the country-side into a vast lake. People living in more temperate climates cannot

[12] i.e., Arab traders from the ports of the Indian Ocean.

[13] This word, from the Arabic Jabal al-Qamar, Mountain of the Moon, could have come only from an Arab source.

form an exact idea of what a heavy rainfall of at least eight month's duration is like. The greatest drawback to Europeans is the high humidity, and the consequent outbreaks of many illnesses. After a while, I began to recover but a new insurmountable obstacle stood between me and my plan: The war, which had broken out between the Beri and the Bari made it impossible for me to obtain the services of the necessary guides for this journey.

However, I learnt that in addition to the Beri road, there was another leading to Quendia, namely, the Liefaran, Machedo [Machedo], Logopi; this road was somewhat longer but equally important, in my quest for the source of the White Nile. Along this road, it takes eight hours between Margiù and Duerù, another eight from Duerù to Kuio, half-a-day from Kuio to Cenderu [Shindirru], and two days from Cenderu to Machedo [Makedo], if a constant southerly course is taken. Pitia, the great chief, of the Beri tribe, has his residence at Cenderù. I first made his acquaintance at Liefaran, where he invited me to his hut, and where I was given a good reception, Machedo, is the largest town in the Bari country, and is situated on both banks of the White Nile. It takes two days to cross this city on foot. Near Machedo, there is a small village called Rego, and here I saw the largest cataract along the Nile, and I firmly believed that this cataract is insurmountable, even during the rainy season. To the south-east of Machedo, two days distance, there is Moroli; from Moroli to Lugufi there are a further two days, always keeping a south-easterly direction. In my journeys to the south, I was able to reach Lugufi and it was my intention to press on towards the source of the White Nile. However, the chief of the Logopi, Gwandoka by name, although most willing to lend me the necessary guides to lead me to the Madi and Quenda, was afraid that the Madi, who were always at war with them would kill both myself and the guides. He thus led me to understand that it would be better if I were to give up the project I had in mind. I knew that the chief was a good man, and that what he said was true, so I agreed, and returned to Margiù, postponing the plan to some future date.

Before returning, however, I gathered all the information I could about the country further south, and particularly about the Madi, Quenda, and Mua tribes, and the source of the White Nile; and these extra details merely served to confirm what I have already written above. Logopi is the last of the Bari tribes, and the inhabitants speak two languages: Bari and another language similar to that of the Cioko, Angwara, and Bari. To the west of Logopi, about half a day's journey away, on the right of the river, there is the large Bari village of Maremo.

One and a half days' distance south of Logopi, also on the right bank, there is the Madi tribe. Here the river is very narrow and flows between high mountains which stretch from east to west. I was told, in addition, that at this place the White Nile joins another big river from the west. From Logopi to Margiù there is no other large river to be found except for the Chit that flows from the mountains of the Madi, and which, after crossing several localities, joins the White Nile at a point between Liefaran and Dueru. Though this river is fairly extensive during the rainy seasons, it is reduced to an insignificant stream as soon as the rains are over.

That, in short, is all I can say about the course and source of the White Nile, and of the principal tribes on its right bank. I cannot go into great details about the people to be found on the left bank as I was only able to make one visit to Gnarcagni, Bekat, and Faglū [Fajulu], which are a good two days journey to the west of Margiù. The great Angwara tribe visit Faglù for trading purposes. (The Nyangwara should not be confused with the Angwara.) The Angwara do not speak the Bari language. The tribe extends to the south as far as another tribe, called the Faglù of Lochi, situated to the west immediately facing Machedo. Further south we find yet another tribe called the Kuku, situated on the left bank of the river facing Muruli. Both the Bari and the Angwara assured me several times, that at about four days journey to the west of Margiù, there is a river which flows from south to north. This was also confirmed by the Cic and the Nuer. Moreover, the Nuer told me that this river joined another large river, the Mislat, which comes from the west.

Having returned to my residence at Margiù, there was little prospect of my undertaking any further trips as the rains were due at any moment, I decided to build a hut of my own, which would assure me shelter and at the same time give me a permanent dwelling-place. I therefore started negotiations to buy a plot of land, and it was only after lengthy discussions with Lenchok, the Margiù chief, that I succeeded in obtaining one. With the help of my servants and the natives, I built quite a sound dwelling-place. As soon as this was finished I was able to make another trip, this time to Laude.

Leghr [?Lugor], the Lirya chief; Lado, the Iyre Chief, and Iban the Loudo chief, were all friends of mine and had often asked me to visit them and stay with them — thus, with this invitation in mind, I set off. On my way, I left the three mountains of Lakoya to the right. The chiefs of these mountains, Leguire, Molere, and Lulupe, are the mortal enemies of the Bari, whilst their language is the same as that spoken by the Lirya, Kumuturù, Ofirica, Naire, Loude and Lutuche. These tribes live on the mountain-tops, as a precaution against enemy attacks. Despite being situated on these heights, the natives have all they need including cattle, and water. They descend to the plains only to work their fields and gather their crops. But even on such occasions they move with great caution, whilst at other times they also descend to go to war or trade with some friendly tribe. The Bejure mountain is half-a-day's journey from Belinyan; Moler is eight hours distant and Lulupe is one day away — all in a southerly direction. Liria is one-and-a-half days' distance to the south-east of Belinyan; Kurmuburu is six hours to the west of Lirya; Ofirica is one and a half days to the south of Kurmuburu; Naire is one day to the south of Lirya; Loudo is two days to the south-east of Lirya; Latuche is one and a half days to the south-east of Loudo. On this journey I made the acquaintance of the chiefs of the Cecere and Liefaran who treated me well.

The heat, except in January and February when there is no rain, at all, is not unbearable. During the other months of the year, the atmosphere is generally damp, dull, and the nights, in particular, are rather cold. With night too there is an additional discomfort, especially near the river, where swarms of mosquitoes attack unceasingly. The natives try to ward them off with the smoke from their fires. Fires are also lit in the huts, with the dual purposes of warming the interior and driving off the mosquitoes with the resulting smoke. In a climate such as this one must obviously expect a great deal of fever. Another common disease is dropsy, or swelling of the legs. This disease is brought about by the rapidity of movement, or rather violence when walking and, in particular, by the strenuous efforts demanded by the frequent dances. Another illness is known as *farendit* (guinea worm) by the Arabs. This is caused by a very long worm, developing in some part of the body, but chiefly in the legs and its origin is chiefly to be found in the poor quality of the drinking water. The guinea-worm is so malignant, that a patient cannot be cured of it, unless the whole of the actual worm is extracted from the affected part. If, for instance, the head were still to remain in the body, the worm would then be able to reproduce itself. The natives are also afflicted by large, running sores, which often prove fatal.

The first-born male inherits the dignity of chief. When there is any matter of public interest to be discussed, both sides taking part sit under a tree and anyone is allowed to attend the meeting. The spokesman of one of the parties stands in the midst and delivers his speech, accentuating his emphatic gestures by the aid of a forked stick. Having delivered his speech he resumes his place amongst his followers and his opponent's turn then comes to dispute whatever has been said. This procedure is repeated again and again until finally the Assembly judges in favour of one or the other side. Once a decision has been agreed upon it is clamourously proclaimed and its purpose is executed without delay. For example, if the discussion had been concerned about some offence that had been committed, the offending person, if a member of the tribe, would be fined and asked to hand over a certain number of oxen and sheep to the chief.

Regarding religion, the Bari acknowledge the existence of some form of invisible divinity which, as they say, resides both in Heaven and on earth. This divinity is usually known as Nun, but sometimes it is also called Juok. They are of the opinion that the divinity does not care unduly about human-beings or temporal things. In addition the Bari are completely unaware of a future life, and of the immortality of the soul. I do not know the exact significance they attach to the sacrifices of oxen and sheep which are offered on such occasions as death and which are called *robanga* by them. Similar sacrifices are also offered where there are serious cases of illness, these being offered by the *bonit* who are also the tribal physicians. Obviously the bonit have the largest share of the flesh offered in sacrifice, but many others are also allowed to join the feast which follows. The slaughtered animals are cooked in large earthenware pots, and the flesh is distributed according to rank, that is starting from the more prominent member of the tribe, downwards. At the same time, much *marisa* is drunk. On some occasions, the *bonit* treat their patients by drawing blood from them. They do this by pressing their mouth over the affected part, sucking hard until the blood flows, spit it out, and then suck again. Wounds are treated by a somewhat similar method. Here the *bonit* licks the wound carefully and even sucks them with incredible casualness, irrespective of whether these wounds are festering or not. Different illnesses are treated, often successfully, with different medicines, which are derived mainly from flowers, tree roots, and herbs. It must be said that such remedies are not without effect. The greater power enjoyed by the *bonit* is that he is consulted on any matter of public or private interest, whether present or past, and this brings him a good income. When interrogated the *bonit* answer by making use of various methods of divination, such as throwing pebbles, making mysterious calculations unknown to anyone else, or tracing unintelligible signs on the sand with a cleft stick.

The people have no idea of the written word and at times, while I was reading or writing, they would creep up to me and whisper among

H

themselves. 'Look, Angelo is seeing whether his family is well or not; whether rain has fallen in his village; how many boats will come here next year, and how many beads they will bring.' And as soon as I raised my eyes from my books they would all gather round asking me for the latest news.

The customs of these tribes are very similar to those of the Bari. On the way, between one tribe and another, there are very wide plains flanked by high ranges of mountains; these plains are either covered by trees or very tall grasses, and are very similar to our beautiful plains of Lombardy. There are many wild animals to be found here, such as elephants, wild cattle, giraffe, gazelles, lions, leopards, hyena, as well as a multitude of different kinds of monkey.

As soon as this journey was over, I once more returned to Margiù, where I found that the merchants' boats had arrived. The Bari at this time were on a war footing and were preparing for a bitter struggle against the Lakoya, and while I did all I could, to avert this conflict, my efforts were in vain. Indeed, they urged me to lead them and threatened me with death if I refused. Similar claims had, on other occasions, been made by the Beri and other tribes but I always managed to override them. Thus in view of the trouble brewing from the tribes and because of urgent missionary work I decided to return to Khartoum with the merchant boats, and I arrived there on 11 June 1852.

Before closing this short report, I believe it would be of interest, if I were to add a few details about the climate, government, religious conception, customs, etc., of the Bari.

The climate of the Bari Country is reasonably good and it is mountainous and in an elevated position. There are no springs and the people living at some distance from the river are forced to obtain their water from wells or reservoirs, but it must be said, that more often than not, such water is bad and stagnant.

Finally the Bari believe that the *bonit* have the power to make rain come and go (although the main authority in this is given to the head of the tribe) to vanquish enemies, to bring prosperity to families in the country, in a word, to dominate insensible nature and the human spirit, as they wish. As regards peace and war, however, the *bonit* have not much say in the matter. The frequent clashes that occur between the tribes are, in effect, merely raids carried out by bands of robbers, and do not really assume the proportions of war as we understand the word. The ultimate aim of such raids is invariably robbery and plunder.

Once a tribe has decided to venture out for plunder, the preparations are heralded by a solemn war-dance, which continues for three consecutive nights. People of all ages attend the dance and their arrival is greeted by the blare of thousands of trumpets and horns. Nearly all of them carry flaming torches made from dried reeds and the spectacle of such a dance is both frightening and beautiful. The young warriors bring their weapons with them. Some brandish one or more spears and carry their shields while others have also bows and arrows. The tips of the arrows are poisoned with the sap of a tree called *niri,* together with the boiled crushed heads of some of the most poisonous snakes known. The nature of the poison produced is so deadly that, once in the bloodstream, death inevitably results.

When all the tribes has assembled at the dance the chief and the very young children stand in the centre where there are other people rhythmically beating huge drums.

Around them stand the young girls, smeared with a red clay called *mege,* which in turn, is coated with ash. Both circles are closed by the warriors who surround them by forming several concentric rows. As each warrior arrives, he places his spear over the girls' head as a token of bravery and as a sign that he is fighting for them and for their country. The girls give answering shouts of joy and applause and then the dance begins, with all the people adhering to their original positions. The dance consists mainly of erratic jumps with each dancer leaping as high as possible.

At the same time, everybody sings, from the smallest child to the most warlike warrior, and the tune is accompanied alternately by the drums and trumpets. A great fire is kept burning throughout the whole of the night. At daybreak the dancers and singers retire to sleep. Dancing is their most cherished passion, in which everything is forgotten. At the end of the ceremony the chief rises to his feet, and the assembly seats itself around him, the women on the ground, and the men on the small stools they always carry with them. There is a deep silence and the chief speaks. He reminds his listeners of the causes of the impending war, praises the bravery of both their ancestors and themselves, belittles the enemy, stresses the importance of being courageous, and holds forth the promise of much loot. In short, the chief makes use of all the rhetoric at his command to spur the hearts of the young warriors on to battle. It is perhaps worth noting here that the same procedure is adopted by the chief during any of his speeches concerning the management of the tribe.

When the hour of battle is near, the chief gives the signal by beating the drum thrice. Every house that hears the signal, immediately transmits it, so gradually, everyone is informed — this is why a big drum is kept in every hut. Fully armed warriors then gather at the chief's hut and all set off to battle. The women do not remain behind in the village but follow their warriors on to the battlefields where they pick up the dead, and render first-aid to the wounded.

The Bari only use iron weapons when engaged in a war against strangers. In cases of tribal war, however, each man is armed only with two clubs, one with which he attacks, the other with which he defends himself. Victory is always followed by dances, and on this occasion, the dancers tie small bells to their legs and leap to the sound of the beat of drums and the blowing of the trumpet.

The dead, whether fallen in battle or elsewhere, are always buried in front of their huts so as to preserve them from the wild beasts. The graves are dug very deep but are not very long, because the dead are buried with their legs bent under their thighs. In the case of a leading personality, however, a mat is placed under the body, as a sign of honour, while all the relatives and mourners press the ground which is gradually placed into the grave. This in fact has a good purpose as it prevents the smell of the decaying body from rising. When one of their dear ones dies the people sob, weep, wail, and shout. Once the body is buried the mourners walk around the grave many times shouting and singing to the funeral beats of the drum. The ceremony is then concluded by a banquet.

Food is cooked by the women and generally consists of a kind of porridge, made from *durra* flour, soaked in water, vigorously stirred without the addition of salt, butter, or any other seasoning. *Durra* is also cooked with beans; the poor eat it in this manner. Wealthier people, however, sprinkle ground or roasted sesame on it, or season it with honey which is in plentiful supply. In general, rather solid foods are preferred, which are placed in small canisters and are then licked. Liquid foods are eaten with the aid of long deep bone spoons. Meat is also eaten when available, that is, when a bull dies naturally, or when it is killed in sacrifice during some ceremonial occasion. Every part is eaten, including the skin, with the exception of the hoofs, hair, horns and splinters of bone. Meat is eaten regardless of whether it is fresh, or has been bad for several days, but though all kinds of animals and fish are eaten, exception is made of hens and dogs because these are known to feed on dung. Rats and a certain kind of red worm constitute a speciality among these people, and if they succeed in trapping a number of them, they are exuberant. The rats are hunted at night by the light of flaring reed torches and are killed with sticks, while the worms are found in the grass.

All, from the chief to the most humble member of the tribe, have the same household goods and kitchen utensils, namely mats and skins on which to sleep; several sun-dried earthenware pots, numerous gourds used as bottles, a wooden mortar to crush the *durra,* and two stones for grinding. A space of ground, or *iban,* surrounds each hut which is protected by a hedge. Here the people pass the cool hours of the day and most of the night. Here also, they have their *gugo* or granary. These consist of several baskets made of rushes raised above the ground on long poles. Private property is so respected that seldom is anything stolen from a *gugo.*

Although there is not a great variety of seeds, the people have sufficient for their requirements. They have two kinds of *durra,* one a local variety, red in colour; the other is white, having been brought here by one of the Egyptian government's first expeditions. In addition they grow sesame, small beans, pumpkins, and tobacco. In some localities there is a variety of millet which they call *coreggia,* and beans known as *giuguat* and a grain smaller than millet known as *leot. Durra* is sown in April, and the others at the beginning of May, while all the crops are harvested in August. During the sowing, the seeds are just thrown to the ground and covered with earth by means of a kind of long-handled metal shovel. The rain, the only crop-producer, starts falling at the end of February and goes on to the end of December. Thus, the natives only differentiate between two seasons, the dry which they call *melin* [*meling*] and the rainy, called *giabe* [*jabe*]. The beginning of the sowing, and the harvest, are celebrated by a solemn public dance. In addition to distinguishing between the seasons, the natives also divide time into months and years. The months are calculated from moon to moon, and the years, by the growing of the new grass, also called *leme.*

All Bari men and women shave the hair off their heads with a small spear, whilst any other hair on their body is plucked with their fingers; even from their eyebrows and eyelids. Similar to the Lakoya and other tribes the Bari males perforate their lower lip and insert a well-finished cone-shaped crystal which hangs down. These are obtained from the mountains. The girls tattoo various drawings of flowers on their stomachs with a knife. It is the custom here to extract the two middle incisors of the lower jaw. The men are very fond of ornaments, such as ivory, or iron rings and glass necklaces. In some tribes, as for instance the Beri and Quenda, the natives cover themselves with sheepskins. As soon as the small girls are able to walk, their mothers hang little bells around their waists. The women cover themselves either with two sheepskins or with garments made from cotton, which grows very well here, or from the bark of trees.

Marriage formalities and ceremonies are very brief and to the point. As soon as the father of the young girl has given his consent, the bridegroom must hand over the agreed number of cows. Numerous guests are invited, a sumptuous feast is held, and the marriage is celebrated. Usually, however, the young man's father visits the father of the girl, and makes the necessary proposal himself. As soon as the first son is born, the husband has again to give gifts to the relatives, in proportion to those he gave on the day of his marriage. The value of the gifts, naturally depends on the wealth of the husband. Love-matches are very rare among the people, for in actual practice the man is really buying the woman, and her parents merely regard her as an object to be traded. When the head of a family dies, the eldest son inherits all the wives, with the exception of his mother. A native is allowed as many wives as he likes, and the more he possesses, the greater he is esteemed.

The care of the homes is entrusted to the women, while the youths, not strong enough to fight, are put in charge of the cattle. The rest, in times of peace, spend their time chiefly hunting or, if near the river, fishing. There are three different ways of fishing: (a) by using a long pole tipped with a sharp iron, (b) by using a spear-shaped iron rod tied to a length of string, forming a weapon which is hurled, and then carefully withdrawn with the speared fish, (c) by the use of osier baskets, used as nets. Much labour and patience is required with the first two methods. However, spurred on by hunger, the people persevere so that by evening their catch is quite substantial.

Although there are many kinds of wild animals, the people seek above all, to kill the elephants with the threefold purpose of feeding on its flesh, making sandals from its hide, and selling the tusks. The elephants are hunted in three ways, the most common being as follows: As soon as a certain place is known to be frequented by elephants, large deep pits are dug along the way. These are carefully covered with sticks and branches. If the animal should pass, it will, inevitably, crash into the pit, from which it cannot escape. The roaring of the trapped monster immediately summons the natives who kill it with their spears. Another time, a hunter will climb a tall, sturdy tree grasping a very large weighted spear. His colleagues form a large circle and loudly blow trumpets and enormous horns and then gradually close in on the encircled elephants who are bewildered by this terrific noise. In the confusion that follows, many of them lumber under the tree where death lurks, for suddenly the hidden hunter will hurl his spear at the nearest, killing it.

There is yet another way which is used by the very daring Beri. Between three and four hundred of them surround these ferocious beasts, blow their wind instruments and draw them close to their huts. As soon as the infuriated animals approach these intrepid hunters fearlessly emerge, and with incredible rapidity repeatedly wound them, until they fall under the incessant blows. Very rarely do the elephants succeed in escaping from the traps laid for them or from the spears of their assailants, but often some of the attackers are also killed.

CHAPTER V

THE WHITE NILE, ITS PEOPLE AND ITS SOURCE, THE STATE OF EUROPEAN KNOWLEDGE IN 1851

by L.G. Massaia

Unlike the other missionary writers whose contributions appear in this book, Lorenzo Guglielmo Massaia (1809-89) was not a member of the Mission to Central Africa. A Piedmontese from Piovà Massaia, near Asti, he entered the Capuchin (Franciscan) Order and in 1848 was appointed first Vicar-Apostolic of the Galla in Ethiopia. In 1884 he was made cardinal.

We meet him in Khartoum as a priest in transit through the Sudan and as a guest in the Mission house at Khartoum. On 12 November 1851 he wrote a memorandum in French to Alfred le Moyne, Consul-General of France in Egypt, which he enclosed with an extract from his journal.[1] In this memorandum he set down all that he had been able to find out about the White Nile from informants in the Mission and the town. The year 1851 was geographically interesting for it was nine years since Salīm Qapūdān's Egyptian government fleet had reached Gondokoro and twelve years before Speke and Grant discovered the source of the river. Traders had already wormed their way into the lower reaches of the Bahr al-Ghazāl but no European or Northern Sudanese merchant had as yet thrust his ship through the weeds into the river Jur in the west or sailed up the river Pibor in the east. The vast rolling country of the Nile-Congo divide was totally unexplored and nobody knew what lay beyond the area of Fr. Angelo Vinco's travels on the east bank of the White Nile. Massaia had never himself sailed on the river, but his résumé of the state of European knowledge which he picked up in Khartoum at this particular stage of African exploration is a landmark in historical geography.

[1] Paris, Ministère des affaires étrangères, Correspondance commerciale, Alexandrie, vol. 34.

I had always thought that the lands near the Equator would be exceedingly populous and that the soil would be very fertile by reason of the seasonal rains. But the opinions of Fr. Pedemonte and Niccolò Ulivi [2] who have themselves travelled up the White Nile beyond 4° 14′ of latitude in the track of the trading voyages from Khartoum have demonstrated that the population of the region is even greater than I originally believed.

The Egyptian possessions upstream of Khartoum extend to about the 15th degree, to a point navigable by ship in the space of five days. [3] From here to the 4th degree, that is, a distance of about 450 miles, a very large population lives in a primitive state. The trading voyages are forced to stop at the 4th degree on account of the cataracts which bar the channel but as the soil on the far side continues to be just as fertile there is no reason for doubting the presence here also of great and flourishing populations. I have also learnt from Fr. Pedemonte that the Shilluk who inhabit the country between the frontier of the Viceroy's jurisdiction and the 9th degree on the west bank of the White Nile form a considerable nation of perhaps several million souls. The same remarks apply to the Dinka who inhabit the land between the White and Blue Niles, as far as the confluence of the White Nile and Sobat at about the 10th degree and some minutes. The Sobat is navigable and along its banks live important tribes according to the statements of the natives and the testimony of people who have gone up the river. After comparing the information supplied by Mr. D'Abbadie [4] and Fr. Pedemonte it is clear that it was not the source of the White Nile that the former discovered but the river Sobat which lies close to the 6th degree less several minutes. The Sobat runs from east to west for a distance of about 150 miles. What gives this view credibility is the fact that the course of the White Nile is known as far as the 4th degree and is certainly navigable beyond that point so that, if the direction of its course, as seems likely, continues southward, it should reach the Equator, a point far beyond that maintained by Mr. D'Abbadie.

On the White Nile, about 25 miles upstream of its confluence with the Sobat, lies a great lake through which the White Nile flows, while on the west of the lake is the mouth of another navigable river,

---

[2] A Tuscan from Pistoia. Like several other Khartoum merchants he had been a pharmacist in the Egyptian state medical service. He died in Khartoum in 1852; Knoblecher officiated at his funeral.

[3] The southernmost Egyptian Government post at that time was Wad Shalā'ī, 90 miles upstream of Khartoum.

[4] D'Abbadie believed that the White Nile rose in S.W. Ethiopia.

called the Bahr al-Ghazal whose course describes an arc originating in
the south-west and divides the lands of the Shilluk and the Nuer. The
latter occupy both banks of the White Nile from its confluence of the
Sobat and Bahr al-Ghazāl up to the 7th degree. Between the 7th and 5th
degrees lie the Cic who dwell on both banks of the river. Upstream
of the Cic the Aliab live on the west bank of the river and the Shir
on the east bank.

These two tribes who occupy the extent of one degree and several
minutes of latitude along the river valley have as their southern neighbours the Bari, the last tribe of which we have any knowledge. The
Bari, like the Shilluk and the Nuer, occupy the hinterland on both banks
of the river. Each of these peoples forms more than a petty tribe and
are nations; each might be regarded as a veritable kingdom by reason
both of the size of territory which they occupy, the fertility of their soil
and the size of the population.

Fr. Pedemonte says that of all these tribes the Nuer have the least
intelligence and drive, though they are by no means devoid of either.
The reason for this is that their climate is unhealthy as they live on
an immense plain covered with swamps. In sailing through the Nuer
country traders are exposed to horrible fevers which require for their
cure enormous doses of sulphate of quinine. The air swarms with
insects including a large sand-fly whose bite penetrates through a linen
shirt and inflames the blood. [5] Besides, the entire territory, known as
the White Nile valley is uniformally flat. The name 'White' derives from
the white-looking surface of the Nile water, a phenomenon which is
easily explained. There is no land feature to retract the light and in
consequence the water reproduces only the vapour in the atmosphere
dilated by the vertical sun.

For the same reason that the country has no mountains and the
inhabitants lack industry, there are many swamps resulting in an unhealthy air. In all this region only a single mountain can be seen and
this is beyond the river Sobat. The mountain is named Jabal Dinka. [6]
It is probable that over the horizon out of sight there are other mountains
as the country abounds in excellent iron ore and in copper deposits. [7]

---

[5] The serut (Arabic *sirūtī*) fly.

[6] A minor slip. Jabal Dinka is on the east bank of the White Nile near Renk.

[7] Subsequent mineralogical surveys have failed to find significant deposits
of copper ore in the White Nile basin, apart from those at Hufrat al-Nahās
in Dār Fūr.

CHAPTER VI

THE JOURNEYS OF FRANZ MORLANG EAST AND WEST OF GONDOKORO IN 1859

Franz Morlang (1828-75) came from the village of S. Vigilio di Marebbe in the Ladin-speaking Val Badia (Enneberg Thal) in the Dolomite Alps. He was educated at Bresssanone and Innsbruck and in 1855 joined the Mission in the Sudan. He served five years among the Bari at Gondokoro and over two years at Holy Cross among the Cic Dinka. In 1863 he returned to Europe. After ten years of parochial duty at home he again went abroad, this time as chaplain to a community of German-speaking immigrants in Peru, where he died of typhus.

The manuscript of his diary in German is in the archive of the Comboni Fathers at Rome. A critical edition containing substantially the whole of the diary has recently appeared in Italian translation: Francesco Morlang, Missione in Africa Centrale, diario, 1855-1863, translation and notes by O. Huber and V. Dellagiacoma in collaboration with G. Vantini, A. Nebel and L. Bano, Verona (Editrice Nigrizia), 1972. The extracts which follow were translated from the German by the late Fr. Huber and cover only Morlang's account of his journeys in 1859 of which a somewhat bowdlerized version was published as 'Franz Morlang's Reisen ostlich und westlich von Gondokoro, 1859' in Petermanns Mittheilungen (Ergänz.) II, 1862-3, pp. 115-24. This and other journals of the time generously acknowledged the geographical importance of the author's travels east and west of the White Nile only four years before the discovery of its source. For a contemporary appraisal see C. Zaghi, L'Europa davanti all'Africa, vol. I: La Via del Nilo, Naples, 1971.

South-Eastward from Gondokoro to the Lirya People, a Two-Day Journey

In the afternoon of 24 July 1859 I set off on my journey with the two boys Igushok and Logo, the former carrying a basket filled with food on his head. Late in the evening we arrived at the Belenyan [Bilinyang] mountain where we camped. Because of the earlier rains we encountered mud along our way, but near the mountain the road was very stony. We came across many skeletons of Bari who had died of hunger. Among them was a girl whose feet the vultures had just eaten and were now attacking the rest of her body. We buried her in the sand as best we could with the aid of our sticks. [1]

[1] On the grisly subject of famine Morlang made the following entry in his diary:

> As in previous years, also this year, the hunger months among the Bari began in the months of April, May and June. Owing to the lack of rain, the people have even been unable to find the leaves and herbs which they normally cook and eat. The cattle, whose blood had been drawn off and sold, were dying of weakness. The girls and the women surrendered themselves to the merchants for morsels of *kisra* and contracted syphilis, and several died a miserable death. The boys, youths and men were robbed and abducted, and the whole country was affected. The guards at the *zariba* were doubled. Every night, the drums could be heard beating out their messages, calling for help. Bands of robbers and assassins were on the prowl stealing cattle. Everywhere there was robbery and murder. Chiefs Medi, Burgodschi, and Cuaka killed several of the thieves with their own hands and threw them into the river. Each day, the bodies, or mutilated parts of bodies, could be seen floating in the river, including those of infants. The people were all reduced to skin and bone and were collapsing one by one. Very many of them, personally known to me, are now lying buried. A short while ago, there were as many as twenty-one *tukul* (huts of straw circular in plan with conical roof and wood frame) in the village of Gondokoro, but on the 20 June there only remained three huts. Everybody, with the exception of one man and a few women had died from hunger. As if this were not enough, the prospects of the future harvest were poor because, owing to the scanty rainfall, the first April sowings on the high ground towards Belenyan were spoilt, while on the plains by the river and on the islands, the ground has been flooded by the river. The Bari were seized with despair. First, they blamed the merchants for their misfortunes, then the mission, then their Bunok diviners and so forth. Hunger became more widespread, and the rains less and less. Finally, the blame was cast on Nyigilò, the rain-maker, the great prince of Belenyan, and his followers. He was forced to flee from Belenyan, where all his cattle were stolen, and his dwelling-place destroyed by fire. Persecuted by all, he was a fugitive for some time in his country, and finally sought refuge with his relative, Medi, near Gondokoro. However, on 21 June, a powerful group of young natives, coming from far and near, converged on Kudshenok

On 25 July we made an early start and at about noon we reached a large wood filled with tall grass where there were elephant grazing. Here the tamarind trees and euphorbia were well-developed and beautiful, and yet there were no signs of cattle or huts because, as Igushok told me, the people were afraid of robbers who often raided them.

Towards evening we reached a small valley to the south-east, lying between the high, rocky mountains and the village of Telegu. The huts situated on and between the rocky crags gave quite a picturesque effect. The wide paths, hedges, soil and mountains reminded me of the villages in the Tyrol. As soon as the inhabitants saw me, they fled, crying: *gwarong! gwarong!* (i.e. a ravenous beast). It appears that the people had never before seen a white man, dressed in European clothes, and with glasses, hat and beard. We stayed with a friendly-looking *monye* (proprietor).

On the following day, we picked our way through trackless stony fields and after about three hours we reached Lirya, living on the southern slopes of a mountain. From here, there is a beautiful view of the Lokoya mountains to the west, whilst the Lauda mountains, which are about two or three days distance away, supply a popular tobacco, which is sold to Laiben.

Just as at Telegu, the natives here first mistook me for a wild animal. It was only after some time, that they dared venture close to me, but even then they would not believe that the hairs of my head and beard, were genuine, they really believed that they had been stuck on. My spectacles seemed to cause great fright among the natives, and I removed them so as to pacify them somewhat.

I was soon surrounded by a host of them, and was questioned on all sides: 'Where do you come from?' 'Do you want to buy tobacco?' 'Do you want to buy ivory?' 'Are there cows and elephants in your country?' 'Do your people also marry?', etc. I answered all these questions, and told them many things about my country, about the sea, the plough, the manufacture of clothes from hair, wool and cotton (also found here), the making of beads (the people had been told by the merchants that these grew on trees at Khartoum, and this is the reason

---

(Medi's headquarters) and angrily demanded to see Nyigilò. He had fled, but was discovered in the nearby village of Ciu-ekir, where he was struck with four spears and clubbed. His stomach was ripped open, and he was fed to the vultures. Thus, Nyigilò, or the Prince of Belenyan (as he was known in Europe) met his end. Following the murder, all the cattle belonging to his family and relatives were stolen. His aged mother died of fright. His wives and children scattered in all directions, otherwise his descendants would have been completely exterminated.

why they are no longer of any value here), etc., etc. They could not be convinced that God (of whom they had a vague idea) was good. On the contrary, they maintained that He was evil (*aloron*), because He sends death, and is responsible for the sun, which burns all their crops.

In the evening, Logo (the Strong) cooked my supper. The chief, named Lege (the Other One) then returned from an inspection of his cattle. He is a wild-looking man, about seven feet tall, with between thirty and forty wives. As there is not much grass growing on his stony soil, he often instructs his men to go on raids to the east, west and south to the Loudo to steal cows, and in this way he is always engaged in wars. He, too, inquired where I had come from, etc. I answered his questions and then asked where the Lirya had originated.

He said: 'We, Lirya and the Bari are but one race. We came from the far south, where the main Bari tribe is situated. They have many cattle there, and three times the numbers of spears of the emigrants here. We left there, because of over-population and continuous warfare. Our children disappeared during the night, and we never knew whether they were stolen by men or devoured by animals. We followed the course of the Chufiri (the White Nile), which has its source to the south, about six days journey from here in a mountain, where there are large dark forests. Another big river also has its source in these mountains, and flows in a westerly direction. The Bari always kept close to the river because of their cattle and the abundance of pasture there. During the journey, most of the cattle were killed, and, by the time they reached Gondokoro and Libo there was only one cow left. Later, they spread northwards to other tribes, whilst those along the northern borders are now known as Shir to the foreigners. Some of the emigrants, namely the Lirya, kept close to the mountains. When we arrived here, we had only one goat left between us, but we successfully put to flight the people who were living here before us.'

The Lirya then showed me the high mountains, which towered above their tukuls. The earlier inhabitants of these parts had previously sought refuge in these mountains, but hunger and thirst forced them to abandon their positions, and they were then either murdered or forced to flee eastwards, which is now Beri country. Since then six *matat* (chiefs) have ruled over Belenyan — the seventh descendant of the Nyigilò family, came with the emigrants from the south. Now the Lirya people live with the Bari along the eastern border, as the Beri withdraw, leaving only a few women and girls behind, who intermingled with the newly arrived natives. Thus, it happens that among the Bari there is a mixture of half-Bari, half-Beri. Similarly, the language (most natives speak both) and the appearance of the people themselves have been affected. The Bari are very tall, whilst the Beri are on the short side. The wheat baskets are not circular-shaped at the bottom, but are square, like those found along the western borders of the Bari. The Beri women wear cylindrical ornaments through their perforated lips, and have large iron rings around their legs, whilst, on the other hand, the rings worn by the Bari women are close-fitting. The ornaments worn on the head by the two tribes are also different.

We stopped here for the whole of 27 July, but we suffered from a great thirst, as we had nothing to drink, and we were not even given a drop of water. On the other hand, we were being continuously pestered by the people with their endless questions. So much was asked for a gourd of milk that the price was almost unpayable.

On the 28 July, we returned to Telegu, where we again visited the friendly *monye*, and spent the day there. We reached Gondokoro at nightfall on the following day.

What I had been told by the Lirya about the origin of the Bari, was confirmed, after my return, by a kinsman of Nyigilò who enumerated thirteen generations of his family and by the rest of the inhabitants, but they could add nothing more about the Bari in the south, apart from the fact that they had been numerous, and that, indeed, they might still be so.

South-Westward from Gondokoro to the Makáraka and Makárayang or Niam Niam or Cannibals

The 20 October 1859 was the date fixed for our departure. Everything necessary, beads and supplies, was ready. The boys, Leghe Floriani (cook), Kungu Alexander, Gwajok Petri and Kinyong (crocodile), were detailed to carry the luggage, whilst Taha, the servant, was put in charge of the donkey. In view of the frequent attacks on travellers, I decided to join the trading caravan of the British Consul Petherick, [2] which was scheduled for the same route and was more than a hundred strong. The members were mostly Bari natives from our neighbourhood. It was late in the afternoon when we got under way, and after a two hour's march, we stopped at Mori, where we intended to pass the night. As usual, wood, water, etc., were bought for beads.

[2] John Petherick (1813-82), a Welsh trader who had been a mining engineer. While trading for ivory he explored the rivers Jur, Yalo and Yei up to the borders of Azandeland.

21 October: For an hour, we waded through boggy water, between five and six foot deep, until we reached a river, and crossed over to the west bank by means of a hollowed-tree trunk (*surtuq*). The ferryman demanded payment, not only for each individual person, but also for each piece of luggage and, to make matters worse, he wanted to be paid with Loudo tobacco, of which we had none. After a three hours march, we reached Tokiman, where we spent the night.

22 October: During the morning our way led through stony fields, and at noon we rested in the open. To the west, there rose the Kuruk mountain, with the Kunufi lying to the south of it; in the east there was the Belenyan mountain, and to the south of this, the Lufet, Berkoka, Koduluri, Ngufi, Lianga, Luluri, Lungi, with the Logwek near the river. The owner of the land demanded payment from me as I was resting in the shade of a tree growing on his property. The porters, who had been quarrelling the whole day long, had gone on and we were unable to move from this spot. The luggage was taken to the nearby *tukuls* belonging to the Tokiman, and we spent the night here. All night long we could hear the beating of drums and songs from the neighbouring localities.

23 October: This morning, our departure was somewhat delayed as, during the night, some of the porters had escaped and had hidden themselves in a corn store. We therefore pushed on until dusk, and then we camped on a high plateau. The people in the neighbourhood were frightened by the braying of our donkey. We obtained milk, sesame etc., from the *monye* of a nearby village. We took on two guides, on the understanding that they should accompany us to Jambara (Yangbara).

24 October: We made our way southwards until sunset, without sighting any hut. Our way led us through a forest where grass was growing eight-foot tall and where there were many wild fruit trees, with mimosas, and deep elephant tracks. We crossed many *khawrs* (seasonal streams), of which the Koda is said to be a perennial stream. In the afternoon, a thunderstorm was accompanied by a little rain. At nightfall we crossed many fields of *durra,* [3] *laka,* [4] and *leot,* [5] until we reached

---

[3] Millet, *sorghum vulgare.*

[4] Laka (Bari, sing lèke), karkadè, *hibiscus sabdariffa,* whose dried flowers soaked in water make a health-giving drink. Increasing tonnages of Karkadè are exported to Europe and America.

[5] *Leot* (Bari, sing *liyiti*), a kind of millet called in Arabic *telabūn,* (*elusine coracana*).

Limu, the first village of the Nyangwara country. The Bari also called this place Fadseho-lu (it is far-away), probably because of the endless forests in the vicinity. As soon as the inhabitants saw us, they raised a frightful cry and stood before us with drawn bows. We stopped and sent some of our men to the village to determine whether we would be well received or not. The people said, that we, the white men, were beasts (*gwuruyin*) and cannibals, and that we must go away. However, having assured them of our friendly intentions, the *monye* invited us to take our luggage to his hut, and cried '*po-ta*' (come along).

The people here seem to be very poor. As ornaments, the men wear a strip of raw skin around their knuckles, a string of beads (bought from a travelling Bari smith) round their middles, six to twelve thick iron rings around the arms, or thin ivory rings, *sollok* rings around the neck (polished shells in the form of shirt-studs), or strings of cowrie shells, a large tin plate on the forehead; a large *sollok*-ring in each ear, while a pipe and a small leather tobacco pouch are fastened around the belly. The women's aprons are made from leaves, fresh or dried grass or fibres. When these aprons become soiled, they look like animal tails, and hang down, almost reaching the ground. Round their ankles, they wear three to six thick iron rings (similar to many of the Liria women); round the head is a strip of spotted leopard-skin, or *sollok*-chain, whilst around the middle, they have different strips of leather and a dagger. The *monye* brought the caravan a small ox, and in order to impress the villagers with the power of gunpowder, a shot was fired in their presence. This method is always used by the merchants, when visiting a locality for the first time, as they say that it creates respect in advance. The natives complained that the sound of the shot had given them headaches, and they retired for a short while. . . . [here follow lists of villages in the neighbourhood omitted in translation].

On 26 October we left Limu, and after picking our way through a forest, where we crossed quite a large stream, we finally arrived at Kakarak. All round us there was towering grass, and it is said that the many elephants living in these parts did great damage by eating the crops. There is a great shortage of milk because the cows do not live long, indeed their cattle in general die off at a very early age, and it is not known whether their premature death is caused by witchcraft, the grass they eat or the water they drink. Many *bunuk* (plural of *bunit*) have been consulted on this matter, but no satisfactory explanation has been forthcoming. [6]

---

[6] Probably the result of a cattle disease, trypanosomiasis, introduced by the tse-tse and other blood-sucking flies.

I

After having found two new guides (the first ones refused to go any further) and having killed and prepared an ox, the caravan struck southwest, making its way through tall grass sesame fields, and small forests, arriving at Tonga on 28 October where we found many herds grazing.

At the sound of our shots the inhabitants fled, and it was only after some time that, little by little, they re-appeared. They seem milder in character than the Bari, and besides speaking the Bari language they have a dialect of their own. The *monye* Panyamok and his people assembled their goods and soon there was a brisk exchange of beads, sesame, corn, *marisa,* etc. In the evening, the porters and natives held a *leri* (dance). The dances of the local people do not appear to be so wild as those of the Bari. The music (for which they appear to possess a real talent) was produced by drums and different kinds of horns, and at times this, coupled with their songs, produced some pleasing variations.

On 29 October, I bought my lads a sheep and a *burma-yawa* (earthenware pot full of corn) in exchange for two pigeon eggs, beads of the same size, shape, and colour as pigeon eggs, and five grains of geneto beads. Towards evening many of the natives and porters were drunk; one of them insisted in giving a gourd of beer to my donkey, as he said that it had told him that it was thirsty too.

On 30 October we left Tonga [Tombur] where a nearby stream passes on its way eastwards. After fighting our way through forests, thorns, and fields, we reached a high plateau. At this point the *monye* and his boys accompanying us refused to go any further as they said that because of previous wars, they would certainly be killed now. Eventually, with the aid of gifts and promises, we managed to persuade another *monye* to provide us with two other guides. After stumbling across very stony fields we reached the small Regong mountain gorge in the Ligi country towards evening. There we halted at the hut of a *monye,* situated in the shelter of a rock. The Regong runs from southeast to northwest.

31 October: At sunrise we were already on the march. One of the local people was supposed to be leading us in a southerly direction to a blind *matat* further in the Ligi country, in an area where the merchants hoped to procure elephant tusks. After three hours, however, our guide refused to go any further and pretended that he had lost his way. He tried to escape but the porters overtook him, ripped the beads, which he had received in payment for his services, from his neck, and only then did they set him free. Fortunately for us another guide was found, a man prompted mostly by the fear of what would otherwise happen to him, who guided us all day through forests, tall grass, marsh lands, and country where no huts were visible, until at sunset, we finally reached the dwelling place of the blind *matat*. He greeted us with the well-known cry of '*magòr!*' (hunger) complaining that his corn, sesame, etc., had all been used up, and that the harvest was still far off. The merchants presented him with noteworthy gifts, but in return they received nothing, not even a single tusk, or ox, or corn or milk. However, he did offer us an old, derelict cowshed, (not having deigned to invite us into his hut), where tired, hungry, and thirsty, we lay down.

1 November: We started off but not before the blind *monye* had unceasingly complained of his hunger, while, from me whom he believed to be a *bunit* he wanted a magic potion which would protect his cattle against war, etc. To his stick was attached a *bunit's* bell to which he gave much importance.

After a brisk march through marshy ground, tall grass, thick undergrowth, and flowering bushes smelling like cloves, we reached Moro or Muru. Towards evening we passed two big *zaribas*, crossed through some *durra* fields and a small forest, and arrived at the dwelling place of the *monye*, the famous elephant hunter, Umba or Weri-Benetit (son of Benetit). However, we did not find him at home as, together with his men, he was away on an elephant hunt and the women did not know when to expect him. Here too, we did not succeed in getting any food, except for some elephant meat, which is stored in baskets, after being smoked. When it is cooked, it tastes like beef-steak. In the evening I bought a kind of nut, which is supposed to be sweet, but in reality, is very bitter. The people eat them mixed with sesame. The wives were afraid to sell us anything else as they feared that their husbands might be displeased and although beads were dangled before their eyes, they remained adamant. I was surprised by such faithfulness among the wives because the Bari wives of the White Nile are exactly the opposite. I walked a distance of a quarter of an hour, to a little river called the Bibè [Bibi] for a bathe. The water here is cool and clear, with a red sandy bed.

On 5 November, I took a trip southwards on the eastern bank of the Yei river. The night was wet and cold, owing to the thunderstorm of the previous day, and the covers and clothes were thoroughly damp. The leading guide refused to go any further unless he was accompanied by two or three others, and the porters, after a long discussion, were of the opinion that the sun was already too high. It was not until the following morning that we travelled direct to the south. After a hard twelve-hour trek we struck camp at a lonely zariba not far from Mordschak. I was exceedingly thirsty but water could not be found in the darkness. I had a few drops of Brinowitzer, [7] which I used for medical purposes. To add to our discomforts there was a slight drizzle, and both the red and white ants gave us much discomfort.

On 7 November, we journeyed for a further six hours and reached Rokon, where the *monye* welcomed us but treated us very coldly. He felt no concern for our hunger (we had eaten almost nothing for the past few days) and put an enormous price on the fowls and goats he tried to sell us. He refused to accommodate us in his dwelling and only offered us a place under a tree. After lengthy discussion, he became more amenable and allowed us into his *zarība,* which was surrounded by a big circular fence. The *zarība* consists of a very strong, and high exterior fence which protects the animals from thieves. Within this fence there is another concentric to it, but not as high and which can be easily scaled. In the area between the two fences, there are the round huts and small corn baskets, whilst between the corn baskets tobacco grows. In the innermost space, there are stakes to which the cattle are tethered.

When our she-ass was brought into the zeriba in the evening all the cattle started bellowing and breaking away from the ropes. So it was decided that the poor donkey had to remain outside. The inhabitants asked me whether all the cows at home were as disgraceful and uttered such wild cries as my donkey (for they called my donkey a cow). The cows here are big and multi-coloured.

Nearby the river Yei flows from south to north and it abounds with hippopotami, crocodiles and fish, while along its banks there are beautiful high trees. The people here old and young, are skilled swimmers. Those going to Mondo in the west, or coming from the opposite direction, jump into the river, and in no time, they are on the other side. They appear to be very superstitious. Thus, the *monye* wanted us to leave his dwelling place because he thought that we had cast a spell upon his cattle. He closed all the entrances and exists and nobody was allowed to enter and sell things. *Monye* Kadini-lo-mere, that is, Mountain Tree, refuses elephant meat because he thinks that men originated from the elephants, and he chased our porters from his

---

[7] An unidentified stimulant or tonic. Can readers help here?

dwelling place when he found that they intended to roast elephant meat they had brought from Moru. A woman, from whom I had borrowed a *sape* (clay pot) would not allow me to cook a chicken in it, and so as to be on the safe side she waited until she saw that the chicken had been roasted on the fire. Elephant tusks should not be brought into the vicinity otherwise, they believe, people would die. Here, we had some showers of rain.

On 12 November, we returned to Moru. This time our direction was more towards the east and after a few hours we ran across a band of elephant hunters, Matat Umba among them. They were preparing to return the next day. The elephant meat has been smoked on wooden frames over an open fire, packed, and the boiled fat had been poured into gourds and earthen pots. Umba's men had killed four elephants in this area. When hunting elephants the hunters split up, part of them driving the elephants along certain tracks, whilst the others take up hidden positions in high places. When the elephants pass underneath, heavy spears are hurled down at them and they are killed in this way. Women and children have been ordered here to carry home the meat. On 13 November, we continued our journey north westwards ploughing our way through forests and grass, and followed by the sickly smell of elephant meat. Late in the evening, we reached Umba's farm at Moru.

A Journey west of the Yei River

14 November: After a tasty fish meal (the people here do not eat fish and dislike it intensely, for they believe it causes one's death) I left, and struck south-west, crossed the river Bibe, which is about 5 foot deep, and quite wide. Bibe (or Bibi) is a torrential affluent of the Yei, which joins not far from here. After an hour I reached the river Yei itself. This river comes from the south and probably flows into the Bahr al-Ghazāl. [8] At this point it is 800 feet wide, and five or six feet deep. It is said to have no less volume even during the dry season. Despite this, the bed of the river is said to be covered with formations of rock which prevent the larger boats from using the river. There are beautiful trees shading the bank, including the dom palm. Amidst beautiful surroundings the village of Woli nestles on the western bank. I noticed that many of the natives there were affected by hernia of

[8] The Yei loses itself in swamps near Yirrol.

the testicles, their scrota hanging down to the calf of the leg.[9] I
enquired whether their habitual jumping was the cause of such a
complaint, but I was told that it was because some malicious persons
had mingled poison with the food and drink of the people so affected,
and that this had caused the hernias.

After leaving Woli, we trudged on for eight hours across fields
of *durra, dukhn,*[10] *leot* and *laka* and arrived at Bibio, a village situated
on a small tributary of the Yei about two days east of the Niam Niam
cannibals.[11] Everything is very cheap here, and in trade beads are
counted singly one by one. I bought plump hens, long-haired billy
goats, corn, butter, flour and indian corn, etc.

On 16 November, the *monye* invited me to his house as he wished
to speak to me about various matters. He mistook me for a *bunit*
(diviner) and asked me to tell him his fortune. He wanted to know
whether he would recover from the stiffness of his body, or die. He
told me I ought to '*momoja ko kume*' (to snuffle over his body like a
bunok). His sons, daughters and kinsfolk were gathered under a *rakūba*
around me and were listening intently to our conversation. However,
the Bari language is not understood by all here (the Bari language ends
at the river Yei) and therefore the *monye* translated my words. The
people here have some inkling of the Great Flood, and they speak of
the one who was left alive. They believe that after death man becomes
a *kududwet* [ködudwo], a shadow which protects men. They call a
superior being *kulan,* i.e. the beginning, the first one. This *kulan* is
said to have created the first elephant from which man originated.
According to the *monye,* to the south-west there is a *Jur lo Tomia*
(Village of Elephants), where these animals are said to lead a domesti-
cated life, like our cows. Furthermore there is a *Jur lo Lopijoki*
(Village of Weathers) also the Village of Hens, where a cock rules like
a *matat* and keeps order. There are no cattle there because of the large
flies, which sting and kill. Far to the south, there is also a *Jur lo Wate,*
or Village of Women. I was surprised to find, marked on a map, on the
other side of the Equator the name Womens' Town. According to the
people the *Jur lo Wate* is inhabited only by women who have intercourse
with dogs and beget either male dogs or girls. Other natives told me
that women, bathing in a nearby stream, become pregnant after their
immersion in the dirty water. Others, however, said that some youths

---

[9] Possibly the result of the disease filarial elephantiasis.

[10] Bullrush millet, *pennisetum americanum.*

[11] The Northern Sudanese were confident that the Azande were cannibals and
called them by the suggestively onomatopoeic name Niam-Niam.

had approached the women and were chased off soon afterwards. To the north there is a village called *Jur lo Kwen*, (Village of Birds). This *monye*, who seemed very superstitious, had a profound knowledge of these doubtful stories. Meanwhile, he ordered a huge jar of *yawa* (beer) to be taken to our dwelling.

After this he came to see me every day. He had come from the Bari country in his early childhood and had settled in the neighbourhood of Weyi, where he had married and became a well-to-do *monye*. He advised me to do the same and stay with him.

During the next few days, more and more natives came to see me and my donkey, and to sell us food. One day a group of them coming from Tubu, about one day's journey away, brought white *durra*, beans, honey, a certain fruit like the *fūl* of Kurdufān, which tasted like chestnuts, to the market and were selling at a cheap price. They were selling twelve cupped handfuls of beans for two *borjok* beads, four handfuls of groundnuts for one *manshur bead*. [12] Only one of the natives amongst them knew the Bari language and he was the one that led the group. From him I bought a knife with an attractive handle. He claimed that he had got it from the Makaraka, the tribes living one day's distance to the west of Tubu. I learnt from him that the Makaraka in the west, and the Makarayang in the south, were greatly to be feared, as they cut all strangers to pieces, roasted them over a fire, and ate them. The Makaraka are said to hunt the elephant, eat the meat but not the intestines which they throw away. One of the *monye* of that place is called Gindschia, his wife Lekituru, and another Dali. They carry only spears and shields, but no bows and arrows. They kill elephants by sharp clubs made of hard and heavy wood. At the sight of an elephant or a stranger they cheer and shout '*idi, idi*', call for their knives and cut them to pieces. Men and women are unclothed. In the latter, the hair round the region of the vulva is allowed to grow long, and when the husband departs, their hair is tied into knots in order to preserve it. The men marry only one wife but she is sometimes shared with guests. A wife is bought for ten hens. (There are whole broods of hens to be found here, but no cows because of the flies.) When a child is born, the husband acts as midwife.

It is said that far away to the west, there are white and red men, who are described as cannibals. Although it is very unlikely that it is

[12] The writer made a name-list in his diary of the various beads in use in the Sudan in 1860 (Morlang, p. 399). No study of origins of these names of the beads and cowries used as currency in the trade of the White Nile basin is known to have been published.

true, I am recording here what a Bari *bunit,* called Lungashu [Lungasuk], [13] told me (This *bunit* was a renowned traveller). He said:

'Three years ago, together with the Bari *bunit,* Lobeke, I, too, travelled as a *bunit* from Mokido (to the south of Gondokoro) and kept a direct south-westerly course until I reached the white man. The white man owns a big stone-house, near a large river, which forms a lake in this locality and then flows on to the south-west. Ships ply up and down the river. In the house, there were eight men and three women. The head of the group was called Air, while his wife, who cooked for him, was called Ile. I was given wine and sweetened coffee. They possessed matches, lamps, and knew how to write. When praying, they bowed their heads to the ground. In their large garden, there was plenty of fruit, including grapes, whilst there were also sugar-canes, and many turkeys. They wore long clothes reaching to the ground. When travelling mounted on horses or donkeys, they carried pistols and guns at their side. They are quiet and speak a foreign language. Their village is called Lokelinge (I looked this place up in an old map, and I found it situated far to the south-west, on the other side of the equator) [14]. Some place-names in that locality are: Malanga (a high mountain), Lo-tschi (a lake), Makarawang, Gumbiri, Kefu [Kep], Bitschoro, Lo-Gume, Kobek, Egamini, Atschera (names of villages).'

Such was the story; and from it one can clearly see how adept the natives are in lying and how they will always frame their answers so as always to please their questioners. Or is the story true, and did this white man to the south really exist?

During my stay at Weyi, there were frequent heavy thunderstorms, while on 17 November the hailstones, which fell, were as big as cherries. Because of the constant rainfall, and the fear of the Makaraka, we were unable to find a single man to act as guide for us not even as far as the nearby mountains, as, for instance, the Malanga to the west, or Tuli to the south. Had I been able to reach these mountains, I would have been able to survey all the country they commanded, but I was forced to retrace my steps and on 21 Novem-

---

[13] Interpreter to Nuqud, agent of the Coptic Egyptian trader Shenuda.

[14] Possibly a clouded memory of a 'coast Arab' settlement somewhere in the interior. There is a Lokalenge at 1° 11′ N. and 22° 40′ E, 150 miles west of Kisangani in Zaire.

ber, I was back in Moru, in Umba's *zarība*. I remained there until the 30th, during which time I gathered as much information as I could about the Nyangwara country.

The Nyangwara Country

Nyangwara (also Yangwara, Yang-bara, Yambara) is the name given by the Bari to the country lying to the west of the Kerek and Kunufi mountains, as far as the Yei river. Thus to the east it borders with the Bari, to the south and west with Makarayang (Makarakak) or Niam Niam; to the north there are large forests with many herds of elephants and the Jur and Arol; while to the north-east it borders with the Mandari. The area involved is equivalent to 1½ degrees both in length and in breadth, with high mountains on the eastern and western sides. There are many streams and rivulets flowing towards the Yei. The villages are generally the distance of one day's journey from each other, and the number of inhabitants of each village is between five and seven hundred people. From Umba's dwelling place, which is situated at the junction of the Bibi and Yei in the Moru country at about 4° N. and 28° 50′ E. the country in front of me was as follows:

To the east: a chain of mountains (about two days journey away) running from north to southeast and called Regong with the peaks of Wer-koka [Wari koka] (son of the leopard) Ridschong, Wododot, Berifat, Gumbo and Lodara. Between these peaks there were also the the peaks of Luturuken, Kero, Kugut, Kurit (giraffe) and the mountain of Mire or Mile, where the Lo-tschi tribe (honey men) is said to live.

To the south: Very far off (probably many days journey away) there are two very high pyramid-shaped mountains. The higher, in the east, is called Tuli, whilst the other in the west is known as Lo-Boyong. The villages of Rokon and Lokwok are situated along this route.

To the west: At a distance of between two to four days journey from the river Yei, the mountain of Lo-Pioko, Dschirimenit, Wowu, Kurubu, adjacent to Koromani, Malanga, Longobe and Ami can be seen running from south to north.

Villages: (*a*) to the south; Kurube, Buku, Kubut, Kune, Lo-Bakela; (*b*) to the south-west and west: Mondo, Tubu, Iye, Baka, Wotshike, Wandshi (Wadshe) Dikibe.

Rivers: The main river is the Yeyi, known as Yei, and only rarely the Bei. Flowing to the north it is said to run between the Jur and Arol to the Bahr al-Ghazāl. Many smaller rivers and streams flow into it including the Bibe or Bibi from the south-east. As to the origin of the Yei I learnt that it was in the Lero mountains, far to the south, whilst nearby the Tschufiri (White Nile) is also said to take its rise. It is thought that the Lokak tribe live in the vicinity of its source.

From the west, the Bukure, Litirimi, Wandschi, Mendsche, Babala, Tore, Ire join the Yei. These smaller rivers, which come from the western mountains, dry up during the hot months. The river which flows by Tubu is so large that it is said that crocodiles and hippopotami live in it.

The climate of the area around the river Yei appears to be quite healthy and the soil fertile. There is only one month a year when there is no rain, and from what I could learn it was most likely to be the month of January.

Products: There are great quantities of iron available but only a few blacksmiths and even these are emigrants from the Bari country who have settled here. However, they are not kept very busy as there is no great demand for their goods.

Copper is also said to be found here but as it is red in colour it is disliked and, therefore, like red beads there is no market for copper rings.

There is no salt available and in its place the people use goats' and cows' urine, after it has first been passed through ashes. Milk is also mixed with urine and seldom with water.

Granite, limestone and flint are to be found almost everywhere. There is an abundance of edible plants and unlike the Bari country there is no yearly famine here. Nearly every shrub has its own edible fruit of different flavour. In addition to the usual types of corn, *bāmyā* gourd (which also grows wild), maize and tobacco are also sown. The young Bari are not very skilled in the art of curing tobacco and when smoked it leaves a sore throat and a cough. Along the river banks there are various kinds of trees, including the olive, dom palm, tamarind, and the so-called iron-wood. Wild vine grows everywhere.

Animals: There are elephants (whose flesh is very tasty) cows, and goats with long black silken hair (much esteemed by the Bari, who cover their arrows and spear handles with goat skin). Much in demand are the hairs of elephants' tails which, if worn around the waist, are considered as a charm against illness. The sheep are few in number and ungainly in appearance. There are many wild animals especially hyenas. As there are no domestic cats, the mice and rats enjoy great freedom and many a time while I was resting they have nibbled at my ears and toes. Mosquitoes and white ants are not so trublesome here as in the Bahr al-Abyad. When I was there few birds were to be seen, but I was told they were more numerous at other times of the year. There is plenty of fish, but as I have already stated, it is not eaten.

Agriculture continues without break throughout the year, and although the main harvests are in July and December, ripe and sprouting corn can be seen at any month.

Regarding the customs and moral standards of the inhabitants, I have already dwelt upon these earlier. The people adorn their bodies in a similar fashion to the tribes of the White Nile. I add, however, that the girls perforate their lips and insert pieces of wood, durra stalks, or stones cut in cylindrical form, rendering their speech difficult. As among all other natives, the favourite drink here, especially at harvest time, is *yawa* (beer). This beer is rendered more platable and intoxicating by the addition of different kinds of plants. Blue is the favourite colour of the Nyangwara, and, *gondshul, franji, manshur* beads are considered to be the most valuable and, indeed, are almost the only ones used in trade here. Tattooing usually consists of incisions radiating from between the eyebrows to the sides of the forehead. The character of the people is placid, and they speak with disgust about the quarrelling grumbling Bari. The more women a man possesses the more he is esteemed. Divorce is rare. The natives are fond of fables and tales, are very superstitious, and for this reason the *bunoks* are highly honoured. They have no boats of any kind. Owing to the lack of iron tools, bone or wooden implements are used in the cultivation of their fields. They use elephants' shoulder blades for these tasks. The *molots* (heart-shaped shovels) are so costly that it requires a whole elephant tusk to purchase one. Love of music, dancing and singing is one of the main characteristics of the natives and they also know how to make all kinds of musical instruments. The Nyangwara people are said to live to a very old age, and I myself saw many old people with white hair. When someone dies, the head is placed between the knees and the body is buried in a sitting position.

The Return Journey from Moru on the Yei to Gondokoro on the Shufiri or from the Nyangwara to the Bari

Towards the end of November the merchants returned, and Umba, the *matat*, or chief of Moro, joined them with seven men. He wanted to see the Mission house, the boats coming from Khartoum, and he also hoped to be able to kill some elephants along the way. I followed them with my five boys and she-ass. The caravan left Moro on 30 November and made its way north-east, first through some villages, and then through a large forest where we spent the night. In the afternoon of 1 December we stopped at a big zariba where we bought an ox. The ox was killed, roasted, eaten and then we slept. This restored the porters' good humour as on the previous day there had been much grumbling because of the heavy loads.

2 December: About an hour after dawn a group of armed Africans appeared in front of us on the plain and they stood and watched us as we made our way to a small wood which was nearby. Then we heard the war drums beating, and our natives well knew the meaning of that sound: we were going to be attacked. We immediately deposited all our luggage in an open space in the woods, and primed our weapons. Our local porters and the merchants' *'askarī* [15] (soldiers) ran forward and took up positions at the flank and stood at the ready with their bows, arrows and firearms. They encountered a disorderly horde who showered their arrows upon the caravan, at the same time uttering dreadful war cries. Our men counter-attacked courageously. At the sound of our rifles, some of the natives ran off, but others rushed in from the right and left, whilst arrows flew in all directions. Meanwhile some of the enemy crept up quietly behind us and were then joined by the cowards who had fled at the first attack. Our people veered round and shouted to the natives to be off, but a shower of arrows was the only answer. One of the arrows pierced my servant, Taha, just above the shoulder, and he fell at my feet. A burst of fire from our guns brought a number of the enemy to the ground and the rest ran away.

We took up our luggage again and a short distance from the wood we rested in the shade of a tree. Nearby were two abandoned farms which had been looted by the Bari. The enemy casualties amounted to nine killed and wounded, while we were unscathed. A group of the

[15] Strictly *'asākir* (plural).

enemy creeping through the grass sent a messenger to sue for peace and he was told that we would negotiate only with the *monye* and we told them that if he did not come the farms would be destroyed by fire and the herds driven off. Shortly after, an under-sized stoutish, elderly man appeared (a bullet had passed through his son's throat). Silently, he knelt on one knee, stretched out his hand, begged pardon and besought us to spare his life. He was reproached for his behaviour and we asked him why we, passing peacefully through this country, had been subjected to such a murderous attack, and why the war drums had been beaten, etc. The *monye* replied: 'We regret everything very much. We had heard that a caravan, laden with many beads and elephant tusks would be coming this way. We believed that among them would be many women (all clothed men are taken for women here, as among the inhabitants only women dress). We did not know that the caravan was well armed, and that besides spears and sticks it also had musical instruments. (Our guns were mistaken for musical instruments.) Therefore we decided to attack the caravan and rob it, but had I known it was you I would never have beaten the war drum.' We demanded that the *matat* should make amends for the loss of time and expenditure of ammunition and arrows by giving us at least two oxen.

The *matat* had already brought along an ox, but we did not accept it because we could not spare enough people to look after it. Instead of this, the Bari porters took some small cattle in compensation for their lost arrows.

After a further talk with the *matat*, peace was made and he provided the caravan with a guide for the day's journey. Whilst he departed grumbling to attend the death ceremonies of the natives killed in battle, we left this village which was called To-ongu.

In the evening, we approached the Regong mountain in the Ligi country and stopped at a village where a marriage was being celebrated. The inhabitants, who had drunk far too much *yawa* uttered horrible cries on seeing us, and threatened to drive us off. As a retaliatory measure we tried to frighten them with our rifle-fire but they were not in the least deterred, and indeed, seemed to be immensely enjoying the noise. They had never heard rifle-fire before. After much trouble we were forced to spend the night in the open under a tree. However, we were immediately visited by the *monye* who told us that he was not afraid of war and that if we did not leave at once he would use weapons to drive us away. We were tired, hungry, and thirsty. The night was pitch dark and we had no guide, what were we to do? We decided to stay, lit a fire in our camp, and kept a careful watch during the night.

3 December: After having crossed a ravine through the Regong, we entered a vast plain where there were many sycamores whose fruit was just ripening and we were able to pick and eat it. Towards the evening we reached Tombur where the well-known *monye*, Panyamok, welcomed us and criticised our appearance by saying, 'this man has put on weight . . . this man has lost weight' etc.

5 December: We made our way to Kakarak; on the 6th via Limu we passed through a large wood near the Koda stream, and being exhausted we pitched camp in a thick wood.

7 December: We made an early start, and after an hour and a half we reached a stream where we quenched our consuming thirst. Late in the evening we arrived at the first Bari village of Kelye. By means of a messenger, the *monye* informed us that if we did not pay him with beads for lying under his tree, we would be stoned. In reply, our porters told the messenger of what had happened when we fired our guns at To-ongu — whereupon no further claim was made.

Next day, after a long trek over sand and stones we were warmly welcomed at Tokiman, although rumours had been spread that we had all been stoned to death. (It seemed as if they had really intended to murder us at Kelye.) Here we received news from Gondokoro that our comrades were safe and that the boats from Khartoum had not yet arrived.

After having rested the night on an open plain, we made our way to the river in the morning, and we were again ferried across by Iguschok. Thus, on 9 December under the strong rays of the afternoon sun, we arrived at Gondokoro in good health and enriched in experience.

CHAPTER VII

ON THE WHITE NILE FROM KHARTOUM
TO GONDOKORO, 1859-1860

by G. Beltrame

Our next contributor was a Veronese, Giovanni Beltrame (1824-1906), from Valeggio sul Mincio. After training at the Mazza Institutes in Verona he came to the Sudan in 1853 and in 1857 went to Holy Cross Mission, since abandoned. In later life Beltrame was appointed Superior of the Verona institutes where he had been a student.

Beltrame's notable pioneer work in Dinka language studies has received recognition elsewhere; we are concerned only with his travel narratives. He was a man who clearly enjoyed travelling; he had the advantage of a fluent pen and all the journalist's skill in noting colourful detail as well as concentrating on essentials. This passage is part of a long published letter, Di un viaggio sul Fiume Bianco, lettera di Don Giovanni Beltrame, *Verona, 1861, pp. 5-46.*

Late in the afternoon of 1 December 1859, aided by a strong west wind, we set sail from Khartoum and started moving rapidly over the rough waters of the mysterious river. During the night we passed by two small mountains, Jabal Awliyā on the right and Jabal Mandara on the left bank, a little removed from the river and almost facing the other mountain. Jabal Awliyā, or as it is sometimes written, Gebel Aule, was thus named by the Arabs because it is the first mountain one encounters on travelling upstream from Khartoum. [1] It is also called Jār al-Nabī after a chief of that name who once lived nearby. [2]

---

[1] Jabal Awliyā' (plural of *walī*, a saint) means Hill of the Saints.

[2] Jār al-Nabī, said to have been a religious teacher from the Yemen, is mentioned in the biographical dictionary of Muhammad al-Nūr b. Dayfullāh *Kitāb al-tabaqāt*, ed. Y.F. Hasan, Khartoum, 1971, pp. 130, 149.

Jabal Mūsā, further to the west, also took its name from a chief, both these men having been greatly respected and honoured by the local people. Jabal Mandara was thus named because its summit, or head as the Arabs say, is flat and round like a mirror.

Always helped by a good wind, within but three days we passed the Egyptian frontier and with it those ancient and impenetrable virgin forests which on the left of the river separate Egypt from the powerful Shilluk. Eventually we reached the mountains of the Dinka which rise on the right bank of the river. Here I could not but heave a deep sigh on looking at one of the highest of these mountains, which reminded me of the happy moment when the late Fr. Angelo Melotto [3] and I, on 17 March of this year, had climbed its height to view that part of Dinkaland which we had explored throughout 20 days with so much labour, from 22 February to 11 March. These particular mountains, placed between 12° and 13° N. are called Niemati [4] by the furthermost Dinka tribe, the Abialang, who are the closest to them. The Arabs call them Jabal al-Dinka since in former times the Dinka extended as far as these mountains, but, as they were being constantly harassed by the Abū Rūf Arabs, they retreated to 11° N. and from there they now extended as far as the capital town of the Shilluk at 9° 50′N., not far from the river Yal at 10° 19′ 54″ N. My old interpreter told me that about thirty years ago the Dinka also inhabited the right bank of the White Nile as far as the Sobat, but they had had to withdraw from there too for fear of the Nuer by whom they were being constantly attacked. Nowadays, the Abū Rūf make frequent raids on horseback among the Abialang, the Agher, to the south of the Abialang, and even among the Abujo, to the south of the Agher, in order to steal *durra*, of which there is abundance among the Dinka. These Dinka, together with the Agnarquei and the Dunghiol, who are more to the south, must also be in constant fear of the Shilluk who, on the same latitude, inhabit the opposite bank of the river. This tribe is called Dinka by the Arabs of Sinnār peninsula, while by the Arabs who inhabit the left bank of the White Nile it is called Gienghe. The Dinka, however, call themselves Gien and this name is given to all the other tribes that speak the Dinka language, although each one has its own particular local name. The Shilluk and the Nuer are, therefore, not included in the name of Gien. At the time of writing,

---

[3] Fr. Angelo Melotto came to the Sudan with D. Comboni and G. Beltrame in 1857. He died in Khartoum in 1859 after a brief stay at Holy Cross.

[4] Jabalayn, Jebelein, on modern maps.

the Dinka of whom I am speaking were still in their permanent dwellings in the interior.

The Shilluk tribe lives along the left bank of the White Nile, on the same latitude as the Dinka and continues almost as far as 9° N. Beginning from the river Sobat, their villages are very frequent and close to one another for about twenty geographical miles. My crew counted in this tract more than one hundred and fifty villages besides those which, they told me, could not be seen as they were further inland. It is true that many wandering Shilluk, given to fishing and hunting, are to be found as far as 14° N. but the true location of this tribe is between 12° and 9° N.

Without encountering any mishap on the journey, we reached Hillat al-Kaka on December 6, at 1 o'clock in the afternoon, and stopped in front of the main village. At this point the river takes a long and sudden bend towards south-west and we began to tackle this bend at dusk. By midnight we had cleared it and were then travelling in a south-westerly direction. The going was neither slow nor fast and at 3 o'clock in the morning we came to the tributary Jal. I had already noted this tributary during my first journey on the White Nile but thought it to be little more than a torrent, swollen during the rains but quite dry during the dry season. On my return to Khartoum from Holy Cross I stopped near the mouth of this tributary as I wanted my interpreter to make many enquiries about it from the Dunghiol who live on its banks. Already here at Hillat Kaka I found out from people well acquainted with the direction of this tributary that for about half a day's journey it has an easterly course and then divides into two branches, one taking a north-easterly direction and the other taking a south-easterly one.

At Mount Tefafan, or Bibb'an, or Kur-Wir (Rock of the River) as the natives call it, [5] which rises to the right of the White Nile at 10° 47′ 34″ N., Mr. Brun-Rollet [6] marks another tributary, which he calls Piper (from the name of Mt. Bibb'an), but which in fact is but a branch of a river called Tarciam and which, after a sweep of about fifteen miles, flows back into the same river. The greatest distance of this

---

[5] Jabal Ahmad Aghā on modern maps.

[6] Jacques-Antoine Brun-Rollet (1810-58), a Savoyard hence a Sardinian subject, was born at Saint-Jean-de-Maurienne with the name of Rollet. As a youth he fled from home as a draft-dodger under the faked name of Brun which he later added to his original name. He first came to the Sudan in 1831. He died in Khartoum. See R. d'Amat, *Dict. de biogr. française*, VII, 1956, p. 518.

channel from the river is from four to five miles and is found at the beginning of the territory of the Abialang.

On December 7, at about noon, we reached Denab. [7] I consider this town to be the capital of the Shilluk country rather than Hillat Kaka for it is more in the centre of the country. Also it is the residence of the *reth* Nyidhok, [8] and is inhabited entirely by Shilluk whereas Hillat Kaka has a mixed population of various tribes. When we arrived, we found that the King had died in February of that year. We also learned that when about to die he had been throttled by his relatives as in this tribe it is considered unworthy for a man of such rank to die by himself. He still lay unburied, well shut up inside a hut, as his successor, who would probably be the son of one of his brothers, had not yet been definitely elected. Such a nomination depends on the vote of the people and only when the successor is established in his post is the deceased *reth* buried. All this was related to us by an old Shilluk who was unhappy about the new election, considering it much better to be without a king altogether.

Soon after midnight, with an almost full moon above us, we saw the river Sobat flowing into the Nile at 9° 11′ 25″ N. This important tributary of the White Nile is called Sobat by foreigners only, the Arabs call it Bahr al-Makhada, there being many places, as I saw myself, where it can be forded. The Dinka call it simply *Kir,* which means river. They also call it *Kiatin,* which is the diminutive of *Kir,* and means little river, in order to distinguish it from the White Nile. Sometimes they call it *Kidid,* meaning big river, from the two words *kir* (river) and *abid* (big) in order to distinguish it from the torrents. I found these names much altered and confused in some maps.

We passed the river Sobat, and after some hours' travel in the westward direction came to a tributary about half the width of the Nile itself. This river is called Bahr al-Zaráf whose banks are inhabited by the Nuer as far as 8° N. It leaves the main river in the Bor country at 7° N., very near a village named Aquak. An aged member of my crew told me he had travelled up the whole of it in a small boat some years before. Many others of my crew, including the *ra'is* himself, knew it in parts and all agreed in saying that the river which left the

---

[7] The Shilluk do not use this name for their principal settlement which they call Pachodo, not to be confused with another village which Turco-Egyptians and Europeans called Fashoda, the present Kodok, 12 miles north of Pachodo.

[8] *Reth* Nyidohok, No. 24 in the Shilluk list of kings.

White Nile at Aquak, in the Bor country, was the same which joined it near the Sobat. I decided to verify this once we reached the Bor country itself.

On December 8, at nine in the morning, we reached the last limit of the Shilluk country and soon came across the villages of the Gianghe tribe which separated the Shilluk from the Nuer.

At noon on the following day we reached the mouth of the Bahr al-Ghazāl, at 9° 18′ 24″ N. An hour before our arrival I noticed, not far from the left bank of the river, the so-called Tekem mountains. To the north west of these live the Baqqāra Humur Arabs. Further north come the Taqalī mountains where the Baqqāra Hawāzma live. These latter mountains, which continue uninterrupted as far as Kurdufān, are also inhabited by many other tribes of Baqqāra Arabs who trade mainly with al-Ubayyid, the capital of Kurdufān. After the Bahr al-Ghazāl, the White Nile, now very narrow, winds slowly and tortuously through the swampy region of the Nuer. These occupy the land on the left bank, a little way back from the bank itself. We were among the Nuer swamps for eight days, while myriad mosquitoes sucked our blood with their wretched stings.

On December 17, at four in the afternoon, we entered the land of the Cic or Ciec, who live along the banks of the Bahr al-Abyad, or White Nile, between 6° and 8° N. The name Cic which I have found written on many maps on the right bank of the river, should be placed on the left, for their permanent dwellings are to be found on the left bank of the river, a little inland. I myself, together with Fr. Joseph Lanz [9] and Fr. Daniele Comboni, [10] visited some of their villages. It is only temporarily, during the dry season, that they come to the river bank and sometimes even cross to the other side for the sake of good pastures. A few Cic, mostly fishermen, are permanently settled on the right bank.

Among this tribe is the Mission of the Holy Cross. On the night of December 22, we reached the Mission station at 6° 40′ N., where I embraced Fr. Joseph Lanz and Fr. Anton Kaufmann, [11] both of whom were in good health and happy.

On the morning of December 26 I set off for Gondokoro together with Fr. Lanz. On the left bank of the river we noticed many more

[9] Fr. Josef Lanz (1827-60), born at Dobbiaco (Toblach) in the Alto Adige, came to the Sudan in 1856 and died in Khartoum after service on the White Nile.

[10] The future bishop.

[11] See pp. 140 ff.

temporary dwellings of the Cic. On the right bank the tribe of Tui, or Tutui, were living.

On 27 December we had the Bor tribe on the right bank and the Aliab on the left; the latter, with their cattle, were in temporary dwellings close to the bank, while the former were still in the interior, by river channels. Towards mid day we reached Aquak, close to where the Bahr al-Zaraf leaves the Nile.

The following day saw a sudden change in what had been for several days a monotonous appearance of the river banks. To the very high grass and reeds succeeded, on the right bank, the beautiful forests of the Bor country. Among the trees we noted the ebony, the *dōm* palm, the gigantic euphorbia, the *alok*[12] and *kacamut*[13] and an occasional *nabak*. We noticed many little channels running from both banks of the river, forming little islands on which the vegetation, owing to the humidity and heat, was dense and luxuriant. These islands are inhabited by poor fishermen who form a caste of their own. At the time we travelled up the river, this — although now quite narrow — was shallow and sluggish, making our progress difficult. Here and there we came across banks of shells over which a falcon or stork often hovered in search of food. We discovered that such a scarcity of water was due to a wide and deep channel which, to the left, leaves the river at 5° 56′ 44″ N. and flows back at 6° 14′ 30″ N. close to Aquak. The island limited by this channel and the river is called Jazirat al-Aliab by the Arabs, and is the largest to be found on the White Nile after that formed by the Bahr al-Zaraf and those in the Shir country.

At about four o'clock in the afternoon of 29 December we left behind us the Aliab and the Bor countries. These limits also mark the end of the region in which the Dinka language is spoken by at least eighteen tribes. On the left bank of the river we find:

1. The Aliab, below 6° N.

2. The Atwot.

3. The Cic or Ciec between 6° and 8° N.

4. The Gok.

5. The Arol [i.e., the Agar. See No. 14 below], to the north of, and contiguous to, the Gok.

---

[12] Alok provides a problem of identification. The Dinka *Alok/Allok* is the grass *Setaria sphacelata* which does not accord with the writer's description of it as 'similar' to the date in shape and size (p. 156, 156n below).

[13] Kakamūt (*Acacia polyacantha* subsp. *campylacantha*).

6. The great Nuer tribe, to the north of the Cic, and widely spread over both sides of the river, speaking a language of its own but knowing and using that of the Dinka.

7. The Gienghe [Jieng] tribe, which inhabits the left bank of both the White Nile and the Ghazal, between the Nuer and Shilluk, and extends well into the interior.

8. The Shilluk tribe, between 12° and 9° N. speaking a language of its own but knowing, and using, that of the Dinka. (The tribes which speak the Dinka language, although occasionally warfaring amongst themselves, recognize a certain brotherhood. The Shilluk and Nuer always consider the Dinka their enemies and are always ready to invade their lands and steal their possessions.)

On the right of the river we find the following:

9. The Bor between 6° and 7° N.

10. The Tuic, to the north of, and contiguous to the Bor.

Continuing on the right of the river, from the Sobat to past 11° N., we find the true Dinka tribes:

11. The Dunghiol [Dongjo].

12. The Agnarquei [Angakue]. [14]

13. The Abujo [Abiong].

14. The Agher [Agar].

15. The Abialang.

All these are small tribes which I, with the late Fr. Angelo Melotto, visited on my return from Holy Cross to Khartoum in February and March 1859.

The wife of my interpreter told me of three other Dinka speaking tribes, situated in the interior at 10° N.

16. The Nyiel

17. The Beer.

18. The Yom.

As well as these eighteen tribes, whose geographical position I was able to ascertain, there are others speaking the Dinka language

[14] A sub-section of the Bor Dinka.

to be found in the upper part of the Sobat and of the Bahr-al-Ghazāl.[15]

From what has been so far discovered, Dinka is the language most generally spoken in the region of the upper Nile. The differences in the language as spoken by the various tribes are very small and those in the pronounciation even more negligible, so that, as I myself was able to ascertain during my study of this language, if one was well acquainted with the language of any one of the tribe mentioned above, it was quite easy to make oneself understood by the other tribes. Proof of this is that my interpreter, himself a Dunghiol, could easily understand and make himself understood by any of the tribes, the Shilluk, the Gienghe, the Nuer, the Arol, the Gok, the Aliab, the Bor and the Tuic. The modest results of my work on this language consist of a dictionary of 2692 words from Italian into Dinka and of 2212 words from Dinka into Italian, the latter accented and with illustrated examples; *Exercises and Dialogues,* on the habits of the Cic, and *General Rules of Grammar.* With this work, carried out over a period of two years, I have tried to organize the Dinka language as spoken by so many tribes.

On 29 December, just before we had passed the island of the Aliab, we noticed two great channels of water, which had left the river at 5° N. flow back into the White Nile. These navigable channels intercommunicate, forming extremely fertile islets, belong to the Shir. These islets are sown with tobacco, sesame, beans, *durra,* and cotton, and we noticed thick clusters of the castor-oil plant, which grows there naturally. Some of the islets are left uncultivated to provide pasture for cattle. The three main channels into which the river divides at about 5° N. are almost totally hemmed in by thick forests, and in these the Shir have their permanent dwellings during the rainy season, transferring themselves to the islands during the dry season for the sake of the pastures. We often met people resting in the shade of huge old trees, looking after their animals, or others guiding cattle across the river or channels to better pastures on neighbouring islands. There were always groups of inhabitants ready to entertain us with clapping, songs and dances in the hope of obtaining a few coloured beads. All this contributed to the splendid panoramas offered to our eyes, for indeed

---

[15] This list is not exhaustive though it is more complete than one would have expected a pioneer to have produced. There is no mention, for example, of the Malual Dinka, the largest of all the Dinka divisions. Also absent are the Rek, Luac and Ngok, though the writer was probably referring to the Luac when he recorded the 'Lau' (p. 153 below). 'Beer' is used by the Dinka of the Upper Nile province to mean non-Bantu, non-Nuer and non-Dinka peoples. A.M.T.

the Shir country is an enchantment of nature! Even the language spoken by the natives, Bari, is beautiful and harmonious.

Early in the morning of 1 January 1860, we arrived among the Bari tribes, when the *ra'is* of the *dhahabīya* pointed out to us a great mountain which rose south-west, to the left of the river, and which was called Gnerkegni by the natives and Jabal al-Hadīd by the Arabs. [16] The reach of the river which flows through the land of the Bari, is called by them Tupiri [Supiri], or better Chufiri (the 'p' and the 'f' are often confused in the Bari language). The Chufiri, of course, is the Nile itself which, according to the people is formed by many branches which unite just before the great cataract to be found at 4° N. Here in the Bari country the woods begin to thin out and the ground to become higher and more sandy, particularly to the left of the river. The river itself, constantly divided by innumerable islets, becomes very wide, making the navigation even more difficult. At about midday, the Belinyan mountains on the right bank of the river came into view, announcing to us that we were nearing our goal. To the south we saw more mountains and at about two in the afternoon we passed a channel flowing into the river from the east, coming from yet another channel which also flows into the river further upstream and which we passed two hours later. The latter leaves the river at Libo, a village where Fr. Angelo Vinco had established his mission station and there had died and had been buried on 23 January 1853. This village is about half an hour's journey from Gondokoro. These two channels form two islands, of which that nearest to the mission station was bought by the late Pro-Vicar-Apostolic, Fr. I. Knoblecher, for its abundance of wood, which could not be obtained at Gondokoro.

At last at 3 p.m. on 2 January we reached the Mission station at Gondokoro, situated on the right bank of the river, where we greeted Fr. Franz Morlang.

On my return from Gondokoro to Khartoum, on 24 January, I spent all my time drawing diagrams and putting some order into the notes I had jotted down throughout the journey on the direction of the river and its main tributaries; on the position of certain tribes and principal localities and on the real names by which the river is called according to the tribe through which it flows, its channels, tributaries, etc. I also marked on a map the journey which Fr. Franz Morlang had undertaken in October and November of the preceding year, 1859, to the south-west of Gondokoro.

[16] Jabal Lado on modern maps.

Comments by the Missionaries of Gondokoro and Holy Cross

The rainy season in Gondokoro usually begins early in March and ends towards the end of November. The rains are heaviest towards the end of April and during May. Some years, however, they are more abundant towards the end of July till about mid-August. In this case the rain during April and May is comparatively light.

The Nile begins to rise at Gondokoro towards the end of February, and reaches its peak height either towards the end of May or during the first half of August, according to whether the rains fall more abundantly in the former or latter period. The river gauge then begins to fall at the end of August, and continues to do so till the middle of February, when it reaches its lowest level.

At Holy Cross the rainy season usually begins towards the end of March, ending in November, and the rains are heaviest in August and in the first half of September.

The river at Holy Cross begins to rise at the beginning of March, reaching its peak height in the beginning of September. It begins to decrease towards the end of September, right up to the end of February, when it reaches its lowest level. Every month during the rainy season the river is given to sudden rise, and more so at Gondokoro than at Holy Cross. It was observed, moreover, that this happens especially during the first months of the rains.

I was assured by my interpreter and by some of my crew that the great tributaries of the White Nile, the Sobat and the Ghazāl, both well known to them, rise and fall at the same time as the White Nile itself. In a letter of mine which I sent on 15 March 1858, I related that there had been a great rainstorm which lasted for about half a day at Holy Cross. I also related that on the 1st of March the river rose considerably but that two days later it was at the previous level, having risen because of rain which had fallen nearer to the Equator.

Concerning earthquakes, Fr. Franz Morlang states that he felt these every year during the four or five years spent at the Mission of Gondokoro. He noticed, moreover, three main periods for these earthquakes:

1. They begin a little before the rainy season and continue for about a month, making themselves felt — mostly during the night — from six to eight times.

2. They are felt again before the heavy rains of August.

3. Again towards the end of the rainy season. These tremors are very slight in comparison with the others which several times brought the plaster down from the walls of the mission and made wide cracks in them. The tremors are more frequent and frightening towards the mountains in the south.

As to the direction of the winds, the northern winds in the Bari country begin towards the end of the rainy season and continue until March. These are followed by east winds which last about one month. They return later just before the commencement of the northern winds. Such east winds bring headaches, loss of appetite and fevers to the missionaries. The south winds blow from the end of April until September while through September and October the western ones prevail. During the first three months of the rainy season, storms come more frequently from south-south-east; during the months of June, July and August they come directly from the south, and in September and October from the west. These last storms, however, like those that come sometimes from the north-east, never bring heavy rains.

CHAPTER VIII

THE WHITE NILE VALLEY AND ITS INHABITANTS

by A. Kaufmann

Fr. Anton Kaufmann (1821-82) was born in the Alpine village known in German as Taufers im Münsterthal and in Italian as Tubre in Val Monastero, a village not far from the Swiss frontier at the Stelvio Pass in the region of the Upper Adige. In 1856 he joined the Central African Mission. He spent a year and a half at the Gondokoro Mission and about one year at Holy Cross, leaving for Europe in 1860. He died at Brixen (Bressanone).

The following are translated extracts from pp. 1-192 of the author's Das Gebiet des weissen Flusses und dessen Bewohner, *Brixen, 1881, omitting the two sections devoted to linguistics: the Dinka language (pp. 95-100), and the Bari language (pp. 156-64).*

General Remarks on the Country and the River

The stranger making his way south from Khartoum, after having crossed a distance equivalent to 3° (or about ninety hours walking-distance) reaches what may be called the boundary of the African region, that is, Jabal Nyemati or Jabal Dinka, two small and not very high conical-shaped mountains.

Here, along both banks of the Nile, the area of the free Negro tribes begins and extends to a vast plain towards the south, which, so far, has only been explored as far as the Gondokoro cataract. It is across this plain that the clear waters of the White Nile and its tributaries wend their way with difficulty. Beyond Jabal Dinka (Jabalayn) until the Sobat is reached, the banks are covered by pleasant-looking woods, hiding wild life of every description. From the Sobat to the country of the Bor and Shir, the banks of the river are low. Woods of mimosa are only rarely found. As far as the eye can reach, there is nothing to be seen but savanna, covered by tall grass, followed by a grassy plain and marshes. During the rains, the river swells and floods the banks, forming marshes and lakes miles wide. These are either covered by bamboo (called *arwor* by the Dinka), or studded by small groups of *ambatch*, a tree whose wood is lighter than cork, ideal for floating, or for constructing boats and small river craft.

There are only a few places in this area where a settlement might be set up. For several weeks, owing to the floods, these look like small islands. Further on, towards the south, the banks of the river gradually rise and in the country of the Shir and Bari the traveller sees villages of considerable size. The river is wide but in many places dangerous for navigation during the dry season when the water level is low, because of the sandbanks and shell-like stones. These sandbanks are principally found, before and after Jabal Nyemati [Jabalayn], and towards the south in the territory of the Cic and Aliab. The names of these places are Makhādat Abū Zayd, Makhādat al-'Anz (Goat's Ford) which is further to the south, and Makhādat al-Kalb (Dog's Ford), where the river widens, becomes shallow and is thus of little use to navigation. At these points it can easily be forded, from which fact it derives these peculiar names. Along the whole of this area, the river has only three tributaries, the sources of which have not yet been explored. The first is the Yal [Khawr Adar] which, coming from the Berta mountains to the east, pours its waters into the river at 10° N. This tributary is not very big and looks more like a stream. In the year 1860 its mouth was blocked by sand for a good part of the way. Much larger is the Sobat which can be navigated for two or three days sailing, this, or at least a branch of it, comes from the south and has its source in the Bari country. The largest tributary, however, is the Bahr al-Ghazāl, or Gazelle River. At its confluence at 9° 18′ 4″ N. it forms a great lake which, during the rainy reason, becomes very extensive. Its banks are covered with gigantic bamboo and ambatch trees, which greatly hinder observation and for which reason, the river bed remained undiscovered for a long time.

Its tributaries come from far away, from the south, west and north-west, but it is navigable only with small boats. While the waters of the White Nile are healthy and pleasant, the waters of the Bahr al-Ghazāl cause illness. This may be explained by the fact that its waters are almost stagnant, and that there is abundant growth of beautiful but harmful vegetation. The so-called Bahr al-Zarāf (Giraffe River) is nothing more than a channel which leaves the river at a locality called

Akwak 6° 14′ 30″ N. It then strikes north, crosses the country of the Tuic and Nuer in several directions and joins the Nile about seven and a half hours' distance to the west of the Sobat mouth. The Bahr al-Zaráf is called Auei in native fable language. There are a lot of small channels; a rather large one in the Aliab country, and one further to the south of Tefafan in the Abyalang (Jabal Ahmad Agha) territory. Finally, to the south-west there are two other rivers which flow northward, and which, without doubt, join further on. They are called Yey [Yei] and Ire or Iri. These two rivers separate the Jur territory from that of the Dinka tribe, and flow into the Gazelle river, if indeed they do not form a principal part of the same. In the same direction, there are two further streams of water coming from the south, the Koda and the Luri, which are dried up during the hot months, but full during the rainy season. The Koda runs through the country of the Mandari and Atwot and it is said that it loses itself in the marshes near Ghaba Sciambil. [1]

Mountains

Nothing much is to be seen at eye-level in this immense plain, and no panorama is visible unless from the top of one of the small hills which rise several hundred feet above the level of the river — precisely those already mentioned namely Jabal Nyemati [Jabalayn], or Jabal Dinka, which seems like five bare heads of rock rising separately here and there in the plain. At 10° N., Mount Tefafan (Ahmad Agha) stands solitary. It is sparsely covered with trees, its steep slopes rising from the eastern part of the plain.

To find more mountains, we must proceed southwards into the country of the Bari. There, we come across the Nyerkarni Lado, standing alone in the plain, whilst to the southeast of this the Luri and the Longi link, then, the Lokoya mountains and those of Lirya and Beri. To the south, the Logwek rises like a pyramid. It stands on an island in the Nile, and so far it is the limit for the Nile boats, because the cataracts begin immediately beyond it. No boat of any size has yet succeeded in passing beyond it.

Pro-Vicar Ignaz Knoblecher made a great effort to navigate beyond this point, but in vain, as he was only able to push a short way ahead. A little earlier, Fr. Bartholomäus Mozgan forged his way ahead in a small boat for two days, but recognizing the impossibility of going any

---

[1] Shambe on modern maps.

further, he had to be content with writing the date of the year on a rock, and ' then returned. According to the assertions of the people, inhabiting a locality three days beyond this point, the river there is full of rocks and not navigable, after which it resumes a smoother course and divides into two branches, one drawing its water from the east, and the other with its tributaries in the west. The Kunufi rises on the western bank, and to the south of this stands the Kerek, both blotting out the horizon to the west of Gondokoro.

A six-day walk from this mission outpost brings us to the mountainous territory of the Nyangwara. Here are many valleys intersected by streams which flow into the Yei in this area. The mountainous district begins here. There is mountain after mountain, each retaining its conical shape. In the foreground is the Regong, which stretches out with many peaks towards the south, and further, on the other side of the Yei, there is a long chain of mountains among which are the Malanga and Jirimenit. However, none of these mountains is very high and all are covered with growth to the summit. Very few are higher than a thousand feet above the level of the river.

Rain and Climate

In this vast territory bathed by a burning sun, the vegetation is entirely dependent on the rainfall, because the people do not irrigate at all. This rainfall is periodical, and the nearer to the Equator the earlier the start of the rains.

At Gondokoro, the first rains, on an average, start at the end of February, whilst at Holy Cross they begin towards the end of March. They cease in early December at Gondokoro, while early November generally sees the end of the rains in Holy Cross.

The rains determine the time for sowing, which is almost identical with that in Germany. Thus, the Beri sow in April, and the Cic at Holy Cross and the Tuic in the month of May, which the Dinka call the 'softening' month. The most abundant rain falls during the first half of the rainy season, that is in April and May, or in August and September. Naturally, the high or low level of the river depends on the respective rainfall; and yet it often happens that the level of the water rises suddenly without a rain cloud being seen at Gondokoro. The river begins to rise towards the end of February, and reaches its maximum level in May or August, according to the start of the rains.

At Gondokoro, where the river is very wide, and the current quite fast, the difference between the highest and lowest level, during the period bekween August 1857 and August 1858, was only $5^4/_{10}$ ft. At Holy Cross, however, where the river is not so wide, the difference during the year 1859 was a little over a pole ($16\frac{1}{2}$ ft.).

Thus the people divide the year into two periods, the dry period, called *Meling* by the Bari, and *Pei-Mai* by the Dinka, and the rain period known as *Kidjer* by the Bari and *Pei-Ruel* by the Dinka. Actually, *Pei-Ruel* means 'the sun month', because the sun reaches its zenith over the Dinka during these rain months [2]. Many will, no doubt, be interested to learn something about various winds, and so I shall just touch upon them.

The winds which blow over the White Nile are fairly regular, and we would not err greatly in taking note of the following general details: after the end of one rain season to the start of another, that is until March, the wind is north north-east. From the end of April until nearly September the winds come from the south: these are followed by west winds in September and October. In turn these then change to the tiresome easterly wind, which gives way to the cold northerly wind during the night. The rains, thus, conform with these wind currents, coming first from the east, and then from the south, finishing up with the storms from the west. The air-currents are similar over the Cic at Holy Cross. From the end of November until March, the north wind is prevalent, especially during the night, whilst, during the day, it often veers north-east.

In the intervening months between the rainy seasons the winds here also blow from the east, but during the rains, the south wind is prevalent. It is a strange thing, however, that if a storm comes from the east it ends with a hurricane to the west, while if a storm comes from the south it ends with a hurricane to the north. We often witness this phenomenon.

It is surprising to note that there are frequent earth tremors at Gondokoro, and, at times, they are sufficiently violent to alarm us in our humble dwellings made of mud-bricks. Such tremors occur several times during the year, especially before the start of the first rains; then again just before the heaviest rainfall which occurs late in the season. Slight tremors are also felt towards the end of the rainy season. These tremors are always preceded by underground rumblings to the south-

[2] We normally say *mai* and *ruel* respectively since it is understood that *pei* (months) are included in the seasons. There are four seasons, not two, according to the Dinka: *ker* which begins about April when the rain begins to fall, *ruel, rut* and *mai.* A.M.T.

east. Often shock follows shock, with everything in the house rattling and shaking, and the inhabitants fearful of what might happen. Two separate earthquakes have been known to occur during the same day and these occurred either towards noon or midnight.

That volcanoes once existed at Gondokoro can be proved by the basalt rock, which can be found scattered everywhere among the land-slides of other stones. This is also borne out by the traditional sayings, and narratives of the Bari, which depict them either as a struggle between mountains, or between earthquakes. They say that Mount Nyerkani was once not in its present position to the north on the western bank of the river, but that it was then near Mount Belenyan. One day, it is said, the other mountains quarrelled with it, and forced it to move away: thus one morning it was no longer to be found near Mount Belenyan, but in the vast plain to the north. Hence, its name *Nyerkani*, meaning "he that is here because of battle".

The elder Bari still recall how, during an earthquake, the ground opened out near Mount Kerek and engulfed several men, later ejecting them full of good beer (*yawa*), much to their disappointment. They say nothing about the volcanoes that were here in ancient times, the exist-ence of which may be assumed from the conical shape of the mountain. However, even the rocks and stones here are not basalt, but granite and gravel-stones.

The temperature here is much lower than in the Northern Sudan — for instance, at Khartoum. In this locality there is no sharp rise or drop in the thermometer, as in Khartoum. Supporting this, here are a few figures, obtained from observations which we made in 1857-8: [Here follow thermometer readings and descriptions of flora, fauna and minerals.]

Population

In these very extensive countries, stretching between 12° and 4° N., the population is not as numerous as one might suppose. Most of the tribes are few in number because of their way of living and, with the exception of the Bari and Shilluk, are all nomadic. As they possess great herds of cattle, they must keep on changing their dwelling-places, ever seeking fresh pastures for the animals. When the rains begin, there is a general move towards the permanent dwelling places in the interior. It is in the interior that the people find better fields for sowing their *durra*, whilst, at the same time, the migratory birds are not so numerous as along the water-logged areas near the river. In the interior, nature offers them wild fruit and abundant grass for their animals; and so, when it is time for the Africans to retire to the woods, it is indeed, a happy time for them.

As soon as the rains have ceased, however, owing to the lack of water, all must return to places near the river, and live very poorly in temporary huts made of bamboo cane, plastered with cow dung, whilst their herds graze on the lush grass.

During the rainy season there is no one to be found near the river, except a few fishermen, and in the dry period there is no one in the interior except a few blacksmiths and cattle robbers. Both men and beasts live in long rows of huts near the river or channel. Consequently, the number of people in each individual tribe is small, but it is impossible to give an exact figure.

The entire population of the White Nile forms four areas of different languages and, for that reason, an equal number of nations which, though speaking the same language, and having the same customs, are each divided into different tribes.

Let us therefore start with the strongest tribe, that is, the Shilluk.

The Shilluk

The dwellings of these people extend uninterruptedly along the left bank of the river, between 12° to 9° N. giving the effect of an immense village, although each different group of huts has its own name. The Shilluks are forced to live in this way because, firstly, they must be near the water (which they frequently lack in the interior) and, secondly, as a measure of defence against the Arabs of nearby Kurdufān. This is the only White Nile tribe to have a common chief. They call him *Makk Reth*. The succession to the throne is hereditary in the family, but it is not the son who succeeds. A near relative is elected, whose first duty is to arrange the funeral of his predecessor. This is because, until a new king is nominated, the body must remain on earth, enclosed in its tukul. We were told that the daughters of such a king were not allowed to marry but, nevertheless, received a dowry of an entire village, whilst, if it were known that anyone seduced one of these princesses, he would be buried alive up to his neck and killed by blows from sticks. Naturally, the king is a tyrant and his word is law. A man who commits a serious crime is beaten by sticks and thrown into the river, but all his goods, including his wife and children, become the property of the king who, if he wishes, can sell them as slaves to the Arabs. This forms part of his revenue and he has also introduced a monopoly on ivory and giraffe tails. When his subjects kill such animals they are only allowed to keep the flesh and skin. The ivory and giraffe tail belong to the king who sells them to the Arabs. These latter seek his favour and make him presents. By means of such gifts from Arabs and Europeans he has come into possession of firearms; but, like the Arabs, he must go begging for powder and bullets. And yet this African sovereign is very proud, so much so that his subjects must walk on their knees before him.

Despite all this, he goes about naked like all his subjects, and it is only when he appears in public that he, like the others, throws a long cloth over his shoulders, not so much for the sake of dressing, but merely to look imposing. The present king is called Gew Kwathker[3] and he resides at Denab, where he holds his court in a tukul made of wood and clay and conical in shape. The number of his subjects is well over half a million. The Shilluk are not handsome; they are thick-set with a proud look and, like all Africans, they are naked.

The women and young girls, however, wear a girdle which is a strip of cloth taking the place of knickers, called *rahat*. The taller of them wear animal skins which, hanging from the shoulders, are tied at the sides, thus covering the whole body. Many of these skins are still covered with hair, which gives the women a strange appearance. The Shilluk are very fond of beads and use them as ornaments around their necks and hands. The hair design of many of the young men is very strange indeed. They let their hair grow long and then plait it skilfully around their head so as to make it look like the brim of a hat, so that head and hat are all one. Others intertwine their hair from the neck right over to the brow which looks like the crest of a dragoon's helmet, presenting a strange sight. Others adorn their heads with white feathers and small ostrich feathers, placing them around the head, giving the appearance of a halo. The Shilluk are lovers of ivory bracelets which they make themselves. Knowing that they are not only numerous but united, they are very proud. The Turks wanted to subjugate them, but they fortified their encampments at the confluence of the Sobat. Later, in 1857, they found that it was wiser to withdraw to safer positions. This tribe has its own language, the root of which is similar to the Dinka, which they nearly all understand.

They live by agriculture and cattle-raising, whilst the poorer fish

---

[3] Gew Kwathker, No. 23 in the Shilluk list of kings.

for their living. They grow *durra*, maize, beans, sesame and a little cotton. The cotton is chiefly grown by the Arabs, who live among them. They are not poor; indeed, they have much grain to sell, as was the case this year. They own many beautiful herds of cattle, and sell oxen and sheep to the travelling merchants along the White Nile. In exchange, they receive salt, spears, copper rings, and even beads of glass.

The Shilluks have beautiful hunting dogs, not unlike greyhounds, which are chiefly trained to hunt gazelles. The women keep many hens, which are eagerly bought by the passing travellers. The last horses and donkeys are to be found among this tribe. These, however, are not reared by the Africans, but by the Moslems living among them.

The Nuer

This is the second principal Negro tribe to have its own language. But the inhabitants also understand the Dinka language. The Nuer live on both banks of the River Gazelle, at 9° 18′ 24″ N., and along the Bahr al-Zaráf. Thirty years ago, they drove the Dinka from the Sobat, and now occupy their territory along the above-mentioned river. They are strong and warlike, and fear no one. As their country is so extensive, they must be numerous, and are only slightly less in number than the Shilluk.

They live more towards the interior, as the plain near the river is very low-lying and is subject to flooding. On the left bank of the river, however, villages can be seen stretching for miles along the bank of the river. They grow a lot of grain, and have ample to sell every year. They are considered to be the chief *durra*-growers of the White Nile area. Here, neither traders nor Turks dare attempt to seize any of them as slaves. As they are very powerful, they are left to live in peace. They have no common chief, but live in a patriarchal constitution — that is, as a large family, gathering all its relatives and goods, and forming a village, where the most important and wealthiest acts as chief, and gives himself the title of *Beng-Did* [*Beny Dit*] (great lord). He does not worry about what happens outside his village. If compared with the Shilluk, the Nuer are more graceful-looking. The facial features of some are surprisingly European. Physically they are very strong. However, it is immediately evident that here we are faced with a different tribe. The individual conception of beauty among these people is very peculiar indeed. This is evident from the way they adorn themselves. We saw chiefs wearing pointed conical hats about a foot long. The hats were completely covered by shells, whilst strings of glass beads hung from the points. From the bead-adorned neck there hangs either a finely dressed goat or leopard-skin. Around their loins they wear wide bands of glass beads, their arms being adorned with ivory bracelets. Some wear a piece of skin around the middle.

The head adornment consists of long red hair, with bent supports holding a double row of shells all around the head. To dye their hair red, and to stiffen their frizzy hair the natives make use of a paste made from a mixture of ash, cow-dung and urine. With this the hair is smeared and arranged like a pointed beret, with the tip sagging backwards. It is worn thus for a year and much in vogue with the men. The women, at least, are somewhat dressed. The younger girls make small strips from the fibre of a special kind of grass, and cover their lower limbs. The older girls also wear skins at the front and back, and tie them round the hips. Some also wear a small skin to cover the breast. The neck is adorned by bead necklaces, while the arms are covered with large bracelets made either from copper or iron. Most of the women wear copper ear-rings — so weighty that the ears are distorted and sag downwards. The young women here adorn the upper lip in a surprising manner — a stick of blue beads, two inches long, passes through the lip and ends in a white bead. The custom of perforating the upper lip is increasingly observed. The Jur and Yang-Bara women perforate both their lips with sticks of gravel, about an inch long and half an inch wide; at times they use both. This is done to attract and hold the eye of the young men. The Nuer tattoo their foreheads with thin horizontal incisions running from one temple to another.

The Nuer country, along the river, is very monotonous, as along its entire stretch only two or three glimpses of the woods can be had. The rest is nothing but grass and innumerable swarms of mosquitoes. During the rains, these are a real plague. Only by completely shutting oneself in a glass case could one escape their attention! However, the fire-fly is seen in unlimited numbers, and the Nuers call them the "lanterns of the mosquitoes".

Things are slightly better during the dry period when there are fewer mosquitoes. At night there is the sight of fires on the steppes. Fanned by the wind, the flames merge into an ocean of fire, burning the parched grass, and killing the concealed snakes, insects, reptiles and other wild animals. The Africans do this so as to promote the growth of the young shoots of grass to pasture their herds and at the same time to destroy the wild animals.

The most striking thing along this stretch of river is the great number of hippopotamus to be found. Between sixty and eighty of these monsters can be seen at a time, amusing themselves in the river. Some emerge, blow water from their nostrils, and make frightening sounds; they splash and leap about, clearing the water with their colossal weight. In particular, they cannot bear the sound of oars, and sometimes hurl themselves at them, splintering them to match-wood. This happened to us on 13 February 1860. A hippopotamus came blowing and snorting to the surface near our boat — the oars had either annoyed it, or touched its back — and then it disappeared under the water again. Not four seconds later, however, it shot up, splintered four of the oars, and then, with a sudden leap, landed on the boat, over a small boy and a goat. The crew shouted and fled with fright, while the geese broke loose from their cages and flapped around in the river. The confusion was horrible. Suddenly, the monster gave another leap and made off snorting down-river. When we finally recovered from the shock of our strange visitor, we were able to recapture our geese, and with the exception of the broken oars, we suffered no other damage.

It was in the Nuer country that a hippopotamus seized the cook of the *Stella Matutina,* and disappeared with him in the water. The poor man had been standing near the fire. The hippopotamus is very dangerous to small boats, which can easily overturn and sink, especially if they are overloaded.

The Dinka

This is the most extensive nation in the White Nile area, and has a language of its own.

The tribe begins from the Gebel Nyemati [Jabalayn], or Dinka Mountain, on the east bank of the river at 12° North and reaches out as far as 6° North; and on the western bank of the Nile it nearly extends as far as 10° North. However, the population is made up of different races, living in a patriarchal community, and not only does it have a common language, but the morale and physical constitution are the same.

To the north, the following tribes belong to this nation: (*a*) The Abialang as far as Tefafan [J. Ahmad Agha]; (*b*) The Ager; (*c*) the Abujo, from Tefafan to the Yal [Adar], and (*d*) the Dunghiol tribe from the Yal to the Sobat. These tribes are small, and it is only in the interior that they join with the Dinka of the south. On the remaining sides, they are surrounded by enemy tribes. To the north and west, they border with the Baqqāra Arabs, and the Shilluk. To the east the Abū Rūf [4] are their neighbours and, each year, mounted on their horses and camels, the Abū Rūf raid them, kidnapping their people, and stealing their grain. The country here is all plain. It is only in the centre, very close to the river that the Tefafan rises. This conical-shaped mount is relatively insignificant, and it has a low range striking out eastwards to the Berta Mountains. The soil is very fertile and yields much grain, enough for all. This is also an indication that they are more industrious than the other Dinka tribes, as, for example, the Cic. In addition, they have to devote most of their time to agriculture, because they have no fruit-yield from their woods. There are only a few *nabak* and tamarind trees, and several bitter *aloks*. They rear cattle only on a limited scale as it would be difficult to protect larger herds against the continuous attacks of the Shilluks and the Arabs to the east and west. Owing to this almost constant fighting, these tribes are more cruel and fierce than the other Dinka. They are always armed with spears and shields; and are suspicious and ever on the look-out for enemy attacks. Many descendants of these tribes live either in the Sudan or Egypt, as poor slaves, or soldiers.

The Tuic

These are to be found between 7° and 8° N, especially along the eastern bank of the Nile, and possess great herds of cattle. During the rainy season they withdraw to the interior where, in the depths of magnificent forests, they have their permanent dwelling-places. During the dry months, they draw closer to the river and take up positions, either along the channel or in its vicinity. The channel is known as Bahr al-Zarāf and joins the Nile a short distance from the Sobat river. This Nile tributary is named Awei by the Cic and Tuic. The Tuic drive their herds across the Awei, and run into opposition with the Cic, who then force them to withdraw to their own side. The Tuic are not so numerous as the Cic but, as they are better organized, they usually get the better of the Cic. They are skilled at agriculture. They rarely suffer from food shortage, and even exchange some of their grain for

[4] The Abū Rūf Arabs, who pasture on both sides of the Blue Nile above Sinnār Town, made periodical raids on the Dinka for slaves and cattle, operations in which they were assisted by the government during the earlier period of Turco-Egyptian rule (R. Hill, *On the Frontiers of Islam,* Oxford, 1970, pp. 7-8, 34-5).

iron with which they make spears, and for hoes which they obtain from either the traders or from the Cic. They must exceed 10,000 in number, and their customs are similar to those of the Kyec.

The Bor

These live south of the last mentioned tribes, between 6° and 7° N., forming about forty villages along the right bank of the Nile. Their customs and habits are similar to those of the tribes we have already mentioned. To the south, they border on the Bari country. Their country is very beautiful, and some of the most magnificent forests are to be found along the river. Here and there, the ground rises slightly, looking down on a most enchanting variety of woods, green meadows, and pleasant hills, dotted with beautiful villages, lying in the shade of gigantic leafy trees. They possess a large quantity of cattle. The population is about 10,000. During recent years they have suffered much at the hands of the slave-traders and merchants of the White Nile. Their grain-yield is such that they too have sufficient over to barter for iron.

On the opposite side of the river — that is to say, on the left side — the small Aliab tribe is to be found.

The Aliab

This tribe is found at 6° N., and only numbers about 8,000. Here, also, the merchants have left their mark, stealing 3,400 head of cattle in one raid. To the south, they constitute the limit of the Dinka language. Some maps frequently refer to the Benduryal tribe, between the Aliab and the Cic. However, such a tribe does not exist and must be attributed to a misunderstanding of the language, because the Cic immediately follow the Aliab.

The Cic

These live between 8° and 6° N., and form many villages. They frequently pass the dry months with their cattle, along the right bank of the river, and this has led to the belief that this area also is Cic territory. However, this is not so: the Cic themselves say that the right bank belongs to the Tuic. As has already been mentioned, these two tribes are always fighting one another over pasturing grounds, and steal each other's cattle.

In 1854, Fr. B. Mozgan of Carinthia founded the missionary station of Holy Cross on Cic territory, situated at 6° 40′ N.

During the dry period, the Cic move westwards, where they have their permanent homes, made up of rows of villages running almost parallel to the river and extending from north to south. It is here they have their best pasturing grounds, while the woods provide them with many different kinds of fruit. The word "woods" is translated by Gok and this name has erroneously been given to the country on the map. There is no such locality. These Africans are rich in cattle, while their number exceeds that of the Tuic and Bor.

Further on, to the west, there are other Dinka groups, namely: the Atwot, to the south of the Cic, the Lau, [5] to the west of the Cic; the Arol, to the north west of the Cic. Further on still, beyond the Lau and the Arol, there are the Gok, marking the boundary of the Dinka language to the west, where there is a big river coming from the south. [6] In this river there are hippopotamus and crododiles, and it can be none other than the Yei, coming from Nyangwara. The Dinka language spreads on along the Yei, and further still to the Gazelle river and on to the tenth degree, which is the extremity of the Dinka tribe.

The Customs of the Dinka

These Dinka tribes are the most handsome among the Negroes of the White Nile; they are tall, well built and developed. Even their looks — though similar to those of other Negroes — are milder than those of other tribes. They are easily recognisable by the tattoo-marks on the forehead. Both men and women, have a deep vertical incision between the eyebrows, from which curved lines radiate towards the hair on both sides of the brow.

They are not keen on long hair. So it is shaved off, leaving only a clump on top of the head, surrounded by glass beads. They cannot tolerate skins around their bodies. The men are naked, but use ornaments to beautify themselves. If a man is wealthy he ties a cord around his neck and hips, and quite a few wear thin ivory bracelets. Otherwise, the majority wear large rings, made either of copper or iron. The poor wear a string of glass pearls round the neck. The men regard any form of

[5] Probably the Luac who have a common boundary with the Agar and Gok and fit the description given in the text. A.M.T.

[6] Unknown to the writer, the Dinka on the western and north-western linguistic boundary comprised in addition the Rek, Tuic, Malual and Ngok, the last in Kurdufān, the others in the Bahr al-Ghazāl.

clothing as an insult to their sex. They would immediately exclaim:
'Do you take us for women?' One chief [7] said quite openly: 'I would
not go about dressed, even if I were made a present of thirty cows.'
Another, who had received a suit of clothes as a gift, immediately
exchanged it for copper ear-rings. If they have anything that could
serve as a garment, for instance wild animal skins or pelican skins,
they do not wear them as clothes. Instead, they twine them to form a
sort of cord, which they then let fall behind them. They derive the
greatest satisfaction from their weapons: spears, arrows, bows, and
pointed iron-covered sticks made from ebony. This last weapon is from
two to two and a half feet in length, rounded and smooth. Sometimes
it is grooved and, being pointed, it can be used for transfixing objects
and for combat. Often there is an inlaid cavity on one side which is
useful for holding tobacco, while at the other end there is an iron-tip
which can be used as a weapon or as a spade. The young warriors of
this tribe — tall, agile, slim, heads adorned with ostrich-feathers, and
equipped with bows and spears — present a handsome sight.

The Abuyo [Abiong], and Abialang, have no arrows, but go into
combat with sticks, and especially with spears and shields made of
buffalo, giraffe — or elephant-hide. The latter type of shield is not used
by the Dinka.

The women, or at least the married ones, clothe themselves. They
do not wear a *rahat*, but tie dressed skins in front and behind them.
These skins are quite long, the wealthier women adorning theirs with
shells, small iron and copper rings and bells, so that they can be heard
from a distance when walking. Quite a few also cover the breast and
back with a different skin. However, the unmarried women and young
girls are not clothed; instead they wear ornaments such as, for instance,
bells on their hips and feet. The older girls wear between eight and
ten rings on their hands and feet. These rings are either of iron or
copper. These are removed one at a time when they are married and are
exchanged for some other necessary commodity.

Generally speaking, both men and women wear ear-rings, not just
single ones, but chains of copper rings which gradually diminish in
size, the largest being on top. To prevent the weight of these heavy
chain ear-rings distorting the ears, the ear-rings are supported by a
small cord attached to the top of the forehead.

This great tribe is neither wild nor cruel by nature, but rather

---

[7] 'Chief' is here used in a general sense. As an administrative institution the
   chieftainship is of recent growth dating back to the Chiefs' Court ordinance,
   1931.

meek and patient in the face of poverty. We were able to observe this among the Cic in the vicinity of the Mission. Throughout the whole of last year the poor fishermen, who live near the Mission's garden, although faced with the greatest poverty, did not steal a single thing. This must also have been the case with the Bor, Tuic and Aliab, before becoming embittered against the white men through the underhand dealings of the merchants who abducted men and beasts from them.

Fr. Mozgan was able to travel extensively in peace among them, accompanied only by a few tribesmen. Now a point has been reached with the Dinka of Tefafan [Jabal Ahmad Agha] when a stranger dare not enter the country without fearing for his life.

It is well known that in general the African is lazy, but there are varying degrees of laziness. In fact, here and there the men also work in the fields, like the Bari and the Dinka of Tefafan; or else like the Shilluk and Nuer, they help their women in this work. However, the Cic, the Aliab and, in general, the Dinka further on, are the laziest. This is especially so with the Cic who, though very proud of their cows, look down on agricultural work as being fit only for slaves. I was once told: 'Am I a slave? Being the owner of so many cows, it would be shameful for me to work. I am powerful! Therefore, that gives me the right to do nothing.' The Cic men only help in the building of houses, where they undertake the heaviest work; otherwise they do nothing else other than look after their cows, and make and stake a few pegs to tether them. Everything else must be done by their wives. These dig the fields, crouching on the soil; they break the clods of earth, and remove the roots with a semi-circular iron implement which has a short wooden handle. It is the woman who has to sow and weed the fields; the man only comes home to eat, driving his cows and drinking their milk — leaving only a negligible quantity for his wife. He spends the rest of the time chatting with and visiting neighbours, sometimes passing the entire day comfortably in the shade with them. When the sun is about to set he returns home, brandishing his stick with joy. The theme of his conversation is, quite naturally, about cows, women, and the Turks, to whom all the white men belong.

It is obvious that, through leading such a life, poverty and hunger reign supreme. After the harvest the grain is only sufficient for a short while and soon dwindles, whilst only the barest quantity is left over for the next sowing period. Moreover, as at this particular time of the year, a great quantity of wild fruit is to be had from the woods, no thought is given to the re-sowing of the grain. They fill themselves with fruit, and are really proud of themselves when their stomachs are full.

With the cessation of the rains, however, the fruit disappears rapidly, being steadily eaten by both men and animals. The dry period approaches and the natives are forced to abandon their Eden in the woods and take up new positions near the river. All that the Cic has to take with him is a small casket of grain, the seeds for the next harvest; the rest he has eaten.

The milk is not sufficient for the whole family, but even so he exchanges it for lotus seeds from the fishermen. These are crushed to a flour and boiled. When there are no more lotus seeds obtainable the wealthier go to the Bor and Tuic and exchange their spears for grain, whilst the poorer rely on fishing and their catch would be quite substantial if they were equipped with better tackle. Whilst, the men are away at the river with their herds, the women remain behind in the woods, laying in further stores of fruit to carry them over the lean months. Such reserves mainly consist of *alok* [8] which is similar to the date in shape and size. Before being eaten, the fruit is cooked in order to soften the bitter-sweet pulp. The stones are later crushed, ground and cooked and mixed with grain of sesame. These stones cannot be eaten alone, because they are very bitter and unhealthy. A little milk is added to the above mixture, and this constitutes the Cic food during the periods of hardship. Their distress could very easily be overcome if they were to pay a little more attention to their agriculture. For instance, the women sow a small plot of ground around their huts with *durra,* sesame and tobacco plants — but they could very well sow much larger fields. Moreover, they could have two bountiful harvests, as the rains fall for six months. A certain kind of maize, which was brought from Khartoum and planted in the Mission garden, grew and matured in only two-and-a-half months — and it was sown up to three times a year. The maize from Vicenza required three months to mature, and the same period of time was necessary for *durra.*

Thus the Cic could easily find a remedy; but they are lazy and, in consequence, lead a miserable life. Another, and indeed principal reason for their misery is something which elsewhere would be a virtue but with them must be considered a vice, namely hospitality.

Hospitality

Not only is hospitality recognized and extended to their own people, but also to strangers. In the latter case, however, they always hope to

---

[8] Possibly the fruit of the dulayb/doleib palm (*Borassus aethiopicum*), or the shea butter tree, *butyrospermum paradoxum* subsp. *parkii.*

receive some present in return. The way it is extended between themselves is, indeed, most comparable to communism. A guest is given all, and when nothing remains, guest and host go to another. However, only grain, tobacco and fruit are considered as common goods, but never cattle. Like all Africans, they are extravagant; there is no question of thankfulness or gratitude; indeed, everyone believes he has a right and the more one gives, the more is taken and requested. If something is given, more is asked for; because he thinks that his friendship is being sought. As a friend, he considers himself to have the right to ask for more, and if we make him a present he thinks that we are afraid of him and, consequently, expects another. This is a serious obstacle to missionary work, because if we give them something, many more come begging; and if we give them nothing, the missionary is regarded as a miser with a heart of flint. For instance, many Africans bring us sheep and goats, outwardly as a sign of respect, but in reality to cultivate our friendship. Obviously, we could not accept such gifts, as with such friends our goods would become common property.

Another characteristic is their greediness as regards food. If an individual has any food, he will eat and feast until all is gone. For this reason, he will not work whilst there is still a crust of food left — not even if he were offered a handsome reward. He eats what he has and enjoys himself, and it is only after he has gone without food for one day that he begins to think. This communism is the reason why there is so little sowing, for if one were to grow more grain, all the others would help him to dispose of it. If he were to have a second harvest, an infinite number of guests, though work-shy, would suddenly appear to give him a helping-hand. This happened to the fishermen living near the Mission's garden. They had cleared nearby a large field and sown maize and sesame. When these were ripe, so many friendly guests appeared that everything was consumed in eight days.

The difficulty of missionary work, under such circumstances, is clearly evident from the above. The native must be helped materially if he is to be rescued from his poverty and hunger, because it is useless to describe the Kingdom of God to hunger-stricken people: words alone cannot abate those pangs. Only when the African has been restored to a fit state can it be hoped that he will aspire to something higher which, for the moment, does not even enter his mind.

In addition to communism, there is also a spirit of particularity in each family. Everything must be divided in the family; each must have so much, each lives as an individual unit. This is so even with the children. No one member of the family would dare trust another with any of his goods; not even a brother. They have no idea of life in community and were never able to understand the brotherhood between the missionaries. According to them, everything belonged to one, while the other members of the mission had nothing and were merely the servants of the superior.

With such poverty, squandering of the harvest, extravagance and complete nakedness, which extends to unmarried girls of twenty, it is little wonder that there is not much morality to be found here. They live among the cattle, are like the cattle, and think like the cattle. Food, women, cows, and dances, these are the sole topics of their conversations. They enjoy dancing and singing the praises of one another, and teach them to their children. The education of their children may be summed up in the following words: "Do as we do. See what we do, and do likewise."

They have no idea of modesty, but are nevertheless reserved in the presence of strangers. After living among them for three years, I must say that I never witnessed or heard anything immoral, although there were many groups of young boys and girls. Very rarely does one hear that a girl has been seduced. This may be attributed to the fact that the girls are sold as brides, while the seducer would have to contend with the vendetta of the girl's father, who would be angry at the loss of cows he would have received in payment from the bridegroom. A more lax and immoral life is led by the older girls who have not found a husband, or by those who have run away from their husbands.

Dances

When the Dinka have something to eat, their most popular form of amusement is dancing. They choose the night for their dances, especially when the moon is shining. These African dances are not as wild and unrestrained as those of the Muslims of the Sudan. They consist of rythmic turns, leaps, songs, wringing of hands, gestures and mimicry. Whoever has seen the bird-dance, *ardea regina,* immediately concludes that the Dinka must have learnt the dance from the bird itself, so similar is it in both movement and effect. The beating of drums always accompanies these dances. The drums are made from hollowed tree trunks, with both open ends covered by a skin. Both ends are beaten, but, as one is much wider than the other, the sounds produced give the effect of two different-sized drums. The men beat the ground with both feet, and then jump up with whistling breath. In fact, this Dinka dance is simple and yet pleasing. The mosquitoes can sting to their hearts content, but the smoking, leaping and dancing continues until everybody is completely exhausted.

The songs are very simple, and are generally about cows, women and girls, although it would be useless to try to single out any verses. They consist mostly of a couplet which is repeated again and again until the singers are tired. As with most orientals, the tunes are sung in a low key and lack a certain grace. The Dinka have a liking for a fast tempo and some of their songs are sung at 6/8-time with great gusto. Many of the songs are solos accompanied by a chorus. The Dinka songs are much more pleasing than the monotonous wailings of the Berberines.[9] Even if there is no dancing, the Dinka will sing spontaneously especially if he has a *tome,* the only stringed instrument he possesses. This is similar to the ancient lyre, and is made from hard tortoise-shell with two branching horns projecting upwards carrying a crosspiece or yoke. The strings are only three in number and are made from either tendons or intestines.

Property

If one were to ask what these tribes possess, the answer would be that more than one would be rich if they had their goods in Europe. Their entire wealth consists of cattle and this is indeed the only thing these African people think of in terms of riches. They know no other wealth; other goods are considered to be of secondary and transitory importance. The wealth of cattle represents something stable to them. They own more cattle than sheep and goats, the last having not wool but hair. The bovine and other animals are of very poor breed. In general the cattle have a high hump, are short in the body, but have long legs. They are rather on the wild side, so that, even if they were numerous, their usefulness would be limited. Even during the best periods very little milk is obtained daily. Even if an African had between 100 and 300 cows, he would not have a surplus of milk; half his animals do not yield any milk at all, and the other half give very little. Moreover, such a owner would require several people to look after the animals, and these too would live off them. Their usefulness as regards meat is also limited because the cows are held as sacred, and may not be killed. They are allowed to live until they die of old-age or illness.

---

[9] '...*die langweiligen Klagetöne der Berberiner*'. The writer probably meant the Barābra (sing. Barbarī) of Nubia.

Father Mozgan, who had a calf killed to provide meat for the household, was sharply rebuked by the Africans. They said that he was like the hyenas, eating cows' flesh. When a cow dies, the mourning that follows is comparable to that accorded a human being. For several days the owner of the dead cow will go about wearing the rope that had once held his beast and tells everybody about his misfortune. Later, he ties the rope around his waist. Thus, the larger owners are always in mourning. Oxen are killed, but only for ceremonial occasions such as the concluding of a peace, wedding feasts, funeral feasts, and in cases of epidemics among men or animals.

They have neither horses nor donkeys. Poultry is kept only by the Dinka of the Tefafan; the other Dinka have none. To obtain poultry for the Holy Cross Mission, Father Mozgan was obliged to travel a long distance southwards to the Mandari. The African's veneration for his cattle is so great that most of the Dinka tribesmen have the name of an ox; whilst their women have the name of a cow. All the animals, whether cattle, sheep or goats, have a special name, according to their colour and size. This is very confusing to anybody trying to unravel the mysteries of the language. Despite all the care and respect given the animals, their increase in number is very little. The fatigue of the continuous journeys they make, lions, leopards, and epidemics, drastically cut down their numbers annually. Last year, for instance, a pulmonary epidemic was responsible for much damage.

The cows are seldom sold. Some time ago it was possible to buy oxen with glass beads or with copper, but now the price is ten times as much and it is very difficult to come across animals for sale. As glass beads and copper are no longer rare commodities and are of little value in the eyes of the Africans, they are of little use for buying the cattle. The people make the horns to the desired shape, as is done in Europe. The shape preferred is where one horn is turned up and the other down. An animal thus embellished is called *mokwe,* and is a favourite among the herd. It is also customary to pierce a hole through the tip of the horn and attach a kind of tassel. Quite often there are cows with no horns at all. The animals are of all imaginable colours. Their skins are used to make mats and ropes, whilst the skins of the smaller animals are dressed and made into garments for the women.

The only domestic animal they have is the dog, which is neither very useful nor beautiful. The domestic cat is missing, although there are plenty of wild cats in the woods.

Dwellings

When speaking about dwelling-places, a distinction must be drawn between the temporary huts erected during the dry season near the river bank, and the permanent huts in the woods, which the Africans regard as their proper homes. The former are only used for a few months and are then demolished. They are built of canes and reeds, plastered with cow dung. They are chiefly occupied during the night as shelter against the north wind, and are filled with ashes to keep out the cold. Many look more like towers than houses, with canes of all different sizes jutting out of the ground. There are no closed walls and many apertures. The permanent houses in the woods present a completely different picture. They are solid round huts, about two poles in diameter, and are constructed by staking a circle of poles, each about a perch in length, and filling the space between each pole with bamboo-canes. These poles and canes are then interwoven with twigs, this giving them the appearance of a round basket. A conical roof is placed on top of the poles, which culminates in a pointed framework of tall dried grass. On the inside the walls are plastered with mud. The floor is rammed down hard and smeared with clay. This completes the African's house up to the door, which is just an oval-shaped opening through which the inhabitants enters or emerges on all fours. There is no need for windows. Plaster drawings, consisting of two figures only, can be found on the walls; the one, an ox-head, symbol of their most cherished possession; and the other, a badly made figure of a serpent as an object of terror. However, it takes a lot of imagination to be able to discern what these plaster objects are supposed to represent. Immediately inside the door there is the fireplace on which the woman of the house cooks, and which by night serves to warm and illuminate the interior of the hut. The fire burns all night and, as the door is tightly sealed, the heat inside is unbearable to a European. The door is sealed with straw matting and closed on the inside.

The Africans do not use flint-stones, and have never heard of sulphur, but start their fires by rubbing a hard and soft stick together until a spark sets the dried grass alight.

These pieces of wood are carefully stored where the cattle are herded together, so that they can easily be found when the herdsmen arrive with their animals. Huts such as these, which must be entered on all fours, have quite naturally, no inside partitions. What kind of furniture is there inside? A cow hide or a mat that serves as a bed;

hollowed gourds, bordered by a zig-zag pattern, used as containers; a few earthenware pots and a tobacco pipe; several baskets hanging from the roof, containing the grain for the next sowing. They have spoons; the Cic use shells, and the Dinka make use of half a small gourd. They would indeed be pleased with European spoons made of metal. In exchange for a spoon I received four quite large hippopotamus teeth. In front of the houses there is a mortar which is used to grind the grain. Among the Dinka the mortars are made from a hard wood, because no suitable stone is to be found in their country. The Dinka of the Tefafan have neither wood nor stones with which to make mortars, so they buy bricks and crush the grain with them but always badly.

Such is the African's house; his bed, his mortar, and his kitchen in which there are only a few earthenware pots. However, these houses are only used by the heads of families; the servants and children always live with the cows. Even the head of the family only makes use of the house during the rainy season to protect himself from the cold and dampness. At all other times his favourite spot is in the cattle enclosure, which is surrounded by a high thorny hedge. Here he can see and enjoy the sight of his cows. He collects the dung with his hands, dries it in the sun, and burns it by night, filling the enclosure with smoke and smells. The heaps of ashes left over are then used as his bed. The ashes protect the herdsmen from the cold and from the mosquitoes. As a further protection against mosquitoes, the Africans sometimes erect structures of two storeys or as many as three storeys in the woods and cover each storey with ash. In the evening they clamber up to the top storey, whilst below they burn all the cow-dung and literally surround themselves with flames. Such constructions are usually erected in the vicinity of the houses and thus serve as a kind of reception room, where in the evening they all like to gather and chat about the events of the day. This is always in the evenings because, during the day each goes about his own business. When it gets late or cold the people disappear into their huts, and bury themselves under a heap of ashes, leaving only the face uncovered. Such a spectacle, with the towering poles and the flames, is surely a page from an adventure book — especially in the interior of the woods, where a fire is also burning on the top storey of these structures, so as to keep the wild beasts at bay.

From this, it can be seen that the Cic are not very concerned about cleanliness. Even if the hut is kept clean inside, and the little square in front of it is kept clear, one must, indeed, be an ardent cow-lover to be able to remain in the enclosure for any length of time. If there is no other water available they use cow-urine to wash the food and drink containers. For this reason the milk smells and seems to be mixed with urine. When the weather is cold the African pours this warm liquid down his back and limbs in an attempt to warm himself. The Nuer colour their hair with cow-dung, and also use it as an ointment. The Cic, too, make use of these two commodities to protect themselves from the stinging rays of the sun. They smear their hair until it takes the shape of a beret, and then whiten it with ashes. They say that by doing this they also protect themselves from parasites.

Any traveller along the White Nile will see in the morning the Africans still covered in the white-greyish ash which is allowed to remain until the sun's rays begin to make themselves felt. Then, if by chance, they come across a stream, they immediately wash themselves, but they are most reluctant to do so if any effort is involved; thus they smell horribly of cow-dung, and their skin becomes almost saturated with it.

The scenes presented by a cow enclosure, after a rainfall, can well be imagined. Men and beasts are walking, splashing and lying in the mud, because no one bothers to make a furrow or ditch to allow the excess water to drain off. If there is too much mud, everything is transferred to another enclosure on slightly higher ground. This involves no great labour, as all that has to be done is to lead the herds out, and take a few goods with them. The huts remain until a more opportune moment arrives for the Africans to return to them.

From all this, one might be led to believe that with such primitive wildness, Africans are similar to the natives of America, who eat everything raw. But this is not so. They cook their grain and eat it mixed with milk. They even cook their fruit and mix it with a little flour to make it tastier. They boil and roast meat, but they are too impatient to wait until it is well cooked and greedily eat it whilst it is still half-cooked. If, by chance, the meat smells, it does not matter for, according to them, the meat is more tender this way. One must not look for any finesse in the Africans' tastes. They eat the flesh of Nile lizards and crocodiles, but do not eat the frog or shell fish, except the tortoise. They use frogs only as fish bait. Besides, they do not eat many kinds of birds as, for example, the heron, because it is known to feed on bad things like toads, frogs and worms. Pelicans and birds of prey are also not touched.

Tobacco

The negroes greatly enjoy their tobacco which is smoked in special pipes. It is customary for the Cic women to smoke the tobacco for their husbands, who, in turn, chew the yellowy-brown smoke-impregnated filter, which is taken from the large stem of the pipe. Tobacco is to be found everywhere, and it is strange that the old name for it here is nearly the same as the one used in America: *tab* or *taba*. [10] Tobacco is held in such esteem that we missionaries made use of it and were almost able to dispense with money. It is easier to obtain something with tobacco than with glass beads. Although tobacco is grown everywhere, there is always great demand for it, because everybody either smokes or chews. Furthermore their pipes are very large, especially those of the Nuer and Dinka. The Shilluk pipe is also quite big.

Marriage

However communistic the practices of the Africans may be, they are very strict as regard their women, who, as we shall see, are precious. The way in which young men bring about their marriage is akin to the eastern rather than to the western idea. When a young man finds the girl he likes, he first tells her of his intentions, and then goes to her parents, where the price he must pay them for her is fixed. The price is in relation to the financial standing of both the contracting parties.

A chief's son marrying a chief's daughter must give the father-in-law ten cows and ten oxen, and also ten cows to the mother-in-law; he must also give presents to his bride's brothers and sisters — such presents sometimes consisting of copper and glass beads. If the bridegroom cannot afford all these cows, a lesser number will do. But, if the young man does not possess any cows — that is to say, if he is poor — then he must be content with looking for the daughter of a poor family, where the price involved is only a few goats. This is the manner in which the poor Dinka fishermen marry. Without payment there is no bride.

Bethrothal exists among the Africans. If a young girl of only seven to nine years of age is promised in marriage, and the price is agreed upon, then the young man must hand over a ram as a deposit;

[10] Correct in the writer's day but *macier* is now the common word for tobacco.

this ram is then eaten at a feast. As in Europe, the girls begin to marry from fifteen years of age onwards, and the young man from twenty onwards.

As regards the rearing of children, they take just as long to develop as in Europe; but the missionaries at Khartoum, Holy Cross and Gondokoro were able to observe that the mental development was premature. At the age of ten or twelve, the children know as much as an adult about life; they know all that is good, and all that is bad; and, indeed, they act in the same way as the adults.

When the day of the wedding arrives, friends of the bridegroom take jars of milk to the bride's father. Wealthier people kill an ox and celebrate with a feast. The bridegroom hands over part of the sum that he has agreed to pay, and the bride now belongs to him. Without much ceremony he takes her home and gives her two skins as garments. However, when the price concerned is very high, the bridegroom only pays a part of the complete sum. He makes full payment only when the bride has become a mother. If she turns out to be barren he does not make any further payments, and often he sends her back to her parents, asking for the refund of his goods. This often leads to trouble, as the bride's parents find it difficult to return the cows they had previously received. Sometimes a couple will divorce, and later marry again. It is a curious fact that the negro women also have honeymoons, lasting longer than ours. Immediately after the marriage, the wife is not allowed to do anything and she is waited upon. Among the Bari it is the wife's mother who looks after the needs of the household: all that the young wife has to do is to enjoy herself and everyone waits upon her. But as soon as the first child is born this delightful time is over for the wife; she then becomes almost a slave and must look after everybody. She must go and fetch water and wood, work in the fields, weed, climb up tall trees to pick fruit, etc. The husband now does nothing at all, and merely looks on. He is the first to eat and the wife receives what is left over. Several men may eat together but not with the women who only feed off the scraps. Going to fetch water and fruit from the woods is not without its dangers. During the dry season, the women must penetrate deep into the woods where lions are lying in wait, and often they become prey to these animals. The greatest danger is after sunset when the wild animals roam in search of food and gather around pools of water and ditches to drink. When picking fruit the women must sometimes fight hordes of monkeys, which attack them and force them to leave the hard-earned fruit behind, and return home empty handed. These tasks must always be undertaken by the women, even if they are in delicate health. They breast-feed the children for two years or more, taking them wherever they go, until a new child comes along. To carry the children, the mother makes a haversack from skin, which is tied to the back and sides. Inside this she takes the children with her to work. While she is working in the fields or woods, this haversack is tied either to the branch of a tree or stick and is left hanging there until the mother has finished. She then returns home — the child on her back and a bundle of wood on her head. These hardships, coupled with the lack of healthy food and long period of breast-feeding, may be the reason why the African women age quickly and bear few children.

From all this, it is clear that the Africans regard their women as servants who exist only to work and bear children. Nevertheless, the women walk freely around, are respected, and are spared the horrors of war. But, as women are so costly, quarrels and wars often arise because of them.

When a woman has aged after such an exhausting life and has no hope of bearing further children, the husband then buys another woman. Polygamy, with all its fatal consequences, exists among the Africans; but, as women are so costly, it is only the wealthy negro who can afford to keep on buying them. The greater the number of women and cows a Dinka possesses, the greater is he esteemed. Thus every Dinka man will buy as many women as he can keep, and sometimes even more. This is the reason why the chiefs are so often poor, and are the greatest beggars.

A woman who has been substituted by another still lives in the house, looks after her children, and receives what little milk the husband can spare her. For each new wife the husband builds a new house.

Hereditary Rights

Connected with this treatment accorded to the women, there is the question of hereditary rights. The woman is considered to be an object — she does not possess cattle — and therefore, nothing is ever left to her. The woman does not inherit, but she herself is inherited. Her possessions consist only if a few glass beads, and copper or iron rings, which she disposes of if the necessity arises.

Before his death the father of grown up sons divides his goods amongst them to avoid any future dispute. The wives and daughters remain with the eldest son, who, when his sisters marry, receives the payment of cows. On his part, he must keep his mother and also his stepmothers if the latter have no sons. In the normal way, when the father dies, the eldest son becomes the head of the family. When the father dies and leaves only small children behind, all is handed over to the nearest relative who undertakes to rear the children. When these children are grown up, they receive the inheritance and build their cow enclosure at the tomb of their father. By this time, however, the inheritance will have greatly diminished.

If, when a father dies, he leaves only daughters or no children at all, the wife does not inherit the property but, together with the cows and all the possessions of the deceased, she is passed on to his nearest relative. The latter acts as he thinks fit, and keeps what is over for himself.

War and Hunting

The theft of a cow or of a woman is a matter of general concern for which the African will go to war. Among the Cic it is generally the theft of a animal which leads to war. This war, however, is not as terrible as that among the natives of other countries. Only the young men and those directly concerned in the theft take part. Most of the Africans are merely onlookers and only remain on the defensive. The men excuse themselves saying: "We have wives and children, and these are sufficient reasons to keep me out of harm's way". The war is only of short duration. Arrows and sometimes spears are used. As soon as two or three negroes have been killed or wounded the affected side surrenders, and peace talks begin. Peace, however, is also of short duration. As soon as the feeling of revenge comes to the fore, the war starts all over again, and this goes on until the rainy season begins. Thus the struggle between Cic and Tuic goes on until they are separated by the changing seasons of the year. An army of this kind is made up of 100 men at the most and generally it is only one village which participates in the war. Between themselves, in their quarrels and disputes, the Cic only use sticks, never arrows or spears. Peace is bought with cows. These people are not very skilled in the art of war. Prisoners are not kept; the African neither forgives, nor expects to be forgiven, and all are killed if they fall into the hands of the enemy.

As yet they have no firearms because, together with ammunition, these are too costly. However, firearms would be extremely useful to them when out hunting, as their arrows and spears are not really suitable against wild animals like the lion and leopard or against large snakes. Only a few are killed, because the animals remain hidden during the day and only emerge during the night. Gazelles and antelopes are killed; they are stealthily surrounded by a group of natives, whilst another group lies hidden in the undergrowth. The animals are driven off towards the concealed negroes, who immediately hurl their spears at them as soon as they are within striking distance. The Africans are quite skilful at spear-throwing and are accurate marksmen. They have a great fear of the buffaloes which are the cause of most misfortunes during a hunt.

They even venture out to kill the elephant, at the greatest risk to themselves.

When on an elephant hunt the Tuic, Bor and other Dinka, set off in groups, surround an elephant, and goad it. Whilst some flee before the onrushing animal, the others hurl spears at it. If the animal then veers round and chases the other Africans, the same thing is repeated, until the elephant sinks to the ground, exhausted through loss of blood. An elephant will run and defend itself, but in vain. However, it claims a few victims before surrendering.

As this kind of hunting is very dangerous, the Africans have another method. Along the roads known to be frequented by elephants, they dig deep pits one after another, both to the right and left. Sometimes as many as twenty pits are dug. These are carefully covered over with leaves and earth. Then, with loud shouts and cries, they drive the elephant along these roads. (Sometimes, they wait for the animal to appear of its own accord.) As soon as an elephant has fallen into a pit, it is killed by spears, although it often happens that a second elephant will pull the first out with its trunk, before the natives have a chance of arriving on the scene. Sometimes, the negroes lie in wait, hidden in tree-tops, until an elephant passes by, and then hurl their heavy spears into its back, generally fatally wounding the animal, which sinks to its feet. This is the way the Cic and Yangbara go hunting.

The Arts

The Africans make their own tools and implements, and, as they like them to be well made, a lot of trouble is devoted to their manufacture. Their spears are beautifully made and razor-sharp. It is really astonishing how they can turn out such finished products, with the primitive means at their disposal. They use a stone in the place of an anvil. Another stone, or sometimes a piece of iron, is used instead of a hammer. Instead of pincers they use a cleft stick. For bellows they make use of a round clay vase, covered by a fine skin, which, on opening and shutting, forces air through a small clay tube on to the fire. They do not know how to weld or solder metals, and yet they are able to produce ear-rings and bracelets of all sizes. In addition, they also manufacture bells for bulls and small trinkets worn by the young girls round their ankles. Fishing-hooks, harpooning irons, small axes and agricultural implements, are also made. They also make a kind of spade for digging the ground. All these articles are produced without the aid of a file — the only tools available being a few stones and pieces of metal. It can be seen that their blacksmith skill dates back to Tubalcain's time.

They also make their own household articles such as saucepans, pots, pipes, etc., and they also have the task of selling them. The missionaries have often bought things from them. In addition, the women also weave straw mats (used for sleeping), baskets for holding and carrying grain, and a kind of interlaced netting, used to carry pots, etc. Apart from the above the Africans have little knowledge of anything else.

They consider the earth to be a vast plain — as they only think in terms of what they can see. Many of the tribes have never seen a mountain, although they know that these exist. The Cic believe that the sun during the night secretly returns to the place from where it rises in the morning, and they say that a native once saw the sun stealthily creeping back during the night. The Dinka distinguish between the brighter and dimmer stars: they call the first 'the shining ones' (*cyer*), whilst the rest are designated by the general word for stars, *kuel*. The comet they call *cyer-a-yol*, the star with a tail. They attach a meaning of disaster, when a comet is seen. We heard of this, when the 1858 comet appeared.

The tribes here have no historical traditions, and so far we have not come across any monument dedicated to bygone glories. As everything is made from clay, it soon turns to dust.

At first the Africans were astonished at seeing white people, but were able to find a plausible explanation to satisfy themselves. The Cic said: 'God created the white men in a clean country and left them there; but the black men, who were originally white, were placed in a dirty country and thus became black.' An elderly native had a better explanation to offer: 'Among the first mothers was one who had several children. When her husband was away one day, she decided to play a trick on him and hid one of the children under a black sooty pot.

When the husband returned, he looked for the child but could not find him, and the wife teased him. Finally, the man discovered the child under the pot, lying completely covered in black soot. And try as they could they were unable to remove the soot. This was the first man of the African race, and all his descendents were also black in colour.'

Religious Conceptions

The Africans are quite indifferent to anything supernatural. Their idea of sublime happiness is to own a lot of cows. However, they know of God, and call him *Den-Did*. They also know that he was the Creator of everything. But as God is good, and can only be good; they take no notice of Him and do not fear Him. They maintain that evil can only come from the devil, and fear him greatly. Whenever, any misfortune occurs, the devil is responsible. They believe that everything ends with death; they do not believe in the immortality of the soul. They regard the soul as only a breath. This is stated in the following Dinka song:

> *Akol ci Deng Dit cak eben,*
> *Aci ruel cak;*
> *Ko ruel aben vei, ko elo pin ko eduok;*
> *Aci pei cak;*
> *Ko pei aben vei, ko elo pin ko eduok;*
> *Aci kuel cak;*
> *Ko kuel aben vei, ko elo pin ko eduok;*
> *Aci ran cak;*
> *Ko ran aben vei, ko elo pin ko aci bi duk.*

> The day that God created all things,
> He created the sun;
> The sun rises, sets and returns again;
> He created the moon;
> The moon rises, sets and returns again;
> He created the stars;
> The stars rise and set and return again;
> He created men;
> Men are born, are buried and never return.

Thus, according to native belief, man will never come back again, and, as far as he is concerned, everything ends with death. It can be seen from this how difficult it is to convert them. They believe only what they can actually see and feel. The Mission will consequently be faced with a long, hard task, and many years will have to elapse before they will be able to have much faith in the preachings of the missionaries.

However, there is something which helps the missionaries to combine their preachings with native beliefs. This is the legendary belief in the blissful state of humanity before original sin. Both the Cic and the Bari say: "God created all men in a state of grace and justice, and they lived with Him in Paradise. But several became bad, God then lowered them from Paradise to the earth by means of a rope. The good were able to clamber up the rope again and regain Paradise. There was much dancing and beer and everybody was happy in Paradise. As time went on, however, the rope broke and now no one can climb to Paradise again, and it remains closed to all men". (The Cic say: 'A little bluebird pecked away at the rope and snapped it.' [11])

This gives them a remote idea of man's original happiness before sin was committed. They not only loathe the serpent but appear to regard it as a symbol of evil. They believe that God is good, but that the devil is just as powerful and evil. They do not offer sacrifices to the good God, but only to the evil devil.

It was on 24 April 1857, that we passed near Cic territory with our boat. As there was no wind, the crew had to tow the boat with long ropes from the banks. Suddenly, a shout was heard: 'The serpent, the serpent!' In fact, a snake was lying on its eggs in a nest. We and the hunter immediately left the boat. The hunter fired and hit the reptile in the neck; it writhed in its blood and then drew itself erect tall as a man its throat swelling. Another shot was fired, and the serpent fell to the ground. We tied a rope around the python's head as its tail was still lashing fiercely. We hauled it up the main mast. After half an hour it was dead, and we removed its skin. It was 19 feet long. In its nest there were between seventy and eighty eggs, and already some small serpents were hatched out. Whilst we were skinning the reptile, we noticed a gloomy expression on the face of our Dinka interpreter. Whilst the others were laughing he still remained despondent. The Pro-Vicar asked him why he was so dispirited, and he answered: "In our tribe it is customary to sacrifice an ox, when such a reptile is in the neighbourhood, and yet you are treating it in this way! It would thus seem that the natives venerate the python. The Bari, too, offer

---

[11] A popular story. The Dinka call the little blue bird *Atooc*.

milk as a sacrifice to this reptile. They say that they only offer sacrifices to the devil, but, as they also offer sacrifices to the python, it points to the fact that they hold this reptile as a symbol of evil — a belief passed on since the original sin of our forefathers. Could it not be that the word "python" with this meaning, reached the interior of Africa from Greece?

The people also believe in a world of spirits. The Dinka believe in good and bad spirits. The good spirits are said to live with God and are called *adjok*. The bad spirits, who live on the earth and cause evil, are called *Djvok*. Generally, they are held to be invisible, but are said to be seen at times. The spirits are also said to take human shapes but are only rarely seen thus. Their proximity is heralded by disasters, because all disasters emanate from them. Therefore, the Africans are great believers in magic and conjuring tricks which, according to them, stave off misfortunes and illnesses. As a consequence, all sorts of magicians and sorcerers are to be found among the natives — even among the women — who charge exorbitantly for their art, and who claim that it is much more effective, if paid for in advance. If their tricks do not succeed, then they blame *Jok* (the evil spirit), or another more powerful sorcerer in the vicinity. The sorcerer is called a *tyet* by the Dinka and is brought in wherever there is any illness. He brings a pot of terracotta and spits on the sick man, especially on the affected part. He removes the sand and mud from the spot, and pats his hands around it so as to ward off the evil spirits. He then takes a piece of wood and places it in the pot. He adds water and then converses with *Jok*. Next he bends over the pot and speaks into it. What he says is unintelligible, but from the muffled echoes of his voice inside the pot he alone is said to understand the answering voice of *Jok*. He then approach the sick man and touches and feels him until, at a given moment he suddenly produces a piece of wood or stone, said to have been withdrawn from the afflicted part and to have been responsible for the pain. He then sprinkles the sick man and those around him with water from the magic pot and declares that the sick man is now better. The sick man believes him . . . and what is stronger than faith? All kinds of prophecies are said to emanate from similar magic pots, but too often they never seem to materialize.

If a sick man is considered to be at death's door, or is gravely ill according to their way of thinking, there is only one thing left to do — and that is to offer a sacrifice to *Jok*. The *Tyet* chooses an ox. The relatives of the sick man kill it. The *Tyet* then takes the contents of the intestines which are still warm, and smears the whole of the sick man's body with it. This is considered to be the last possible cure. However, the *Jok* only receives the smell of the sacrifice, because a good portion of the flesh is taken away by the sorcerer and the rest is eaten by the relatives. And yet it is believed that such a ceremony is capable of warding off the evil spirit. After all, since it is such an esteemed animal as an ox that is killed, surely it is a tremendous sacrifice.

If, however, all this is of no avail and the sick man dies just the same, then his head is shaved. A hole is dug near his hut. The head is then bent forward between the knees and in this sitting posture the deceased is buried. The negroes have their graves near the house, otherwise they fear that the hyenas will uncover and devour the bodies. The grave-digger fills his ears with earth so as not to hear the cries of the deceased. The future heir seizes the weapons of the deceased and brandishes them in all directions, to stave off the evil spirits. All the relatives are in mourning and shave their heads. They tie a cord around their necks and hips. Should the deceased be a man, the relatives fast for three days; should it be a woman, the fast goes on for four days. Afterwards, a fire is lit on the tomb and once more the sorcerer arrives. This time he brings a lamb which is to be offered in sacrifice. He leads the lamb around the tomb. The parents then seize it, throw it to the ground and, sitting on it, slowly strangle it. Meanwhile, the sorcerer makes mystical signs and sprinkles them with water. This sacrifice is made to the *Jok*, so that he should not come and take another member of the family. The wealthier Africans kill an ox instead of a lamb, and this is eaten in merry company. In some places, on similar occasions, the sorcerer will lead a ram or lamb around the tomb, and then let it run off into the woods, where it falls prey either to the wild animals or to robbers. When in mourning, all ornaments like glass beads and rings are taken off, and are replaced by a cord made from tree fibre, which is worn for nearly six months. If the deceased has left much property behind him, the mourning-cord is worn for a year. Such is the custom of the Dinka tribes.

We observed the following at the house of an old woman: before eating, she took a portion of food and some drink, and threw them near a stick planted inside the hut and near another outside. This was done so that the evil spirit would not harm her. Among the Africans too, the older people are the most superstitious. They know of no prayer to God or to *Jok*. They observe no feast days, whether national or religious. To them every day is the same.

Time according to the Dinka

The year, *run*, has twelve lunar months and two seasons; the dry
season, *Pei mai*, and the rainy season *Pei ruel*. They do not know how
many days there are in a month. Their day is divided into: dawn,
morning, noon, afternoon and evening. They are not very advanced as
regards counting, and only a few can reach ten. Anything over ten is
described as 'many' or 'numerous'. The negroes count with their fingers
and, when answering a question, they simply hold up the required
number of fingers, without replying verbally. It can be easily understood that the negroes do not know how old they are: they have not
the least idea. It must not be believed that they do not grow old. In
most families there are grandchildren to be found between twelve to
fifteen years of age, and from this one may deduce that the grandfathers
have reached quite an advanced age — especially among the wealthier
people. If the older people were better looked after, and did not
suffer from hunger and poverty for six months of the year, they would
certainly grow much older. We came across people who by their looks
seemed to be between sixty and seventy. Many certainly die early, owing
to their extreme poverty, and because their children, who are similarly
placed, cannot help their parents. As the younger people are stronger,
they are able to overcome the more drastic effects of poverty, but the
older, being weaker, just succumb. Whilst in general the childen love
their parents, the parents, especially the mother, love their children
dearly.

Politeness

One might well believe that among people like these, there are no
compliments and formalities; but this is not so. Like all other races they
have their formalities and words of politeness.

In the mornings the Bari greet each other saying: 'Did you sleep
well?' — *D'adoto?*' The Dinka: '*Yin aci nin?*' In the evenings the
Bari say: *Farana! Do farana!* — peace be with you. They are atten-
tive of others and ask: 'What is there new?' '*Acin-ke-do?*' — 'Has anything evil happened to you?' If there has been a misfortune, they express
their sympathy. The Bari exclaims: '*Oddio! Oddio!*' — the Dinka:
'*O-makii! O-makii!*' 'Oh, dear!' They console and give advice. They
inquire about other people's families whether the wife is well, and ask
how the children and animals are faring. When a visitor leaves, they say

'*Iti Lor!*' 'In peace!' The departing visitor turns round and says: 'Remain behind!' '*Dong-ee.*' It is the African custom to go out and meet a stranger who is visiting them, lead him into their huts, and offer him a skin or mat to sit upon. When he leaves they accompany him for part of the way, and again say: 'This place is blessed' — '*ee thiei!*' and then they return home. If such a ceremony is over-looked, they are insulted because, although an African may be naked and poor, he is very proud. Experience has proved, however, that the more polite an African, the worse he is.

The Dinka Fishermen

From the start of the Cic and Tuic territories, to the last of the Dinka, the Bor and the Aliab, many small villages are to be found along the river. Further to the south of the Holy Cross Mission, there are larger villages, where very poor people depend mostly on fishing for their daily food. They live in a patriarchal fashion and have very few domestic beasts. If any African in these localities should own a few heads of cattle, he pastures them with the herds of the nearest chief. As they are very poor, they are held in contempt by the owners of large herds, although they probably live under the same conditions and perhaps a little more comfortably. They are not nomadic, but live in their small villages. Although they have the same customs, they work harder than the nearby owners of cattle; necessity forces them to work harder. They live by their fishing, and their catch would be much more abundant if they had better tackle. They use a hook, which is nothing more than a pointed, curved piece of metal without a barb. They attach several hooks to a long cord, which is held by a floating plank of wood, or else fish with one hook only. The rope is made from a fibrous plant and is very like our hemp rope. They use meat, animal intestines, or frogs, as bait.

In addition, they make use of a small harpoon, which is plunged into the body of the fish. This iron is attached to a very long cord and is thrown out towards the middle of the river, a stick being used to give it impetus. When the fish is struck, the stick falls away from the harpoon. The fish remains attached to the rope and is pulled out. This harpoon is also used on boats, and is flung to the left and right by a man on the prow, who then gathers it in by the cord. Although the river is alive with fish, this method of fishing is lengthy and tedious. If the water is shallow, the fisherman jumps in and, attaching the harpoon o a long pole, flings it right and left, until he strikes some fish. Often as many as twenty fish are caught by this method. The women also help. They immerse large baskets into the water, and try to catch fish that way. They have no knowledge of nets, but they make a kind of cane interlacing, with openings behind which they attach long baskets. By using this method, their catch is often quite heavy. If the level of the water is very high, it spreads into the tall grass and even reaches the woods, so that the fish remain trapped in the grass among the growth. In such a case, there is much more fish available. They roast the fish on their fires, and dry them in the sun, and then exchange them for milk with the cow owners.

These fishermen are very daring, and even hunt the crocodile and hippopotamus. They use a large iron harpoon, about 7 or 8 inches long, attached to a strong rope. This is hurled out into the river by means of a long pole, which then breaks away from the harpoon. This method of catching crocodiles is not very dangerous. The fisherman cautiously approaches the amphibious reptile, until he is within good striking distance. If the blow is well delivered, the crocodile cannot escape, and although it may snap its jaws and thresh, it is quickly killed by spears. The negroes eat the meat around the neck, whilst the other parts are sold to traders.

There is much greater danger involved in hunting the hippopotamus. The fishermen go out in groups, with more than one boat. If they come across a hippopotamus on land, they very quietly approach it, launch the harpoon into its side, and withdraw the pole. Angered the beast turns looking for its enemy — in the meanwhile the hunters are straining to hold the beast with the rope, whilst another harpoon is plunged into the other side. If possible, the rope is tied to a tree. The wounded hippopotamus savagely fights back, roars terribly, and tries to break the rope with its teeth. If the animal succeeds, then the hunters must flee, and the hippopotamus, with the harpoons embedded in it, makes for the river, where it dies. The hippopotamus acts in a similar way if wounded whilst in the river; it furiously hurls itself against the hunters in the boat, and should the boat be overturned, the men are in real danger. When on the river, the rope is short, and a floating piece of wood at one end, tells the hunters the exact position of the beast, provided it has not bitten through the rope. They then follow it, and strike again until they can corner it in some small channel, where they hold it with the rope. If the beast is not able to break away from the rope, harpoons and spears are embedded into it until it slowly dies. Sometimes, the struggle goes on for six hours.

The roars of the enraged animal during the struggle are terrible to hear, but like a swarm of bees, the fishermen hit it again and again, until a triumphant shout announces that the animal has been killed. What a feast for the hunters! They now have more than one ton of meat to eat! The hunter, who was first to harpoon the animal is honoured like a hero, and receives the prize share of the flesh. The remainder is shared by the whole village. After two or three days there is nothing left, not even the skin. Only the teeth are sold. On their return from such an expedition, the hero of the day heads the procession of boats and uninterruptedly sings about his own daring deed. The others echo hits song and later relate the whole story to their families. The empty pots are quickly filled, and the day is rounded off by much feasting and dancing.

In such a poor country, only the wealthier heads of the families can afford a large harpoon. The poorer can never hope to have one of their own. The harpoon ropes are made from tree fibres or from hides. It can be seen that the Africans are very courageous in the face of such tremendous odds, especially as their equipment is so poor.

To them, a greater treasure still is a boat, the most precious thing they build. A fair-sized boat costs between nine to ten cows, and even the smaller ones cost four cows. These boats are nothing more than hollowed tree trunks, pointed at the front. The crews must remain seated, otherwise the boats would capsize. A few oars, fore and aft, push the boat at great speed through the water, and its usefulness is enhanced by the fact that it easily makes its way through the marshy grass. Thus a boat owner is considered a wealthy man. All the Dinka, Bari and Nuer tribes have this kind of boat, but the Shilluk have two kinds. They have a boat made of ambatch canes, tied together with the thin ends coming to a point in the front, and the thick ends appropriately shaped, forming the stern. These boats are so light a man can carry them on his head to the river and back. However, they do not hold more than two persons.

The largest kind of boat the Shilluk possess is similar to the Venetian gondola. It is made from two hollowed tree trunks, bound together with rope, pointed at the bows, with raised sides. This type of boat is very long and narrow and can hold eighteen persons. There is no tar available along the White Nile, so rope is used instead of metal and the joints and cracks are filled in with mud. There must always be someone in the boat to bale out the water which seeps in through all the cracks. The Cic boats are similarly constructed, but better finished and more durable.

The fishermen on the White Nile are the only boatmen to be found, hence they are sought by all who wish to cross the river, and a good price in grain and milk is asked for such service. The boats are also used when gathering lotus seeds (*helumbium*) which are carefully picked and exchanged for milk. Some years there is an abundance of this seed, providing the fishermen with their living. Otherwise they grow very little, with the exception of a few tobacco plants. In many of these fishing localities the ground is very low and is subject to flooding. However, the fishermen who, for three years now, have taken up positions near the garden of the Holy Cross Mission (where there are twenty houses) have begun to cultivate the soil, and have successfully grown the sesame and maize seeds which were supplied by the Mission. As they were able to reap two harvests, they were very enthusiastic and said that they were going to enlarge their fields. . . . However, the moment had come for us to leave them, and on hearing this they were very sad. They tried to persuade us to remain with them and brought sheep and goats as gifts. They were beginning to realise why we had come amongst them, whereas at first they had taken us for traders. In short, the fruits of the Mission were beginning to appear. While we cannot say that we achieved much, we can no longer say that it is impossible to civilise these peoples. But the supreme grace is not yet visibly spread among the Africans, which is urgently required if they are to change from pagans to good Christians.

This is how things stood at the beginning of 1860 when the Mission boat, on the orders of our Superiors, came to take us to Egypt.

The Bari

Beyond the lands of the Bor tribes, the ground rises slightly; the marshes disappear, and magnificent forests are to be seen to the right and left. Here, we are among a totally different tribe, the Bari, who live along the 6° 14′ 30″ N. and the south. The south is unknown and the Bari themselves say that there are many peoples living to the south in addition to themselves and the Shir, as far as Logwek.

This race is not nomadic and has permanent dwelling places. The northern Bari and the so-called Shir (between 6° and 5° N.) live on the pleasant and fertile river islands which they cultivate. Their villages are built on the river banks, one near the other. They grow *durra*, sesame, small beans, and tobacco. The herds are guarded by only a few men necessary for their protection.

Towards the south the country of the Bari proper becomes increasingly sandy, and in the Gondokoro area, to the west and east, the soil is also sandy and barren. It is as if the river has chosen this area to jettison the heaviest of its alluvial deposits, not being able to carry them any further; whilst the finer soil is deposited along the lower parts of the northern sector. Only the low-lying land and the islands are fertile, but subject to flooding. Within the space of four years floods ruined the harvests at least twice. The Bari do not only live near the river, but in the interior of the country near streams, where they also dig wells. Here too, the Bari do not live a nomadic life, and only have a few young men looking after the herd. The panorama of this country is beautiful, with its alternating woods and plains. Pleasant villages lie under the shade of gigantic trees. A circle of green-covered mountains fill the horizon as if painted by an artist, while the rushing stream twists like a silver snake through the plain. In the months after the first rains, it is truly an enchanting picture; the eye can see from east to west, and from south to north; whilst further on towards the north the view is blocked by many trees. Village after village, and wood after wood, follow each other till lost to sight. Everywhere there are beautiful things to be seen. The eye is gladdened by the hedges surrounding the huts, and especially by the cow enclosures where the euphorbia is as tall as trees, all covered with yellow flowers. Nearby is the imposing *krurulung* tree, [12] which resembles the walnut. The fruit of this tree is cooked by the Bari and made into an oil which is used to grease their bodies, whilst the Dinka use butter specially made for this purpose. This is done so that, when the strong winds blow, the skin does not crack and cause pain.

It is the population, however, which attracts attention. Here there is no shyness or fear as with the Dinka, who flee at the sight of a stranger. On the contrary, the boats are warmly welcomed here, and natives with their spears, bows and ivory bracelets come forward in greetings. Their chief wears white feathers, a heavy ring, and a belt of glass beads encircles his loins. Even his feet are covered with shiny brass rings which are polished every day. Ash-covered men are rarely seen here, instead the wealthier and noble smear themselves from head to foot with a mixture of oil and red-ochre earth, so that they look almost like glowing devils. According to them, not only is the colour of this mixture beautiful, but they maintain that *krurulung* oil strengthens them. Therefore everybody, including the women and especially the

[12] The wild olive tree, probably *Olea hochstetteri*.

M

younger people, make use of it. The women cover themselves with a *rahat*, that is, a few strips of cotton or fine chain, and sometimes only with a leather strip which falls to the heels and thus looks like a tail when they run. Neither the men nor the women wear ear-rings, but only rings on their hands, and copper or ivory bands round their feet. They adorn the neck, chest and loins with glass beads, preferably coloured vivid red, blue or white. In addition to the *rahat*, the women also cover themselves with skins which they themselves have dressed. The young girls add to their beauty by tattooing themselves. They incise a pattern on the skin and then rub the cuts with the sap of a certain tree, so that the wounds swell whilst healing, leaving a swollen scar made up of tiny blobs and forming fantastic designs. However, in time, these become smaller and smaller. The men do not do this. They, or at least some of them, carry fine straps around their shoulders. These straps have two uses: the first is for carrying a small stool which can be used at any time and in any place; the second is for the punishment of women and children. These stools are about nine inches high, are very smooth, and finely cut from one piece of wood. The Bari men do not like to sit on the bare earth, so if they have no stool they carry a round piece of hide with them. They even wear a kind of sandal made of buffalo skin during the hot months, so that the hot soil does not harm them. The pipe is even more important to the Bari than to the Dinka, and is the faithful companion of both men and women. The tobacco habit has become so strong that even if there is no tobacco obtainable, the Bari are content with charcoal. They do not prepare the tobacco in leaves, but in cake form which lasts longer. The most appreciated tobacco is that from Lokoya and comes from the Loudo tribe. A certain quantity of tobacco is obtained in exchange for a ram. The tobacco is inhaled deeply from clay pipes which are quite well shaped and fired by the women.

Among the Bari it is possible to distinguish cow owners by their build, because, being fed on milk, they are taller and more developed, than the poorer people.

As we have already said, the Bari are impudent, noisy, and quarrelsome. They will immediately say *ju lio*, 'My friend', to anybody they have seen for the first time, and immediately beg for something, shouting '*Magor*', "Hunger". When begging they say '*Nan ko magor duma!*', "I am very hungry." They retract the stomach and rub their hand over it to make the meaning more evident.

The names of the men and women are according to the circumstances at their birth. Many bear the names of months, and it is customary to give each other nicknames so that many have two or three.

These people also live in a patriarchal fashion, but, if some of the elders are to be believed, half a century ago Shir and Bari still had a monarchical regime under the rule of a forefather of the chief and rain-maker Nyigilò. They also say that, as far back as six generations ago, this race immigrated and, coming from the south, drove the Beri from the Lokoya and Lirya mountains, pushing as far as the large islands of the Nile which they still inhabit today. It is said that most of this people still live to the south of Logwek. The chief here is called *matat* (plural *kimak*). Nevertheless an owner of any importance bears this title and carries a stick with two points which is recognised as a sceptre.

War

This tribe is more quarrelsome than the Dinka. Very often village fights village, western villages fight eastern villages and villages on the opposite banks of the river clash. The theft of a woman or of a cow, which often happens, gives rise to a fight. According to the natives, there was better order in the country when they had their common king, who lived at Belenyan. He dealt swiftly with robbers and murderers, had their hands severed, and sometimes even ordered their heads to be cut off. At the present time, however, each village has to look after itself. The three chiefs at Gondokoro are called Ulibari, that is 'allied to Bari or Bari friends. (Uli-Bari is not the name of the place, as is erroneously marked on some maps.) In view of such insecurity, the head of each family has a drum with which he passes on the news of invasions or peaceful events. If the drum is used to summon the others to war, the message is repeated by all the villages and, within a short space of time thousands of warriors gather together. If a war threatens, all the people meet late in the evening, and discussions go on far into the night. Then all the chiefs appear, accompanied by their men. The young men sit in a large circle, the chiefs take up their position in the centre, and each concisely tells the audience of the grievances suffered at the hands of the enemy. The audience silently listens and then debates whether it would be preferrable to go to war or sue for peace. Added weight is given to the arguments by beating the weapons on the ground and leaping around. Generally, those who shout the loudest get their own way, and the day for going to war is decided upon.

It is customary for the Bari women to accompany their men to war. They carry food supplies, tend the wounded, and mourn for the fallen with high pitched shrieks. The women come to no harm, for it would be considered a shameful deed to kill a woman on the battlefield. However, war here is similar to that among the Dinka. As soon as a few have fallen, peace is made. Unless directly concerned, the young warriors do not give evidence of any great bravery or courage. The chief is often obliged to kill one or more oxen for his warriors, otherwise they will not go to war and fight. It is a different matter however, if there be rich plunder in view, as was the case, for instance, in the attack against the Piedmontese Consul, Vaudey, and in last years' aggression against the merchants. Lured by the booty, the natives become fearless, run blindly into the fray, and slay right and left with their spears. In this way, they killed 120 to 156 Egyptian soldiers this year. Only thirty Egyptians escaped death, and many of these were wounded. If provoked, the Bari are savage and aggressive.

This hostility between themselves is also the reason why they know little of distant areas. Their stories are based only on suppositions and are often just fabrications. The traveller must see for himself.

Their Occupations

To understand the Bari well, one must remain among them for a whole year. At the beginning of the rainy season one might be led to believe that the Bari are a well-organised people, the only drawback being that they are naked. At this time of the year there is feverish activity everywhere. Along the river in the already green fields men can be seen working everywhere. They begin at sunrise and work without interruption throughout the whole day until evening, and only stopping now and again to drink milk. This is work in earnest. They are bathed in sweat, but relentlessly continue, clearing the grass with a metal hoe. If, by chance, there is any *marisa* available, the work is executed with joy and clamourous shouts and songs until evening. Then, and only then, will they return home with their tools on their shoulders and eat a pudding made from *durra* grain, or from a mixture of flour and the leaves of certain trees.

Durra is the main crop of the Bari, but in the sandier soil they also grow sesame and small beans. One must not forget that this work is very laborious (Europeans could not endure it), especially in view of the poor quality of the food available, and thus it only goes on for two or three weeks, sometimes less. The men then rest for two or three months, and the most they do during this period is to repair their huts which threaten to collapse under the rains. They tend their cattle, lying down

amongst them during the day at least, because at night they have to
defend the growing crops from the menace of the hippopotamus. They
keep guard shouting and clanging pieces of metal so as to keep the beasts
at bay, for the Bari have not the proper equipment to fight them and
are not as skilled in this as the Dinka fishermen. When the grain begins
to ripen they stand guard over it day and night, armed with bows and
spears; otherwise there would be nothing left for them to reap. Not
only must they contend with the hippopotamus, but also with the
numerous thieves who want to gather the crops without sowing. If thieves
were to succeed in breaking into a field of *durra*, they would remain
there for days, making gluttons of themselves, and it often happens that
they fall ill and die because of this overfeeding.

The Bari's greatest joy is at harvest time, when every member of
the family helps in carrying the ears of corn in a basket or special container called a *gugu*. The corn is not all thrashed at once, but a little at
a time when required. The women do this work. The men rest for a few
weeks and enjoy themselves. Then they start thinking about the second
sowing. The Bari are the only tribe who sows twice during the year.
Only a little *durra* is sown the second time, but they plant more beans
and a little tobacco. By now the first harvest has all been consumed,
whilst the second yields little, and is eaten even quicker than the first.
In the new year few will have any grain left, apart from the little that
is kept back for the following season. Hunger and poverty then set in,
and the people become more harsh and spiteful than usual. After the
first harvest the Bari are generous and wasteful, but the second harvest
is followed by war and tribal quarrels, which continue for months.

Poverty

Poverty, hunger and disaster follow in the wake of these quarrels every
year. During such times, no business is transacted without an extra
something being asked for. It is truly characteristic of this hunger-
stricken land that the 'extra' demanded in their sales and purchases, is
denominated by the word hunger, *magor*. Nothing is done without a
magor. But what are the reasons for such hunger and misery that recur
every year? The first reason may well be that the soil is not very fertile,
as we have already pointed out, because the good earth has been washed
away by the floods, and the only fertile localities are to be found in the
low-lying areas. Moreover, the entire country is thickly populated, especially near Gondokoro, and it would take a very industrious people to

cultivate sufficiently to meet the requirements of the entire population. However, it must not be believed that there is any waste ground. Each plot is divided by bundles of grass. The work in the fields is badly done, and when sowing, the drill holes are barely deep enough to receive the seeds. Thus, the tender seeds are either dried up by the burning sun or choked by the grass. If a week goes by without rain, the entire sown fields dry up, as the sandy soil requires abundant water. Besides, a grower cannot sow too much because he would never be able to protect all his crops from the thieves. Even when the harvest is rich, the natives lavishly waste it; having been hungry for such a long time, they now wish to make up for it, and liberally cook and eat the grain, and make beer from it. The vainer natives exchange their grain for glass beads, with which they adorn themselves. Generally speaking, there is nothing left after three months. On the average, half the population has no grain for six months of the year. The Bari have less fruit than the Dinka, and their few heads of cattle are undernourished, owing to the small and poor pastures, thus yielding very little milk.

Some go to the Shir and the Beri to buy grain in exchange for beads and iron: iron is also used as an article of exchange by the White Nile traders who arrive in December each year. Some are employed to take goods to the interior of the country, and thus escape from the miserable life. The greater number of these Bari carriers stay away as long as they can. Indeed, some stay away altogether, as they find they are better off away from home.

When the first rain falls the last few seeds of grain are sown, and then misery and poverty are at their height. During the months of April and May, the inhabitants visibly grow thinner and become more emaciated, especially the children who have been driven away from their parents. Many are killed and thrown into the river, even the mothers throw their children into the river because they cannot feed them. Many die of hunger. Everywhere one hears of assassinations, abduction, theft and killings. Indeed, the law of the strongest is in force. They fear death less than the whip. A Bari will reason as follows: 'If I am dead, I am no longer hungry. But the whip hurts and I suffer both from the whip and from hunger'. Thus the Bari will risk anything rather than die of hunger.

He who possesses a little milk sufficient to keep him alive, is indeed happy, because most of them feed only on the leaves of certain trees and herbs which they cook during the evening and leave to soften during the night. Even the beasts have to suffer, but they are not killed because they represent the only wealth of the Bari. As the country is so thickly populated, there is no wild life. The poor go fishing, but as the river is so rapid along this stretch, and as they have such bad tackle, they catch only a few fish.

The fishermen and blacksmiths are known as *tomonok,* but they are looked down upon by the cow owners, who do not go fishing or do smithy work because such occupations are considered degrading. During the hunger months, the Bari humble themselves, are patient and things are said which at any other time would give rise to spite and quarrels.

With the coming of June, the miserable conditions begin to improve, the sesame ripens, and more milk and better vegetables are available. Soon the *durra* will be ripe, but before this happens some of the Bari go south, where this grain has already ripened, begging and stealing. Later, the inhabitants of the south, in their turn, do the same and come here demanding the same treatment. However, the Bari are generous and will give freely whilst they have it to give.

Merry-making follows the harvest.

Merry-making

Great as was the misery they have just experienced, boundless now is their joy whilst they have plenty. If seen at this time, one would be led to believe that the Bari are always drunk. There is merry-making and singing nearly every evening; and when there is beautiful moonlight, dancing goes on far into the night. The Bari dance is not immoral in itself but is rather of a warlike nature, and disorderly conduct sometimes occurs, which is not really surprising in this time of plenty. Their dance is wild and daring and is accompanied by a deafening clamour. The greater the noise, the more beautiful and attractive the dance, according to them. The dance is held in a sandy plain, cleared of trees and stones, near the village. A withered tree around which they dance is planted in the middle. To get an idea of this dance, here is an account of what we saw on 25 July 1858. The first announcement of the dance had already been given by the drums in the afternoon. Again at seven in the evening the measured beats of the big drum invited all the neighbouring villages to the dance. At nine o'clock, when the moon was riding high, bathing the countryside in its silvery light, the revelry began. After having eaten plenty, all the people from the neighbouring villages came to the dance.

As in times of old, the arena was situated alongside a gigantic *kurulenghi* (oil tree). Everything was illuminated by the beautiful light of the full moon. Around the arena, fields of flourishing *durra* concealed

the dancers' huts. When we arrived the drums were already being beaten
and there was much noise. 'Are you here?' *'Ta apo?'* 'Good evening!'
'Parana!' 'There is dancing this evening.' *'Leri kata.'* 'Is not the dance
beautiful?' *'Leri alobut?'* *'Taba kata?'* 'Have you any tobacco?' Thus
shouted many of them in chorus, calling us by our names. This was
our welcome. In the centre of the area stood the old tree surrounded by
a garland (*vore*) made of twigs and grass, the sign of a feast. Also around
the tree were the young drummers and a group of children who were
leaping and jumping and throwing their hands and feet into the air.
The dance began. Men, women and children, young and old, came
forward, shouting and cheering with great noise. Finally they formed
a circle around the tree and started to move into a double ring. The
smaller ring, on the inside, was made up of women and girls carrying
spears or sticks and *durra* stalks. The outer ring was formed by the
fathers, young men and boys. All were armed with bows, arrows, and
spears. Distinguished men carried shields made from elephant skin.

The best possessions of the Bari were brought out on this occasion
to create an impression. Everyone was adorned with white feathers, some
having them arranged in the shape of a helmet, while others had them
hanging downwards from the neck, like a bird's tail. Rare furs could
also be seen like those of the ichneumon, civet and small leopard, and
were either worn by the people on top of the head or on the chest.
Naturally the beads were not absent. One of the principal necessities
required by the dancers is a chain of small iron bells (*waryakan*) which
is tied round their feet up as far as, or above the knee, with which they
produce a deafening sound when the dancers rhythmically stamp their
feet. The young girls also adorn their necks and hips with pearl beads,
while the women display their new aprons. Those lucky enough to be
smeared with red from head to foot were considered really beautiful and
raised much enthusiasm. Medi, the chief, paraded pompously, wearing
the yellow tin belt which he had bought the day before for four hens,
two of which he still owed. Being in possession of such a treasure, he
was the envy of all eyes. One after the other the natives all said that
he was great — *lu-aduma*. The front of his head was adorned by the
beak of a marabou, in his hand he carried a shield made of elephant
skin, while a leopard skin hung from his back. In addition, his many
brass rings around his arms and legs were brightly polished. He was very
merry as, no doubt, before coming he had emptied several containers of
beer (*yawa*).

Beyond the two circles of dancers there were rows of spectators,
waiting for a dancer to tire in order to take his place. At the same time,

these spectators kept back a multitude of children, to prevent them from mingling with the dancers.

The dance itself consists of the rhythmic beating of feet, with the dancers assuming fierce looks. The movements are cadenced with the dancers swaying to the right and left, and swinging back whilst the iron bells jangle deafeningly. The women, inside the circle, wave and throw their arms about, bend swiftly forward and back, jump high into the air with both arms outstretched, cheer, shout and scream to the chorus of the men. At a sound from the drum the rings break up and there is great confusion. The dancing stops and only the children keep up their incessant noise. There is an apprehensive moment for the men when, with ferocious looks, they start to attack each other, brandishing their spears as if in deadly combat. The women scream. However, the spears fall to the ground; it was only a mock battle, and continuous cheering echoes through the air. The drum beats again. With his spear raised, the chief appears followed by the dancers, while in a circle the warriors also advance as if going to battle. In the same manner, the circle of women advances.

Whoever wishes to see handsome, gigantic but wild warriors is granted the sight here. Bundles of burning straw are then placed among the dancers and, by the light of the flames, the warlike dance begins again but takes on a more gruesome aspect among the pandemonium.

As dances are seldom held without musical accompaniment, the Bari have also their own musical instruments. The principal part is played by the drums, made from hollowed-out tree trunks and covered with skins at both ends. This instrument is always heard among the Bari, as with it the head of a family gives the signal to water and milk the cows, to feed the calves, and to return home. The drum is also sounded to summon the natives whether to dance or to war. . . . There is also the lyre, which is called *tom* and is similar to that of the Dinka. The Bari have also a wind instrument which is to be seen everywhere. It is made from the small horn of a ram with three holes to modulate the sound. It is carried by all the young men and is played on all occasions. The Bari have also a larger horn with a lateral hole. It is extended by an ever-widening tube made of skin, which terminates in a kind of terracotta funnel, curving gracefully upon itself. This kind of horn has only a low note and is not very musical. However, such horns are indispensable to the Bari because they help to increase the noise at their ceremonies.

Their songs are chiefly about deeds of war, the tunes being very lively and quite pleasant to the ear. These nocturnal dances are continued almost uninterruptedly from the end of July to the middle of November.

When a Bari has enough to eat, he dances in the evenings and eats and sleeps during the day.

Marriage

It is precisely at this time that the Bari, and Africans in general, think of getting married. They make new acquaintances and, if already engaged, the marriage contract is now arranged. As with other African races, the woman must be bought. As the Bari have very few cattle, the price for a woman is less; and even the most distinguished Bari women only cost about ten cows plus a few small gifts to the relatives. The poorer are able to buy their wives for a few goats. The first year is very expensive for the bridegroom because he also has to keep his mother-in-law, who looks after his wife during the honeymoon and until the birth of the first child. [13] Thus, the bridegroom must have a large supply of grain. Apart from the wedding feast, there are no other ceremonies. Each man may have as many wives as he can keep, while chiefs here have more wives than those of the Dinka. Those who wish to do things in style take a new wife every year; for instance, that fraud of a chief Nigila [Nyigilò], who had more than twenty. During the hunger months, many of the chiefs only keep a few wives, but as soon as the harvest is in, the original wives are taken back and a new one is added, as was the case, for instance, with Chief Medi near the Mission.

Even among the negroes where every woman lives in a separate house, polygamy gives rise to hatred and jealousy, as can be seen from the following episode which occurred on 10 June 1858. Near the Mission lived a man who had two wives, one of which he loved more, the mother of a young girl of about four or five years old. The other woman gave vent to her jealousy and sought revenge on this little child in a terrible manner. One day, when the mother of the child was away, this second wife killed the infant, and took it some distance away from the house, tore out the intestines and the heart, removed the eyes and left it under a tree. She then returned home. Meanwhile, the father heard of the story from a man who by chance, while making his way

[13] A widespread custom, e.g. among the Copts of Egypt.

through the woods, had seen the child in this horrible condition under the tree. The father went home and asked the second wife where the child was. She replied that it had gone towards the south with some other people. She then went to hide herself in another house. Troubled in his mind the father made his way to the woods and saw that the child was indeed his daughter. He rushed home to look for his second wife, but she could not be found. At last she was forced to come out, but immediately ran away again. The father then learnt from other people that the murderer of his child could only have been this second wife. The news so infuriated the father and the other men that they sought and caught her, and beat her to death with sticks. They did not bury her but left her lying near the road, where she was devoured by the birds three days after her death.

As already mentioned, the women are often the cause of war when: (*a*) they leave their husbands, who in turn demand the cows back from the wives' parents; or when (*b*) the women return to their parents, saying that their husbands have ill-treated them, and demand that steps be taken against them. This, however, only happens among the wealthier natives. The poorer also have their disagreements, but these do not occur so frequently. On the whole, there is nothing lasting about marriages here. Sometimes, especially among the poorer, they are broken after only a few months, and usually when food is scarce. Bitterness then sets in, and the husband drives his wife away, accusing her of not having been thrifty. At times a wife will leave her husband of her own accord, when there is nothing left to eat in her house. She runs off and hopes she will have better luck with another husband. Marriage ties are not observed when hunger is rife. Everyone is on the move, looking for something to eat. When harvest time comes once more, many married couples are no longer united, as the wife has married another man and the husband another woman.

In general the women are more insolent and corrupt than the men. Adultery is widespread, especially in view of the permanent stay of the traders and their servants. Prostitution was once almost unknown here, but it was not long before the vice began taking its toll, and the infections associated with it spread among the Africans, who called them the 'illnesses of the French'! [14] In the areas inhabited by these merchants, nearly all the Africans are affected by some venereal disease.

---

[14] *Morbo gallico* and *mal francese* were also common Italian variant terms for syphilis.

Step-children

In view of such conditions, it is little wonder that the children grow up so uncontrolled in their ways and manners. When these women have children, they also bring with them the children of the previous husband. When hunger comes, the stepfather gets rid of all his step-children — or at least the stepsons, as the daughters are kept back so that they can be sold to their future husbands. Of late, there have been cases where the stepfathers have sold their stepsons as slaves to merchants, who take them and later re-sell them. These stepchildren, cast out by their parents, have no one to look after them; no house will take them in. Rejected by all, like birds of the woods they must fend for themselves. The Bari call them the 'children of the woods'. Many die from starvation when they are still young, while those who manage to live are forced to become thieves and murderers. Those who die of hunger are left where they fall, to be devoured by the jackals, or are thrown into the river. The survivors also find their way to the grave as thieves and murderers. When they are caught thieving, no mercy is shown them; they are either beaten to death, or have their throats cut and are thrown into the river. Even among the parents no spark of human pity exists for these unhappy children. To quote an instance, here is what occurred in May 1857: as usual during that month, hunger was widespread. The missionaries saw two boys carefully picking from the mud the waste seeds of grain thrown to the chickens. Father Uberbacher pitied them, took them into the house, gave them food and hoped to teach and educate them. But they continued stealing, and although they were repeatedly punished, they still persisted. Finally, the missionaries became aware that these two boys had even stolen the little sugar which the Pro-Vicar had brought for the Mission. Their cunning in stealing was incredible. Later the stolen sugar was found buried in the garden, and the two boys had to be asked to leave. A short while later we were told by another boy that the sugar thief had returned to this locality with his hands and feet burnt. When we saw him he was indeed a pitiful sight. His toes were no longer visible, while all that remains of his hands were scorched bones. Out of sheer pity, we gave him to eat and drink, and asked him what had happened to him. He replied: 'When I left here, I went to my father's village, and, being hungry, I hid in my uncle's *durra* field and ate some of his grain. But my uncle saw me, seized me and dragged me off to his hut. There he held my hands and feet in the fire until they were charred. He then threw me out, and for three days I have been crawling back here.' This was how his own uncle treated him! We carefully tended his burns and he improved. As soon as he was feeling better, however, he began stealing again. The Pro-Vicar, who daily sent him some tit-bit, was himself robbed of pigeons and poultry. We had to turn the boy away again. He died a few days later, and was eaten by the birds.

These 'children of the woods' are incorrigible thieves, as we experienced with at least forty of them. They are thieves and bandits, and as this is their only occupation, it can well be imagined how skilled they are in their wicked deeds. The theft that occurred whilst we were stationed in Gondokoro cannot even be imagined. The thieves are organized in teams, have look-outs, and are a real curse in the Bari country. If one was caught he was beaten to death, without the least pity. Now they are frequently sold to the traders.

Hospitality is less generous here than with the Dinka, and all owners have to hide everything they possess. When something is sold, it is always during the night, so that others do not get to know about it and claim a share under their communistic customs. If a beast is killed, it is done during the night and it is hidden, so that no one knows that there is meat available. The meat is secretly cooked and eaten behind locked doors with only the family participating. This is done because it is the law of the strongest that prevails, and as soon as it is known that there is any meat available, neighbours, friends, and thieves, all come and, like vultures, watch night and day, in the hope of obtaining even a small piece of meat.

The rights of inheritance are almost identical with those of the Cic, with the difference that the young heirs are robbed of everything, both by their relatives and strangers. This is what actually happened to the orphans of the brother of Nyigilò, who were sold as servants to the traders at Khartoum.

Dwelling-places

The Bari dwelling-places consist of round huts similar to those of the Shilluk and Dinka. Here they are slightly lower, but more striking to the eye, as the roof slopes down to within two feet of the ground, thus forming a kind of circular passage around the hut itself. This passage is used by the children for sleeping, and for the storage of wood. The huts have two doors, one leading into the round passage, and the other into the dark interior, and can only be entered on all fours. The furniture among the Bari is the same as that among the Dinka, with the exception that the Bari have a grinding stone which they use for grinding their grain in the Arab fashion. The far end of the stone rests upon the ground, and the women, on their knees, crush the grain by rubbing another stone on it. The Bari also have a mortar to grind their grain. No hut is complete without its low stool, which is used as a seat during the day and a head rest during the night; whilst mats and skins are used as beds.

There is also a peculiar large basket granary (*gugu*) which the Bari use to store their grain. These 'baskets', which are found near the huts, are made from plaited twigs. They are round and very large, coated with clay on the inside and kept up by strong poles. Round, pointed covers are placed over the top of the baskets, thus protecting the grain from the rain and dampness, and offering better protection from the termites. If there is any foodstuff in the basket it must be guarded. Consequently, by night, especially during dark nights, the owner sleeps under them.

The Bari women cook all their food in terracotta vessels which they make themselves, and each of these utensils has a different name according to its shape. As salt is available here, their food is tastier, although they like their milk to smell of urine. Now and again the richer natives eat meat, including the skin, horns and hoofs. Even the bones are crushed and eaten. Thus, there is not the slightest trace of an animal having been killed. Like the Chinese, the Bari eat mice and rats, go hunting for them, catch them in traps, and by the light of flares kill them with sticks. The glowing flares of the hundreds of rat-catchers, rushing to and fro in the dark evening, are very striking. These small rodents are so numerous in Africa, that whoever possesses a cat or two, is considered very fortunate. It is sometimes impossible to sleep because of the rats running about everywhere on the ground, whilst in many cases they have been known to bite people in the night. One can well imagine what ravages they cause amongst the foodstuff. But they very rarely have much luck, since the Bari country is one where hunger prevails for both man and beast. Although the starving Bari are not very particular in what they eat, and even eat rotten fish and stinking meat, they do not eat frogs, which at times are very numerous.

Blacksmiths

In the Belenyan and Kerek mountains, the poorer Bari earn their living by working as blacksmiths, as there is much iron to be found there. The metal is worked after it has been smelted, and is turned into agricultural implements and spears, which are then exchanged for grain. In these modern times, the merchants purchase these implements with grain and then resell them for ivory. Like the Dinka, many of these blacksmiths carry their tools with them and go from locality to locality looking for work. They repair spears and other equipment, and make bells, bracelets, small chains for barter, receiving food in exchange. Like the fishermen, the blacksmiths are looked down upon and have no say in public meetings, nor do they possess any cows. Here they are called *tumunök*.

Religion

The Bari believe that there is a Creator and call Him *Man*, but treat Him indifferently. The tradition of the rope which led to Paradise and which finally broke may be what is left of the sacred story of the Fall of Man and of his happy state before the Fall. Many of the elder Bari offer milk in sacrifice to the black viper, believing themselves to be descendents from it, and so call it 'the grandmother' (*yakanye*). Otherwise there is no sign of religion among the Bari. They are so stricken with poverty that they care for nothing except eating. It is only when they have had sufficient food that they give way to uncontrolled joy. They do not believe in the immortality of the soul, and say that after death there is no hunger or pain. We were told that there have been some suicides, but we ourselves never came across any.

As among the Dinka, the evil spirits are blamed when any misfortune occurs. Their witch doctors, called *punok*, [15] indulge in their usual tricks and duplicity, and even some of the women deceive the people with their magic pots and other more stupid devices. Similar occurrences took place near Gondokoro during our stay there. There was the case of an old grandfather complaining of rheumatic pains in the back. The *punok* was called in. Having been examined, the old man was given a rib-shaped piece of wood in exchange for a considerable sum, and told never to part with it if he wished to get better. Thus, as each day went by, the old man could be seen gripping his piece of wood, never letting it go for a single moment, either when sleeping or eating. Gradually, as the weather improved the pains began to dis-

[15] Elsewhere *bunok*, *bunuk* which the writer translates as *Zauberärzte* (plural), now, with greater understanding of the *bunok's* role in society, sometimes (where applicable) translated as diviners.

appear, and this was attributed to the magic powers of the wood. The wood was then joyfully handed back to the *punok*, together with a further gift.

The belly skin of wild animals such as leopards and panthers is also believed to possess magical curative properties. Thus, the *punok* are very quick to buy this part of the skins and hire it out to the credulous people, as was done with the rib-shaped wood. For this reason it is impossible to buy a complete wild animal skin among the Bari.

One day, the small grandson of the above mentioned grandfather fell ill. As he had already attended the Mission and had been baptized, we offered to cure his fever with the medicines at our disposal; but the grandfather refused us permission. The small boy was kept at home, and the *punok* was called in. But we later heard that the boy was not getting any better. After a few days we passed by the boy's hut, and immediately outside it we noticed a grinding stone attached to a rope, which had almost been reduced to powder by almost constant friction. We were told that this had been put there by the *punok* to drive off the evil spirit so that the child would get better. Meanwhile we continued to send him good soups, hoping that it would do him good. Two days later, however his younger brother told us that he had died. The grinding stone certainly did not help him, and at the same time prevented us from being with him.

These tricksters even distribute amulets as protection against death, and the poor Africans believe in them. The Africans are so superstitious that they believe a man can produce or withold rain. The rainmaker is held in high esteem. But although the work is lucrative, it is fraught with danger. After a rainmaker has succeeded in leading the natives to believe that he has produced rain, he demands many head of cattle and sheep as a reward. Generally, these rainmakers are very observant people who have some inkling of the atmospheric conditions and are, therefore, able to guess when rain is due. However, this trick does not always succeed and consequently the fields become parched and the rainmakers run very serious risk of revenge from the natives. If they are not fortunate enough to escape in time, they are seized and generally their stomachs are cut open at a point where the rain is though to be hidden. Death in this manner befalls one or two of them. Last year even that great mendicant and rainmaker, Prince Nyigilò, fell victim. He was killed by spears, having accepted payment while the sown fields were scorched by the sun. Nyigilò was always in flight, and once even reached Khartoum where he lived at the Government's expense in Brun Rollet's house, returning home in the latter's boat. Nyigilò was a descendant of an ancient family of kings, who knew how to win favour by flattering strangers, and who was a first-class beggar. He left many children, having had more than twenty wives.

Death and Burial

As soon as a dying person has expired, the heir or father of the family takes up his weapons, runs out and around the house, shouting and waving spears and sticks in all directions so as to ward off evil spirits. Everybody comes shouting and crying. The grave is dug in the same manner as among the Dinka, and the body is placed in it. A messenger gives the news of the death to the relatives, who then all come to the grave, sprinkle sand on it, and sit around weeping. They then have the hair shaved off their heads, and the mourning is over. However the tears shed must be paid for with meat and the heir must give a banquet, which is sometimes a burden for him, taking as many as three oxen, and still the mourners are dissatisfied.

CHAPTER IX

A DINKA PRIEST WRITING ON HIS OWN PEOPLE

by Daniel Deng Farim Sorur

Fr. Daniel was the first of the Dinka nation to enter the Catholic priesthood. His was a remarkable career. While he was a boy in the country of the Bahr al-'Arab where the southern border of Kurdufān meets the province of the Bahr al-Ghazāl, he and his mother were caught by slave-hunters and brought to al-Ubayyid. There he was freed by Bishop Comboni who had him educated at the Khartoum Mission School and later, in 1876, at Verona. He completed his studies at the College of the Propaganda in Rome from 1877 to 1883. Between 1883 and 1886 he studied at Beirut where he taught French and Italian at Ghazir on the Lebanese coast between Beirut and Jibail. His academic career was consistently brilliant. In 1885 he was ordained priest in Cairo and after working four years at the Catholic School at Sawākin he toured Europe with Bishop F.X. Geyer collecting money for the Central African Missions.

Daniel Sorur was a competent linguist adding Italian and French to his native Dinka, and he had a fair mastery of literary Arabic. Never very robust he died in Hulwān (Helouan), a health resort near Cairo, in 1899. Of the many references to his life and work in the missionary literature of his days and since, the best short biography is 'Daniele Den Farim Sorur' in Alma Mater, Roma, Nos. 9-10, 1930, pp. 87-94. *The following passages, written in 1888, were taken from the author's manuscript notes in Italian preserved in the Archive of the Comboni Fathers in Rome. Some of these notes were translated into German as 'Daniel Sorur Pharim Den, Neger aus dem Stamme der Dinka', in* Bericht Negerkinder, Köln, 1887, pp. 17-97.

FROM THE NOTEBOOKS OF DANIEL SORUR

The Dinka or Gienghe

Dinka is a name, foreign to our language; and if it is in the Dinka vocabulary, then it can only be a corruption of Gien — Gienghe to Dgin — Dghinghe, which, for the sake of euphony, has been changed to Dinka, either by the natives themselves or by the Arabs.

According to all maps, it appears that the Dinka once occupied a very extensive area. The name Dinka is common to all the tribes included between 6° and 12° N., and between 26° and 34° W.; that is to say, from the Bari tribe to Bahr al-Dinka, near Dār Fāzūghlī in Sinnār, and from the River Chol Sobat to Dār Fertīt.

I have no proof by which I can establish the extension of the Dinka tribe along the right bank of the Nile. To my way of thinking, Chol or Yol is a Dinka name, and means 'tail' or 'extreme point'. This leads one to suppose that, in days gone by, the Dinkas were masters of this river, and to indicate the source of the Sobat tributary, they named it Chol or Yol Sobat.

The names *Alwal* and *Agot* are also Dinka, and thus it would appear that in past times the Dinka occupied the villages on the right bank of the Nile, as far as Bahr al-Dinka. I do not know if there are still tribes belonging to this race in these districts. Certainly the Dinka are the most numerous in number, and speak the same language in the whole of the Sudan, thus showing sign of having the same origin.

The disappearance of the Dinka from Sinnār, must be attributed either to their mixing with other races or because they were forced to retire before the continuous attacks from the Abyssinians, Kaffa, Galla, and Jallāba. [1]

All these people seem to recognise the Dinkas as brothers, despite the fact that they have adopted the Arab language instead of the Dinka, which at one time appears to have been the language of their country.

The name Dinka also applies to that south-western area which has as its neighbours the tribes of Dār Fertīt, and Dār Niam-Niam. It is certain that the Rek tribe is one of the Dinka tribes. The Dār Fertīt are not Dinka, and I cannot explain their presence in our terri-

---

[1] The name usually given to petty traders, pedlars, from the Northern Sudan. Here the writer seems to mean armed merchants who made raids on the Dinka.

tory, except by saying that it is probably due to some intrusion. Niam-Niam is a corruption of our word *cham* (to eat), and repeated as *cham-cham*, as is our way.

Both the Dār Fertīt and the Niam-Niam form different families to ours as regards their physical constitution and customs. They are rather small in build and sturdy. The Nuer and the Shilluk especially, do not like to be called Dinka, although their type, language and many customs show them as belonging to this race. Many times the Shilluk go to war with the Dinka, as in the time of Ismā'īl Pasha, when they joined forces with him to fight the Dinka inhabiting the right bank of the Nile, from Dār al-Funj to Sinnār.

Customs of the Dinka

The population generally follows pastoral pursuits and the cultivation of the soil. Young men look after the animals, that is the oxen, cows, goats, and sheep. When they are in the grass-lands their sisters or relatives prepare their food. The parents look after the cultivation in the fields. Cattle constitute the main source of wealth of the inhabitants.

Agricultural instruments and produce

The Dinka have primitive tools which they use in the cultivation of their soil. They are made either of iron or of bone, and shaped like a shovel, about 50 cm. long. As soon as the sowing season starts all the dried grass is gathered and burnt. After the first rain, the father, mother, sons and daughters, who are able to work, go to the field where they work on their knees. As soon as the ground is ready, sowing begins. Our grain is a kind of very hard buckwheat.* The soil is fertile and there is an abundant yield of maize, cotton, sugar-cane, ground nuts, sesame, bananas and beans.

We have some fruit-bearing trees: the tamarind, the *heglig*, [2] and a kind of tree whose fruit in time of famine, we dry and grind to make flour, from which a kind of bread is made. [3] This tree can be found between the Gienghe and Nuer tribes. Harvest is reaped twice yearly. The first cutting is made from the roots, which are left to provide fresh shoots. The second, takes place two months after the first, during the

---

* Perhaps *telabūn*.
[2] Arabic *hajlīja, Balanites aegyptiaca.*
[3] The nut of the dulayb palm.

period between the rains and summer. However, this harvest does not yield much, and the wealthier do it more to provide food for their cattle.

GOVERNMENT

There is no organized central government, but in each village certain people are elected by those who are mainly engaged in affairs concerning war. Otherwise everyone is his own master, and does what he likes with his goods. Sons are always subject to their parents until they marry, and if they do not marry they remain in the family.

CLOTHES

Generally men and boys go naked; married women wear two skins tied to their loins one hanging in the front, and one at the back. Girls are completely naked.

TRADE

As money is unknown all trade is carried on by barter.

HOUSES

The shape of the huts is round. They are made in the following way: a hole about half a metre in depth is dug: poles about two metres in length are stuck into the ground. These are plastered with a mixture of mud, hay or straw to make it more consistent. Planks are then placed on the poles forming a cone. All this is a man's job. Women do all the thatching. This is so nicely done that huts are waterproof. The door is about half a metre high and one must stoop to enter. The stall which shelters the cows, bulls and goats has a higher door, this being about one and a half metres in heights. The windows, if such they can be called, are the size of a baby's head. The Dinka have a lot of cattle and therefore require much pasturing ground. A large part of the population remain in the open country for most of the year, and do not return to their houses until the rains begin. Only the aged and very young are left behind in the villages.

BEDS

The women and those who sleep indoors make their beds on the ground. They lie on ox skins cut in half and well arranged. The men who look after the cattle lie on the ashes of the cow dung, which they first dry and then burn, to keep the insects away from the cattle.

MARRIAGE

As soon as the son or daughter has found his or her choice the parents are consulted. In the absence of parents the nearest relatives deal with the matter. As soon as an agreement is reached the wedding day is fixed, and religious ceremonies take place. On the day of the wedding the bridegroom must give the bride's parents and relatives ten cows and a bull; ten cows to the mother, five to each of the brothers of the bride; he must give beads to the sisters as well as rings of brass, copper, or other metal. The bride receives no dowry from the husband nor from her parents unless through inheritance in the event of their death. From this it can be understood that a poor man or woman, cannot marry a wealthier one. Polygamy is allowed among the Dinka, and it is very rare to find a wealthy man having only one wife. This multiplicity of wives and consequently of children does not deprive the first wife and her children from having the first place in the family. When the father is dead, one of his brothers or nearest relatives is obliged to take the widow as his wife; and if there are more than one, he must at least take the first, and give the others their freedom and goods, with which they can feed their children. As no authority exists to settle disputes, the strongest is always in the right. This also happens in other disputes, apart from matrimony.

It is the custom here that the young people cannot get married without the explicit consent of their parents or nearest relatives. When two young people want to get married, they must inform their parents of their intention to marry so-and-so. The parents on both sides, then go into the matter and, if they are in agreement, they fix the date for the marriage.

There is, of course, class distinction. Rich cannot marry poor, or vice versa. One is not allowed to marry outside the tribe, unless the stranger has settled in the village or is considered to be a citizen of it.

It often happens that the parents agree to a union of their children and, as a guarantee, each of the parents fixes a ring to the ear in the case of a son, or bracelet in the case of a daughter; this was done to me and to my eldest sister. These promises are generally kept, and the father who breaks his word is considered to be unfaithful.

Despite the custom of asking the parents' consent it often happens that young men, spurred on by love, marry against the wishes of their parents.

Marriages between near blood-relations are prohibited. I have never heard of nephews or cousins being united in marriage.

DIGNITY OF THE DINKA WOMEN

I have often heard it said that negroes do not believe that their women have immortal souls, and therefore the men merely make use of them on a purely material basis. This is not true with us Dinka. It is true that we do not leave the women idle and often it is they who take on the heaviest tasks. But considering their public prayers, the religious ceremonies they hold in families in the absence of the father, and the sacrifices they make after his death, such an assertion is untrue. The father is the head of the family, then comes the mother. The women look after the welfare of the family and enjoy the esteem of their husbands. Their authority over the children is respected.

CIRCUMCISION

Circumcision is practised for the male sex only. I do not know in what circumstances it was introduced. I believe it was done because it was thought to be a sign of progress. There is no fixed period as with the Arabs who perform it between the ages of five and ten. There are no people who specialise in it. Generally it is the father. Among the Dinka circumcision can take place at any age, and is not accompanied by a religious ceremony. I have known young men of eighteen and twenty, and fathers of children, to be circumcised. [*]

TATTOOING

Tattooing is not practised by us, but the four incisor teeth of the lower jaw are removed from the children as soon as they are ten or eleven; perhaps to give them a better chance of pronouncing the language.

BURIAL OF THE PARENTS

The burial of parents is the duty of the eldest son. When the father or the mother dies, he chooses a spot near the parental home. Here a grave is dug. All the nearest relations are invited to weep for the deceased. Before laying the body to rest, the hair is shaved off, the body is washed,

---

[*] We are informed that circumcision is now practised only by the Rek, Malual and Ngok of Kurdufān, possibly under Muslim influence. Among the other Dinka listed on pp. 134-5 above, circumcision is a social disability and is never practised.

covered in cloth, and generally placed in the grave in a sitting position. After three days of mourning, a lamb is let loose to be devoured by the wild beasts. This sacrifice is made so that the evil spirit (*jiong-dit*) does not take the soul of the deceased to the house of fire (*pan de mac*). All the relatives also shave off their hair.

CARE OF THE SNAKE

Among the Gienghes the python, is not feared and, although not worshipped, is held in respect. Generally it is to be found near the dwelling-places, hidden under the straw or among the canes. The fact that they are such quiet neighbours seems to have earned them this attention, and each family always prepares a little grain, seasoned with butter, placing it at the spot where the python usually appears.

THE SACRED COW

Among the objects worshipped is the sacred cow. This is solely reserved for sacrifices or public prayers, which take place during times of disaster such as famine or war. These sacrifices and public prayers are reserved for the women, who must not drink the milk or eat the flesh of these cows. Nearly every family has a sacred cow. When disaster befalls the country, all the women meet and the chief hands over one of the sacred cows. The women lead it to the river, and together sing '*Yen dig ayan wir o yen dig ayan pan de kir*' ('I am leading the heifer to the river, I am leading the heifer to the land of the rivers', etc.). I do not remember the rest. This chorus is sung after each stanza, which is sung by some of the women as they push the cow towards the banks of the river. As soon as the cow is in the water, the women silently return to their homes without looking back. Often the cow returns to its herd and this is a sign of great calamity and the ceremony is repeated until the cow does not return. At another time it is a bull — sacred, because born of a sacred cow — which is offered in sacrifice to placate an evil.

I well remember having watched similar ceremonies during my childhood. For some time, smallpox had been rampant among us. The greater part of the people had crossed the river with their animals in search of pasture ground. The disease continued to spread. Many sacrifices and prayers had been offered but without effect. Then, one day, a man who said he was a compatriot of ours presented himself to the chief and asked leave to speak to the people. This was granted. At about nine o'clock, all of us in Wen de Meren gathered in the courtyard of the chief. The mysterious man appeared with his eyes blindfolded, and spoke at length through the medium of an interpreter. The gist of his speech was to persuade us to do what he said if we were to be freed from the curse of this disease. We listened to the speech with great attention. The suggested remedy was that all the men, boys and girls, women and children, should run after the bull pushing him forward, and going once round the *zarïba*. As soon as the speech was over, all the people careered madly, according to the prescribed instructions. The first who were able to follow the bull at close quarters and return to their point of departure, would infallibly be cured of the disease. Those who lagged behind had to resign themselves to a miserable death from smallpox. When the chase was over and everybody had returned the animal was killed and burnt on the spot. The mysterious man disappeared with his interpreter but the smallpox remained.

Every man who has a sacred ox is held in esteem. In the evenings after supper, the man takes his ox round the *zariba*, singing its praises, that of his forefathers, or the beauty of his ox. More praise is sung if the ox bellows during the song.

BLESSING OF THE FRUIT

Among the religious ceremonies I remember, there is the blessing of the new fruit. No one of the family, including the children, must taste the new fruit until the father, or the mother in his absence, has scattered some round the courtyard, asking the blessing and protection of *Deng dit* or *Goran* (God) on all the family.

THE BLUE NILE

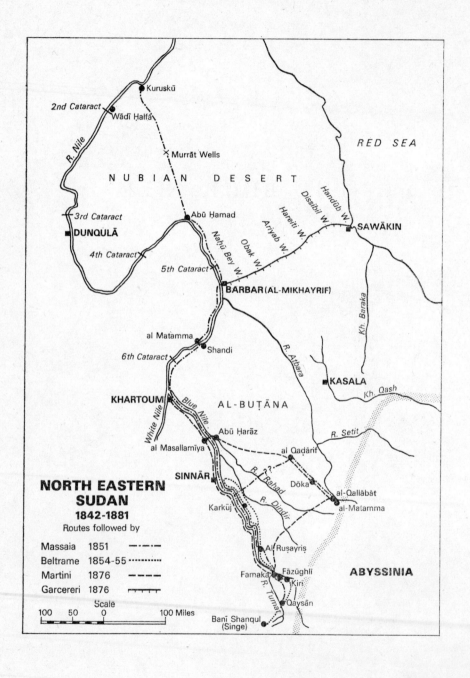

RED SEA

Kurusku

2nd Cataract
Wādī Ḥalfā

Murrāt Wells

N U B I A N   D E S E R T

Ḥandūb W.
Dissibil W.
Hareiti W.
Ariyab W.
Obak W.

SAWĀKIN

3rd Cataract

DUNQULĀ

4th Cataract

Naḥū Bey W.

5th Cataract

BARBAR (AL-MIKHAYRIF)

R. Atbara

Kh. Baraka

al Matamma

Shandi

6th Cataract

KASALA

Kh. Qash

KHARTOUM

White Nile

Blue Nile

AL-BUṬĀNA

R. Setit

Abū Ḥarāz

al Masallamīya

al Qadārif

SINNĀR

R. ? ?

Dōka

al-Qallābāt

R. Raḥad

al-Matamma

Karkūj

R. Dindir

NORTH EASTERN SUDAN
1842-1881
Routes followed by

Massaia	1851	—·—·—
Beltrame	1854-55	··········
Martini	1876	– – –
Garcereri	1876	⊢⊢⊢⊢⊢

Al Ruṣayriṣ

Famaka

Fāzūghlī

Kiri

ABYSSINIA

R. Tumat

Qaysān

Scale
100   50   0   100 Miles

Banī Shanqul
(Singe)

CHAPTER X

KHARTOUM TO THE GOLD WORKINGS
OF FAZUGHLI, 1851

by L.G. Massaia

In Chapter V Mgr. Massaia was at Khartoum reporting the local information on the White Nile in the course of his journey to Ethiopia. Now he continues his way from Khartoum up the Blue Nile valley with the intention, or at least the hope, of penetrating to the Galla country through the Banī Shanqūl. Defeated in this he succeeded in entering Ethiopia by the trade road through al-Qallābāt. The narrative of his itinerary in this region is of interest because he is an important witness of the condition of the government gold-extracting enterprise at Qaysān after the departure of the Russian mining engineer, E.P. Kovalevski, who had examined the workings and made recommendations for their improved exploitation three years before. Massaia's impressions should be compared with those of the French architect P. Trémaux who accompanied Kovalevski to the goldfield. Massaia was no mining engineer but a practical observer who quickly recognized maladministration when he saw it. This short passage is extracted from the writer's reminiscences, I miei trentacinque anni di missione nell'Alta Etiopia, Roma, 1885, II, pp. 77-100; 104.

Now and again, as we continued our journey, we passed by large and small villages, on both sides of the river; some were deserted, and others had only a small population. Many of the inhabitants abandoned these villages, fleeing from the pillaging of Egyptian soldiers when, at the time of the conquest, they lost their independence and liberty. This long stretch of the Nile is, undoubtedly, the most tedious and also, the most dangerous, part of the journey, tedious on account of the many turns of the river, to the east, north and south. Not only is the distance

immeasurably lengthened by such tortuous winding, but also the traveller
is prevented from taking advantage of the north wind, so that a journey
of only a few kilometres, as the crow flies, and which could be done in
half a day, is prolonged for several days. Dangerous, because one is
forced to fight continually, the innumerable crocodiles and hippopota-
muses, that infest these waters. Also one has to be on the look-out all
the time for the reefs, against which the boat is often dashed, compelling
us frequently to pass the night, either near to the shore, or on a sand-
bank in the middle of the river. Thus, it took us twelve days to reach
al-Rusayris, a small town situated on the right bank of the Nile.
Standing on picturesque hills, thickly covered with palm trees, which
obscure the view of the city, are scattered groups of huts, five or six
in number, enclosed by rushes. Here there is a cataract, which the
boats can pass only with great difficulty during the months of the crest
of the flood. At this point, my boatmen stopped; they to return to
Khartoum, while I stayed on for some days looking for a camel with
which to continue my journey on land.

Some miles away, on the opposite bank to al-Rusayris, is a large
market village to which come the natives of the Dinka and Tabi mountains [Ingassana]. From what I heard, this market was very much
frequented, especially by the independent and warlike population of
Tabi, whom the Egyptian Government had been unable to subdue, and
with whom they were continually at war. . . .

Having procured the camels, I left al-Rusayris for Famaka, in
company with some merchants from Khartoum carrying grain and rice,
and other merchants from al-Qadārif, with coffee and salt. On the first
day, we passed through forests of extraordinarily large ebony trees, and
further along came across the most beautiful which, however, had been
spoiled by travellers, who had cut pieces from them. Other trees were
already cut into lengths, awaiting transport to al-Rusayris and thence
to Khartoum and Egypt. In the evening, with the forest behind us, we
stopped near a rivulet whose spring was at a nearby village, abandoned
on account of robberies by the troops. We had intended to spend the
night in these huts, but finding them full of snakes and horrible insects,
we kept away. Thus, we were forced to sleep in the open, and finding
some dry spots free from grass and bushes, we laid our skin
mats.

In these hot places, one cannot sleep in safety where there is grass
and bushes, for the snakes and scorpions nestle everywhere amongst it,
and are especially dangerous at night. One frequently comes across
snakes, such as the boa and the asp. The first is about two metres in

length, is as thick as a human arm, but is not as deadly as the asp. Nevertheless, both are to be avoided. That night, I became very much aware of the harm done by white ants. These insects, which are extremely numerous, infest these hot and arid soils remaining hidden under the earth, and only emerge from their holes at night in search of food.

That night after the evening dew had fallen I spread out my skin mat, and settled down to sleep under the light of those magnificent stars. Being extremely tired, I soon fell asleep, and for half the night I slept deeply. But when I awoke, with bites and stings all over my body, I felt such a burning sensation that I thought I was amongst thorns, which almost made me mad with pain. As it was pitch-dark I lit a match and saw, to my great surprise, an army of white ants furiously assailing me from all sides, so that my skin was riddled like a sieve. I awoke my companions, and even with their help it was with great difficulty that I could get rid of those loathsome insects creeping about my body. While this was happening I noticed that they did not go near my companions at all, and so I asked them the reason for this. I was told that their skins had been sprinkled with a certain oil, from which the ants run away, and that the skins were spread out before the dew fell, and not after, as I had done. Placing it on dry ground keeps the ants away, as they prefer damp places.

In the morning we continued our journey towards Famaka following a path winding up and down, over hills, valleys, shallow and rushing streams, dotted here and there with rocks, stones and brambles, making the crossings very tiring for me, as well as for the animals. Finally, we again came to the Nile, which we had left at Rusayris, and then to Famaka. At this point the river makes a curve from west to east, opening out from a valley between two small hills and flowing between two rocks very near to each other, forcing the camels to cross it lower down, while we passed through in a boat. Continuing together again, we ascended to the villages of Famaka, whose huts scattered here and there, presented a pleasant panorama. Here, before the war with Turkey, Muhammad 'Alī had built a beautiful little place, to be used as a refuge should he have been defeated and forced to leave Egypt. It stood on a small hillock, overlooking the Nile and surrounded by charming gardens. It was never inhabited, and began to decay before it was completed.

We stayed the night at Famaka, and early next morning resumed our journey. In a short time we arrived at the small town of Kiri, the chief town of the Fāzūghlī Province. This place, built by Muhammad 'Alī, might be better termed a military headquarters. The inhabitants numbered scarcely a thousand in addition to the garrison, and were mostly slaves and prostitutes. I had no doubt that I would receive a favourable reception in view of the recommendations I had brought from Cairo. I was, in fact, received with every possible courtesy by the commander, who offered me the hospitality of his house which had a small enclosure where the master spent a few hours of the day, and also a large hall, used as a parlour for eating and sleeping. In the evening, after a delicious supper, we had a long conversation. At bedtime, the master summoned a page to undress him, and to keep him company during the night. The young page helped him to undress, then sat down at his feet and, to induce him to sleep, began to tickle them. A page was also put at my disposal, and for the two other officers sleeping there, but I declined his assistance, so he went off to my servant. This custom is considered an act of courtesy in these places.

My aim in going to Fāzūghlī was to ascertain whether there was a direct route to the Galla regions without having to pass through Ethiopia. Therefore, as soon as I arrived, I sought all the information I could on the matter. From Kiri, standing on the western bank of the Blue Nile, the Galla regions to the east were pointed out to me. These regions were, according to some people, a distance of some five or six days' journey over dangerous and impracticable roads. According to my calculations those were not the Galla regions but those of the Goggiam, which I knew well. Living at Kiri was a septuagenarian who had been an orderly to Muhammad 'Alī Pasha, and afterwards an officer under the command of Ibrāhīm Pasha. He had fought in the Syrian war but owing to his advanced age was retired and put in charge of the old arsenal at Fāzūghlī, established also by Muhammad 'Alī. This old Muslim, who spoke Italian well, passed a considerable part of the day in my company. He had been in Ethiopia twice as ambassador of the Egyptian government at the court of Rās 'Alī. [1] Thus knowing the place, he advised me to take the northward road which would have brought me to Lake Tana, and thence to Galla. Although this was an easy journey and free from dangers, it was, nevertheless, unsuitable for me. By entering Ethiopia, I would have infallibly exposed myself again to the old persecutions of Salāma, [2] without the hope, perhaps, of getting into Galla. My intention of going beyond the Egyptian border was, the old officer thought, only a sham, for he believed me to be a secret spy

---

[1] A Galla magnate from Begemder who was dispossessed by the future Emperor Theodore II in 1853.

[2] The same archbishop of the Ethiopian Orthodox Church who drove Fr. Luigi Montuori to seek refuge in the Sudan.

of some government. Nevertheless, he told me I could reach Fadasi, whose market was frequented by numerous Galla merchants, in half a day by going through Qaysān. From there I could get to these regions in the company of Galla merchants. According to other merchants coming from al-Qadārif to sell salt and coffee, I could go direct to the Galla country, by way of al-Matamma with the caravans of Dunkur, going round Abyssinia.

Being unfamiliar with these places and people, and being confronted with all these differing opinions, I was undecided as to the route to follow. Finally, I decided to go via Qaysān, being the shortest and most direct road to the country which I much desired to visit, which for six years had been the object of my anxiety and labour, and from which I was kept away by the wickedness of men. I thought the best way was to join a company of soldiers who, every week, travelled between Kiri and Qaysān as escort for the mail to and from the gold workings of Qaysān. I asked the commander for his consent and to supply the necessary animals. My request was granted, and after taking the usual tamarind decoction and quinine, I prepared to start.

On account of the frequent ambushes, laid by the indomitable Tabi population, on the Turkish and Egyptian caravans, the three-day journey from Kiri to Qaysān is very dangerous. Leaving Kiri, a group of mountains to the west comes into view and rises majestically over the great Dinka plains. From these mountains come these warlike natives, the terror of Egyptian soldiers. I had been informed that the whole group of mountains was thickly populated by robust and audacious people who were subject to a petty king. In addition, some neighbouring villages of the Dinka were also subject to him and paid him a tax. All the mountain-dwellers speak a curious dialect, which bears considerable resemblance to the Dinka language. They cultivate the land and breed cattle. The climate is very healthy, but higher up, I was told, it is very cold. For this reason the inhabitants cover themselves with very heavy clothes which are both strong and durable. Before the Egyptian domination of these parts, the Tabi maintained friendly relations with their neighbours (there were families at Fāzūghlī who were also related to the Tabi) but after the Egyptian invasion, relations between the inhabitants and strangers were broken off, and in the protection of their mountains they preserved their own independence, waging furious war against the invaders. Many, also from the Fāzūghlī region retreated to those impregnable fortresses, to enjoy that freedom and independence, of which others wanted to deprive them. Their united force cost the Muslims very dear in their thirst for domination, slaves and money. At first, being without firearms, they were afraid to descend the heights. Later they obtained firearms from the Egyptian soldiers themselves, who sometimes, in order o obtain their freedom, climbed the heights with their military equipment. The tribesmen obtained a further supply by continual ambushes on the enemy. By these means they became very strong and fierce, to such an extent that whereas previous fifty soldiers had been adequate escort for the caravans plying between Kiri and Qaysān, afterwards not even 100 were sufficient.

The soldiers and caravans being ready, we started off after shaking hands with the commander who paid me so much respect and gave me so many favours. We travelled the whole day without incident, but towards evening we began to see human bones scattered here and there along the road; this made the soldiers march more cautiously. At dusk we halted in an open place to pass the night, not daring to travel in the darkness, fearing some surprise from those audacious people of Tabi. The soldiers made a circle around the women and children for protection, while I placed my tent near the leader of the company.

As we continued on our way we saw skeletons and human bones in great number. The soldiers, I was surprised to see, could clearly distinguish the skulls of Egyptians from those of the Tabi. On examination, I found that the occipital development of the latter was larger than that of the former. At some distance from the road, we saw a great number of elephants which alone, or in separate herds, grazed on the plains. Not a tree was left untouched; they were all either broken or beaten to the ground by those giants who feed on their foliage. Going along, the soldiers fired now and again into the air, and on seeing this I asked why they did not direct their shots towards the elephants to better advantage. They replied that it was not prudent to irritate them, otherwise they might attack us and make it difficult for the caravans to pass that way in future. So they continually fired into the air to keep them away, and also to frighten the Tabi.

As we continued, the Tabi mountains appeared more clearly towards the north-west. About noon next day we came to a small stream, and here we stopped for dinner. Someone pointed out to me a heap of human bones lying some distance away; they were those of a company of soldiers who had been ambushed and cut to pieces by a band of Tabi five years previously. After dinner, we resumed our way, but those cowardly soldiers proceeded with such fear and trembling as to invoke within me a feeling of both compassion and anger at the same time. By the evening we had left those mountains so far behind that a sudden surprise attack was thought improbable. So the soldiers, now fearless, began to sing and dance. . . .

To revert to my journey: We left in the early morning and arrived at Qaysān before noon. This town is situated on the southern slope of a hill, surrounded by high mountains and close to the right bank of the Tumat, a river flowing into the Blue Nile near Famaka. I was immediately introduced to the garrison commander who invited me to stay in his house, come what may, although I constantly urged him to find me another house so as not to inconvenience him, and also to leave me more freedom for my affairs. Later I was visited by the director-general of the mines, Muhammad Efendī, and one of the companions of the Bey with whom I had become acquainted at Khartoum. He had already received letters of recommendation concerning myself from his old colleague, and did his utmost to keep me in his house. As he had a European education and was still following its manners and ways, I should undoubtedly have had more freedom and hospitality. But the commander, an Albanian, who was very fond of foreigners, would not give in, but promised me a separate room in which to sleep and attend to my business, on condition that I dined with him. I was visited also by all the officers of the fortress and by all the employees of the mines.

Qaysān owes its importance to the gold mines which were discovered, or rather developed, by Muhammad 'Alī. [8] In addition, there was the mines administration consisting of eight senior officers, three of whom directed and supervised the works on the river Tumat where the sand was purified for the extraction of gold. The others supervised the excavations of the gold mines nearby, as well as about 100 miners working under them. The Administrations' accounts were sent to Cairo by a director-general at certain times, after having been checked by a superintendent living at Qaysān. Furthermore, a special administration dealt with the purchase of gold from the natives and its exchange on behalf of the government principally for glass beads and other goods of equal value.

As I still remained incognito, the people were convinced that I was on some secret government mission. As a result, there was a continual flow of senior and junior officials, with information to which

[8] Government forces made a first reconnaissance to the gold-bearing sands in the Tumat valley in 1821. An Austrian mineralogist, Joseph von Russegger, visited the site in 1838 and a Russian mining engineer, E.P. Kovalevski, explored the region in 1847 and set up sand-washing plant. This 'Klondyke' episode in Sudanese history attracted no gold rush but gave rise to much writing.

I was an unwilling confidant; so much so that there was not a single intrigue or swindle in that administration that was not brought to my knowledge. In view of the small profit derived by the administration, the Egyptian government wrote angry letters to the management threatening the closure of the mines and the recall of all employees. The output was, in fact, not sufficient to cover the expenses of the garrison or the labour. On its part, the management excused itself by asserting that the existing workings were almost exhausted and that very little gold was obtained from the sand. Fearing, however, that the government would definitely decide to close them, a proposal that the garrison should be augmented with 200 additional soldiers was made. The intention was to advance into the interior to discover new mines, thus yielding a greater profit for the administration.

As I have already said, I was all against being drawn into similar questions and quarrels; but it was no use. Consequently, I was obliged to see all and hear all. I was brought forcibly to the mines and shown in great detail the excavations and machinery on the river Tumat. In view of what I saw and heard, the government had every reason to be dissatisfied. To tell the truth, the administration cared more for its own interest than for that of the government by whom they were paid. The profit from the mines went into the pockets of its administrators instead of to the government. Still under the impression that I was some authority of the Egyptian government, they offered me gold in the hope of persuading me to sign certain acts and accounts with which to justify themselves. I refused to do so, telling them that I did not want to be involved in their affairs.

Thirty years have elapsed since I visited those mines, and twenty since they were closed by order of 'Abbās Pasha, so I can now say something regarding them. Muhammad 'Alī was a great and tactful man, able to undertake such operations, organise administrations and select the right people to run them. Thus he was confident that all would progress smoothly. In fact, he drew millions of piastres annually from the principal mine. This mine consisted of a small isolated mountain, round and treeless. In addition to the excavation of the usual gold-dust, nuggets of pure gold were found. The mountain had been almost entirely worked out when I saw it, yielding only some pieces of quartz mixed with yellow sand. One million [piastres] were obtained in the beginning from the river Tumat installations where the sand was purified by machinery. At the time of my visit I am sure that it yielded a profit no smaller than the above. Moreover, the gold exchanged for glass beads and other goods from Sinnār and elsewhere could be calculated at more than 1,000 pounds, even in the last years of Muhammad 'Alī.

In 1855, at Gudru, I had the opportunity of seeing the quantity of this precious metal which came from those countries. In fact, several thousands of pounds were paid yearly into the market of Asandabo, and an even greater amount was brought to Goggiam and al-Matamma by those people not desiring to enter the Galla regions. I came to know that the metal was collected by the people of Fāzūghlī, Qaysān and Galla countries without much labour or industry. All that was required was to purify the sand brought by the floods and heavy rains in that extensive territory between the Galla regions and Qaysān, a distance of less than a geographical degree, in a direct line. Any government judiciously using scientific and appropriate machines, as did Muhammad 'Alī, would have found great wealth in that rich soil, as was shown by the gold uncovered by mere superficial washing.

The works at Qaysān went on for some years longer, but finally the Viceroy 'Abbās Pasha, seeing that the profit did not cover the expenses, closed them down and recalled the administration. The government certainly had reason for this step because, as I said, the superiors and those working under them looked after their own interests, and not those of the government. Whereas if they had conscientiously done their duty, the yield would not have failed, as the fields were rich with gold. Instead, what happened? The miners passed the long days either in idleness, or occupied in cultivating the gardens for their superiors on the river Tumat, or even gathering wood for their families and grass for their cattle. The senior officials, instead of concerning themselves with their office business, spent the time amusing themselves, and molesting the neighbouring peoples. Had they honestly handed over to the government even the small profit they could have made, undoubtedly the result would have been different. Also the buying and selling with the natives had almost come to an end. Instead of attracting them with good manners they oppressed them to such an extent that they preferred to trade elsewhere.

In 1879, when I was banished from Abyssinia by Emperor John, I came to al-Matamma where I met an old man, a former pupil of Clot Bey,[4] who had been a doctor at Qaysān. Speaking to me about the mines, the old man regretted their closing for the simple reason that,

[4] A.B. Clot Bey (1796-1868), a French physician who went to Egypt in 1825 and for many years was responsible for the medical training of Egyptians. He has been called, not without reason, the founder of modern medicine in Egypt.

without even having been involved in the affair, he had himself gained half a million, simply for keeping silence on the misdeeds of the employees. For all these undoubtedly reasonable motives, the Egyptian government abandoned the enterprise, which had prospered so much under Muhammad 'Alī, and which could still have continued to earn a good profit, had it been managed by an active and honest administration. In my opinion, its closure was a mistake. Had that dishonest management been dismissed and the business placed in the hands of honourable persons, it would have continued to prosper. Even supposing that the government did not want any further responsibility in the matter, it could have conceded it to some private company to their mutual advantage instead of winding it up. But it is always the case with weak governments, afraid of everything, and 'Abbās Pasha was not Muhammad 'Alī.

Since my arrival in Qaysān, my thoughts were occupied more with the continuation of my journey to the Galla regions, than with the mines. The director-general thoroughly disapproved of my desire to go to Fadasi. 'There would have been no difficulty', he said, 'if you had come some time ago, but now it is impossible. Only two days ago, two Egyptian merchants were murdered in that market. As a result of this there is a kind of war between us and those people. If you go there, you do so at the risk of your life and we do not want to be responsible to the government, if anything should happen to you. Instead', he added, 'so that you can hear all the news and information we will assemble here all the people you desire to question.' The director's apprehension was fully justified, for not even the Khartoum merchants who came with me from Fāzūghlī had the courage to go there after the murders, preferring to wait at Qaysān for traders from the south to come and exchange their goods.

These southern traders, bringing gold, musk and other goods for sale and exchange to the Khartoum merchants, were not strictly, from the Galla regions, but from Fāzūghlī, living at Fadasi in order to trade with the Galla. Consequently, the news I would have received from them would only have been vague and indirect. They told me that a caravan would take seven or eight days to go from Fadasi to the Galla boundary where the Galla brought their merchandise. I questioned two Galla about their country, and was told that it was not too far. One of them came from Baccare [Baccara] and the other from Nonno [Nono], places I had come to know by correspondence when in Goggiam. From them and from other information received, two contrasting conclusions emerged: the first, favourable, indicated that the Galla regions, where

I desired to go, were not very far from Qaysān, Baccara and Nono; the second, unfavourable, showed that the Galla did not allow the merchants coming from Turkish or Egyptian countries to cross their borders. Other black tribes dwelling beyond Fadasi, as well as the Galla, would not permit any white man, believed to be a Turk, to cross into their country. The murder of the two merchants at Fadasi market was not, in fact, committed by the inhabitants of that place but by people of the district who had come to the market.

If I was determined to go to Fadasi at any cost, the commander and director offered me an escort of 100 soldiers. 'But we assure you', they said, 'that all will run away on your arrival, with their slaves and merchandise for fear of reprisals, except perhaps for a few inhabitants of the place who are on good terms with us. They are afraid that we are going to take revenge for the crime.' These proposals were made by the two gentlemen who anxiously wished to avoid the onus of responsibility in the event of anything happening to me. Believing me to be a spy, perhaps in their hearts they wished I had gone to those parts, caring very little for my fate. Who knows but they would have felt great satisfaction had some accident befallen me, in view of what I had learnt of their swindlings.

I resolved, finally, to return to Kiri, seeing that so many obstacles prevented me from entering the Galla country via Fadasi. There I would make new decisions. This conclusion caused some consternation among those people, who held a meeting, and with the intention of securing my friendship still more, they confidentially offered me some presents. Thus they would have been sure that I would not have revealed their secrets which would certainly have exposed them to severe punishment from the government. This unexpected generosity put me in a great quandary, for if I accepted their gifts it would appear that I was in collusion with them and their robberies, or at least outwardly condoning their misdeeds, a dishonourable action which was against my conscience. On the other hand, if I refused them I would have been under even greater suspicion, and as I was returning to Kiri, it would have been quite easy for them to have tricked me, even trying to avoid responsibility, to the government. These people are masters in that art!

I thought of revealing my identity, showing them that I was a missionary, in order to convince them that they had nothing to fear from me, and how wrong they were in assuming I was a spy. But this revelation exposed me to many and grievous difficulties. Indeed, there were some merchants from al-Qadārif and al-Matamma at Qaysān who, had they learnt of my identity, would have undoubtedly spread the news that I was to re-enter Abyssinia, and thus the Coptic party would have been up in arms, and recommenced the persecution.

When the day came for my caravan to start, all of them came to accompany me for a part of the way, giving me most profuse demonstrations of homage and friendship. The next day we travelled in great haste in order to avoid the danger of being caught by the Tabi; only at noon did we stop for half an hour for some food, then resumed our march immediately so that we would arrive before evening at the place where we rested on the previous journey. In the evening, the soldiers, tired already by the forced march of the day, and more so by the drunken orgies of the previous night, ate some bread and went to sleep. In the morning it was a real business to wake them! Finally, before sunrise, we resumed our journey and arrived at Kiri at 2 o'clock in the afternoon.

On that journey I dressed in the guise of an Arab clerk, and had my beard shortened so as to be unrecognisable by anyone in Ethiopia who might have seen me before.

It is impossible to make an exact and detailed description of the places I passed through and that long journey. I remember, only, that always following a north-easterly direction, I arrived at al-Qadārif for Doka, then the last military station on the Egyptian frontier and, like Kiri, the residence of a commandant. He received me in his house with great kindness and politeness. Much against my will I was obliged to remain there for a few days to look for other camel-drivers, as the others who had accompanied me this far dared not go beyond the Egyptian border. I was assured by some merchants whom I met there, that I could have entered the Galla region via Dunkur, by travelling from al-Matamma with the Lukha merchants, skirting the Ethiopian borders. They warned me, however, that it would be necessary for me to go dressed as an Arab merchant, and not as a European traveller, as Europeans were not welcomed by those people. This was no trouble to me, as I was willing to go dressed even as a beggar, provided I could attain my goal of entering my Mission. I followed this advice and left for al-Matamma, arriving there three days later.

CHAPTER XI

UP THE BLUE NILE VALLEY FROM SINNAR TO BANI SHANQUL AND BACK, 1854-1855

by Giovanni Beltrame

This chapter is of interest to the student of Islamic heterodoxy in that it contains the first detailed recorded account by a European of the people of Abū Jarīd, a small community who live in the country on the right bank of the Blue Nile between Karkūj and al-Rusayris.

Shaykh Abū Jarīd, a late seventeenth-century sūfī teacher, is briefly mentioned in the Tabaqāt of Muhammad al-Nūr b. Dayf Allāh, a biographical collection in Arabic of Muslim saints and men of learning and letters written about 1800. [1] *The merit of Beltrame's account is not that it is accurate in every doctrinal detail but that it is original. What was known of the People of Abū Jarīd before Beltrame was hearsay. Even so intelligent a man as the trader J.A. Vayssière could jot down a reminder in his notebook: 'To find out the name of a tribe originating in the Sudan (from Dar Dongola, I believe) which now lives near al-Qallābāt on the Abyssinian border. This tribe denies everything that Islam stands for except for the name, curses the Prophet, deeply reveres Ayesha, has all property — as well as women — in common, and subjects candidates for admission to the tribe to long and searching tests.'* [2]

This garbled account of the People of Abū Jarīd — if in fact Vayssière was referring to them — is far different from the version which Beltrame has presented to us. In a sympathetic and sensitive paper by S. Hillelson written forty years later, the People of Abū Jarīd are described as an extreme wing of Sūfism who venerate the palm

---

[1] *Kitāb al-tabaqāt,* ed. Y.F. Hasan, Khartoum, 1971, p. 162, 162n.6.

[2] J.A. Vayssière, Notebook, f.2v, Paris, Société de Géographie, Ms. 8° 23.

tree and regard Shaykh Abū Jarīd as interchangeable with the Prophet.[3]

The following extracts come from the author's book Il Sennar e lo Sciangallah, *Verona/Padua, 1879. I. pp. 142-93; 197-9; 255-97: II. pp. 31-39 (extracts).*

The kingdom of Sinnār once consisted of the greater part of the country bounded by the White Nile and the Blue Nile. Now, it is divided into two parts, the northern part which forms the Khartoum district, whilst the southern part is known to the Turks under the name of Sinnār. The town of Sinnār, which has between ten and twelve thousand inhabitants, is the capital of this province. The language spoken is Arabic, and the dominant religion is Islam.

The climate of Sinnār is hot and unhealthy, but less so than that of Khartoum district. The rainy season starts at the beginning of May and sometimes lasts until October. November and December are the months of the harvest, especially of wheat and *durra,* and the inhabitants of the Khartoum district come to make their purchases as the prices are low. The people of Sinnār are exposed to numerous fevers and other illnesses, attributed to the unhealthy miasma in the air arising from decaying matter and from the marshes and pools caused by the flooding of the Blue Nile.

For six or seven months of the year, Sinnār presents a grim picture of barrenness but, as soon as the rainy season starts, the scene changes entirely: one or two heavy rains are sufficient to produce a complete change with the ground covered with vegetation. The soil is fertile. The inhabitants of Sinnār cultivate only a very small portion of their land: the harvest is sufficient to provide the country for at least three years. The principal products are: *durra,* wheat, maize, beans, lentils and tobacco. In the plains, watered by the Dindir, the finest quality cotton and sesame are easily grown. The gardens, irrigated daily by the water from the river, produce pomegranates, oranges, lemons and figs either in flower or fruit practically all the year round. The people

---

[3] 'The People of Abu Jarid', Khartoum, *Sudan Notes and Records,* I, 1918, pp. 175-93. The sect also roused the interest of two officials who served the former Egyptian Government, Emin Pasha (his unpublished diary cited in *Der Islam,* IV, 18, p. 160, entry dated 4 October 1881, and Na'um Bey Shuqayyir (*Ta'rīkh al-Sūdān,* 1902, I, p. 57).

of Sinnār who live along the banks of the river are mainly engaged in agriculture but their methods are primitive.

There are great forests stretching mainly along the right bank of the river. They abound in buffaloes, elephants, leopards, giraffes, rhinoceroses, foxes, monkeys, wild cats, ostriches, gazelles, and antelopes. Reptiles are very numerous.

The inhabitants of Sinnār are of regular features, medium height, slim build, and with a phlegmatic temperament; one seldom comes across a hunchback, a lame person or a dwarf. This is due, in some respects, to the healthy way in which they bring up their children. Very soon after birth the mothers expose them to light and air. They wash them frequently, taking hold of them by a foot and plunging them head first into the river. They let them crawl freely on the ground even when they are very small, and it is only when they see that they begin to get sleepy that they put them into a goat or sheep-skin, folded over and suspended by two ropes from the walls of the hut, or from a tree.

When a mother has to take the baby out with her, if he is still of a very tender age, she bundles it into the same skin and hangs it round her neck in such a way that it rests on her back like a knapsack. When the child is a little older, the mother carries it on one of her shoulders and it steadies itself by holding on to its mother's head with both hands. With such care the children grow up vigorous and robust.

In December 1854, while I was in the town of Sinnār, I twice saw the ceremony of circumcision. At the head of a long procession, there were four sturdy young men, each mounted on a handsome steed and holding four long whips made of hippopotamus skin. Two by two they lashed each other, bare-skinned, to see who could endure it longest, until they were torn and bleeding, while the curious crowd kept shouting: 'hurrah, long live the friend of the girls!' (*akhū al-banāt*). Behind these youths followed eight camels adorned with green garlands, multi-coloured cloths and rattles. On the camels were seated the brothers and friends of the youth who was to be circumcised; then there was a motley company of drummers, fife and cymbal players; then there followed the dancers and several girls beautifully dressed and carrying small vases on their heads, from which arose fragrant perfumes. In the midst of the girls were two young boys, mounted on horseback, covered with leaves and ribbons, through which it was just possible to see their brown faces. It was a scene not lacking in beauty.

I saw also the ceremony of a new bride being carried in triumph by her parents and friends to the house of her future husband. The procession which precedes the fiancée is similar to the one for a circumcision; here, however, the bride does not sit on a camel or horse, but walks very proudly and sedately, wrapped in white, all perfumed, with a crown of green leaves on her head, her nails tinted, her lips and eyebrows blue, under a canopy, held up by four or six of her girl friends. A girl walks backwards in front of her, fanning her face with ostrich feathers. Another girl follows holding a wooden stool upon which the bride sits every now and then to rest. Then the dancers gathered around her hop and skip to the sound of the *darabukka*[4] and castanets, and praise her beauty in song. Now and again these praises are interrupted by impatient gestures from the friends of the groom. Once the bride reaches the house of the groom, she enters alone and two sturdy youths with whips in their hands zealously stand guard over the door to stop anyone attempting to enter. Even the groom, who is impatient to see his wife and embrace her in his home, is prevented from going in. A battle then ensues; this goes on until the two guards admit defeat and abandon their posts. The triumphant groom then rushes into the house, shuts the door, and is alone with his conquered bride. At this juncture strident shouts and applause arise from the throng that accompanies the procession. To the sound of the *darabukka*, the fifes and castanets, many of the youths and girls beat time with their hands, and the dancers take up their dance again. Towards evening the music ceases, the dancing stops. The nearest relatives and the friends remain sitting on the ground: enormous platefuls of *kisra*[5] *and mulāh*[6] are brought in as well as roast chicken, mutton, and other foods; the supper goes on until midnight.

Marriage is a duty, and all must fulfil it, or put up with general mockery. It requires the consent of both sides; sometimes the father marries off his son although the latter is still under age; but as soon as the son is of age, the act must be ratified otherwise the marriage would be declared null and void. The ceremony is carried out in the presence of witnesses; generally, the couple are represented by their families. The *feki* presides over the marriage and writes down the conditions of the contract. The nuptial gifts are compulsory for the man; the woman only brings with her a few pieces of furniture, if she has any.

According to Islamic law there can be no marriage between relatives, nor can a man marry a woman with whom he has sinned, or his slave, unless he intends to free her. Divorce can take place by

---

[4] A kind of drum.
[5] A pancake of unleavened bread baked on a griddle.
[6] A thick stew of meat and vegetables.

mutual consent or by a judicial decision. After divorce, the bride who has already received half the nuptial gift at the marriage ceremony, receives the other half.

In Sinnār every new bride on the eve of her marriage goes to the bank of the river with several of her girl friends in the evening, takes off her clothes, and plunges into the water three times with the intention of cleansing herself in the eyes of her future husband.

In the large villages, and above all in the towns, all the young women destined to be married, must, before reaching puberty, undergo a very painful operation, which in Sinnār is called *kheitat* (sewing) which serves as a guarantee to their future husbands. When the marriage takes place, a woman expert in this kind of work restores them to their natural state. 'It is an evil custom', the *qādī* used to say, 'it is contrary to the spirit of religion; yet, on the other hand, if my daughter does not undergo it, she is condemned to life-long spinsterhood'.

In the southern part of Sinnār (province), the women, especially the married ones, tattoo the uncovered parts of their bodies. But their skins cannot take the deep incisions, such as I have seen among other tribes on the White Nile, where such incisions are, at times, true scars. More often, they are made on the face and serve to differentiate between the various tribes.

Funerals must be carried out as quickly as possible; this is prescribed for every Muslim. In the town of Sinnār the dead are buried in public cemeteries which are respected as sacred grounds. The most precious object of the deceased is placed above his tomb, and no one will ever dare touch it. The people of Sinnār carefully wash the bodies and take great care of the graves. They patiently decorate the tombs with small coloured pebbles gathered from the desert, and arrange them to form charming patterns.

As soon as a person dies, the dancers are called and the parents and the friends of the deceased are invited. Once the body has been washed it is wrapped in a new mat, put on a bier and taken to the grave; during the journey the body lies on its right side with the face turned towards the east. The men cry silently and the women lament loudly, and make gestures of desperation. They cover themselves with dust, scratch their faces and breasts, and pull out each other's hair, and after some time the closest relative remains alone. Placing his head on the bier, crying and singing in low tones, he recalls the happy time he spent with the dead man and laments that he can no longer answer him. He asks the deceased a hundred times to forgive him for all the wrong he did him and makes excuses for his faults. He promises that, while he still has a breath of life, he will never forget him, will frequently speak well of him and will often come to visit him, and wash his tomb with his warm tears. . . .

The inhabitants of Sinnār believe in the transmigration of souls. In this connection I wish to refer to a conversation I had with a very rich old man of eighty named Shandaloba, whom I visited several times, accompanied by Mr. Peney, [7] in order to have from him letters of recommendation to *Fekī* Musā'id, a relative of his, and to several chiefs of the Shangalla whom he knew very well. After supper we had a long discussion on many things, among which was transmigration. I asked the old man:

'When a man is dead where does his soul go immediately?'

'When a man is dead I believe that his spirit remains dormant until the body has rotted away, and that it then tries to find a new body until it has been purged of all the sins it had incurred in life; and I suppose that this is *barzakh*, or purgatory, between death and resurrection.'

'I understand; and if the soul of the dead man is free from sin, where does it go then?'

The old man smiled and, with a characteristic inclination of his head which meant 'it is impossible', he replied: 'If this were possible it would go to the Paradise promised by our great Prophet.'

'If a child dies?'

'If a child dies, its spirit would either stay near its tomb or in the infinite sky, would await until the sounding of the trumpets of Israel, from the temple of Jerusalem, resurrects the dead, and then it will go to Paradise.'

'If a man dies having only committed small sins in life, into what body do you think his spirit would enter?'

'Without doubt it would enter into the body of an animal like, for instance, a bird or a monkey, that is not wild.'

'And if he had sinned greatly?'

'In such a case, God and the Prophet would keep far away from him and his spirit would, for instance, enter the body of a crocodile, a hippopotamus, a hyena, a lion, etc.'

'Why is it that animals are sometimes killed by your people if you think that in some of them there is the soul of the dead?'

---

[7] Alfred Peney (1817-61), chief medical officer to the Egyptian Government in the Sudan.

At this observation of mine, the old man stopped a little confused, and then continued: 'You will never have heard that any of us has killed any monkeys because we firmly believe that in nearly every one of their bodies is the spirit of a dead man.'

'Don't you kill the crocodile, hippopotamus, or the lion, the hyena, or other beasts?'

'You will have noticed that we only take the lives of those animals that can do harm to man, or those which are needed by man as food; and this is a good thing, because everyone's duty is to defend and protect himself. . . .'

On the morning of 22 December 1854, all was ready for our departure. A north wind was in our favour. I affectionately kissed Peney and shook hands with the Governor who, from the divan, accompanied me, together with some Turkish officials, as far as the bank of the river. I got into the boat for al-Rusayris. The boatmen sang a prayer to the Prophet for a safe journey and we were off. . . .

The distance between the town of Sinnār and Karkūj is about 80 kilometres. We arrived at this locality only at about noon on 27 December, the tortuous conditions of the river making it impossible to take full advantage of the North wind. Beyond Karkūj progress was difficult owing to the persistent calm, to the continuous winding of the river, and to the rocks against which the boat kept striking every moment. In my journal are marked on the right bank the little villages of Dontai, Bunzuqa Mumin [unidentified], Kayran, Umm Barid, Saoleil, Hamda, Bados, Abū El Garef [?al Jurayf], and to the left the two large villages of Sīrū and Abū [?Hajar].

The soil as we slowly proceeded southwards was not so well cultivated. Each family only cultivates what is necessary for their livelihood and to pay the tribute to the Government. The huts are badly built, housing a confused mass of men, women, children, and domestic animals. In the villages there are no public cemeteries or mosques. The five daily prayers are generally forgotten and ablutions ignored. . . .

On 2 January 1855, I arrived at al-Rusayris, a town of about 7,000 inhabitants, on the right bank of the river. I stayed there until 13 January. Accompanied by the aged Abū Shanab I went round the neighbourhood observing and interrogating the people; I carefully recorded my observations in my journal, as well as the answers that were given to me and this is what I can report:

From al-Rusayris, the ground rises perceptibly and as the traveller proceeds southwards towards Fāzūghlī and the Shangallah, the way becomes increasingly mountainous and difficult owing to the many streams. From the top of the hills on which the little town is situated the eye of the observer takes in the most pleasant prospect and ranges over ground covered with young crops. In the woods and forests, which for the most part are made up of gum-producing acacia, palms and similar trees abound; and here and there the enormous baobab rises. This tree appears first about 12° N. To get a true picture in one's mind of this giant of tropical vegetation, one must see it. This exceptional tree is spongy, has thin slender branches, a smooth trunk and is copper coloured, with greatly developed roots, some of which make comfortable resting places for tired travellers. The leaf, as is indicated by the name of this tree (*adansonia digitata*) is digitated and is very small in relation to the tree itself. The foliage is sparse, and during the winter season the tree is bare; but the fruit hangs from its branches even during this season. I have seen it in the month of January. It is oblong and about a foot in length; the peel is solid and green in colour, and contains seeds here and there among the pith, the taste of which is acid. The natives place this pith in water and leave it for some time until the water acquires a taste. A decoction is made from the leaves, and the water is drunk as a remedy against fever.

The inhabitants of al-Rusayris have a darker skin than those of Sinnār. In nearly all the places I visited along the banks of the Blue Nile from Khartoum to Fāzūghlī I saw that newly-born babies have considerably lighter skin colour than their parents. The parents told me that when their children grew up and were obliged to remain in the sun all day tending the cattle, their colour would deepen.

The life of the inhabitants of al-Rusayris is very simple. At dawn they all get up, milk the sheep, goats, camels and cows, make butter, drink the bitter milk that remains, and eat *logma*. [9] They drink out of small saucers, made mostly from palm-leaves, so well woven that there is no danger of the liquid seeping through. Then the men and boys lead the cattle to pasture and do not return until dusk. The women go to draw water and gather wood; they grind the corn; they weave enough cotton cloth for the needs of their families; a little before sunset they see that the supper is ready. As soon as the men and young boys return from the pastures, they water the cattle, have their supper, and then go to sleep on their *'anqaribs*. Sometimes, after supper, one of the older men tells a story that lasts for many hours. The clothing of the men and

---

[9] Presumably the Arabic *luqma,* bread or pastry fried in oil, or any kind of sweetmeat.

women consists only of a piece of ragged, dirty cloth; the young girls are naked until they reach the age of puberty. Puberty is very early in these hot climates, and we have seen some instances where girls of ten have become mothers and boys of about twelve fathers.

The men do not shave their hair, as is done in Sinnār, but let it fall from the nape of their necks, crisp and curled. This also applies to the women who are greatly concerned with their make-up. Because of the old layer of camel-fat that is smeared over the hair, they lose, if seen at close quarters, the grace and elegance they seem to possess at a distance. Girls and women are tattooed from the shoulders to the loins.

Circumcision is not practised here. In order to be valid in the eyes of the public, a matrimonial contract has to be made in the presence of several elderly witnesses. Very few people have more than one wife. This is due to lack of means; some, however, keep a concubine either in their house or elsewhere. It is very rare that a woman is unfaithful to her husband, but if this should occur, she is immediately disowned by him.

These people are by nature placid. But if anyone is either injured or killed, the family of the victim seek blood in revenge, not only of the attacker but also of all the males in his house. Thus it sometimes happens that an entire family have to leave their own country to avoid the endless vendetta.

The elderly Abū Shanab told me that these inhabitants never attack other tribes; but if they are provoked they are capable of defending themselves with heroism. You would see the enthusiasm that animates them when they set out to meet an enemy! The brides, the daughters, the sisters, and even the mothers delight in the thought of their husbands, fathers, brothers and sons going to war. They accompany them with cymbals and drums, and urge them to fight hard, never to turn their backs on the enemy, to win or to die. Here they firmly believe that a man killed in war and in the defence of his country immediately goes to Heaven and that from there many blessings shower upon the family of the deceased. The warriors are armed only with spears and shields; on their right arm, above the elbow, they tie a tooth and they say that this protects them from the enemy's blows.

It often happens that they must defend themselves against the sudden attacks of the Gumuz tribe, situated to the southeast, and the natives of Jabal Tabi, in the southwest who, spurred on by hunger, at times raid the territory between al-Rusayris and Fāzūghlī. The merchants of Sinnār and al-Rusayris who carry their grain to the

P

Shangalla to trade must travel in big groups made up of two or three hundred people so as to be able to overcome any attacks by the natives of Tabi. It sometimes happens that some merchants are forced to leave their goods and cattle in the hands of the enemy in order to save their lives.

Beyond Karkūj, public cemeteries are not seen. The body is buried in the place which suits the nearest relative best. The funerals are noteworthy for their simplicity and they take place as soon as the dying man has drawn his last breath. When I was in al-Rusayris, a shaykh died, leaving a young bride and a little boy. The *fekī*, having performed the rites over the dying man, calls the wife, who is crying nearby, and tells her to listen for her husband's last breath, which she takes from the lips of her husband with a kiss. Then she closes his eyes and mouth; she waits a little and then calls him several times.

Quietly one goes through the town telling the parents and friends of the death of the chief. These gather quickly round the wife. Only one woman is allowed to enter the dwelling-place to comfort the widow and this is the one held most dear. The beating of the big drum is heard, while relatives and friends recall the virtues and goodness of the deceased. The body is not washed, but wrapped in a cloth, and the following morning before sunrise it is carried without ceremony to the burial place. The young widow follows it from afar; and when it is laid in the grave, with the face looking towards the east, she is the first to throw in a handful of earth, then she draws to one side until he is buried and all have gone. Remaining alone, she kneels, bows her head on the tomb and relieves her sorrow by crying. She then strips off the leaves of the nearest tree and scatters them over the tomb, where she also places the saddle and a few other simple belongings that her husband had used frequently when he was alive. She calls him several times by name — and laments because he no longer answers — she tears her hair — she covers it with dust, she scratches her face and her breasts — and emits shrill shrieks and desperate shouts of anguish. On her return home she stops in front of the doors of the houses, and at the top of her voice she shouts: 'No woman is today unhappier than I! if anyone claims to be, come forward, and my grief will challenge her.' Numerous women with their hair all dishevelled and covered with ash come out of their houses to embrace her, holding her to their breast and calling her the most unhappy of women. They all follow her, echoing her lament and expressions of anguish. They then enter the courtyard of her house and stay there until dusk. This funeral ceremony lasted for three days. . . .

On the morning of 13 January 1855 I left al-Rusayris with three camelmen and my servant. At two o'clock in the morning we arrived at al-Damazīn ... and the following day at al-Barīs [ʔal-Buraysh], my camelmen's village. al-Barīs is a small village with not more than 300 inhabitants, and is situated in the woods about two kilometres from the river. I cannot describe the great welcome extended to us by these inhabitants.... They had been assured by the camelmen that we would not be hostile to them. They thronged around us; boys and girls of eight and ten years of age completely naked, lively and pretty, danced around us.

We left al-Barīs at about eight o'clock in the morning and we reached Obsogola [Abū Zaghulī] shortly before noon. On the way, I said to my escort 'I hope that the inhabitants of Abū Zaghulī give us a good welcome.' 'There is not much hope of that', was his answer. On our arrival, several of them, who were lying in the shade of an old sycamore, disappeared, and each of them stood guard over his hut, refusing to help the camelmen in unloading the boxes. We erected a tent. In the meantime, Fath Allāh was lighting the fire. I myself went up to one of the Arabs standing at the door of his hut and made him a present of three rows of beads, asking him to obtain three or four chickens for which I would pay. He accepted the gift, ran away and never returned. The water had already been boiling for some time now. The soldier said to me: 'Please, give me leave to act in my own way, and I swear to you on the Koran that in the twinkling of an eye we will have a lamb at our disposal.' 'No', I replied, 'it is better to be careful; we shall not die of hunger.' We hurriedly ate a little biscuit-bread soaked in water with onions from al-Rusayris; I had the tent dismantled and the camels loaded, and we departed. We walked continuously through woods of *sunt*, perspiring under the intense heat.

The village of al-Sharīf, towards which we were heading was, according to the camelmen, still about four hours away. As I was afraid of the many wild animals I was looking around for a place where we could pass the night. Finally I saw a flock of sheep being led by two natives towards a stream. At the same time several young girls carrying on their shoulders, skins (*qirāb*) full of water drawn from the stream, ran across the path in front of me on their way to their huts which could not be far away. 'Thanks be to God', said the camelman, 'there must be a tribe of nomadic Arabs encamped here.' In the meantime the soldier, without a word from me, had already run on and stopping one of the people leading the flock, asking him to guide us to the encampment. He returned with an Arab, between thirty and thirty-five years

of age, slim and tall; his colouring was not yellow or brown like that of
other Arabs, but red copper. He had lively penetrating eyes, a fine nose,
a pleasant mouth, thin lips, a small beard and very long blond hair
falling down to his shoulders. We followed him a good quarter of an
hour till we reached the camp. I asked the soldier, 'But what kind of
people are these?' They are thieves and murderers', he replied. 'The
Arabs call them Abū Jarīd, but they call themselves by another name;
they are worshippers of fire, and sacrifice lambs and bulls to it.'

Their camp was in the midst of the woods. Each tent was made
up of three or four poles stuck into the ground and joined transversely
at the top, above which was a large mat, overhanging the side to
screen the sun. The tents were arranged in a semi-circle. When we
arrived, the men had not yet returned with their cattle from the pasture,
and with the exception of a few old men and babies, there were only
women to be seen; the girls were all busy grinding *durra* and preparing
supper for their families. The old women were lying quietly on the
ground keeping the children amused.

As they saw us appear, not one of the girls stopped her work or
showed any sign of surprise. They too, like the men, allowed their
blond hair to grow long and smooth, but dressed it with greater care.
They were clad only in ragged cloths round their loins.

Two old men approached us, saying: 'Welcome in the name of
God; put your cases down, for the time being; our chief will shortly
return and he will show you where you can rest for the night.'

When evening came, the men and boys returned from the pastures.
The chief, who had been speaking to the two old men for some time,
came over to me and said:

'Welcome, in the name of God.' Then he continued: 'Is it true
then that you are not a Turk?'

'No, I am not a Turk.'

'Is it true that in your soul you do not conceal any evil towards
us?'

'As God sees me! I am not going to do you any harm.'

'Well then you and your servants are at peace with me, and may
God bless you all.'

He went away and came back almost immediately, but not before
I had lit two candles and laid a mat on the floor. The small flames from
the candles filled him and the tribesmen with awe, as they could not
understand how the candles remained alight, without using wood as
fuel. I asked the chief to sit down on the mat. I had a *chibouk* and
coffee brought to him; I gave him a piece of cloth and a pair of

slippers, which pleased him very much, and thanking me he said that he did not know how he could repay me. Several of the tribesmen who were present enjoyed the gifts I had made to the chief just as much as if they had received them themselves.

I then had the following conversation with him:

'Tell me, O chief, what is the name of your tribe?'

'Everyone calls us by the name of Abū Jarīd, but our real name is Zabala'āt.' [10]

'Are there many of you?'

'No, not more than 300 people counting men and women, and we are divided into three groups each of roughly the same number of people. These here form one group; the other two groups live in this wood not very far away.'

'Have you been in this area a long time?'

'Among the Arabs we are the oldest inhabitants. We kept a pure language, pure blood and a primitive way of life.'

Where did your ancestors come from?'

'They came from that part where the sun rises.'

'And why did they leave their country?'

'Our fathers were shepherds like us, and above all they loved their liberty. They lived in the desert. They were molested by continuous strife with strangers who claimed to have conquered them. For a long time they resisted the enemy, but finally, tired of the bloodshed, they left their homeland and came to these woods.'

'Are you Muslims?'

'No, we are not Muslims.'

'And what is your religion?'

'We observe the religion of our fathers.'

'Do you believe in God?'

'Yes, we believe in one God only, *Allāhu wāhid* who manifests himself especially in fire and in the stars.'

'Therefore you adore fire and the stars?'

'Certainly, in fire and in the stars we adore God.'

'Who created all things?'

'All things were created by God.'

'And who created man?'

'Man was created by God.'

'In what manner did He create man?'

[10] By a slip the writer has transposed the words Abū Jarīd and Zabala'āt. The community call themselves Nās Abū Jarīd (People of Abū Jarīd). Muslim critics of their tenets refer to them by the opprobrious name *al-Zabala'āt.*

'We do not know. We do know that on earth man is condemned to live a life of continuous struggle to defend the freedom and peace for which God created him. This is why our fathers have separated themselves from human society, among whom there is no peace.'

'How many men did God create in the beginning?'

'We do not know.'

'Did He also create spirits?'

'Without doubt God created spirits, which exist in Heaven.'

'Do you believe that there exists a Great Spirit, who is the cause of evil, and, if so, what do you call him?'

'There is a Great Spirit who causes evil, and we call him *al-shaytān al-kabīr*, the Great Devil, and other less powerful spirits depend on him. These we must propitiate with sacrifices.'

'And what do you sacrifice?'

'We sacrifice a few lambs, and each year a bull, to the fire and stars, because God is manifest by light and heat.'

'Where do you pray?'

'We pray near the fire, looking at the stars.'

'Will this world have an end?'

'Yes, this world will have an end, and everything will be destroyed by fire; but then everything will be born again.'

'When we die, what will happen to us?'

'When we die, we shall be happy if we had always loved peace, otherwise God will punish us.'

'And will the reward or punishment given to man be eternal?'

'We do not know, only God knows that.'

'And is God eternal?'

'Yes, God is eternal; He always was and always will be.'

'Has God a body?'

'No, God has no body; He is everywhere, and rules everything.'

After supper the chief came again to see me with his elders. I said:

'I thank you sincerely, O chief, for the supper you have given me and my servants, and may God repay you. I was pleased to eat meat and fresh *durra* bread. You get the meat from your cattle but how do you manage to obtain *durra* as you have no fields?'

'As soon as the proper season comes several of our tribe go to the river banks with young cattle and exchange them for a quantity of *durra* sufficient for each family for the whole year. Apart from this, we never see a strange face.'

'Do you marry women from other tribes?'

'We do not and I hope that it will never happen.'

'So all your families must be inter-related?'

'Certainly, and that is why we live in peace. If by chance there is some slight dispute between families, it is quickly settled by the elders.'

'Have you no priests?'

'Our priests are the elders, who bless the newly-born, marriages, the dying, and the tombs of the dead.'

'What blessings do the elders give your babies?'

'They placate the evil Great Spirit, *al-shaytān al-kabīr,* and the lesser spirits, and impart the blessings of the Good Spirit.'

'And for the marriages?'

'It is they who arrange the marriages, who bless them, and advise the young couple to love each other always, and preserve the peace.'

'And at what age do you marry?'

'The elders do not allow marriages until the parties are grown-up.'

'When one of you is seriously ill, what do you do for him?'

'The elders gather round his bed, bless him, and realising that medicine can no longer help him, exhort him to patience, telling him that such is the fate of man, who is condemned to suffer and die on this earth, then to be re-born later to a better life.'

'Of what does this better life consist?'

'We do not know, but it is known to God who holds all in His hands.'

'When a man is dead what are the funeral ceremonies?'

'When a man is dead, the elders fix the hour and place of the burial. The body is carried by four men or four women or by four boys or four girls, according to the age of the deceased person. The body is carried upon the mat on which the person died, and is clothed in the same garments that he wore while he was ill. When they arrive at the burial place, the body is laid in a deep hole, with the face looking east. Covered with sand and then earth, it is well rammed down to prevent any possible unearthing by hyenas. Then above the tomb a big fire is lit, around which dances take place, accompanied by mournful songs.'

'How is the chief of the tribe chosen, and by whom?'

'The elders are the ones who choose the chief. He must be intelligent and kind and it does not matter to what family he belongs.'

'Do you take more than one wife?'

'No, we cannot do this as the number of women is almost equal to that of the men. However, it sometimes happens that a girl without

a husband or a young bride left behind with no children is given as a
concubine to the nearest relative.'

'Does it ever happen that a brother marries his own sister?'

'This has happened, but in very rare cases.'

'When a husband dies without leaving sons, is his cattle left to
the widow?'

'No, in this case the property belongs to the nearest relative,
whose duty it is to keep the widow, and sometimes he takes her as a
concubine.'

'And if the widow has very young sons, do they inherit the
cattle?'

'Yes, as soon as the boys have grown up, their father's cattle are
restored to them.'

'Do you circumcise your young boys?'

'No, though it is said that our forefathers did.'

At dawn on the 16th, after a friendly farewell from the chief, we
departed.

After two hours, on the road towards the south, we reached the
foot of a mountain, covered with gum trees with tall whitish trunks.
The soldier collected a few drops from the trees and offered them to
me, suggesting that I kept one or two in my mouth and told me that
they would quench my thirst a little.

At ten o'clock in the morning we entered the village of al-Sharīf
and the chief welcomed us with the most courteous manners as if he
had known us for a long time. He insisted on helping us to unload
the camels: he immediately had the mats laid under his *rakūba* [11]; he
had *abrè*, [12] the refreshing drink of the country, brought to me, and
he ordered his servants to kill ten small pigeons and to prepare
food.

This chief was respected not only by the people of the country,
but also by all travellers. I had already heard of him when I was in
al-Rusayris, in Sinnār, in Wad Madanī, and in Khartoum. He was also
a *fekī*.

At three in the afternoon, we left our host and made our way
towards Surayfa, where we arrived at one o'clock in the night. This
small village was completely enclosed behind a great wall of straw
(*shukkāba*) preventing the inhabitants from any contact with strangers.
We were forced to spend the night outside the *shukkāba*.

[11] A lean-to shelter.
[12] For a recipe see, *On the frontiers of Islam*, pp. 114n. - 115n.

On 17 January, we made an early morning start towards Khawr al-Janna. This village is situated on a hill, and it takes its name from a stream nearby. The way between Surayfa and Khawr al-Janna was very rough, and crossed by rocky streams, which proved very difficult to ford. I shall never forget the Hadabat stream. As we were going down towards it, the cases fell off the backs of two of the camels. I immediately rushed forward to try and save one, which contained fragile objects, and it fell on my right foot. At first I thought the foot was fractured, but later I discovered that it was only bruised; I had to hobble along for at least ten days. It was two o'clock in the afternoon when we arrived at Khawr al-Janna. This village, too, like the one at Surayfa, is closed in by a *shukkāba* and we were forced to remain outside, under the shelter of a poor and badly-built *rakūba*. Hungry as we were, we had to leave at four in the afternoon for Famaka, where we were just able to arrive at nine in the evening.

I confess that it is quite impossible to describe the rough path between Khawr al-Janna and Famaka. It wound its way up and down hills and valleys, barren except for a few patches of acacia.

In the morning I rose early with the intention of carefully observing the position of Famaka, which lies at the beginning of a chain of mountains called Fāzūghlī. The village, placed on the top of a hill, offers a fire view of the neighbourhood. The *tukuls* of other villages, are scattered here and there in small groups all round, either on the top of a mountain, on a slope, or in a valley. Most of the inhabitants of Famaka are made up of the families of soldiers which the Egyptian government keep there to collect the taxes from the inhabitants of the neighbouring mountains. The population does not exceed 400 people.

I crossed the Blue Nile in an old boat, accompanied by an escort of three soldiers. After a difficult journey we arrived at Adassi [or Fadasi] and then at Jara [?Yaradda], a little village on the left bank of the river, where we spent the night. The following day we were at Kiri.... We stopped there a couple of days and then we left for Qaysān. We crossed the stream which separates Fāzūghlī from the primitive tribes and at sunset encamped beyond the mountains of Agaru. One hour after midnight we started off again, following a very narrow path which was constantly lost in dry stream beds, and we arrived at Qaysān on 23 January as guests of Delī Mehmed *ikinji yūzbāshī*[13] who treated me very kindly.

I remained fourteen days in Qaysān. I had to spend the greater

---

[13] Turkish *ikinci yūzbasi*, junior captain.

part of this time disputing with the officers who did all they could to prevent me from continuing my journey to Shangalla. I managed to take note of many other things, and to record them in my journal.

Qaysān, surrounded by high mountains, is situated on the right bank of the river Tumat. When I arrived it was inhabited only by soldiers and their families. 'Abbās Pasha had posted a garrison of 200 soldiers there because of the gold mines in the area. Sa'īd Pasha who succeeded 'Abbās Pasha, heeding to repeated advice of the local military authorities, recalled the garrison to Kiri.

As soon as the Egyptians had settled in Qaysān the local inhabitants withdrew to the neighbouring mountain where they built a new village also called Qaysān. I visited the chief of this Qaysān several times on the mountain. My visits cost me a few presents, for which, however, I was repaid as it opened the way to introduction into his household where there were also chiefs of other neighbouring villages.

Here, is the report of conversations I had with these chiefs:

'What language do the people speak?' I asked them.

'Like the Agaro and the Kashangaro, they speak the language of the Berta, who extend for a good way south south-west of Qaysān, on a long chain of mountains, which rises here. It is a beautiful language, slow and soft but poor in vocabulary; as rich as the Arabic language, which we chiefs speak.'

I asked him to speak to me in the language of the Berta; I transcribed the numbers from one to a hundred, a few names, a few verbs and a few prepositions; but all these and other notes were lost on my return in a forest in Sinnār. The inhabitants of Qaysān were quite amused when I greeted them in their tongue with the word *angiarata* and called them '*Ide!*' 'O man!'

'And how is it that you chiefs alone know Arabic?'

'Because we are descendants of Arabs. Our forefathers conquered these mountains by arms; and since then we have been considered chiefs. Our counsels are accepted and our orders obeyed.'

'Do they cultivate the soil?'

'They do not like agriculture; they are nearly all shepherds and live in the mountains. Before there were Egyptians in lower Qaysān, they used to sow a little *durra* along the fertile banks of the Tumat.'

'What do they live on now?'

'The greater number of them live on *durra* which they get from the *jallāba*, in exchange for gold-dust found in the sandy beds of the stream.'

'When does the rainy season start here?'

'Usually in the month of March, but sometimes it begins in February, and ends in September.'

'Do you pay tribute to the Turks?'

'Yes, we pay them an annual tax in gold-dust.'

On 3 February, there arrived at Qaysān the *Faqīh* Musā'id and the great chief, Wad al-Gharbī, of Banī Shanqūl. From the very first day of my arrival at Qaysān, the Egyptian officer, Deli-Muhammad, told me openly that I would not be able to continue my journey, but I was determined to leave. It was only after endless discussions with the commandant that he gave me permission to join Musā'id, and Wad al-Gharbī. . . .

'How shall I dress, great chief?'

'With a simple under-waistcoat, and a cotton band round your head' . . . 'exactly as the *Jallāba* dress.'

At noon on 5 February, I left Qaysān, our caravan joining Wad al-Gharbī and Faqīh Musā'id. Our way was very uneven and covered thickly with trees. . . . Sometimes there were deep rushing streams, very troublesome because of the baggage on the camels' backs. One hour before sunset, we crossed two streams and I asked Wad al-Gharbī:

'Do all the streams that we have crossed flow into the Tumat river?'

'All', he replied, 'and the Tumat is the largest of the streams, which during the rainy season, overflows and floods its banks; but in the dry season it holds only a few pools of stagnant water.'

'What is the name of this chain of mountains from north to south, to our right?'

'The Berta mountains', he said.

Along the way, conversing with Wad al-Gharbī, I asked:

'How do the Bertas live on the mountain?'

'They live very poorly; they have a little *durra,* and to obtain more they exchange gold-dust with the *jallāba.* They also eat herbs, boiled in water, the fruit of wild trees, meat mostly from dead animals, and they drink the milk of their sheep and goats.'

'And why is it that, at least during the rainy season, they do not come down into the plain, which is so fertile, and grow their grain?'

'Once they used to come down to the plain and gather an abundant harvest. But since the Turks came and inhabited Qaysān they do not venture to come down.'

'Did the Bertas trade with this province before the Turks conquered Fāzūghlī?'

'Not only with the people of Fāzūghlī but also with those of al-Rusayris and Sinnār.'

On 7 February at midnight we arrived at Singe. The village was all illuminated. Before each hut there was a great fire. Later I got to know that these fires were a demonstration of the great joy that every-body felt at the coming of a white man, never seen by them before.

All was silent, and as I slowly went along with my boy I could hear only the noise of our steps. It seems that all the life in Singe was reduced to the two of us. Suddenly, in that profound silence, I heard the blowing of a horn. I turned in the direction whence the sound had come, and there was Wad al-Gharbī followed by a throng of natives, who had gathered at the blowing of the horn, and who were anxious to see the white man at closer quarters. Soon three or four hundred people were gathered around us, even the women with their children on their shoulders. All were shouting as loud as they could, clapping their hands, and stamping their feet. When we arrived at a hut, which formed part of Wad al-Gharbī's house, and which, we were to use as our lodgings, the people nearly knocked me over. Some tried to touch my feet, some my legs, my hands and arms, while some even pulled my nose and ears. Some kept caressing me, while others raised their fists at me. All the time, I was watching Wad al-Gharbī hoping that at any moment he would ask the people to move off, so that I could rest, as I was dead-tired. But Wad al-Gharbī was only thinking of amusing his people, and before allowing me to go to bed, he wanted me to fire off the rifle which I had slung over my arm, to see the effect of the explosion.

I was forced to please him, and fired into the air. All fell on top of each other, giving wild shouts. Their heads were turned to me; they were dazed.

Having recovered from the shock, they wished me good night and returned to their own huts.

But the day was not yet over for us. Just as I was turning in, I heard a voice calling me from the open door of my hut. It was the voice of Wad al-Gharbī, who was asking me to go to his mother's hut, as quickly as possible, because she was lying there ill, and wished to greet me that same evening. As she was the mother of the chief, I willingly accepted the invitation. I took with me a very beautiful garment and about a dozen small mirrors.

After some forty paces we arrived at the Great Lady's hut, and inside lay the sick woman stretched out on an ox-skin and covered up to the shoulders in a dirty garment. Led by Wad al-Gharbī, I approached her and, according to the custom, squatted down. I shook her hand and kissed it, and she shook and kissed my hand also. This was followed by an exchange of *angiarata* (greetings); she asked me if I was married ... and why I was not married.... She said that it would have given her great pleasure to see a white woman. She felt my hands, my cheeks, nose, ears, eyes, mouth.... 'Oh yes', she exclaimed, 'he is really made like us'. She then again asked her son, Wad al-Gharbī, who was acting as interpreter, if it were really true that the whites eat human flesh: assured that this was not so, she said: 'I am glad that things are as this gentleman says, and not as we believed up to now!'

As soon as an opportune moment arrived I thought I would light the candle, but when the match flared up all the other women, who were there watching with their eyes and mouths wide open, took fright and rushed to the door to flee. The sick woman, threw away the cover under which she was lying and stood upright, terrified, while Wad al-Gharbī, laughing like a madman, tried to quieten her as best he could.

Reassured by the presence and words of Wad al-Gharbī, the women returned smiling, and the sick woman resumed her position on the ox-skin. I then covered her with the dress I had with me and told her that it now belonged to her. I also gave a small mirror to each of the women who were present, and these gifts were greatly appreciated. Before retiring to my hut Wad al-Gharbī made me an offering, according to the custom of the country ... which I did not accept. In the morning I got up at sunrise.

The inhabitants of Singe were still nearly all asleep. I walked to the highest place of Singe and remained there rejoicing in the grandiose spectacle that was unfolding around me. There were high mountains, deep valleys and immense plains covered in thick, high grass. A fresh, invigorating air was gently rustling the leaves of the trees near me, and birds of all sizes were greeting the new day. Suddenly I saw eight widely-staring eyes looking at me; there were four natives seated on a rock nearby who wanted to know what I was doing alone on these heights. When I returned to my hut, Wad al-Gharbī told me that several Galla merchants were waiting for him at the foot of the mountains and that my cases had to be fetched.

At about nine o'clock we arrived at the tents of the Galla. We stopped, in the shade of a group of trees where there were also between twenty or thirty of the strongest young men of Singe, armed with spears.

The Galla merchants, who were grouped a little distance away near their cattle, threw their spears to the ground on seeing Wad al-Gharbī and came to kiss his hands, and then offered their hands to be kissed. In the meantime I was observing these people. They were medium-built, with small round heads, yellowish skin, crisp black hair, sharp lively eyes and regular features. As soon as this first ceremony was over, Wad al-Gharbī, through a Galla interpreter, told them a few things about me. They then all looked at me and kisssed my hands and clothes. I was astonished and could not guess the reason for such attention. Wad al-Gharbī then told me that they professed the same religion as myself — they were Galla Christians coming from a country two days away to the south-south-east. They had come to exchange iron, sheep, horses and oxen, with the Bertas, for gold-dust and beads.

I asked them several questions and they replied that they knew Bishop Massaia and other white men with him who possessed many books, wrote on paper and often prayed to God. They could not tell me more.

At three o'clock in the afternoon, I went with Wad al-Gharbī to Banī Shanqūl to visit *Fekī* Musā'id, and the two great chiefs Shaykh al-Fadlī and Honkong. Towards four o'clock we were already seated in *Fekī* Musā'id's *rakūba*.

The news of my visit to the *Fekī* was known to the whole village in a few minutes, and natives came out from all directions. Without exaggeration, there were between four and five thousand people to see the White man. They were to be found on the roofs of huts, the tops of trees, and from any vantage point they could find. Others were being lifted high in the crowd so that they could see better.

At last, *Fekī* Musā'id and Wad al-Gharbī were able to persuade them to return to their huts, and told them that I would be returning to Banī Shanqūl another time.

'We have only been in this area for a short while', *Fekī* Musā'id told me. 'We are the people of Shandi and Halfaya having fled from these places when Muhammad 'Alī sent Egyptian soldiers to avenge the death of his son Ismā'īl Pasha, who was burnt alive in Shandi.[14] Many then sought refuge here in Banī Shanqūl. Some went to Fadasi and others dispersed in the neighbouring mountains. The black people that you have seen here are the ones who were already living here when we came, and some of the Berta who surrendered to us. The chief of all these blacks is Honkong, whom we shall visit. . . . If you are

---

[14] An incident in 1822 which touched off the Sudanese revolt against Turco-Egyptian oppression and the resulting savage repression by the occupying forces.

willing, let us go to see Shaykh al-Fadlī, the great friend of Nimr, who had Ismā'īl Pasha burnt alive in a hut in Shandi.'

What a charming old man he was, of about eighty years of age. He was lying still and half asleep on a mat in the *rakūba* in front of his hut. *Fekī* Musā'id went up to him first, took his hand and kissed it reverently; Wad al-Gharbī did the same, and I, too, felt compelled to do so. 'How fortunate I am', I told him, 'to be able to shake and kiss the hand of the hero of Shandi.' These words of mine stirred the venerable old man. He lifted his wrinkled brow, raised his chest and with two black shining eyes he looked at me and started speaking: 'That great night; that great night in Shandi; Ismā'īl Pasha, that man who thought he could torture us with his wild caprice, was to remember that night; the scoundrel was claiming three hundred slaves from us or he would have killed my friend Nimr. That great night . . . that great night in Shandi . . . I remember as clearly as if it were today, how with our valiant soldiers we solemnly swore to burn Ismā'īl Pasha alive in his tent. I remember the moment we attacked him, in the darkness of the night, suddenly and swiftly. We killed the guards and officers who were guarding him, and shouted 'Revenge on Ismā'īl Pasha!' Then, as we had sworn to do, we burnt him alive.'

The old man spoke with incredible strength of voice, and at the same time maintained a certain dignity. I have never seen a more terrible and yet more beautiful old man than Shaykh al-Fadlī.

We drank coffee with him, and before leaving I offered him a pinch of snuff as I had seen him making use of it several times. Seeing that he liked my snuff, and the box containing it even more, I let him have the lot.

Before sunset we found ourselves at the hut of Chief Honkong. This was a little way off from that of Shaykh al-Fadlī. Honkong was seated on the ground outside his hut, surrounded by cattle manure, and was expecting my visit, as *Fekī* Musā'id had already informed him that I was coming. He never received anyone except the servant who brought him food. *Fekī* Musā'id told me that the chief prayed continually, thinking of God, of the future life and human misery.

I shook his hand, kissed it, and pressing it over my heart, I said: '*Es salāmu 'alayk, ya shaykh al-kabīr, Allāh yubārak fīk*' ('Peace be with you, O Great Chief; may God bless you'). He then placed my hand over his heart and said: '*alayk as-salamu, yā sīdī, kattar ala khayrak* (May health be with you, Sir).

I then asked Wad al-Gharbī, and *Fekī* Musā'id: 'Why is the chief left in the midst of such dirt?' Honkong understood what I asked, smiled and said: 'Now that I am an old man, and as I am getting weaker each day, I wish to lie here in the manure, crawling with ants. The ants are my only company on this earth where I have lost everything, and where only my hut remains, which will receive my bones when I am dead, and that will be soon. I no longer have any wife, sons, cattle or gold. All have been taken from me by the God whom I worship, and by the Turks whom I hate. However, I must say that all my nephews and my people would have me with them, but I prefer to remain here alone in my hut. My dearest ones died here. Here I once buried my gold which I had to hand over to the Turks. They wrenched the teeth from my head and cut the tips off my ears and tongue. *Allāh yana'lhum!* may God curse them. I was born poor in this place and here I wish to die poor. Such is the way of the world. 'Be at peace', I said, 'and trust in God, for He is very good, sees all and understands.' 'Yes', he replied. 'my trust is in God alone, who is good and just, and sooner or later will avenge me.' We left at about eight o'clock and we did not reach Singe until about ten.

On 8 February, I got up at dawn to go to places where I could visit several points, take note of the geographical position of the country, and with the help of Wad al-Gharbī record the names of the principal mountains and streams. I did this for three days, not returning home before eleven in the morning.

The Shangalla country is bounded by Fāzūghlī to the north, and the Bahr al-Azraq and Dabus to the east. The Dinka tribes of Sinnār to the west and the Dabus and the Galla people to the south.

From north to south this country is crossed by the great chain of Berta mountains and is called by different names according to the different tribes inhabiting it. The main tribes in the area are: the Agaro, the Kushankuru, and the Berta (the strongest and largest of the tribes) and the Banī Shangalla. All these tribes speak the same language, which is also called the language of the Berta.

The main river that flows in this land from south to north, to the east of the Berta mountains, is the Tumat, one affluent of which rises in the Andu [?] mountains, and another in the Bibi mountains. After a course of about 150 geographical miles it flows into the Blue Nile between the two streams, Hadabat and Khawr al-Janna. On the same slopes of the Shangalla, there is also the river Dabus, the source of which is still unknown. This river is part of the eastern and southern boundaries of the Shangalla, and flows into the Blue Nile at about 10° N.

To the right there are many streams which during the rainy season swell the Tumat and all flow from east to west. The names of the principal streams going from north to south are: *Khawr Baba,* perhaps so named because it indicates the boundary of Fāzūghlī with the great Berta mountain range; *Khawr al-Qaysān,* named after a nearby village; *Khawr al-Jāmūs,* so-called because of the buffaloes along its banks; *Khawr al-Ramla,* the stream of sand; *Khawr al-Dhahab,* the gold-bearing stream.

These streams were thus called by the Arabs, even before the Egyptian invasion, and Wad al-Gharbī assured me that the Arabs only translated into their own language the names given to these streams by the natives. I was anxious to know if, from the western slopes of the Berta mountains, there flowed streams along a westerly course.

Wad al-Gharbī spoke of a small stream having its source in the Berta mountain range, about half a day's walk to the north of Singe, and flowing from east to west. He was unable to tell me its name. He also spoke of a large stream between Singe and the little river which had water only during the rainy season. I took notes of what Wad al-Gharbī said, and hoped that they would become useful later on. Such an occasion arose in February 1859 when, on my return from the Bari tribe, I visited the Sobat river up to Pan-e-Lang and the Dinka tribes on the right bank of the White Nile. At the time, I questioned the Dinka of Pan-e-Lang. All were unanimous in stating that the Sobat has two main branches. One comes from the south, and the other from the east. I do not doubt that this branch of the Sobat is the small river pointed out by Wad al-Gharbī. [15]

The climate here is not as hot as that of Sinnār. This must be attributed to the greater altitude, and to the longer duration of the rainy season, which lasts from March to September. In this season, the streams swell quickly and the Tumat overflows. As soon as the rains stop there remain only pools of stagnant water.

The Banī Shangalla are generally all shepherds. Since the Turks occupied Qaysān, they have not cultivated the soil though it is very fertile. They feed on cooked herbs, fruits of trees, flesh of dead animals, and on what *durra* they get from the *jallāba* in exchange for gold-dust.

The character of these inhabitants is proud, indomitable and aggressive. Any small passion arouses them. They cannot tolerate any

[15] With the limited knowledge which Europeans then possessed of the head streams of the Sobat, the writer was led into error as to the western tributary, the Baro, which rises on the West Ethiopian plateau 200 miles south of Banī Shanqūl. The *khawr* which Wad al-Gharbī pointed out probably flowed westward towards the White Nile.

wrong done to them and are eager for revenge. The Shangallah are divided into tribes, each one independent of the others. Each recognises a chief. When he dies the elders meet in council and agree on the choice of a new chief. Their choice is then made known to the tribe, and is generally accepted.

The garments of both the men and women is very simple: a strip of cotton cloth tied round the loins, and another joined to this at the navel, and passing through the legs is joined to the strip at the back. The men do not wear any ornaments; the women have an iron ring at the top of their left ear and a small round plate of metal on the sides of the nose supported by a twisted wire, which passes from the nostrils. On certain solemn occasions the women dye their bodies red.

During my stay in Singe, Wad al-Gharbī was building a large hut. I wanted to help him with my tools, and I made the three steps for the entrance to the hut and two chairs.

The floors of the huts in the Shangalla are formed of poles and canes covered with clay, and are raised about three feet above the ground, supported on large stones. The circular walls rise from the floor, and their exterior is strengthened by long poles embedded in the ground, rising about eleven feet above it. The roof is conical and rests on two walls. The inside of the walls is coated with a reddish mud. On the outside, this is done to a height of about five feet, while the upper part lets through air and light.

With regard to marriage, I have to add something interesting: the three wives of Wad al-Gharbī were once his slaves. One evening I asked him: 'Why did you marry slaves rather than choose a free woman, the daughter of some Arab chief? And what do the other chiefs usually do?' To this he replied: 'If a chief wants to marry the sister, or the daughter, or anyone of the family chief, it is necessary for him to have a sister or a daughter or another girl of his family to marry to any near relative of the bride. If this exchange cannot be made, he can still make the marriage, but the children of it do not belong to the husband but to the family of his bride. Now, as I had no daughters, sisters or near relatives to effect the exchange, and wishing the children that were born to be mine, I chose three girl slaves, who became free as soon as I married them.'

'If the husband of these wives died....?'

'If I were to die', he replied, 'no one could enforce his rights over them and their children.'

'Do the women ever inherit any of the goods left by those who die?'

'Never, always the man.'

'And when the children are still very young?'

'A guardian is then nominated to take care of them and protect them and their property until they have reached a mature age.'

In some of their illnesses, these people resort to violent remedies. They stab the swollen parts, running the risk of cutting an artery; they run a lighted firebrand over a wounded arm, with a steady hand, and blow away the smoke from the burning flesh. Sometimes, they use a red-hot iron. These remedies, although applied so brutally, often have admirable results.

One night I was awakened by the voice of Wad al-Gharbī. I got up immediately, and I asked him what was the matter. He replied: 'You must come immediately with me to Banī Shanqūl to heal a girl about nine years old who has been stabbed. She is the daughter of Sheikh al-Fadli'. I lost no time. I took with me bandages, sedatives and medicaments. I left for Banī Shanqūl with Wad al-Gharbī, and six spearmen.

It was one hour after midnight when we arrived there, and a large crowd of natives awaited us. All was silence. Everyone was looking at me, waiting to hear from my lips the sentence of life or death.

I entered the house where the girl was lying near a fire with her head on her mother's breast. She was crying. I carefully examined the wound, which passed a little above the left arm-pit, where it joins the shoulder. As no important vein had been touched, I hoped that in a few days the girl would be better. I dared to say: 'She will certainly get better.' I carefully cleaned the wound and dressed it as best I could. I recommended the mother to take care that the girl would not dislodge the bandage when she moved. I had to delay my departure from Singe for several days. Every evening I returned to dress the wound, until 25 February, when the girl was better.

That day, a long column of girls, between twelve and twenty years of age, all dressed in festive clothes, came to greet me. They were dyed red, they had iron rings in their left ears, metal plates on their noses and branches of evergreen on their heads. Certainly, these were the most beautiful women of Banī Shanqūl. The young woman who led the rest had a smile on her lips and walked gracefully towards me. With both hands she held a wooden bowl containing a little milk. She said: 'Take it, sir, and drink it. It is from my goat, I milked it this morning. May you live for many years, and I hope to see you again shortly among us.' Then all the girls joined hands and formed a circle around me and, accompanied by singing and the sound of the big drum, they began a graceful dance. Now and again they paused and a great shout went up: 'Long live the white man, who is able to cure illnesses! Hurrah!' I can still see and recall that novel spectacle.

At noon on 26 February, the *Fekī* Musā'id came from Banī Shanqūl to Singe to accompany me with Wad al-Gharbī towards Qaysān. Woods, hills and rocky mountains, a vast plain looking towards Abyssinia, small and large dried-up streams — such was our road.

I hardly slept that night in Qaysān. A lone Egyptian soldier was singing: '*Fī'l-jinayna, fī'l-jinayna* — One of the most beautiful of the Arab girls, pale, tired, with her hair rumpled, is in the woods plaintively singing that she has been betrayed by the one she loves dearly.... She calls him again ... she will call him every morning, every evening, and in the darkness of each night, while there is breath left in her body....' Strange music. The continuous exotic lament haunted me....

We left Qaysān, and arrived at Kiri on 6 March. The sky was blue and the soil freshened by rain the day before. I proceeded to Famaka and left there for Surayfa at dawn on the 19th, accompanied by the Egyptian commandant till, after an hour's walk, we met some soldiers coming from al-Rusayris with several Egyptian prisoners condemned to exile for crimes they had committed in their homeland.

From Surayfa I began to draw away from the river, making my way to the north-east to visit the nomad Arab tribes, encamped between the Dinder and the Blue Nile. I made about thirty halts among the Arabs, and always lodged under their tents where I could study their customs.

All the Arabs, whom I visited between the Blue Nile and the Dindir are shepherds. Their language is Arabic, but preserved here in all its purity. Neologisms and barbarisms have not affected it in the least. More than once I heard sentences which recalled to my mind some of the verses of the Koran. I noticed too that when the shepherds made grammatical errors, or used less pure pharases, it was when they were speaking to strangers, in their efforts to make themselves better understood.

The voice also of these Arabs is soft and agreeable. Their appearance is gracious, and the features of the face are amazingly regular. Their bodies are perfectly proportioned in all parts. Both men and women are generally vigorous and agile. They have great power of resisting hunger, thirst, tiredness and sleep.

In general, these Arabs are poor and each marries only one woman. Whoever has a lot of cattle is in a position to marry more than one woman, and he considers himself fortunate because he increases the number of his relations, and so adds greatly to his influence.

Marriages nearly always take place by mutual consent. Nevertheless, a father will never allow his daughter to marry a man he does not hold to be his equal. Rape is sometimes the upshot of a refusal, and the offender is then sought by the parents of the young girl. Once in their hands, the offender must redeem himself by handing over young cattle, and this then gives him the right to marry the girl.

Women's work consists in looking after the beasts that are not taken to pasture, making or repairing household goods, and preparing food for the family. In the evening the girls, after having milked the camels, goats or cows, make butter by shaking a vessel full of milk; they also grind grain and help their mothers in the domestic work.

Like the men, the women tie the cotton aprons round their loins; one end of the apron is attached to a thin leather belt, and the other thrown over the shoulders. Girls wear the *rahat*.

Dancing is a distraction which the Arab girls always afford the guest who receives the hospitality of their tents. In this case some kind of present must be given to the dancers. Among the presents which I gave, the most appreciated were the small looking-glasses. The women of these Arabs not only allow themselves to be seen, but it was they who met me, who introduced the family and who prepared my food and supper.

As soon as I had reached their dwelling-places, I was given a pot of *marīsa* and, after about half an hour, I had to eat *mahrāra*, [16] national delicacy, with which the guest is always entertained.

If an Arab has no ram ready to celebrate the arrival of his guest, he will go to his neighbour's enclosure and, without anyone's permission, will choose one and kill it on the spot. He then takes it to his tent, leaving a trail of blood along the way, which serves to tell the owner of the man who took it away. The owner then goes to claim at least part of the animal when it is cooked and roasted. Hospitality is sacred to the Arabs, and they regard as a guest anyone who takes part with them in a meal. They say: 'We have bread and salt between us, which prevents us from becoming enemies.'

On the morning of 27 March, I crossed the Blue Nile. The town of Sinnār was near. . . . The Vice-Governor procured me the camels to go to Wad Madanī. 'Be careful', he said, 'to keep a north and north-westerly direction, and move away from the river. Take the path that

---

[16] An hors d'oeuvre of sliced raw offal.

leads into the great woods of Sinnār, and here and there you will find
camps of the Abū Rūf Arabs.... '

After two days, I was among the Abū Rūf Arabs.... Their customs
are more or less the customs of the Arabs on the right bank of the Blue
Nile, but they show greater attention in raising and training their
horses.... The horse is the inseparable companion to these Arabs;
their best defence in war, and the source of their wealth....

I left the Abū Rūf on 30 March, and the chief with whom I stayed
came a good part of the way with me through the woods. On the
evening of 31 March I was in Wad Madanī. ... At daybreak on 5 April
1855 I at last saw Khartoum.

CHAPTER XII

FROM KHARTOUM TO AL-QALLABAT AND FAZUGHLI, 1876-7

by G. Martini

The author of this itinerary, Fr. Gennaro Martini (1843-1915) was a Piedmontese born at Beinasco, a small town near Turin. He received his education for the priesthood first at the Seminario delle Missioni Apostoliche in Turin and afterwards at the seminary in Biella. In 1874 he came to the Sudan with Bishop Comboni, and two years later made a journey in the Nuba Mountains recorded in Chapter XV below. Here we follow him on an assignment in the Ethiopian borderlands. Fr. Martini has an observant eye for picturesque detail but, either because he was insensitive of ear or, as is more likely, his manuscript was butchered by printer and editor, his recorded place-name spellings are sometimes difficult and even impossible to identify. The account which follows is derived from his report, 'Relazione intorno alla sua esplorazione sul Fiume Azzurro', Annali del Buon Pastore, No. 16, 1877, pp. 36-58.

Fr. Martini retired from the Mission in 1879 and spent the rest of his life in his native Piedmont. In addition to his parochial duties he lectured at the Istituto Umberto Primo in Turin where he taught among others the future King Fuad I of Egypt. He died at his birthplace, Beinasco.

We left Khartoum on the 21 September 1876, and took the road, which for the most part flanks the White Nile and extends to the desert between the White and the Blue Nile. The road running alongside the Blue Nile is actually the shortest to al-Masallamīya, but it was still bogged down by the marshes left behind by the rains. There was yet another road running between these two, but I chose the former, because from there I knew that I would be able to make a close study of the cultivation in the desert. Because of the accumulation of sand blown by the winds, this stretch of desert remains uninhabited for almost the whole of the year. At the beginning of the *kharīf*, [1] however, it is taken over by the Arab agriculturists from the localities along the river. These quasi-nomadic people, accompanied by their herds of cows, goats and sheep, once more take possession of the land they abandoned during the dry season. Shortly before the rains are due, they come to repair their old huts, or erect new ones made simply of matting, as a protection against the hurricanes and rainstorms. A large ditch is dug by each group of people in some low-lying spot and this serves to catch the necessary rain-water for them and their beasts. As soon as this is done, work in the fields begins.

Here, briefly, is the way they proceed. First of all, they clear the fields of the dried grass and old *durra* stalks of the previous year. The refuse is then heaped up and set on fire. Once the soil has been cleared, parallel rows of small holes at intervals of 30 to 50 cm. are made. After the first rain has sufficiently moistened them, a few seeds of *durra* are placed in them, and they are filled up with soil pushed in by the feet. With this the sowing is completed and nothing more is done until the harvest except to clear the fields once or twice of the quick-growing grass, so as to prevent the young *durra* shoots from being suffocated. Once the grain has formed, the battle against the winged-tribes then begins, for swarms of sparrows and other grain-eating birds continuously attempt to settle on the fields. As a counter-measure, small platforms are erected on the forked branches of trees, and on these boys sit, continuously shouting and waving sticks with rags in an effort to scare off the hovering flock of birds.

There is little cultivation in the stretch between Khartoum and Arribeh [? Wad al-Turābī], so Kalākla . . . Etman and other villages in this area cannot be properly called agricultural. Here they depend on their herds of cattle for a living, or take up jobs as camelmen. A few of the smaller towns where water is not obtainable remain uninhabited. Arribeh is an agricultural village, and the Arab inhabitants do not emigrate because they can grow sufficient *durra*, the stalks of which supply the needs of their cattle. It is at this point that a vast and florid cultivation opens out, and, although I have been to many parts of the Sudan, I cannot ever remember having seen anything to compare with this. I stopped at Arribeh for two days and spent my time inspecting

---

[1] The rainy season.

the fertile fields, entirely covered by the quick-growing white *durra*. I picked a few stems, some of which were 40 cm. high.

The stretch which I visited between Arribeh and al-Masallamīya is remarkable for its number of small towns, some permanent, or some inhabited only during the rainy season, and for its remarkably flourishing cultivation.

On my way I visited [?] Gasel Udeab and [?] Abiselab. The countryside between these villages is completely denuded of trees, and even the *heglig* and *nabak* bushes, and the acacia, met with along the previous stretch, are not to be found here. The inhabitants of these villages make use of sun-dried cow dung as fuel for their fires.

One day, as I was proceeding on my way with my camel, I was suddenly startled by the noise of shouting and clapping of hands. I turned my head in the direction of the noise, and became aware of a dark mist almost blotting out the sun. At first, I thought that it was a village in flames. On arriving there, however, I saw that men, women and children were madly stamping on the fields of *durra*, crushing it to the ground. Others were hurriedly setting fire to bundles of dried grass, and soon, fanned by the wind, the fields were covered in thick black smoke. They were fighting their most deadly enemy — the locust. Locusts had appeared in great numbers that year. Woe to any field on which they settle, for in a matter of a few hours the crop would be entirely destroyed.

In general, the people are quite hospitable, communicative, and generously offer guests their *kisra*, milk, *mulāh* and roasted *durra*.

I arrived at al-Masallamīya on the 28th, and stopped at the house of Wad Madanī, [2] ex-shaykh of the country. He was a very courteous, honest man, and looked after me with great care. The town is quite extensive and is inhabited by merchants and farmers. There is a beautiful mosque, and for the most part the houses are made of earth, but are quite pleasant and clean. The wells are large and supply drinking water all the year round. As the water is somewhat ferruginous, however, the wealthier people have their water brought to them daily from the nearby Blue Nile, which without doubt is the best water in the whole of the Sudan. I wandered through the town, questioning the people and entering the *zarība*, and I think that I am correct in stating that two-thirds of the population are slaves, mainly Shilluk, Fertīt and Dinka.

---

[2] Probably al-Hājj Madanī Shanbūl (R. Hill, *On the Frontiers of Islam*, pp. 32, 32n., 168, 200).

After a long trek through prosperous cultivation, we arrived at Abū Harāz from al-Masallamīya. About two kilometres away from the river, the cultivation ceases abruptly. All that can be seen are the thick bushes of *nabak, heglig* and other thorny shrubs, often covering the narrow pathways. I reached Abū Harāz and stayed at the house of the shaykh of the camelmen, al-Sālih 'Abdullāh, who was very kind and looked after all my requirements.

Abū Harāz stands on an elevated and healthy spot on the right bank of the river. It is one of the oldest villages in the Sudan, but is now somewhat deteriorated. However, a market is held twice a week, and the inhabitants are farmers and traders. From Abū Harāz to al-Qadārif there are two principal roads used by travellers; one flanks the river Rāhad for quite a long stretch. This stream takes its rise in the mountains of Ethiopia above Fāzūghlī and flows into the Blue Nile near Abū Harāz. The other road, further up, crosses this uncultivated area in an easterly direction towards al-Qadārif.

Generally, the first road is used during the dry season because of the convenience of the nearby water and the agricultural villages along the Rahad. The second is used during the rainy season both to avoid the marshes formed along the first, and because the deposits of rain-water along this road are extremely useful to the travellers. As my journey took place towards the end of the rainy season I naturally took the first road.

As soon as I had left Abū Harāz, the scene changed considerably. Apart from a few small fields near [?] Idelcfhe Andelmehet, and several insignificant villages, all that could be seen now was an unending growth of a kind of *qashsh* — small, thin, sturdy reeds about three metres in height. These reeds are so dense that when a camel passes through, it opens a small path, over which the other camels follow. This part of the journey is very tiresome, because even on camel-back the traveller cannot look around him, but must be careful to avoid being hit in the face by the towering reeds.

For three days I kept up a steady pace until I reached Gala [?Buwayda al-Qal'a] I felt quite tired, as during the previous nights we had been unable to sleep because of the brief but violent storms that had occurred. At the first rumbling of thunder and darkening of the sky towards evening, we had to hastily erect improvised tents, supported by tree branches so as to protect our supplies of dom. At Buwayda al-Qal'a, there are large wells and cisterns; here we refilled our waterskins and rested in one of the numerous villages which formed a kind of oasis in the midst of these desert steppes. After Gala Bang

[?Qalʿat Arang] — a long chain of mountains to the south of the road — and before Buwayda, there are the Rargen [?Sarjayn] and Janis [?Fanays] mountains, together with other smaller ones, and these are studded by the small towns of the Arab farmers. Here the fields are larger and more flourishing and we could see stretches of *durra,* beans, and many other kinds of vegetables. From Buwayda al-Qalʿa I made my way to Sūfī, a large village near al-Qadārif, and the intervening countryside was similar to the previous one, the same steppes and the same reeds. However I was able to visit Jabal ʿAtāsh, Jabal Ummat Rumayla, Jabal Umm Qurūd.[3] The latter hill is covered by many leafy trees, and infested by scores of monkeys — hence the name Umm Qurūd, Mother of Monkeys. At the foot of the hill there was also a kind of a grotto, where we found very clear water seeping through the ground, and which the camelmen said never dried up throughout the year.

Although it was October and the season was quite advanced, storms occurred every night along the whole of this part of the journey.

al-Qadārif, or rather Abū Sinn, is a second-rate town situated on an elevated and healthy spot. A short distance away it is surrounded by small barren hills except to the south where there is a large stream. There is little cultivation in the surrounding countryside. During the *kharīf* there is a dense growth of tall *qashsh,* which is immediately burnt as soon as it is dry.

To the south, however, only a few minutes away from the town, there are beautiful gardens with lemons, *qishta,* pomegranates, prickly pear, dates and many other varieties. These gardens flourish because of the water drawn from the *sāqiyas,* whilst deep wells, eight metres down in the rocks, provide drinking water throughout the whole of the year.

Most of the houses are *tukuls* made of straw, and enclosed by thorny *zarība.* However, some are made from stone and lime-mortar, while a few are of brick and earth, plastered with lime on the outside. Stone can be obtained in large quantities from the nearby mountains and even nearer to the town, it consists mostly of a hard granite, dark in colour, and of natural rectangular-shape. The merchants, whether Greeks or Arabs, construct large storehouses, which they then hire out

---

[3] On modern maps Jabal Ummat Qardūd. *Qardūd* = rugged, elevated ground within an outline like the back of an animal. Did our writer, possibly seeing the monkeys on the mountain, conclude wrongly that the name was Ummat Qurūd, Mother of Monkeys? L. Montuori also passed by a 'mountain of monkeys' (p. 32 above).

to traders. Abū Sinn is a town with numerous inhabitants and is a trade-centre owing to its central position among all other towns. It is also a meeting place for the traders of Khartoum, Kasala, Judda and al-Qallābāt. From Khartoum, Judda and Kasala, many caravans arrive bringing linen, drapery, salt, spices and other Arab goods. From al-Qallābāt comes coffee, beeswax, honey, horses and skins bought by the Sudanese from the Ethiopians. The markets are filled with quantities of *durra* and bales of good quality cotton from the neighbouring towns, in addition to numerous heads of cattle, sheep, goats, etc. The market or bazaar is held twice weekly. On such days between forty and eighty oxen, ten to fifteen camels, and five to ten *kharūf* (large sheep) are killed in the market square, and each family buys its requirements of meat, because during the non-market days only a few sheep are killed. The climate is good, even after the *kharīf* [the rains], when fever is rampant in the Sudan. It is true that I came across many sick people, but the cases of fever were few, and even then were of short duration.

al-Qadārif is the headquarters of a *mudīr* dependent on the *hukumdāriyya* of Khartoum. [4]

Continuing south, we arrived in three hours at Atar [?'Assār], a village, which recently sprang up during the Abyssinian War, when groups of soldiers were stationed here. The inhabitants are a mixture of people from Egypt and the Sudan. As it lies in a valley, surrounded by medium-sized mountains, it is quite warm here, and many beautiful gardens are to be found.

On 10 November, I left Abayo by camel and continued my journey. Towards evening, we reached the boundary of the territory between Shaykh Abū Sinn and Shaykh Wusai, who lives in Tāka, and whose land extends as far as al-Qallābāt. Until Alobras was reached, about a day's journey from al-Qadārif, all that could be seen was barren ground, often rugged, and covered with layers of stones and pebbles, making the way ahead very difficult; there are no trees, with the exception of a few *nabak* shrubs, and little or no vegetation. Further on, the ground begins to be studded with groups of *heglīg* and red acacia. The latter yields a limited quantity of gum, which the inhabitants of these parts collect by cutting the tree about a metre from the ground. A day further on towards Doka, begins a large forest of varied and pleasant trees. One can admire the acacia, *nabak*, and *jummayza*, and their extraordinary size offer the weary traveller a welcome rest under their

---

[4] The Turco-Egyptian-occupied Sudan was divided into a number of administrative regions (plural *mudīriyyāt*), each governed by a *mudīr* who was responsible to the *hukumdār*, the equivalent of governor general, in Khartoum.

shady leaves. Lower Doka stands on a small hill, covered by a flourishing vegetation. Here one can also see a maze of valleys and small hills, dotted with pleasant groups of huts. The surrounding plains are covered by a luscious growth, broken here and there by dense woods, as far as upper Doka. This attractive town is made up of numerous *zariba,* and groups of huts, nestling on the slopes and plateaux of the mountains.

There are very many villages all around, and all are agricultural. On the market square, *durra,* sesame, beans and other local produce are sold at a quarter of the price of that sold at al-Qadārif. This is because of the abundance of the harvest, and the difficulties of transporting the goods elsewhere. There are many hyenas in these mountains, and they are bigger then any I have seen elsewhere. During the night, they roam the public highways in search of food but they leave the inhabitants undisturbed.

The sun was just tipping the barren peaks of Dhanab al-Kalb, a high mountain, to the east of Doka, when I took the main road leading to al-Qallābāt. There are only a few villages on the way, but these are surrounded by well-cultivated fields, and the inhabitants are very hospitable. For most of the way, the road winds through beautiful forests, crossed here and there by large streams, which were now dried up. The principal one is the so called Kakamut, near Ra's al-Fīl, whence a long chain of green-covered hills can be seen. Travellers have to burn a path for themselves through the undergrowth, consisting of very tall grass which hinders their progress. It often happens that virgin forests are damaged in this way.

There is much wild life to be found here: guinea-fowl, gazelles and antelopes of various kinds. A day's distance from al-Matamma, near the mountain of al-Qallābāt, the terrain becomes mountainous, and is often intersected by deep streams. The mountains are quite high, but do not form continuous chains. Their slopes are covered for some distance up with leafy trees. The groups of mountains seem to follow one after the other, giving the traveller the impression of being enclosed in a long narrow valley. At the end, the horizon opens out a little, the mountains at the side draw further away from each other, and the smaller hills are covered with numerous dulayb palms. Here we reached the old town of al-Matamma also called al-Qallābāt, from the mountain that dominates it. Part of the inhabitants are natives of the country, part are Arabs who settled here after its conquest by the Khedive of Egypt, and the smallest part is made up of Ethiopians who came here to trade. The dwellings are nearly all built from *qashsh,* and enclosed by thorny *zaribas.* The climate is unhealthy because of the long duration of the rainy season and the low-lying terrain where the town is situated. The air in the town is therefore warm and damp and is responsible for much fever. I had fever for eight of the ten days I stopped here.

The market is busy only during the dry season, during which time it is frequented by Arabs and Ethiopians trading their goods. The roads are completely impassable during the rainy season. The Ethiopians bring in large numbers of horses from their country, which for the most part are bought by the Baqqāra. They also bring large quantities of coffee, honey, bees wax, butter and cattle, especially bovine. The Arabs bring cotton, linen and *durra*. Both buyers and sellers pay a tax to the shaykh of the place. In his turn, the shaykh pays an annual tribute either to the Khedive, or to the King of Ethiopia — since al-Qallābāt is not strong enough to maintain complete independence. When I was there, during the early part of November, the market was closed, and the inhabitants were in great fear because the Ethiopians were threatening to invade the country. However, this danger was overcome by the payment of a large sum. *Durra*, sesame and linen are generally cheap; but it is not so with linen articles, and other imported goods, after the market has been closed, for then their prices increase substantially. Above the town there is a large fort and a garrison of soldiers, kept there as a guard against a possible invasion by the Ethiopians. The forests encircling the city abound with wild animals, particularly lions, which during the rainy season roam around the city during the night. I was shown a spot where a few months earlier a *feki* was devoured by a famished lion. Usually only a hungry lion will attack a man.

We made our way towards Jabal [?] Caefi, a short distance from al-Qallābāt, and we took the same road as we had previously taken when we arrived, but veered slightly to the west and passed the villages of Melca and Aorbella. For about a day we followed the course of the Rāhad, which we reached at Ottegian. We crossed without difficulty, as the level of the water was low. Having crossed these two streams, we made our way towards the south-west, and arrived at Nesciscia [?Abū Shunayna], a large Arab agricultural village. The countryside here is mountainous and skirts a large marshy area, which holds the waters from one *kharīf* to another. This was the last hospitable village that we came across on our way to Fāzūghlī. From Nesciscia we followed the course of the Blue Nile for a day until we reached Fāzūghlī. The journey at times was quite wearisome. Everywhere are acacias of different types, together with *nabak* and other thickly-covered thorn trees. For hours on end I had to wade through marshes, with water lying more than a metre deep in the tall grass. Truly this was a difficult part of our journey, especially as there was always the danger of being bitten by some poisonous snake. At times the slopes of the mountains are so precipitous and the streams so deep that we had to descend from our camels and laboriously forge our way ahead on foot.

I was journeying towards the end of the *kharīf*, where for the greater part of the year there was only sand blown by the winds; now there was grassland. The climate was quite agreeable and the atmosphere clear.

At about two days' distance from Famaka, the roads became increasingly difficult owing to the numerous streams that followed one after the other, and the deep precipitous valleys, through which a small path was barely discernible; thus the camels were hindered in their progress.

Famaka, like al-Matamma, stands on several hills rising from a large valley, surrounded by the river and medium-sized mountains. The natives of the country, who are dark in colour, are Muslims, and form two-thirds of the population. They are very courteous. One-third is composed of Arabs, who are mostly employed by the government. The town is made up of huts enclosed by *zarības*, but it has deteriorated since its domination by the Khedive. There is scant cultivation, and cattle are few. The Blue Nile flows near the city, at the foot of the Fāzūghlī mountain, through several cataracts which make navigation impossible.

Hippopotami abound along this stretch of river. Towards evening and in the morning, twenty or thirty of them can be seen going down-river, with their heads above water. There are also a lot of crocodiles, some of enormous size.

There is little or no trade at Fāzūghlī. I noticed a complete difference of customs and ways of life as between the Arabs and negroes at Fāzūghlī, al-Rusayris and other villages I passed on the way. A negro will very rarely go to an Arab's house; he does not seek his assistance or trade with him. The negroes have their own markets and trade only among themselves, as I had already noticed above al-Rusayris. I crossed the river to a village at the foot of Jabal Fāzūghlī to visit the ancient settlement, wherein resided the *makk* [5] of that district. All I saw was a small village in ruins. The old *makk* was away with the *mudir*.

Having left Famaka, I made my way back and hugged the river as

---

[5] The title of certain senior tribal leaders, usually hereditary, in the former sultanate of Sinnār. Under the Turco-Egyptian regime the title tended to become ceremonial.

best I could. I visited the villages of Kassab Abū Shandī, Brra [ʔButaba] and others inhabited by Arab shepherds, or native negroes. I noticed little cultivation at these villages, and only scanty pasturing grounds. However, there are thick woods of different types of trees: I saw adansonias, and *jummayza* of extraordinary size. I stopped several days at al-Rusayris, where the local commander treated me with great kindness. Some time ago, al-Rusayris was densely populated by negroes, but now there are only a few houses and huts. I then continued my journey by boat from al-Rusayris, as I wished to see some of the villages along the banks. From al-Rusayris to Khartoum, the two banks of the river are inhabited mostly by Arabs. As far as Karkūj on the right bank and Sinnār on the left very thick woods can be seen inland, together with intermingling shrubs and grass. Three or four days' journey towards Khartoum from the above-mentioned places, a vast treeless plain opens out dotted with agricultural villages.

In general, there are very few *sāqiyas* on the river, because normally the banks are high and precipitous. The villages in the woods above Sinnār and Karkūj are enclosed by very high and thick hedges or *zarības*, because of the numerous lions in this area.

I passed Sinnār and left the boat near Smaad [ʔUmm al-Sant], as it had twice threatened to founder. I continued the journey by camel, and once more keeping close to the river, I returned to Khartoum. I was able to see the many beautiful agricultural villages like Fadāsī, Abū Furū', Abū 'Ushar, Nādī and Wad al-Turābī, surrounded by vast fields. It is from these villages that Khartoum market receives most of its grain. Some of these villages grow cotton quite successfully....

NUBIA

CHAPTER XIII

NUBIA IN 1861

by Giovanni Beltrame

Here Fr. Beltrame writes an essay on Nubian anthropology, on the distribution and customs of the non-Arab peoples who live along the banks of the Middle Nile, whose lands were then frequently known as northern or lower Nubia (Nubie inférieure) to distinguish it from southern or upper Nubia (Nubie supérieure), a territory stretching from the region of Berber to the southernmost limits of Arab settlement. The use of the word Sudan to cover the entire territory between Upper Egypt and Uganda was slow in coming. These passages appeared in the writer's book, In Nubia presso File, Siene, Elefantina, *Verona, 1893.*

The inhabitants of Southern Nubia are descended from the Arabs, and speak their language, but those of the northern part, in the Nile Valley, although they know Arabic, speak a dialect of their own. This dialect is sweet, harmonious and without aspirates and, as far as I could make out, bears no relation to Arabic.

The true origin of these Nubians has not yet been established. The Egyptians call them Barābra, which is the plural of Berberī. In Algeria and Morocco, the name Berberī is also given to a race which lives apart from the Arab race, and which, in addition to Arabic, speaks another language. However, the similiarity in the names is not sufficient to prove that these two races are of the same origin.

Although the name Berberī has been given to them since time immemorial, and although accustomed to being so called and using it of themselves, it is not their true name. The inhabitants of northern Nubia repeatedly told me that their true name is Kennu or Noba, and I know that the Barābra of Algeria and Morocco actually call themselves by the name of Sciluh or Amazigh, that is, free men.

It may be that either one or the other was called by ancient Egyptians by a name meaning Barbarians, as we know that the name of barbarians was given by them to all who did not speak their language. The Greeks and the Romans may then have translated this term into their languages. Granted this hypothesis from barbarians, translated by the Romans, there emerged Berberī (plural Barābra) in the Arabic language. The comparative study of the languages spoken in Africa will alone solve this and similar ethnographical problems.

From the studies so far made on this subject, the language spoken in several of the oases to the south of Algeria is said to resemble some of the terms used by the Barābra of this area. But could not such similarity derive from the frequent and intimate relations existing between these two people, rather than from a common origin?

Some of the leading writers on Africa have expressed the view that the mother tongue of the Bishara, or Bishārīn living in the Tāka area (to the north-north-east of Abyssinia) is the same as that of the Nubian Barābra of the north. As a matter of fact, several of the Bishārīn merchants I knew in Aswan all spoke this Nubian language in place of Arabic, but in order to prove that the origin is identical, it must also be proved that they possess no other language of their own, apart from Barābra of the Nubians. Actually among themselves they employ a dialect which is not understood by the Nubians of the north. Moreover, their character is completely different.

The Bishārīn had been described to me as wild unfriendly people, who drink the warm blood of living animals, and feed only on the flesh and milk of their beasts. However, the wealthiest of them come two or three times a year to the banks of the Nile and exchange their cattle for supplies of *durra*.

When I saw them for the first time in Aswan, I was most agreeably impressed. They are truly handsome men with regular features and large, expressive eyes, and their build is lithe and elegant. The colour of their skin is dark chocolate. Their hair falls a little below the ears, arranged in straight locks, each of which is curled at the ends. Their hair is impregnated with grease and so matted that it would be difficult to pass a comb through it. However, they are careful not to disturb their hair, and always have with them a sharp piece of wood in the shape of a large needle, with which they scratch their heads.

I was most anxious to know the original language of the Bishārīn, and to learn as much as possible of their customs. As I earnestly wished to visit them in their tents, I managed to persuade my companion

Fr. Dal Bosco to follow me in my new exploration as soon as Pro-Vicar Matteo Kirchner, who was in Europe, had arrived at Philae.

When I heard that a few Bishārīn had arrived in Aswan, I hastened to make their acquaintance. I had several meetings with them and before leaving I asked: 'Would it be possible for me to accompany you, without incurring any danger, to visit your tribe and make friends with your chief?' 'Certainly', they replied, 'you will be welcome ... why not? However, as we are returning tomorrow, perhaps you would not be ready in time to leave at such short notice, but we shall be back in Aswan in three or four months. In the meantime, we will tell our paramount chief of your wish to visit him, and you can be making the necessary arrangements to accompany us the next time.' Before leaving them, I gave them a magnificent *chibuk* as a gift to their chief.

It was on 4 January 1861 that I had this conversation with the Bishārīn, and on the 17th of the same month, the Austrian Consul, Schreiner,[1] arrived in Aswan. On this occasion I acquainted the Consul with my desire to visit the Bishārīn country, and he kindly offered to obtain a firman from the Viceroy of Egypt, Sa'īd Pasha, which would guarantee me a safe journey. While I was more than content with the new and interesting life at Philae, I was nevertheless impatient to leave so as to be back by the month of June before the great heat set in.

In the meantime, I was learning as much as I could about the ways and customs of the Bishārīn. Many strange things were told me about the perils of the journey, and the pride of these people. Some said that I would be attacked on the way, and that white men in particular were the targets of the Bishārīn. I was told of the spiders, scorpions and snakes which I would find on the way, and in my tent. They spoke of the moral stupor, acute ear-aches and violent pains. However, these reports, given to me by Aswan merchants, I considered to be exaggerated.

Towards the middle of April, the Bishārīn returned to Aswan, but the *firmān* which the Austrian Consul had promised to send me had not arrived. In fact, he did not return until June, when the Bishārīn had already left. This was disappointing to me because it meant that I would not be able to visit them in their own homes. Moreover, the Pro-Vicar had to return to Europe to hand over the Mission to the Franciscan fathers.

---

[1] G.F. Schreiner (1821-83), Chancellor in the Austrian consulate general at Alexandria in 1851-3 and Consul General in 1858. He was made a baron in 1870.

The word *bishārī* (plural *bishārīn*) bears without doubt traces of an Arab name, and the same can be said for the words Amar, Umrān, etc., by which names several Bishārīn tribes are called.

I am not going to touch upon the customs of the Bishārīn which are identified with those of the Abū Zayd Arabs. From what was told to me by several Nubians, and repeated by some Egyptians who had visited them several times, the likeness is so remarkable as to make it difficult even for expert travellers among Arab shepherds to decide if they are among Bishārīn or descendants of Abū Zayd.

In my opinion (*a*) the Bishārīn, who have the same customs as the Abū Zayd Arabs; (*b*) the Barābra of Northern Nubia, who are almost identical in their ways, with the inhabitants of southern Nubia, descendants from the Arabs, and speaking their language, and (*c*) the Barābra dispersed among the Arab populations of Morocco and Algeria, and whose customs are confused with those of the Arab shepherds, were all natives races intermingled with the Arabs, and perhaps especially, with the Arab shepherds, who are found to the north and south of the Tuareg and Tibu. These people preserve their native language, while the Arabic language was easily introduced owing to their continued relations with the Arabs, by whom they were invaded or surrounded.

The Nubian Barābra are slightly over medium build. Their slender limbs, long thin hands and arms, although in proportion to the rest of the body, do not, at first glance, betray that vigour and elasticity which I frequently saw. Their limbs, devoid of excess flesh, showing only bone, muscle and sinew, are capable of great effort and labour. The oval and rather long faces of these Nubians are very much like those of all the other tribes of Upper Nubia. Their features are attractive and delicate, although deeply tanned by the rays of the tropical sun. Their eyes are keen, black and sparkling. The nose is straight and regular, while the whiteness of their teeth equals that of their ivory. In fact, the Nubian Barābra and their women could be called beautiful, despite the general narrowness of their brows and slenderness of the muscles. Their ways are graceful and dignified, although at times they give way to sudden fits of temper.

Customs of the Barābra

The Nubian Barābra, like the ancient Egyptians, have a reddish-brown skin, oval face, aquiline nose, slightly rounded at the tip, thickish lips, but not protruding, prominent chin, thin beard, lively eyes, hair curled but never frizzled, and a perfectly proportioned body. On seeing them,

Blumenbach, the traveller, was greatly struck by the marked resemblance they bore to the figures depicted on monuments of ancient Egypt. [2]

The Barābra women do not tattoo or paint the uncovered parts of their body. However, like the men, they often have scars on their shoulders and backs. These scars are caused by a red-hot iron, used surgically by them to combat contagious diseases, especially prevalent among the younger people, or to stop a dangerous inflamation. This cure is not new to Africa, because Herodotus tells us that 'when the young nomadic Libyans reach the age of four, the veins at the top of the head, and those of the temple, are scorched with raw wool. I cannot say whether all these nomadic people do the same, but it is practised by some of them who claim that it guards them against the phlegm coming from the brain, thus assuring them of perfect sanity.'

There are only very few Nubians in the north who practise circumcision, saying that it is praiseworthy but not a necessary obligation. Some of these Nubians subject their daughters, before they have reached the age of puberty, to a very painful operation called *kheitat*. This is generally practised among the Arabs situated in Kurdufān and Sinnār, and it is an operation which guarantees to their future husbands the virginity of the young Nubian women.

Although the Barābra of Nubia are courageous and full of vigour, they have only the weakest idea of personal valour. If goaded by a Janissary they react feebly like a flock of sheep, as they are convinced that any retaliation against a representative of the government would be in vain, if indeed it did not have serious consequences.

They know nothing about patriotism as we understand it. Nevertheless, the similiarity of the language, the desire to be valorous in war, so as to earn the title of 'friends of the girls' (*ikhwān al-banāt*), and the adoption of a similar worship, have brought about a certain moral tie between them which, in some way, makes up for patriotism.

As for such feelings as respect and love, which could inspire people to sacrifices for their supreme chief, such sentiments do not exist in these feudal countries. Without patriotism, without respect for their sovereign, and all professing the same religion, living in the same area and having the same customs, the Barābra warriors fight only for booty. Once they have obtained it they care little or nothing for the victory or defeat of the person who called them to arms to defend his state. Like all barbarians, they go to war without stores or supplies, and live entirely on the country they occupy, consuming and destroying everything.

[2] J.F. Blumenbach (1752-1840), Austrian physician and anthropologist, professor of medicine at Göttingen and a pioneer of the anthropology of Africa.

Few are the Barābra who stay in their own country to work the land. The majority of the young boys, once they have reached the ages of twelve or fifteen, take up navigation, and in this they are adept. Many go to seek work in Alexandria, Cairo, Khartoum, etc. There they are employed as house servants or caretakers and, when they have grown old, they return to their native country telling of their strange adventures.

The Nubians are romantic. Many times, seated amongst them, I have heard their chatter as they rested during the heat of the day. I have heard them telling of the splendours of the cities of the Caliphs, of the marvel of the Suez Canal, and of the immense ships of the *Frangi* (Europeans). All great events fire the enthusiasm of the men and women. But the main attention was, above all, given to stories of war and hunting, and still more to the descriptions of animals and people of Central Africa. They were especially interested in the pigmies (whom they had not yet seen) no higher than three feet with beards down to their knees, armed with spears and so agile that they were not trapped by the trunks of elephants. In their conversations they evoke memories (although under different names) of Cyclops, Automolfs, pygmies and of legends which are to be found in the most ancient Greek literature. I listened to them, greatly impressed by what they said.

Here is what Schweinfurth writes, after he himself heard the narratives while passing the long evenings on the Upper Nile lying on the poop of his boat: 'Thinking of the traditions referred to during the conversations between my boatmen, I was puzzled and could not make out how much could be attributed to the inventive powers of the Nubians and what was their actual experience, and I said to myself: "How could they know anything about the works of Homer? How is it that they make the Shebber-Dighintu (dwarfs with long beards) fight the cranes, sometimes giving victory to the latter, and sometimes to the pigmies, as did the poets of ancient times?" '

The Date Palm

The limits of this precious tree in the interior of Africa are the 12° and 37° N., while along the coasts the tree is to be found as far as the Equator.

The date palm is no lover of rain, but nevertheless it must be repeatedly watered at the root to make the fruit grow plentiful and succulent. It is sometimes to be found in the desert, and a traveller sighting it sighs with relief for he knows that there must be fresh water nearby. For it to thrive well, the soil must be of a particular kind. Thus it is not surprising to find that there are numerous oases to be found to the south of the mountain ranges along the 33rd parallel, and this long chain is named Balad al-Jarīd,³ the region of the palms. It stretches from the Atlantic to the banks of the Nile; then it branches out towards the south, and finally crosses from north to south, the whole of the palm area which flanks the river Nile.

In Egypt and Nubia, as in all other areas, water is the essential element governing the fertility of the soil. Irrigation is necessary, and, if this is not provided naturally by the flooding of the Nile, it must be provided artificially. It is true that the mud of the Nile has some fertilizing value, but perhaps this value has been rated too highly. In the great oases of the Sahara, water and sun make up for the Nile mud. The gardens of Neftah (Balad al-Jarīd) yield in no way to the gardens of Rosetta. Moreover the slimy mud of the Nile seems to be less favourable to the date palm, as the fruit is not so tasty and abundant as it is in Neftah. It is also true that the Egyptians, especially along the Nile, are more interested in the cultivation of rice, grain, beans, cotton, sugar-cane, etc., almost neglecting the palms which are generally not watered.

On the other hand, in the oases of Balad-al-Jarīd the growing of palms is intelligently planned. Here the plantations are nearly always in the form of an equilaterial triangle, around which there is a narrow ditch, always full of water.

The palm is propagated either by seed or cuttings. The seed, sown in spring, germinates after three or four months, forming a solitary leaf; in the second year, two or three equally simple leaves are formed, while in the third year, pinnated leaves begin to appear. But as the shoots from seeds do not yield fruit until they are between fifteen and twenty years of age, and moreover as the seeds often produce male shoots, which cannot be distinguished until they begin to flower, propagation by cuttings is preferred. Thus in this way the standard of the trees is preserved, and in some cases even bettered, and they begin to fruit after five or six years at the latest. Even though they are female shoots, they are nevertheless pruned, in order to prevent them bearing imperfect fruit.

It is true that this tree takes a long time to grow, but on the other hand, it can have a life span of almost 250 years. If left to itself, it

³ Usually written in the plural, *bilād al-jarīd*, literally Lands of the Palm Branches.

reproduces from the saplings coming from the roots, but after eighty years the fruit is scarce and of bad quality.

Once the date palm has reached this state of decay, a sweet sap, milky, refreshing and agreeable, can be obtained from it; this is called date palm milk, and is procured by first cutting some of the branches of the top of the tree, and in spring three or more deep vertical cuts and a single circular one are made, under which bowls are placed to catch the liquid, which flows out in great quantity. However, this must be drunk as soon as possible because it quickly turns sour. The bowls are emptied each morning and they hold between 12 and 15 litres of this healthy drink, which only dries up after two or three months. The drink is quite similar in colour and taste to that of the coconut, and is called *luqma* in Arabic. Very early in the morning, the children sell it in the streets, shouting: '*luqma maliha yā luqma*'. Because these cuts infallibly cause the death of the tree, they are only made in superfluous male trees or in female trees which have become sterile and incapable of yielding good and abundant fruit.

The trees blossom in spring, and the fruit is picked either in October or November, according to the type of palm. When the date palms grow together in woods, as in some parts of northern Nubia, fecundation easily occurs, and the pollen from the anthers of the male tree is so abundant that at sunrise the woods appear to be covered by a yellowy mist. But cultivators concentrate only on female trees, which give a greater yield and rely on the wind to spread the pollen. The Arabs say, perhaps with exaggeration, that in the desert this pollen can travel distances of almost fifty miles, and that a single male tree can fecundate 200 female trees. However, as it is most important that fecundation should take place, to rely on the wind alone would be risky because one cannot estimate its strength or direction, so the growers resort to artificial fecundation, such as has been practised since ancient times and of which Theophrastus spoke. With this end in view the pollen sacs of the male palms are gathered when they are ready to burst with pollen. They are then vigorously shaken over the top of a female tree, scattering the pollen. This operation is essential, and if not carried out could lead to a complete lack of fruit. This actually happened in the neighbourhood of al-Bāsra in 1779, when the soldiers of Kārīm Khān did their utmost to carry out the idea of their sovereign to devastate everything. They destroyed all the male date palms and reduced the population to extreme poverty. In 1800, a similar tragedy befell Egypt, when the French and Muslims together ruined the fertile fields and obstructed the peaceful work of agriculture. In view of such disasters, which are not infrequent in the eastern lands, the growers do not forget to store some of the pollen every year; they have learnt from experience that it can be kept for several years in storage.

If a tree is not very high it is shaken and the fruit falls on mats or cloth so as not to bruise it. If, however, the tree is high, the picker climbs to the top, aided by the scaly nature of the bark. When the date is fresh (*tamr*) and newly-picked, its flavour is exquisite. The dried date (*balah*), differently prepared, forms the principal food of the inhabitants of the areas where it grows spontaneously. The people living near the Atlas mountains grind their dried dates into flour, which they mix with a little water. This is the only food they take with them on their long treks in the deserts. Sometimes the pulp of the dates is mixed and kneaded with flour, and *bisaysa*, a kind of bread-biscuit, [4] is made. This is health-giving, nourishing and pleasant to taste.

At times, the fruit is crammed into large earthenware containers and reduced to pulp under pressure; this, separated from the skin and stones, emerges from holes made in the bottom of the containers. The pulp thus obtained is greasy but has a delicious taste. It is called date-honey, and is used in place of butter to season rice and other foods.

In some places, like Nubia and Egypt, the dates are fermented with water and a kind of wine, vinegar and brandy are obtained, great use of which is made especially by the Copts.

In Nubia I was told that if the hard stones of the dates were ground, softened and boiled in water, they could serve as food for sheep and camels, but I have never verified this. I have also read that burnt date stones are used by the Chinese as an ingredient for the making of Indian ink, and that the Spaniards make their toothpaste from these stones.

The spadices, denuded of their flowers, are made into brooms, and the spathes are made into vases of various shapes. The old leaves are cut each year, and after they have been dried in the sun, serve as a valuable fuel in these districts. The fibres on the base of the stems are used to make rope and rough cloth. Mats, carpets, baskets, hats and other domestic articles are made from the leaves, softened and made pliable by immension in water.

The wood of the old trunks is very hard and durable, and is used in the construction of rustic buildings. In those countries where this useful tree abounds, it is generally the sole provider of building materials.

---

[4] A short, sweet pastry, an Egyptian delicacy.

Date wood burns slowly and without flame, and its charcoal gives off intense heat.

The wild date palm is always found in sandy and damp places. Groups of palm trees are to be found in the vast ocean of sand, stretching from 30° N., ever more arid, to within a short distance of the Equator. The traveller finds welcome relief from the sultry heat in the shade of these trees, under which fruit and grass flourish, while many and different kinds of birds gather in search of food and water.

The types of date palms are numerous, and the fruits of each are different in shape, which may be oblong, rounded, oval, cylindrical, etc. The dates also differ as regards consistency, size or colour. They can be yellow, brown, red, white and the like, while the taste also varies.

The best fruit are the largest semi-transparent, sticky variety, golden-yellow in colour and sweet in taste.

The shape of the fruit is generally the same as that of the stone it contains, and an expert grower, by merely looking at the stone, could tell the quality of the fruit and the type of tree which produced it.

Among the numerous known varieties of the date palm, the *degle*, [5] grown in the Balad al-Jarīd, is considered the best — the queen, or rather the king of dates. This is the type of tree which grows to the greatest height, and it is not uncommon to see some of them about eighty feet tall.

The *degle* palm is more productive than all the others, bearing its fruit in October, giving eight or ten clusters, each of which may weigh between 12 to 20 pounds. Its fruit is only eaten by the wealthy. The poor must be content with other varieties, mainly the *karlig* which is the most common of all

The *monakhir* (nose) date, which is held by some to be better than the *degle*, was reserved solely for the table of the Bey of Tunis, and it is not marketed.

The *trunga* date is one of the largest, but its taste is only mediocre.

The *ameris* is the first to bear fruit, and the *lagu* the last.

The *tafilet* [6] dates and those of all the oases of Morocco are of great renown.

The *sultānī*, — *saʿīd* — *freyeh* — *kaiby* — *uaedy* — *gazaly* varieties grow in the Siwah oasis.

---

[5] *Deglet Nur,* grown mostly in Algeria and Tunisia, introduced to the Sudan since the writer's time. As a soft date it is held in the Sudan to be only slightly superior to the Sudanese *Bint Ahmōda.*

[6] Read *Tafilalet,* a variety originally from the Algerian oasis of Tafilalet.

The *sultānī* date is of good quality and is in good demand commercially.

The *saʿīd* date is exported and sold to Egypt.

The *uaedy* date is the most inferior, and this is given to animals. The last kind, the *gazaly*, bears abortive fruit.

The following varieties are to be found in Sukkōt in Nubia: *kuntela*,[7] *berekāwi*,[8] *bettamudi*,[9] *dogona kedeventa*, *mursaye*, *shidda*. The *shidda* kind gives the most fruit. The best dates are those of the *bettamudi* and *barakāwī* palms.

In general, the Sukkōt dates are exquisite, rather small, and the stone thin and pointed. These dates are rare and are not often exported. On the other hand, the common varieties are found everywhere in Nubia.

At Wādī Halfā and Khartoum there are more than a million trees, and a tax of more than a million piastres was paid to the Egyptian government. The Nubia dates are sold by Nubian merchants in the Sinnār, Kurdufān and Dār-Fūr.

I have already stated that this palm extends as far south as the 12th parallel in the interior of Africa. Within this latitude it fruits like the vine, twice yearly. The first time it only yields an under-sized fruit full of sugar, which is picked in May after the dry season. The second fruiting is more prolific but with little sugar and so moist that it cannot be kept for long. These are picked in August, after the rainy season.

Writers, and especially poets, have praised the palm throughout the ages, dedicating it to heroes and victory, and regarding it as the emblem of conjugal love, health and the stability of empires.

From what we have said about this precious tree, it is not surprising that the Arabs hold it in great esteem. For this reason, its premature destruction is considered a crime by them and by all those who profess Islam. The caliph, Abū Bakr, a simple man, despite the splendour by which he was surrounded, ordered his lieutenants, as they were leaving for the conquest of Iraq, not to destroy the fruit-bearing trees (palms) upon which the people relied for their food. Moses also prohibited the destruction of these trees: 'Do not cut the fruit-bearing trees', he said to the Israelites, 'because each tree contains the life of a man' (Deuteronomy).

[7] *Gondeila*, makes an excellent soft date, a speciality of Wādī Halfā district before the drowning of the palms under the waters rising in the reservoir of the Aswan High Dam.

[8] *Barakāwī*, a fine dried date, sold in Egypt as *Sukkōtī and Ibrīmī*.

[9] *Bint Ahmōda*, similar to *Gondeila* but in the Sudan considered even superior.

But these words are not always heeded by the Muslim warriors. 'Abd al-Qādir b. Mahī al-Dīn in a few days thus destroyed the fortunes and hopes of the inhabitants of 'Ayn Madhī because they refused to open the gates of their city.

These trees are, in fact, like a pledge which the inhabitants of the oases cannot withhold from the enemy, and if there is no sacred order prohibiting the destruction, then the inhabitants may as well surrender or resign themselves of all they possess, even their country, as they would be forced to abandon a soil which for many years would no longer yield fruit.

Unless one has actually experienced this, it is impossible to have any idea of the temperate coolness and serene beauty of a cluster of palms in the middle of the desert. It seems as if the palms are rearing their slender and elegant heads, surveying the ocean of sand surrounding them. All around is deep silence broken only by the rustling of the wings of some birds or the murmur of a small turtle.

The Camel: a Study based on visits to Arab Shepherds

Buffon, writing of camels, said that they were the ships of the desert, but the Arabs, who are better acquainted with camels than with ships, say that ships are the camels of the sea.

Anyone who has seen these ruminant animals will have noted the following characteristics: long head, cleft upper lip, nostrils obliquely divided, prominent eyes, small ears, long neck, one or two humps, medium length tail, two jointed toes underfoot, four udders, wool-like hair, callosities on the chest and on the legs. The legs are long and unshapely, and terminate in feet which are apparently out of proportion. Altogether, these characteristics are anything but elegant, and in fact the appearance of this animal is quite grotesque. However, as we shall see, this deformed mass of flesh and bone is one of the wonders of nature which must impress even the most indifferent of observers.

One cannot sufficiently describe how aptly the characteristics of a camel satisfy the peculiar demands of its environment. If, for example, one wanted to build a living machine, designed to serve all the purposes such as are served by the camel, the problem could only be solved by the invention of a machine built from the blueprint of the camel itself. The thick skin under its wide feet is divided into two toes which are not separated externally, so that they are able to balance the entire body with their expansive elasticity, thus preventing the animal from sinking into the sand, over which it proceeds with slow, silent steps. The nostrils are formed in such a way that the camel can close them at will, so as not to breathe in the sand whirled up by the scorching *khamsīn* or *samūm*. The strong incisors of the upper jaw are able to bite the coarse, dry, prickly plants of the desert. The wonderful power of nature is above all evident from the cellular formation of the stomach of this extraordinary ruminant. In its stomach the camel has two appendices in which the glandular system almost continuously separates a natural fluid, similar to water, or if necessary, retains the freshness of hastily-drunk water for a considerable time. Thus, whether the water is produced and separated, or merely stored in the rumen, it suffices the camel for many days on its long treks across the arid deserts.

The seven callosities on the joints and chest, and a single or double hump on the back, specifically meet the requirements of the camel, which is considered to be the slave of man. These callosities bear the weight of the camel's burden when it kneels to be loaded. I must add, moreover, that the hump, or humps, are nothing more than secretions of fat, which are absorbed in the event of the camel being deprived of food, thus serving the camel in good stead in case of emergencies during a life destined to be spent in the desert.

The camel has various uses. The Arabs eat its flesh and drink its milk. From its hair they weave clothes, and from its hide they make shoes and sandals. Its dung is used by them as fuel, and the soot obtained produces sal-ammoniac after sublimation in well-closed vessels. In the east, camel hair is made into cloth and exported to make painters' brushes.

The hair of Persian camels is held in great esteem. There are three qualities: black, red and brown. The black is the most valuable, then the red, while the brown is only worth half as much as the red. But all these advantages are as nothing compared with the great usefulness of this ruminant as a means of transport. They are indeed the living machines by which communications are maintained across the most barren of deserts. Without them man would never have crossed these wastes. The tiring journey across these arid and inhospitable areas are made comparatively easy by the camel's natural gifts and nature. The camel is gifted with a very keen sense of smell, and often on long journey, exhausted by fatigue and thirst, it will break away and head straight for water, which had escaped the notice of the other quadrupeds and of the men themselves.

There are two different kinds of camels, the *camelus bactrianus*, with two humps, which is not found in Africa, and the *camelus dromedarius,* which has a single hump and is to be found everywhere in this continent. The Asian camel, which I do not intend to dwell upon, is hairy especially under the throat. It is generally dark brown in colour, and shorter and more muscular than the African camel.

There are very many different varieties of the *camelus dromedarius* in Africa. As with horses, the form and size depend a lot on the climate and the care taken by the owner. There are saddle camels and transport camels. The former are very fast, and often their trot is easier than that of our horses. I say our horses, because Arab horses never trot. The transport camels are more robust and walk slowly, swaying their wide shoulders.

The Arabs call all their saddle-camels *hajin.* Here too there are many varieties, and the special types are more the outcome of good food and rearing than the influence of the climate.

The Arabs train their *hajins* for quite a long time, and with incredible patience. They are saddled when quite young. At an early age, the *hajins* are easily broken in, and little by little obey the movements desired by the Arab.

The Arab, as I have already said, is always gentle in his treatment of the camel he is rearing, and gives it loving care. With certain actions or gestures the Arab calls the camel to him, pats it, scratches its ears, neck and belly, and by means of a small whip, teaches it to bear left or right. The various movements of the dromedary are always preceded by a certain intonation in the voice of its master.

As soon as the *hajin* has mastered the first steps of its training, knows how to bear left or right, start, increase speed, halt suddenly, kneel and rise, a bridle is then placed on the camel and he is taught to go at a short but fast pace, a movement greatly favoured by the Arabs. Finally the camel is taught the easy and fast trot.

Among the Arabs on the right bank of the Nile, I saw some dromedaries with a reddish hair, whose movements were easy and springy, and while running, their noses appeared to be skimming the ground. Among the Arabs on the left of the Nile I saw camels running faster than horses.

'Tell me', I asked an Arab one day, 'are your *hajins* fast?'

He replied: 'If you were to meet an Arab mounted on his camel and greeted him with *al-salāmu 'alayk* (may health be with you) and he replied *'alayk al-salāmu* (and may health be with you), the words would hardly be out of his mouth before he was far away, because the speed of his *hajin* is like that of the wind.'

Another Arab told me: 'Do you know that I have a *hajīn* which has covered enormous distances more than once, and it was only after four or five days of almost unbroken running that I allowed him to rest for a short while, but even then he did not seem to have the slightest need of it.'

'And how were you able to stand up to such a long journey without resting?' I asked him.

'Ah', he replied, 'we people of the desert are not like you who can only rest if lying on an *'anqarīb* (bed), or on the ground. We are able to eat, drink, smoke and sleep on our camels.'

I often saw the Bishārīn camels, and their elegance is surprising. They are generally brownish in colour, and rarely reddish. Sometimes they are markedly similar to a giraffe; the lower lip droops, the ears are short and erect, the brow is wide and curved, and the eyes are intelligent.

The feet of the *hajīn* glide through the sand giving the body a pleasant movement. Over stony surfaces, however, they are not so sure on their legs, but here too they never fall. They are easily led and can stand up to the greatest strains. In addition to the slow, measured step during moments of respite, there is a special step of their own which is aptly termed '*hajīn's* pace' or amble, and in addition they have an easy or fast trot, which can prove rather unsettling to an inexperienced rider. I tried it only twice, and I really thought I was going to die from such discomfort. I was jerked up and down like an acrobat on a tight-rope, my stomach felt as if it were being pulled to pieces, my head was whirling, my back felt broken . . . in short, I was finished.

Like all camels the *hajīns* are always ready to obey their master's voice. There is no need to use the whip on them. If well treated they are duly grateful, but if ill-treated they have a curious knack of getting their revenge. I once saw a Bishārīn camel, which, according to the owner, was the best he had ever possessed, but I was told that it must not be irritated, otherwise one would have to pay dearly for any wrong done to it.

This animal, the Arab went on to say, had belonged to a different owner a few years before, a man of violent temper who at times used to beat the camel unmercifully and even deprived him of his fodder. For a time the camel showed no resentment but waited for an opportune moment to seek its revenge — and such a moment was not long in coming. One fine morning, while pasturing, the camel observed that his master was passing nearby without his whip. He immediately attacked

S

him, seized him, threw him to the ground and trampled upon him with his feet tearing his limbs to shreds.

The saddle-camels are held in great esteem by the Arabs, not only because of their speed, but also because of their endurance on the longest and most exacting of journeys.

Some of the *hajins* can continue twenty-four hours without respite. During this time they cover a distance equivalent to five days' ordinary march, and they are also able to average about sixty miles a day for six or seven days running. . . .

The *hajins* are guided by a kind of halter made either of a simple rope or elegantly woven in leather. One end of the halter is fixed around the neck and over the top part of their head, and the other end is held by the Arab guiding the animal. This latter end is first passed through an iron, copper or silver ring attached to one of the camel's nostrils. If the *hajin* belong to a great tribal chief, these rings are never removed.

The saddles generally used by the Arabs to mount the camels are not very different from those which we use on our horses. Sometimes, the saddles are fitted with stirrups, but it is more comfortable and practical to cross the legs in front of the first pommel, resting them thus on the neck of the animal. In this way the camel is guided by the heels in the same way as a horse is guided by the knees of the rider.

The saddles of the Nubian Arabs, which I preferred to all the rest, are filled with straw and are placed on the camel's back. A small cushion or kind horse-cloth is then placed on the upper part. The more ingenious Bishārīn cover their saddles with a concave wooden seat, wide at the front and open in the centre, so that the top of the camel's hump remains free. This seat is covered in leather, and a sheepskin is placed over it.

In general, the saddles have two wooden pommels, and some Arabs place two iron spikes at the top of each pommel. However, this is very uncomfortable and can sometimes prove very dangerous. The saddle is held firm by a girth, a breast-strap and a girdle around the belly, but a crupper is rarely used under the saddle.

To mount when the *hajin* is kneeling, one first takes hold of the bridle, the right hand is placed on the back pommel, slightly bent, the right leg is then quickly swung over the first pommel, with the body leaning slightly forward, while the left hand is then placed on this same pomel; a slight tug on the bridle will then bring the camel to its feet.

However, if the traveller is not very experienced, and fears that the *hajin* might suddenly rise just as he is about to mount, it is wise, before swinging the right leg over, to get someone to place a foot on the camel's neck or on one of his folded legs; otherwise he runs the risk of being thrown backwards — I speak from experience.

Another precaution which a traveller must take, whether he be mounted on a saddle-camel or transport-camel, is to grip the pommels of the saddle firmly at the moment when the camel is rising to begin its journey, or is about to kneel at the end of its trip. To make a camel kneel one has to give the bridle a sharp tug, and at the same time making certain guttural noises, which convey to the camels or dromedaries the wishes of the rider.

The Arab or experienced traveller can mount a *hajin* even when it is on the move. In such cases the camel obviously does not kneel. The bridle is seized, and the head is lowered until it almost touches the ground; the left leg is placed on the neck; the first pommel of the saddle is gripped, and this is held until the right leg is swung over.

To get a *hajin* to trot it is only necessary to give the bridle a slight shake, dig the heels into the neck and repeatedly urge the camel on with the sound of '*ich, ich*'; this sound is produced by filling the lungs with air. Towards evening songs also greatly help the camels and dromedaries along their way, for the camels know that these songs are quickly followed by rest.

Arms are generally carried hanging from the saddle straps, but the sword normally dangles from the back pommel of the saddle, while to the left there hangs a *zamzamiya*.[10] This vessel is always hung in the same way, but on the side less exposed to the sun. On both sides of the saddle there are two small leather bags containing food and other drink. The traveller is also careful not to forget his *chibuk*, which he often fills and lights up, helping him to overcome the fatigue of the journey.

In Egypt, where the camels are well-nourished and well-watered along the banks of the Nile, these ruminants are more energetic than those of the Nubian desert. They easily carry loads of between seven and eight quintals, and the same is said of the camels along the Mediterranean basin. But as such camels are accustomed to regular and abundant feeding, they would be unsuitable on the long tiring journeys across the desert, and this is the reason why many camels die on the caravan routes from Cairo to Mecca. This never happens in the Nubian deserts, although the journeys are longer and more exacting.

---

[10] A portable canvas water vessel which keeps its contents cool by evaporation. *Zamzam,* name of a spring near Mecca, typifies the delights of drinking from it.

Although the Nubian camels are thinner, and less vigorous than those of Egypt and the Mediterranean basin, they have greater powers of endurance and a greater resistance to thirst and hunger. However, they can only carry between four and five quintals, and if the journey should be long and fatiguing — for instance, like that between Dār Fūr and Asyūt — then the load carried would be even less. Many times, in Nubia, I saw camels which refused to budge because they had been overloaded, and some cases it was by only a few kilogrammes. They only consented to move when the excess weight had been removed.

A caravan, composed of good camels, on a fifteen to twenty-day journey, can average from twenty-five to thirty miles per day. Depending on the season, the camels can go without water for between three and seven days, and for about two days without food. If a completely barren desert is being crossed, the camel-men take some grain with them and give some to their animals every two days.

The various kinds of grain which are best suited to the camels are maize, *durra* and *dukhn;* beans, unless there is nothing else available, must not be given to them. Dates are not good for camels, and they are fed with fatty foods only during the evening so as to give them time to digest them properly.

As soon as an Arab sees that his camels are ready to endure the hardships of a long trek across the desert, he begins by giving them a purgative. They are given several litres of marisa and quantities of green-stuff, such as clover. In the evening the camels are then given some well-pounded grain moistened and mixed with a little salt. Such feeding, called by the Arabs *deriscia,* [11] excites the camel's appetite. The Arabs then keep the animals away from their drinking places until the day of departure, the time of which is normally in the afternoon. An hour before (the hottest of the day), the camels are allowed to drink, and they swallow enough to enable them to carry on for several days without suffering from thirst until they come across a *bīr* (well), where they again drink. In order to protect the camels from scabs and sores caused by exposure to air or insect bites, the Arabs smear their skins with a kind of tar.

On coming back from a long journey, the camels are quite thin, and their hump, which previously swayed gently, has become almost motionless. In such a condition they would not be fit to start on another journey; they must be looked after, and sometimes it takes two or three months to restore them to their former strength. Should

---

[11] Probably *daris,* dried Egyptian clover, berseem.

the camel be old, then it is quite possible that it will never be restored and it thus loses all its value. This depreciation in the value of camels after long journeys results in a corresponding increase in the cost of the hire. Thus in Kurdufān, where the price of a camel is not more than 25 francs, the cost of hiring it between al-Ubayyid and Dongola, a journey of between fifteen and twenty days, is more than 20 francs. If hired between Dār Fūr and Asyūt the cost would be twice the price of the camel itself. It is not rare for two or three camels to die under their loads on these long journeys, while others arrive at their destination so exhausted that they are unable to make the return journey.

THE NUBA MOUNTAINS

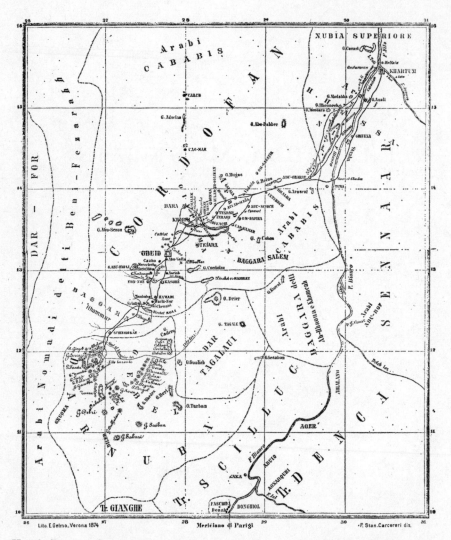

Kurdufān and Gebel Nuba (illustrating S. Carcereri's journeys of 1871-3).

CHAPTER XIV

IN THE NUBA MOUNTAINS, 1873

by S. Carcereri

Fr. Stanislao Carcereri, a member of the Camillian Order, had joined the Catholic Mission with other members of his Order, in 1871. After making the journey described below and taking part in the founding of missionary stations at al-Ubayyid and Dilling he was elected Superior of the Camillian house at Berber.

Carcereri was an unusual character, an intelligent observer, a competent geographer, a good map-maker, but a rather independent colleague whose differences with Bishop Comboni over mission policy caused his resignation and return to Italy with his fellow-Camillians in 1877. His notes on the Nuba Mountains which we print below were published in Annali del Buon Pastore, *No. 8, 1874, pp. 7-27. It is probable that, had he stayed with the Mission, he would have attempted a journey into Western Ethiopia, if we can judge by a letter which he wrote from Berber to the Italian explorer, Carlo Piaggia, begging him for a French or Italian translation of Ernst Marno's report in German on his travels to Fadāsī in 1870.[1] To our loss, Carcereri never made the journey.*

---

[1] Carcereri to Piaggia, 4 Dec. 1876. (Lucca, Archivio di stato, legato Cerù, n.32). Carlo Piaggia (1827-82), an explorer who brought the first intelligible description of the Azande people to the attention of Europe and also explored the Equatorial region. Ernst Marno Bey (1844-83) of Vienna, who afterwards entered the service of the Egyptian government, had made an unsuccessful attempt in 1870 to penetrate the country of the Galla. R. Gessi, the future pasha, with P. Matteucci similarly failed in 1877.

From al-Ubayyid we took a southerly direction and soon left behind us the villages of Wad Abū Safīya, Kaba, al-Muraykib, Barakin, Fekī Dai al-Nūr, and many other smaller ones. All were inhabited by the Kināna Arabs, who were always most generous to us with their hospitality. They own a good number of cattle, and have excellent pastures, but this year the high mortality among the animals which devastated Kurdufān, also had its effect on them, and many of the inhabitants were reduced to misery. The largest of these villages is Ebn-Noc [?Idd al-Nimr] which is situated on a height, and a little distance away it is almost surrounded by a large stream which takes its name from the village. This stream is full of water for a good part of the year, and waters the neighbouring woods. To the north-east lies Jabal Kurdufān; to the south-east, Jabal al-Daiyir, and to the north-west, Jabal Abū Harāz. On leaving the village one enters a very thick and thorny wood with many ebony trees. This wood stretches as far as the village of Fekī Dai al-Nūr where the scene changes to one of flourishing vegetation of different kinds, and where there are many *fūlas*, [2] and huts of the Arabs.

On the morning of the day following our departure we arrived at Birkat-Keli, the southern boundary of Kurdufān. Here there is a large pond of which the water is fresh and drinkable, and it is said to be as deep as the height of two men. Its greatest length is from east to west, and it is fed by the waters of the streams, which are swollen during the rainy season, in that area. During the dry periods there is practically no water in this pond, but the inhabitants nearby dig wells into its bed, and a little way down they always come across sufficient water for them and their beasts. For this reason the population is very numerous around al-Birka, and I was told that more than thirty villages depended on the water from the pond. There are good fish to be had here, also wild ducks and an abundance of other water-birds. On the northern shores of the pond a market is held each day.

After the Birka, I entered the Baqqāra Humr country; al-Ubayyid people urged our being accompanied by an escort, but I refused to accept their offer. The heavy downpours of the preceding day forced our guide to take a route which he did not know very well; when we arrived at al-Birka, he begged me get in touch with a government official, who was in this part, to ask for help on our way. I thought it wise to do so, and I asked for a second guide, who knew the area well. The official replied that he had received orders from the Governor of al-

[2] Rain-water ponds.

Ubayyid to lend me soldiers; I answered that I did not need them, as I and my companions did not fear anyone. He then said: 'If that is so I cannot guarantee your lives, either among the Baqqāra or among the Negroes.' 'I will take the responsibility', I said, 'all I need is a guide; you need not fear for us.' He consented, and in the early morning we made our way towards the west. To some, my refusal may seem presumptuous, and so I would like to say a few short words about it. It must be understood that the Baqqāra, and the Negroes, do not trust anyone who does not trust them. If they have any reason to fear for themselves, then they become savage. But if they see that a stranger trusts them, and if they have no fear of him, then they are the most pacific and hospitable people in the world.

Perhaps better than many, I knew their character well. I had made a special study of it during my stay in Kurdufān. In addition, I was out to explore all I could, even to finding out whether the way was safe or not, and this would not have been possible had I been accompanied by armed soldiers, as everyone can understand.

We journey on steadily, much to the admiration of our guide who had difficulty in understanding that fear cannot live in the hearts of a missionary. After walking for two-and-a-half hours we reached a forest, well wooded, and sheltering lions, leopards and many wild animals, but all we came across were bees, busily engaged at their hives in the trees. We tried at least three times to cross the forest, but we were unable to do so each time because of the thick growth, and had to resign ourselves to going round it. As we skirted it, we had the opportunity of observing ebony trees, tamarinds, jummayza, dulayb palm, adansonia, and many other kinds, which we had never seen before. At this moment we saw a group of Baqqāra approaching us. They were of different ages and all armed with muskets and spears. They passed near us, looked at us curiously, but nothing more. Further along we saw mats hanging from trees. It was a Baqqāra village and in it there lived the shaykh of that tribe. At the moment he was holding a meeting with other leaders. He was named Muhammad Ashosha, [3] and as soon as he saw us he greeted us, and invited us to eat with him. In order not to give him any reason for distrust in us, I accepted immediately and was first to get off my camel. A group of courteous, gay Baqqāra then sat down and looked at us curiously.

In the meantime, the shaykh had three plates of wild rice brought

---

[3] Muhammad Ashosha. Possibly Hamad Asūsa (died about 1875), chief of the 'Abd al-'Alī branch of the Hawāzma Arabs, who lived near al-Birka.

in. It was seasoned with great quantities of milk and butter. Roast chicken with sauce followed, with *keshra*, [4] and sour milk to drink. To all this I added coffee, which was very welcome to these people, who had not long known about it. After having rested a while in this lonely romantic spot, we continued our journey and crossed the great forest. On the other side there was a great wood, also full of thorny trees, which made our progress laboriously difficult; it took us a good sixteen hours to cross it, and we had to mount and dismount several times. The main obstacles were the many streams across our path, and the fact that, at many points, we could not ride our camels.

When we reached the outskirts of these woods it was evening, so we decided to wait until the following day before going any further. We placed all our belongings around us and before settling down to snatch a few hours sleep, we lit the customary fires round us, and saw to it that they would burn all night. This was done in order to protect us from wild animals. In this torrid zone, sunset is immediately followed by darkness, and we were soon dropping off to sleep. Suddenly we heard a noise in the distance, growing louder as it came near. Then we could make out the sound of horses coming our way. We all got up to see what would happen; we thought of putting the fires out, but it was too late. We were in two minds as to whether we should run away or hide, but we decided to hold fast and see what was in store for us. Soon a handful of mounted Baqqāra came into view, armed with spears, shields and muskets. They dismounted, tethered their horses to trees and laid down their arms, and each lit their own fire. Soon afterwards one of their leaders left the others, and accompanied by three or four servants came towards me. We could then make out that it was the shaykh who had invited us to eat with him on the other side of the forest. I welcomed him warmly, and had coffee brought to him. He told me that they intended spending the night with us, and that they would be leaving the next morning for the mountains where they had some business to attend to.

When day came we said good-bye and again took up our trek into the woods. On the following morning we drew clear of them. Nothing of importance had happened during our journey through it, except that we came across a herd of wild boars, and several very large multi-coloured gazelles. Before drawing close to the Dilling mountains we had a frugal lunch of biscuits, sardines and onions. Then we made our way on foot for quite a long stretch through the thorny trees. It is almost as

[4] Read *kisra*, unleavened bread pancakes.

if nature had intended to defend the inhabitants of those mountains, with such an abundance of mimosa and prickly *haraj*. [5] At times, we were forced to push back the branches of trees so as to open the way ahead. At a spot where the woods opened on to a valley, which offered an easy way to the native villages; we halted waiting for our mounts. We soon saw people coming to meet us from the mountains. Some were on horseback and some on foot. The news of our arrival had preceded us, and Fr. Franceschini [6] was able to recognise the *kojur* Kakum, who, a short while before had visited the Mission at al-Ubayyid.

The *kojur* is the temporal and spiritual chief of various villages united under his authority. Each village has its chief but all recognise the sovereignty of the *kojur* called in their language, Weru. He summons them to war by the beating of drums. He settles the differences arising among his subjects. Without him nothing is done. Nevertheless, it must not be thought that he is surrounded by formality and pomp; there is nothing like this about the *kojur* of Dilling. He is like the father of a family, one of the ancient patriarchs; he receives everyone and, like others, works for his daily bread. He does not levy taxes; has no tribunals, or any guard of honour, or permanent army. He has only a few distinguishable garments, which he puts on for solemn occasions. He was mounted on a white steed saddled with a leopard skin when he came forward to meet us, and was dressed in blue with a scarlet cloak on his shoulders and a hood of the same colour on his head. At his side were four halberdiers with their spears; he was followed by his *wakīl*, [7] dressed in a white robe with a red neckpiece, also on horseback. Then came the chiefs of the villages. They were all dressed in white. Finally, there was a group of people from the villages, their bodies half-covered; some mounted, and some on foot and all armed with spears and muskets. As soon as they had reached us, they all dismounted, and fired their rifles into the air in salute, and shouted with joy. The *kojur* then came up to us, embraced us and warmly welcomed us. The others gave us their hands, and the young men offered us their right arm and shoulder to be touched. After all this tumultuous welcome, the *kojur* thanked us and told us that they had been anxiously awaiting us, and added that three days ago he had sent people to al-Ubayyid to fetch us. A new burst of musket fire expressed the joy of all at our arrival. Having thanked the *kojur* and everyone for their welcome, we remounted

[5] *Haraj,* undergrowth.
[6] A Camillian Father and the writer's travelling companion, he had come to the Sudan with Bishop Comboni in 1871.
[7] Arabic for assistant, deputy or agent.

and, riding between the *kojur* and his *wakīl*, and surrounded by the crowd of followers, we continued our journey to the villages.

Our entry to Dilling was triumphal. Continuous rifle fire in salute, shouts of welcome, hand-clapping, games, horse-racing, everything they could think of was done to express their joy. I was almost moved to tears by the sight of the women with their children lined up on the surrounding mountain heights, jumping with joy, clapping their hands and echoing with their songs the clamour from the valley below.

Finally, we arrived at the foot of the fourth of the five mountains which make up Jabal Dilling. We dismounted and began to ascend that mass of stone, up to about half-way. Here was a spacious plateau, shaded by numerous trees, and with five large huts and a *tukul* on it. Before the entrance we saw a *khayma*, a circular tent of coloured canvas. This was the residence of the *kojur* of Dilling, and here we were warmly welcomed and looked after during our whole stay. As a mark of distinction we lived in the tent. The *'anqarībs* were immediately made ready, and we were given a refreshing drink of water and honey, *durra* canes as sweet as sugar; this was followed by *marayq*, mutton, chicken, goat, plenty of milk and honey, and even a *dukhn* pastry, a delicacy made with honey, butter and eggs. All the *kojur's* servants and women did what they could do please us during our stay there. The only exception was late at night, when neither the *kojur* nor the village people ever left us alone. They always remained, curious and pleased at what we told them, repeatedly exclaming together with their *kojur*: *'ajā'ib!'*, *'subhāna'llāh!'*. [8]

In addition to the present report, I will try to send a map, [9] showing the route we have followed, and the special features of the locality we have reached. In the meantime, I think it might be useful if I described Jabal Dilling and its neighbourhood — including the nearby mountains which are all inhabited by the great family of Nuba.

Jabal Dilling, which the native people call Waku in their tongue, is situated near 12° N. and 30° E. It is a mass of pure grey granite, of various heights. The first four mountains are united; the fifth, to the south, which is also the highest, is separated by quite a long valley, which circles round all the other mountains and isolates them. Their base is in proportion to their height, and although they seem to form huge steps towards the sky they are not easy to climb. On these steps

---

[8] 'Wonderful!', 'God be praised!' (Arabic).
[9] See his map at p. 282.

and on level stretches of the mountains the people have built their huts. These are of all shapes and sizes, some square, some round, some rectangular and some even look like bottles, being narrow and very tall. The Nubas also make use of the many caves and natural cavities of the mountains as hide-outs. The *kojur* himself has his divan in one of these recesses, which are very cool and dry.

In this way the Nubas live scattered among the mountains in numerous groups. They once lived in the valley below, but there they only had their natural courage and crude weapons to defend themselves against attack. When firearms were introduced into the Sudan and they were unable to obtain any due to lack of means, they could not stand up to their more powerfully armed enemies, and were forced to withdraw up the mountains to seek shelter. In the evening, their animals follow them up the slopes, and only the sown fields remain exposed in the valley, and these are often stripped clean by the Baqqāra. These mountains contain natural reserves of rain water; in addition the people have built large cisterns and small wells which guarantee them a sufficient quantity of this necessary element. Near Jabal Dilling there is a stream called al-Nile, whose banks are flanked with gigantic trees and flourishing vegetation; during the rainy season it is filled with the waters from the mountains and other streams which run into it; its bed is large and quite deep. Even after the rainy season, when everything seems dried up, fresh clear water can be obtained by digging down a little way into the bed. I sampled it many times, and was told that the water is present the whole year round. According to what I was told, this stream flows into the Birkat Rāhad, which is to the south-east of al-Ubayyid, between Jabal Kurdufān and Jabal Dayir, a little above 13° N. This lake is always full of water and contains good fish. It is larger than the Birkat Koli. Jabal Dilling is the first mountain inhabited by Nuba that one comes across on the way from Kurdufān towards the south-south-west. Some distance away it is surrounded by other mountains of differing heights, all of which are inhabited by the same tribe of negroes. From the heights of Dilling, a very curious panorama unfolds itself, and the mountains seem to describe a circle towards the north-east.

Due east, the Kadero mountains stand out prominently with their principal peaks Kororo, Kafeir, Koldagi, Kortala and Debatna. This group is about two days' caravan journey from Dilling, that is, some 50 miles; it is thickly populated, and stretches in a north-south direction. Like Jabal Dilling it is of granite formation.

A little further south come the Jabal Habīla and the Jabal Wata.

Then in the form of a crown, between the south-east and the south, rise the mountains of Turda, Karkandi, Kottang, Nynya, Numma, Sigada, Kurgal, Morun, Julud, all about a day's journey from Dilling; these mountains are themselves surrounded by smaller hills, also inhabited by the Nuba.

To the south, about half a day's journey from Dilling, rises the Ghulfan group, with its main peaks Jokon, Katla, Temein and Kabila. This group of mountains is perhaps the highest and most extensive that can be seen from Dilling, stretching from north to south. It is said that natural springs are to be found here. To the south-west lie the following mountains: Salara, Giacobha [?], and Fagu, the Tandiya with its minor chains, and finally the Nyima and the Burne. All are only a few hours away from Dilling. To the west are the Fanda and Karko groups, where natural springs are also found. To the north-west are the Giogob, 'Adlān and Sabai mountains. Finally, to the north is the little Kador mountain. To the south of the Ghulfān the great tribe of the Dileb has established itself, and to the south-west the Nyuoma. These tribes differ from each other, and each has its dialect. It appears that some time ago they were the enemies of the Nubas on the mountains I have described, but now it is certain that they are friendly. Some time ago, the *kojur* visited them and he was well-received by the inhabitants.

I shall now describe the character and customs of these people. From what I gathered they are frank and sincere, and very intelligent. The enthusiastic welcome with which they greeted us was not a momentary warmth. They were very sorry when we left: they accompanied us along a good stretch of the way, and repeatedly begged us to remain with them. The *kojur* offered us his residence, and any other place to our liking, and he was not satisfied till I showed him the place where they should build huts for our return. The final farewell was very moving. They told us that they were going to start building our huts immediately. Endowed with a robust and sturdy constitution, they possess an intelligence capable of being well-educated. They quickly assimilated and understood all they heard and saw, and were soon teaching others what they had learnt.

They are exceptionally industrious. During the rainy season they sow their fields with a variety of grain, such as *dukhn*, maize and black corn, white and red *marayq*, groundnuts, beans, marsh-mallow, tobacco, etc. They spend the greater part of the day cultivating their fields. As soon as the harvest is in, they gather honey from the woods, build huts, look after their animals, weave mats, or make plates and bowls from a blackish and very consistent clay. They exchange these for other goods they need such as salt and clothing. They have their own language, but many understand and speak Arabic. With the exception of the boys, they are all clothed, or at least half their bodies are covered. The Nubas are polygamous by tradition, but there are many who, either by choice or by necessity, have only one woman. They live soberly and drink no spirits except on solemn occasions, their usual drink being *marīsa*.

As far as I could understand, their religion is limited to a few practices akin to magic. There is a special word for God in their language, *Belebt;* there is also a word for the devil — *Tighni*. They mention the name of God with a certain sense of fear, but I never came across any act of adoration or sacrifice. However, one morning when I was looking at the neighbouring mountains, I heard shouting from the hut. It was the voice of the *kojur,* and I thought he was reprimanding a servant, but I soon realised that this was not so. I approached. The *kojur* was lying on an *'anqarīb* with his head bared, and he was wearing a red and white shirt. He kept shouting *'giran! giran!'* In front of him was his *wakīl* with his red neck-cloth, reciting something from memory, which I could not understand and could not get explained to me. The chiefs of the other villages were seated around, silent and with their heads bared. After some time of praying and shouting, the *kojur* fell silent, but let out a few moans like a tormented soul. Then, one of the village chiefs shook his head, and like a man possessed he gave vent to an inarticulate shout. He then took his stand by the side of the first two, still shouting and gesticulating like a madman. In the meantime, the first two were holding a conversation in undertones and, when this conversation was over, the ceremony was over too. A little water was sprinkled outside the hut. All then left, doffing their prayer-robes and saying that they had been assured of a good harvest and that they all longed for us to live among them. No one was able to tell me the meaning of that *giran;* they told me that they acted in this way because the custom had been handed down by their forefathers.

I was able to gather that they are not Muslim. They keep pigs and eat pork; they have no ablutions or Islamic prayers, and they know nothing of the Koran. We were among them on the first evening of Ramadan and for several days afterwards. They ate the same as we did during the day, and drank and smoked as usual. When babies are born, they have a rite which can be said to reflect faintly on a long-lost memory of Christian baptism. On the eighth day after birth, the *kojur* goes to the house of the newly-born and anoints its forehead with

T

dihn. [10] On the fortieth day the parents take the child to the *kojur's* house, and the *kojur,* dressed in white, solemnly receives the child and, together with it, enters into a tank of water where he prays for it. He then again anoints the child with *dihn,* and hands it back to the parents.

I asked how the Nuba expressed the words Paradise and Hell in their language, but they did not understand me. When I explained to them the meaning of eternal reward, they replied that it was the same to them whether they were good or bad. I found that they do not bury their dead, but throw them to the hyenas in the woods.

[10] Fat or edible oil.

CHAPTER XV

PEOPLE AND GOVERNMENT
IN THE NUBA MOUNTAINS

by G. Martini

In Chapter XII above our Piedmontese missionary was observed on his way from Khartoum to al-Qallābāt and Fāzūghlī. Some months before, when he came to the Sudan, he was posted to the Nuba Mountains. At the beginning of 1875 he was at Dilling (Delen) where he carried out a reconnaissance in the mountains in the course of helping to found the Mission station at Dilling. These passages are taken from Annali del Buon Pastore, fasc. 13, 1875, pp. 3-17.

Jabal Nuba is that part of Central Africa which, to the north, marches with Kurdufān, to the north-west with Dār Fūr, to the south with the Shilluk country and the Gienghe, and to the east with the Banū Salīm. It is a vast plain crossed by streams at many points, covered with forests, with numerous small mountains inhabited by various tribes who for the most part speak the Nuba language. The immense forests which surround the mountains are made up of various kinds of trees, such as the ebony, tamarind, adansonia, gum trees, and the like. In the forests there are elephants, lions, tigers, hyenas, giraffes, gazelles, wild boar, ostriches, and wild hens. Here one also hears the incessant song of the birds, and the bees produce wax and honey of excellent quality. The Jabal Dilling, which is part of the mountains of Jabal Nuba, is like the centre of the crown formed by the other mountains around it. To the west, it borders the Jabal Karko and Jabal Fanda, to the south Jabal Ghulfān, to the east Jabal Ovosa Kadero, to the north-west Jabal Gador [?Kudr] and 'Adlan. To the north-east, the wooded part stretches as far as al-Ubayyid, capital of Kurdufān. The situation is pleasant, and despite the burning sun, the forests, mountains and winds maintain a cool temperature.

293

Jabal Dilling is a group of five mountains of medium height situated to the north-east; their masses of granite form arid summits, vast caves and strange gulleys and steep slopes. Wherever there is soil, the wild fig tree can be found with large leaves similar to those of the ivy. Only three of the five mountains are inhabited. The dwelling-places are small, round huts, made of earth and maize straw, and covered with grass. The outhouses are simply formed by poles stuck into the ground without any lateral walls, with flat roofs under which the inhabitants shelter during the heat of the day. The grain is stored in large earthen jars. Hedges, formed by high thorns, protect the herds of goats and cows from the nocturnal attacks of wild animals. These small dwelling-places, which are dotted here and there in the shade of wild fig trees on the slopes of these bare-topped mountains, form a strange picture. In the valleys, at the foot of the mountains, are stretches of ground, clear of trees and cultivated. According to the inhabitants, the soil is very fertile when the rainfall is normal, and yields rich crops of cotton, fodder, vegetables and sesame. Once the rains are over, water — so necessary to life, industry and agriculture — is scarce everywhere. To obtain the minimum quantity of water necessary to live, one must go on a quarter of an hour's journey and draw from wells near a dried-up stream. When it is very dry, one has to dig between 14 and 16 metres before reaching water in these wells.

The Religion of the Nubas

They are neither Muslims nor idolaters. They have their own religion made up of different ceremonies, which they believe honour 'one only God, sovereign ruler and provider of all things on earth', as well as some of their protecting spirits. It seems probable that their forefathers, who once inhabited Nubia, and who came to these mountains after the Arab emigration from the Hijāz, were Christians. Their religious ceremonies are celebrated by the *kojurs* of whom there are five at Dilling. One of these is also head of the government, and officiates only on very solemn occasions affecting the interests of the entire tribe. They have no temples, but each *kojur* has his own hut which is reserved for religious ceremonies. Inside the hut four poles are fixed into the floor, about a metre high, and planks of wood are fixed across forming a narrow platform. On the side of the hut hang several cow skulls, the use of which is unknown to me. Here is the way the religious ceremony is performed. All the tribe remain outside the hut; the *kojur* steps on to the platform and lies down on it. He begins to blow heavily, turning from one side to the other. After a short while his face begins to go red, his eyes widen, and he lets out several heavy groans. Gradually he raises his voice, and emits curious shrieks. All this time he is twisting and turning, foam gathering round his mouth and his voice becoming hoarse. At this point, the spirit entirely possesses the *kojur....* The tribe, standing silently nearby, await the oracle. A representative of the *kojur* stands at the door of the hut to hear what he is saying. Then in a heavy voice he begins to speak, according to the circumstances, reprimanding the people for their faults, foretelling the future, giving answers according to the intention of the ceremony, and repeating what he says several times. The word of the *kojur,* while possessed by the spirit, is sacrosant to everyone, and is received with great faith and respect. When he has finished speaking, the *kojur* remains lying down for a short while, then he jumps to his feet as if coming out of a deep sleep. As if he did not know what the spirit made him say, the *kojur* listens to his representative who tells him what took place. It is not clear what is meant here by the spirit. Each *kojur* has his own, and the great *kojur,* in addition to his special spirit, is assisted by those of the other *kojurs* who are in the hut where the ceremony is held. Often these ceremonies end with an orgy of *marīsa* . . . so that disorderly scenes of drunkenness follow in the wake of the religious ceremonies. These ceremonies are very frequent, and govern both public and private affairs. Here are a few examples which I will describe in detail.

At the beginning of the May moon, the rains begin and the ibis is seen. As this bird is the signal for the coming of the rains, it is greeted joyfully, and this is a happy event for all. As soon as the ibis has been seen, the great *kojur* is informed and he watches until it alights near the huts. He then has a bowl of water placed under the bird. Naturally, the ibis looks down, and then resumes its flight. The Nubas say that by this act of lowering its head, the ibis blesses the water so that it may be abundant, rendering the fields fertile. The great *kojur,* assisted by his representative and lesser *kojurs,* mounts the platform and, possessed by the spirit, speaks of the coming rain, in the presence of the elders of the country who are eager to attend this ceremony held at daybreak. During the evening of the same day, all the heads of the families bring the *kojur* half a gourd of grain and sit round him in a circle. Then one of the lesser *kojurs* enters the circle, takes the grain from the gourds, and puts it into a large basin, mixing it together. This completed, he picks out a handful of grain and places it in half a gourd. At the same time, two other *kojurs* take half a gourd of water and half a gourd of *marīsa;* then the great *kojur* stands up and, followed by all, walks a short distance towards the thorn hedge which surrounds the dwelling-places. There the elders dig a hole in the ground and the great *kojur* places the grain into it. Then, taking the half gourd of *marīsa,* he raises it to his lips but does not drink any, and empties it over the grain. At the same time, some of the elders come forward, and over the grain they cut the neck of a chicken, taking great care that all its blood drops on the grain. Finally, the hole is covered and the great *kojur* washes his hands in water over it. This formality is repeated every day until the seed has grown to a certain height.

Once the ceremony is over, they all return with the great *kojur* to his house and drink *marīsa* until they are drunk. If the seed grows, it means that there will be a good harvest that year; if it fails it will be a lean year. If, after the first rainfall and the ground has been sown, fifteen or twenty days elapse without further rainfall and the harvest is endangered, another ceremony is held.

The women, festively clad, are summoned by the sounding of the drum, and go in procession to the *kojurs,* visiting the chief first. Along the way, they emit piercing shrieks, similar to that of the *kojurs,* and violently strike their throats. On arriving at the *kojurs,* the hut to be used for the religious ceremony is immediately closed. The women continue to shout and beat on the outside and then prepare to dance. They dance in the following way: one of the women hops a little distance away with her feet together, and clenching her hands she clasps her body with her arms, then slightly bending the knees and raising the hands above her head, she makes quite a high jump, which she repeats three or four times; this is taken up by another. Once the dance is over, the shouting ceases. Then one of the women, begins to sing the praises of the spirit of the *kojur,* accompanied by the beating of hands. This song is taken up by all the women. The *kojur* is then begged to consult the spirit. While the *kojur* lies shouting on his platform, the women continue to yell and sing until the hoarse voice of the priest tells them that he is ready to speak. He reminds the people that in their misery they must think of God, of the spirits and the *kojurs,* but as they have not done so they have incurred the wrath of heaven — drought, hunger and all evil. Drawing a comparison between the riches and wealth of the past and the present poverty, he says that the tribe is thus suffering because it has not faithfully observed the religion of its forefathers or has followed the precepts and customs of the Muslims. He concludes the ceremony by promising rain for the following day. If all the *kojurs,* or the greater part of them, hold out the same hope, then the dancing, shouting and singing go on until nightfall and start again the following day. I must point out here that although these people are not Muslims, they have a great inclination towards the precepts and customs of the Muslims as they see these practised by the Baqqāra living on their borders. Many of these, when they go to fight and plunder them in the mountains, have tied on their arm and neck pieces of paper covered with Arabic characters written by the fakirs. These are worn as talismans, not only to guard them from danger, but to ward off the spears and bullets of their enemies. I myself saw one of these fakirs writing a few words on a piece of wood. The words were then scraped off and mixed with some water which was given to an invalid who, full of faith, drank it and paid well for it. The Nubas have learnt from the Muslims to swear by the Koran, to weep for the dead, to call Muhammad the Prophet of God, and some other things.

Government

The inhabitants of Dilling, like the greater part of the Nuba people, pay a small tax to the Viceroy of Egypt, who, in all other ways gives them complete freedom of government. The government of the Nubas is a kind of republic presided over by the great *kojur*. A little common sense, strength and fear are all that constitute its legal code. The ruling of the *kojur* is always sought in differences between interested parties. Often, however, the people reach a settlement among themselves or through the help of their neighbours. They rarely make use of their sticks, and less still of their knives and spears. If by chance one of them is killed, his family holds itself responsible to take revenge by seeking the life of the killer. The latter, knowing full well that he can no longer stay in his native country, escapes and seeks refuge among some other friendly tribe. It is certain that the rancour towards him will remain hereditary in his victim's family. Up to the third generation, the sons believe it to be an honour for them to kill the persons responsible for the death of their great-grandfather. The great *kojur* has the right to declare war or make peace with the enemy after having previously conferred with his senate, which is composed of the elders of the country. In the event of war, all the young and sturdy men are mobilised. If, during the war, the mountain is attacked, even the old men take up their arms, and shouting they hurl themselves *en masse* against the enemy. At the beginning of hostilities, twenty or thirty young men, armed with spears and muskets, hide in the forests of the nearby mountains, and when they are ready they seize the horses, cows, sheep and, if they can, women, children and soldiers. If the tribe becomes aware of such an attack, it sounds the call to arms, and they throw themselves at the attackers who either flee, or if in sufficient numbers, give battle, killing without quarter and, above all, endeavouring to capture slaves. These slaves are then taken to the *kojur* who makes his choice, leaving the rest to the victors. The parents of these unfortunate beings hurriedly barter for their release with cows, goats and grain, otherwise they are taken to al-Ubayyid and sold to the slave traders. Sometimes, instead of selling them, they are kept in the house and are made to work the soil. In such cases, they are treated as any other member of the family. Owner and slave work together and eat the same food. The slaves, like the others, take an equal part in the tribal festivities; but so that they should not escape, an iron or wooden ring is placed round their necks A long wooden stick is fixed to this ring, and sometimes it is tied to a stake. Hostilities between the tribes sometimes last for several years, until one of them sues for peace. Once peace has been established, the tribes respect and help each other until some future occurrence breaks the peace once again. Both peace and war are solemnly announced to the tribe by the great *kojur*. In the evening towards nightfall, or at early daybreak, the *kojur*, who normally lives in the more thickly populated part of the mountain, stands on top of a high stone and, for a few minutes, sings at the top of his voice. As soon as the Nubas hear this song they hurry out of their houses and silently await the word of their chief. After a moment's rest, the *kojur* breaks the news of peace or war, and gives what advice he thinks necessary. The great *kojur* does not live in any great luxury. He has no need of material means to be obeyed, nor does he levy any taxes, or have prisons or gallows. He is like a father who with all his heart desires the good of his whole tribe. Before giving any outstanding order, he consults the elders, respects the will of the majority and announces the decisions reached to the tribe. His words become law. If at times the *kojur* deems it necessary to utter some reproach, the Nubas feel deeply hurt and ashamed.

Customs and Habits

The men have a girdle round their loins or they cover themselves with a white cloth. Some wear trousers in Arab fashion, and *jallābīya*[1] with wide sleeves. Nothing is worn on the head. Their feet are shod with leather soles, tied with thongs. Their wrists are adorned with iron or

[1] Arabic for a long shirt.

brass bracelets, while from their ears hang one or more ear-rings. Up to and beyond the age of twelve, the young boys go completely naked, but round their thighs they have a cord of horsehair or brass wire. The women have many ear-rings, while round their necks they have neck-laces of various coloured stones. Enormous brass bracelets with ten or twelve twists encircle their wrists. A cord round their loins supports a piece of cloth, about two spans in length and width, worn in the front, and sometimes at the back. On solemn occasions or dances they adorn their heads with brass leaves, and wear bracelets on their ankles. The elder people of both sexes have their hair cut short, while the younger let their grow long, forming tresses piled one on top of the other, covering the whole of the head.

The Nubas are polygamous, but they have no divorce. The husband, according to his circumstances, must give the father-in-law a certain number of cows and goats, and a certain quantity of grain.

The Nubas have no industry. They are agriculturalists and shepherds, and their lives are sober and very simple. Their only problem is to obtain the barest necessities of life with the least possible exertion. The work in the fields is slight, and quite simple. When the rainy season draws near, the Nubas go to their fields, cut the shoots left from the previous harvest and clear the weeds. As soon as the first rains fall they use an ebony tool pointed like a spear to make holes in the ground for their seeds. They leave the rest to nature, to make the seeds germinate, grow and ripen. When harvest time approaches, they cut, thresh and store the grain, as I have already said, in large earthen jars to which they come each day in order to take out sufficient for their daily needs. The rest of the year they spend in weaving mats and repairing their houses. They have no servants except slaves, and in order to eat they must work. Each cultivates, for himself, his own field. Their furniture is simple: a shield, several spears, a few firearms, one or more 'anqaribs, mats made with dom *dulayb* [2] leaves, and several *būrmas* or round earthen basins in which they keep water, flour and *marīsa*. A few hollowed-out pumpkins, which are used as plates and drinking vessels, a few earthenware utensils for cooking, and finally a *murhāka*, a millstone which they use, together with another stone, for grinding grain.

[2] The *dulayb* (*doleib*) palm.

THE DESERT ROADS

CHAPTER XVI

KURUSKU TO KHARTOUM, 1851

by L.G. Massaia

Cardinal Massaia continues his reminiscences of the Sudan in the days of his early manhood and takes us over the well-trodden camel tracks from the Nile at Kuruskū to Abū Hamad, which enable the traveller to avoid the great bend of the river, its cataracts and delays. From Abū Hamad he rides along the river bank through Berber to Khartoum.

There is nothing strikingly original in this itinerary undertaken during the doldrums which marked the term of office of 'Abbās I, vālī of Egypt. But at least this intelligent narrative adds to our knowledge of the desert road during the middle years of the Turco-Egyptian occupation, when the 'Abābda camel contractors were at their most efficient and, for the time, at peace with the government. The writer's remarks on the ruins of Soba are tantalisingly brief. The Cardinal's narrative comes from I miei trentacinque anni, II, pp. 49-59.

After twelve days' navigation (July 1851) from Asyūt we reached Kuruskū. Nothing worthy of mention occurred during the voyage. There was always the same monotony, the same weariness and the same danger from crocodiles, which forced us to stop during the night and only push on during the day. [1] However, my boatmen did their best to cheer me up and distract my mind.

At Kuruskū we stopped, bought something to eat, and for the first time for many days broke away from the dull routine of having the same kind of food at every meal.

---

[1] The Cardinal's memory has failed him in this small particular. Pilots on this reach of the Nile who did not sail by night did so for navigational reasons such as absence of moonlight, the formation of new shoals or unfamiliarity with the channel.

Kuruskū is a small place, situated at the foot of a bare rock, and lying on the right bank of the Nile. It is a commercial centre and its importance lies in the fact that the boats coming from Cairo to Dongola, and the caravans arriving from the desert, converge here.

Travellers who intend to press on further (whether following the course of the Nile, or crossing the desert) must cross a cataract near Kuruskū to a nearby village which is the starting-place of the caravans. The cataract itself is only a small one and it can be crossed at any season, but that is the business of the *ra'is*. We crossed the cataract in the morning and we were thus able to reach the village comfortably during the same day. At this point, my contract with the boat ended, and so, together with the head-boatman, we visited the *Efendi* (a government clerk) to verify the clauses that had been drawn up with the former in Cairo. He gave me a cordial reception, having previously received a letter from Hannā Messarra concerning me. After this verification the contract was then annulled in the *Efendi's* presence after I had expressed satisfaction with the fulfilment of the conditions. I dismissed the *ra'is* giving him a letter for Cairo in which I again expressed my satisfaction for the service rendered to me, and giving full liberty to my Procurator to give the boatman the promised reward. Really, how well those boatmen served me!

The traveller coming from Upper Egypt to Kuruskū with the intention of continuing the journey to the Sudan has here to choose between two routes: the first, that of the Nile, which is very long and wearisome; it forms a semicircle and goes through Dongola by crossing the cataract. When the river is at low water, this passage is impossible with a boat, and it is only during the three months flood that the boat can be pulled across. The second is that of the desert, which, going in a straight line, joins the Nile at Berber. Those wishing to go to Khartoum, ordinarily choose the latter unless they have some business on the other route. If the desert route is chosen, the following practice is observed; one has to see the Egyptian concessionaire in charge of the desert traffic whose business it is to provide all the necessities for the journey. According to the number and needs of the travellers, he determines the number of animals, and men required to look after them. He receives payment and fixes the day of departure.

The same *Efendi*, therefore, assumed the responsibility of looking for the caravan which was to accompany me. He found some camel-drivers, as well recommended as the boatmen who had brought me from Cairo. Three of them with their camels were to be my companions; one camel for me, another to carry the water, and the third for the luggage. This was reduced to two full boxes ... containing my personal belongings, and two baskets containing food and other accessories necessary for our protection from the sun during the day, and from the cold during the night. The *Efendī* himself came and presented the bill for the charges. I paid him the sum agreed upon, and obtained a receipt upon which he also noted the number of persons, camels and pieces of luggage that composed the caravan.

We left the village of Kuruskū on the following day. After a short distance, the road branched in two directions, one leading to the desert, and the other to the Nile. One of the camels, seeing that we were taking the way through the desert, lay on the ground and would not move. To tell the truth, this disconcerted me as I thought that either we should have to return to get another animal or we should have to change caravans. But the head camel-driver, quite unperturbed, ordered the animal to be taken to the water, where it had a good drink. It then peacefully returned to the others, and the journey was continued.

I asked for an explanation of this, and the camel-driver told me that before undertaking a long journey, the camels are led to water for a drink. This is an indication of a forthcoming journey, so they drink in order to have sufficient for the time when they have to go without. This particular camel, having failed to understand the signal, drank only what was necessary for the day; but as soon as it perceived the way it had to go, where no water could be found for four days, it rightly made its protest.

The Kuruskū desert is perhaps vaster than that of St. Anthony. Nothing but a sea of sand confronts the gaze, broken only here and there by stony rocks or hillocks. In fact, we saw no sign of vegetation for four days on its northern edge, and only towards the south did we find some oasis, or some mimosa. Thus the prospect of that vast and arid plain, the immensity of its horizon, the monotonous uniformity, the deep silence that surrounds everything, all have the effect of producing a feeling of profound sadness, unless one lifts the mind to God.... For those travelling through these hot places, the first care is for the water-bags, which must be carefully kept, for should these fail there is nothing save death. Great attention must be paid to them at halts. The best method is to hang the water-bags from trees, and should there be no trees, to put them on the ground, with some skins underneath, to prevent the insects, attracted by the humidity, from boring them. In addition, it is necessary to protect oneself against the rays of the sun, which at certain hours become unbearable and even dangerous. It is preferable to travel at night, if there is moonlight, and the drivers know the way, and to pass the day under the tent. There is no fear of thieves or wild animals, neither is any fraud to be feared from the camel-drivers for they are generally faithful, especially if they entertain hopes of getting some reward. Moreover, as they have to give an account to the Egyptian authorities, they are careful not to commit any offence against the traveller.

My three camelmen were Bedouin, of good character, simple and rustic, living far away from the corruption of the city, and very affectionate towards me. The son of one of them, a lad of about fifteen, was of childish simplicity and most earnest in rendering me all the services I needed. He wore a small cloth round his loins, but when the sun rose, he put it on his head like a turban, and walked quite naked, with the childish indifference of a three-year-old. The two old men recited their Muslim prayers at fixed hours. When they had no water for the prescribed purification before prayers, they sprinkled themselves with sand. To keep them cheerful along the road and to ensure their goodwill, I gave them dates and biscuits, on which they feasted. Thus we travelled quite cheerfully. It was delightful to travel at night, while during the day the sand got heated and the air burned like fire.

About 3 o'clock in the afternoon on the fourth day, we saw in the north a rising storm with frequent flashes of lightning, and in the distance, we heard crashes of thunder. At first I gave it little thought, knowing that rain never falls in the desert, but when I saw the anxiety of the camel-drivers, and heard, now and again, some unusual laments from the camels, I too began to realise the danger. As the storm approached nearer and nearer we stopped and unloaded the animals; the men told me to get between the two boxes, wrap myself in the covers, and if the storm were to come over us, to shake myself now and again. Suddenly we were enveloped in intense darkness, and thick sand began to rain down. Placed between the two boxes, I thought only of freeing myself of the sand that fell in great quantity and dropped like water on both sides of me. Shortly afterwards, I began to feel an ever increasing weight on me, despite my efforts to shake it off, and free myself from it. Being wrapped in the covers I was unable to see whence this came, and to tell the truth I was confused, not knowing what to do. At this moment there came into my mind the story I had heard of the thirty Egyptian soldiers who had been buried alive in that very desert. This thought was so frightening that I began to make greater efforts, and so I managed gradually to raise myself and shake off that mass of sand under which I was buried. The storm lasted about twenty minutes, then gradually passed off, and the sky cleared. My boxes, I was surprised to see, were buried under two spans of sand; of the water-bags there was no trace at all! ... I thanked God for having given me that inspiration, otherwise I would surely have been a victim. The young man, more experienced than I in this, had stood erect, and shaking his head and shoulders easily freed himself of the sand that fell on him.

Then we began to search for the water-bags and other equipment; it proved a great task to find it and dig it out. When all was over, the headman mildly reproached me for not having followed his advice, principally for having refused the help of his son, sent expressly to me as he was so experienced with regard to these terrible storms. He was right in making this complaint, for not only did he warn me beforehand, but he was so thoughtful as to send me his son as my companion and help.

Apart from any other reason the hurricanes of sand that rage furiously over the desert are sufficient to make them uninhabitable. This explains the great difficulty of exploiting canals and railways [2] in those extensive territories of Central Africa, for everything would be buried by sand. Some advantages might be obtained by bringing water through pipes for irrigation, for the sand is not mere silica but contains also some humus which could be easily put under cultivation. But who is going to attempt such an undertaking?

As soon as the weather had calmed down and the luggage was dug out and assembled, we ate some bread and then continued our journey. It was nearly sunset, but we hoped nevertheless to advance for the greater part of the night. Along the desert, I kept finding skeletons of men, camels, donkeys and other animals. I could not account for this at first, but after the peril of the storm, from which I had been miraculously saved, I then understood, and realised that all the skeletons were those of the victims of the desert, first buried, then unearthed, by those terrible hurricanes.

It was already midnight, and feeling really tired, we decided to stop, eat and have some rest while it was still moonlight. I gave dates and biscuits to the camel-drivers; I myself had some with cheese. Having refreshed ourselves, we slept, but before daylight we were again on the

---

[2] A widely-held prediction at the time but since proved wrong. Driving sand was a minor nuisance along parts of the Suez Canal and on some desert sections of the Sudan Railways. The only line which had to be annually cleared of a minor mountain of sand was the short Tokar-Trinkitat Light Railway built in 1921. This disability was one of the reasons for its closure in 1952.

move, and finding here and there some mimosa sprigs, I prepared coffee for all. Before sunrise we resumed our journey, expecting to reach the oasis, inhabited by the Bedouin, in two hours.

On our early arrival, we unloaded the animals and approached a place, apparently cultivated. Although cultivation was scanty, places such as these seem like heaven to those travelling through the barren deserts. The inhabitants consisted of two Bedouin families, who lived on the milk provided by fifteen goats, and several camels. Their dwellings consisted of rough huts, built with poles, upon which was spread out a large cow's skin. The oasis, situated on the route to Berber, suffered from a scarcity of water. Consequently, these Bedouin had to travel far with camels in order to fetch it. The water was sold afterwards to the caravans, and some pieces of bread and other eatables were received in payment. There was a well, admittedly, but with so little water, that after an hour it was exhausted. [3] Consequently we had to spend the whole day round that well, needing it both for ourselves and the camels.

The depth of the well was only three metres, two of which were through sand, and the remainder excavated out of stone, through which the water continually filtered. Our poor boy was there the whole day until evening with a mug in his hand, but he could collect barely half the quantity we needed. We had, therefore, to offer something to those good Bedouin in exchange for the water. I noticed that during the day, the filtering was abundant, while at night it almost ceased. This led me to the conclusion that it was due more to the heat, than to the internal spring.

We left in the evening, and travelled the whole night and the next few days without any notable incident, until we reached Berber, a provincial headquarters and residence of a *mudīr*. This town, situated on the eastern bank of the Nile, marks the northern boundary of the Sudan, and is one of the most important places in that region. Not far away there once existed the ancient Meroe of which some remains can still be seen. The rainy zone begins here and, as you gradually ascend the Nile, it increases in intensity, so much so that at Khartoum the rain is as abundant as in Ethiopia. Berber, where the rainy season is moderate, enjoys a healthy climate, whereas Khartoum and all the Sudan are infested by the most deadly fevers. I took lodging at the *wakāla*. [4] In addition to the payment agreed upon and given to the *Efendi* of Kuruskū,

[3] The Arabs call these wells *Abyār al-Murrāt,* The Bitter Wells. Camels drink their water reluctantly; it tastes through tea.

[4] Arabic for rest house.

I also gave a good tip to my camel-drivers who had served me so well. I thanked them cordially and dismissed them, but the boy had become so affectionate that he would not leave me. So the father remained for two more days to satisfy his son's desire, and then departed.

Next day three camels were ready, together with some persons who, having to go to Khartoum, were to accompany me by the orders of the *mudīr*.

As I have already said, the Sudan is generally infested with fevers, and it was now September, the most unhealthy season. I should have remained at Berber, at least until the end of November, to avoid them, but this long stay would have greatly delayed my plans. The missionaries working in the interior might have been alarmed at my non-appearance. I decided, therefore, to take every possible precaution, place myself in the hands of God, and depart. Accordingly I took a good dose of tamarind decoction, and the next day fifteen grains of quinine. The tamarind, next to the palm tree, is the most useful and beneficial that God has given to these people, for its fruit is the most efficacious and innocuous medicine that can be found there. It is abundant in the Sudan, and much better than that of India, which is red, sour and fermented. The natives eat it with bread, but in cases of sickness it is taken in the form of a decoction which immediately produces its purgative effect, leaving the stomach free and cool, and the patient not much weakened.

I could have gone to Khartoum from Berber by boat with less expense and more comfort, but I thought it better to stay on land to avoid the miasma of the river. [5] The camels and men being ready, the *mudīr*, himself came to estimate the charges. . . .

After seven days of good journeying, we arrived at Shandi, a large town on the Nile, and chief town of another province, with a Bey and garrison of Egyptian troops. The river divides the city into two parts, as the Seine divides Paris. I followed the road running along the west side of the Nile, stopping at Shandi opposite to the place where the officials and soldiers resided. At this point the river is so infested with crocodiles that the people dare not go near it to wash their feet, and I was told of a tragedy that had happened some time previously to a young couple in this connection. The son of a rich Muslim had married a young woman from another place, and on his return to Shandi with a large train of attendants he was given a great welcome. The first Muslim purification of the young couple was to take place at noon,

---

[5] The *mal'aria* which was then universally associated with malarial fever.

and all the people went to the Nile to witness it, and to feast. On their arrival, the *fakir* [6] and the young married couple straightaway entered the water to perform the ceremony. Suddenly, a crocodile, under the water, seized the leg of the bride and dragged her away. At this unexpected disaster, the bridegroom bravely dashed into the water and did his utmost to save her, but he too disappeared. Not knowing what to do, the stupified onlookers called them, waiting the whole day for their return but to no avail, and thus the feast ended in great lamentation.

Having heard that a European was in Shandi, the Austrian Consul * together with the Bey sent me an invitation to visit them on the other side of the river. I went at once, and found the Consul giving assistance to the Bey in a mock battle between camel soldiers and cavalry. It was the first time I had seen the camel used in military drill, and came to the conclusion that, on the point of agility of movement and readiness to obey, a well-trained dromedary holds its own against the horse. I also saw magnificent and beautifully made saddles, comfortable both for men and animals. Twenty-five years later, when I saw the very bad harness of horses and camels in Shoa, I mentioned it to King Menelik, and persuaded him to use saddles like those of the Sudan, for the couriers and those fighting the Danakil.

Before starting my journey, I repeated my preventive cure at Shandi as I had done at Berber by taking a good decoction and the usual dose of quinine. Shortly afterwards, I made my departure, always following the river, but at a distance. It was the end of September: the water was still at a high level; the banks covered with beautiful vegetation, and here and there, on the left side, were pools of water, into which enormous crocodiles plunged on seeing us.

By land, it takes no less than seven days to reach Khartoum, whereas by boat it would take only three or four.

On arrival at Khartoum, the European finds a great city with all the facilities of Cairo. However, if he is not careful in the choice of diet and in taking the necessary precautions, it may easily become his tomb. This city, situated at the confluence of the White and Blue Nile, is therefore subject to miasmas which rise from the two rivers. Generally, for the first few days, the traveller feels quite well, but he may be stricken quite suddenly by the virus of fever. If his stomach is not clear, the disease affects the brain, causes congestion, and he falls a victim within forty-eight hours or even less. Typhus develops, sometimes,

---

[6] Read *feki*.   * K. Reitz (1819-53).

in three or more days. Six years after my arrival there, our missionary
Fr. Giusto da Urbino followed the same route on his return from
Rome, and came to Khartoum. He felt a certain uneasiness after dinner
and, without having time to use any remedy, died after the first attack
of fever. [7] Up to the time of writing, over one hundred of my acquaintances — missionaries, nuns and travellers — have fallen victim to these
deadly fevers. . . .

As I had arranged to travel on the Blue Nile, I asked my friend
Fath Allah Mardrus to make all the necessary arrangements, and looked
for a boat which would take me to the first cataract. He got everything
ready for the journey. In addition, seeing that I was not yet fully
recovered, he gave me one of his servants to act as interpreter, and he
himself accompanied me over a long stretch of the river. Then, on the
morning of the last day of November 1851, I said good-bye to the
Khartoum missionaries, thanked them for their kind hospitality, and
was off. The journey was indeed begun under good auspices, for a
favourable wind gave us three days of good navigation. We continued
without stopping, except for short periods, at any of the numerous
villages situated on both sides of the Nile, until we reached the ruins of
Soba, an ancient city on the left bank. We cast anchor near a small
village to the right. Here we met an Egyptian officer with a company
of soldiers, who had been sent to raze to the ground whatever remained
of the city, and to transport the material by boat to Khartoum to be
used in the construction of the governor's house.

The fever, which had never ceased bothering me, returned again
here, and forced me to stop for two days. I had recourse once more,
to tamarind and quinine. Although weakened, I went nevertheless to
see the famous ruins, little of which remained. They had all been
demolished and transported to Khartoum for the building of houses,
following the decision of Muhammad 'Alī to reconstruct the city, or
rather to found the new one.

A few days after my arrival two tombs containing human remains
were discovered, which had been exhumed and scattered by the people
without regard. Among the bones were found two crosses, one of copper
and the other of silver. The copper one was of Latin form, and had

[7] Giusto da Urbino (1814-56) was born Giovanni Iacopo Cortopassi; Giusto
was his name in religion while he added the name da Urbino as he belonged
to that province of his order. He died in Khartoum while on his way to join
Massaia in Ethiopia. For his life see G. Sforza, 'Un lucchese compagno del
P. Guglielmo Massaia in Africa (1846-56)', *Mem. R. Accad. d. Scienze di
Torino*, 2 ser., LXIV, No. 1 (Scienze morali), 1913, pp. 1-24.

nothing remarkable on it; the silver one, also Latin, had rays and semi-circles on the four extremities. In the centre, and in the middle of these rays and semi-circles were small round cases which could only have served for holding relics: this I believed to be a bishop's or an abbot's cross.

The interior of each tomb was formed by four great brick slabs, about one metre in length and half a metre wide, fixed on a surrounding wall. Some were still intact, but the others had been broken by the demolition of the wall. I saw some Coptic and Ethiopic letters in the inscriptions which covered them. Not being very familiar with the language, I copied an entire line, keeping it in my bag with the intention of deciphering and studying it, but this, together with other documents, was lost in the persecution of Kaffa. I thus remained in ignorance. I tried at least to obtain the crosses, but they would not give them to me. As I had to resume my journey, I requested Mardrus to do his utmost to get them as soon as he got back from Khartoum. . . .

At Soba, Mardrus and I parted company, much to the regret of both of us. He was to return to Khartoum, and I was to ascend the Nile towards the city of Sinnār, the capital of that ancient kingdom. [*] I did not pay it a visit, but from what I heard very little remained of its former granduer and prosperity. In those glorious days, it was the commercial centre and capital of that kingdom which included the vast regions drained by the two rivers, the White and the Blue Nile. However, when Khartoum was founded, this kingdom was divided, and commerce lost, for the caravans from al-Qadārif brought their eastern merchandise to Khartoum instead, but Sinnār nevertheless still kept up some traffic with the south and the rest of the delta. Sinnār was then also the residence of a *mudīr*, and had about twelve thousand inhabitants, mostly Muslims. Its climate and that of the neighbourhood is very hot and unhealthy, but certainly not so unhealthy as that of Khartoum.

---

[*] The early history of the town of Sinnār is obscure. By the sixteenth century it had become the seat of a dynasty of rulers of indeterminate origin called the Funj. These Muslim sultans ruled a loosely-organized state which at the time of its greatest extent stretched from the Red Sea to the interior of Kurdufān and from the region of the Third Cataract to the Ethiopian border. The last sultan surrendered his decayed sovereignty to a Turco-Egyptian invading army in 1821.

CHAPTER XVII

SAWAKIN TO BERBER, 1876

by S. Carcereri

In this short passage Fr. Carcereri describes his journey over a Sudanese desert road at the height of its importance. For long a pilgrim route, the cession of the port of Sawākin by the Ottoman Sultan to the Khedive Ismā'īl of Egypt in 1865 immediately increased the economic importance of the Berber-Sawākin road. The opening of the Suez Canal in 1869 brought Sawākin within shipping range of the world's markets and further increased the camel traffic on the road. Within eight years of Carcereri's journey this main commercial artery would be closed by the Mahdist revolt, and the road thereafter sank to the level of a furtive contraband route for Sudanese traders matching their native cunning against the Mahdist customs police. The road finally died in 1906 when the new Sawākin-Berber Railway linked the Red Sea with the Nile.

We take the following lines from Fr. Carcereri's paper published in Nigrizia, No. 1, 1883, pp. 145-9; 165-70, with map (by H.G. Prout Bey) at p. 152.

    Sawākin is a very important Red Sea port, but it is quite a risky affair to land there because of the numerous reefs. Steamers enter the port by passing through a narrow channel between the reefs. These are indicated by large pillars, but no steamer dares enter the port after sunset.

    The city is divided into two sections. In the first section is the port, almost forming an island, and this is considered the better of the two sections. The houses here are mostly stone-built [1] with wooden ornaments brought from Judda. A low stone bridge connects this part of the

---

[1] The building material was probably coral from the Red Sea coast.

city with the second, which is made up of huts inhabited almost entirely
by the nomadic Bishārīn. Sawākin has about 4,000 inhabitants. The
Sawakinese are copper-coloured, but there are also many negroes from
the interior. The Europeans consist chiefly of Maltese and Greeks. The
inhabitants are zealous Muslims, which is probably explained by their
constant contact with the people of Judda, whose zeal for Islam is well-
known throughout the whole of the East.

The climate is hot and conducive to sleep, and this probably
because of the phosphoric-evaporation of the sea, the water of which
contains 35 per cent [2] of phosphorus. Even the pools, a quarter of an
hour's distance from the sea, are said to contain phosphorus.

The importance of Sawākin is increasing daily, because the caravan
traders are becoming more and more numerous along the Kasala and
Berber routes. Sawākin would become even more important if the railway planned for the Sudan included the port.

One of the principal routes taken by the caravans is the road from
Sawākin to Berber on the Nile. The desert between Sawākin and Berber
is called by its inhabitants, the 'desert of the Bishārīn', and it is possible
that it is a continuation of the great Nubian desert between Wādī Halfa
and the mountains of the coast. The Bishārīn tribes extend between
Sawākin and Berber (between the Red Sea and the Nile), and from the
Tropic of Cancer to 15° N. (the Ethiopian border). The Bishārīn are
shepherds who have their own language which the Arabs do not understand. In outward appearance they are handsome. These sons of the
desert are tall and straightly-built; they have superb chestnut-coloured
hair, neatly arranged; they wear a cloth which covers the entire body
with the exception of the arms and legs, giving the appearance of a
magnificent Roman statue.

In addition to their shepherd life the Bishārīn also look after the
transport of caravans from Sawākin to Berber and vice versa. Two
chiefs allot the goods to be transported to the camelmen, and both live
in the vicinity of Ariab, a large well, half-way between Sawākin and
Berber, where the caravans have their longest halt. Thus near Ariab is
the chief or great shaykh for the Sawākin-Ariab stage of the route,
while his *wakīl* (representative), 'Osmān Moltasen, [3] is at Sawākin. Near
Ariab is also the great shaykh for the Ariab-Berber tract, while his *wakīl*,
Muhammad Muhammadayn, is at Berber.

Having overcome the natural lethargy and laziness of the camelmen

---

[2] A slip for .0035 per cent.
[3] Read 'Osmān Multazim, Osman the Contractor.

by threats (left to themselves they would never be ready at any time) our caravan took up its journey again on 4 February 1876 at 7.0 a.m. After a four-hour journey along the gently sloping coast, we came across a few hills and the Handub wells. Leaving the Jabal Waratab group of mountains to the left, the way ahead is through narrow valleys and sun-scorched mountains. In the valleys are a few water-holes, and goats, sheep and camels graze there, while timid gazelle flit in and out of the wild thorny acacia shrubs. We arrived at Otao well. Until now we had taken a north-westerly direction, and from the tops of the mountains we could still have a final glimpse of the far-away sea. We then entered Khawr Ossot and proceeded south-west. The greenish colour of the rocks surrounding the valley indicated that they were metalliferous. At 37° W. there is a road curving to the left which, after passing through narrow valleys, reaches Sinkat, the villages of the Sawakinese. The flora of Sinkat is such as to attract botanists even from Europe.

Dissibil is the third well on the road from Sawākin. It is inaccessible during the rainy season because it is then covered by torrents of water streaming down from the summits of the Jabal Erba (or Sotriba), situated to the south-west. A little further on is a large rock, shaped like a sphinx, with a head very similar to that of a cat; there is a small cemetery nearby, and the tomb of a Muslim saint named Tager; the camelmen coming from Sawākin visit this tomb of their patron saint and pray for a safe journey. At this point the rising valley of To Blal [?] begins, and this is the most beautiful that one comes across. The road is formed by the sandy bed of a stream flanked by wild acacia, while euphorbias and other succulent vegetation, including the so-called *eusclapia* ('*ushar* in Arabic), grow by the wayside.

Three hours further on, the scene changes. There are no more trees, but only colossal rocks scorched by the sun. These gigantic masses, with their yawning cracks and crevasses caused by the sun's heat, impart a sombre and truly African atmosphere. To the right lie the mountains of Kurn [?] and to the left the isolated Jabal Amit, which further along to the south-west takes the name of Jabal Odrus. Wādī Amit (or Wādī Odrus) is one of the broadest valleys between Sawākin and Berber, but as it is higher than the other valleys, it can be called an upland, rising to about 920 metres above sea level. It took our caravan four-and-a-half hours to cross this valley.

In the evening we halted at Wādī Hareitri, narrow and thickly-covered with thorny shrubs; here are many wells. Near the first that we came across was a hut made especially for the caravans by Gordon

Pasha. The water at Hareitri is pure and very warm; at six o'clock in
the morning it registered 26° C., whilst the air temperature was only
9° C., the lowest we had come across during the whole journey. Outstanding among the vegetation which abound in this valley are the
euphorbia officinalis, a thorny plant similar to a chandelier with many
branches, each spreading out into smaller arms. The white pulp of this
plant provides the inhabitants with the poison with which they tip
their spears and arrows. Hareitri is the pasturing ground for the herds
of the Bishārīn, who live behind the mountains hidden in remote valleys
and away from the caravan routes. Further on in the wādī, at the foot
of a rock, is Bī Mabua. After three hours journey towards the south,
we drew clear of Wādī Hareitri and after making our way up stony
hills, reached a plain called Ariab (or Wādī Tereb Aria [?]).

After Ariab we reached the upland (in Bishārīn dialect called
Okley-Da [Okilidada]) which ends in a rocky ascent. After having crossed
several hills covered with stones and pebbles, in a south-westerly direction, we descended into the narrow valley of Hayaba. To our right
there is the Bīr Salalat, which is at the foot of a rock. Large vultures
hover around the rocks, while small turtle-doves and wild ducks wheel
around the well.

Water is more or less abundant, according to the season. In March
we found a small lake there, and when we returned in June the water
was almost a metre below the surface of the soil. On our return, we
found that several wells at Wādī Hareitri had completely dried up.
The villages are far away behind the mountains. Opposite the well is a
big cemetery. A government guard of two soldiers, is always on duty
near this *bīr*, [4] attending to the needs of the caravans and keeping order.
In the same valley there are leafy and very shady trees, growing often
from a thick undergrowth. The hills at the end of the valley form a
picturesque scene to the left, and if they were covered by shrubs and
plants, they would indeed rival the most beautiful hillsides of Italy.
These are the first groups of the Kokreb mountains. To the right, at the
end of the valley, the black mass of the Badab ['Abādāb] mountain
rises to the sky. After a long climb, through Wādī Habr [?Hayaba],
towards the west, we halted at Kokreb. Water is plentiful among these
mountains.

Like Hareitri, Kokreb has several wells, and they are Kokreb, to
the north, the Bīr of Badab in Wādī Kokreb to the west-south-west,
the Bīr Matree [?Magwala] and Bīr Adelhabit. Beyond Kokreb, the

[4] *Bīr* = well.

road branches out: one branch towards the west-south-west to Rawai, and another to Ariab where water is plentiful. The road to Rawai is shorter but there is only one well until Bīr Obak is reached.

We took the road to Rawai. From the summits of Jabal Badab and the highlands of Jabal Wowitte (the main summit of the Kokreb group) the vast valley of Wādī Lagag opens out. After two-and-a-half hours' march the barren soil is transformed into fields of *durra*, surrounding the Bishārīn village of Ellajam [?]. To the right there is an isolated granite rock, which both from its position and shape can be likened to a tower, and can also be seen from far off. Vegetation flourishes here: there is the high *panicum turgidum*, the yellow straw of the *crysopogon* and among them on the ground are wild pumpkins. The soil becomes flooded during the rains and cracked by the heat during the hot season.

After a further two hours journey over sun-blackened rocks, we found ourselves in the great plain of Tongul [?Tongwil] which took us three hours to cross. Here, for the first time, we came across a kind of snake of the lizard and crocodile family, yellowy in colour, called *waral*. The camelmen told us that their colleagues in Kurdufān eat these reptiles with great relish.

At 11 p.m. we stopped at Wādī Darunga (or Durungerat) which begins from the Makadieh [?Mekadio] mountain, near Ariab and extends west-south-west (along the road to Ariab, the northern entrance of the wādī is passed). Wādī Durungerat is one of the largest and the ground is entirely covered by thick grass. The direction of the wādī (from the north to south-south-west) convinced us that it led to the Atbara.

Having left Wādī Darunga, after four hours march among the blackened rocks, we descended through a narrow, bare and rocky valley, to Wādī Rawai. A few acacias and the structure of the rocks told us that water was to be found here. Wādī Rawai narrows towards the north, and on the left of our road the colossal rocks are pitted with clefts from top to bottom. Here are the wells, which take their names from the valley, and they are the deepest yet encountered.

Among the clefts were Bishārīn with their cattle, while overhead large desert birds were circling. After a further two hours' trek, through valleys surrounded by hills, there opens out a long wide hill-flanked plain. This plain is covered by tall yellow grass, almost giving the impression of a field of ripened corn. It is a continuation of the great Wādī Laiameb, which is to the north on the way to Ariab. To the south-west, Jabal Ofik was becoming visible. After another four hours we climbed a hill and, between the small heights enclosing the *wadi* below, we could make out a long strip of golden yellow in the far distance stretching away towards the horizon. These were the sand-hills, where Obak wells are situated. After five hours, we descended the sombre Ofik and Rawai mountains, in a west-south-westerly direction, and reached a large plain named To-Karaiet, where we spent the night.

After Kokreb, the road splits into two branches. So far we have described the one taking a south-south-westerly direction; now we shall describe the one that runs west-south-west.

We passed the great plain of Lagag-Auey (or Eiameeb [?Ayamab]) and left the peaks of Badab to our right. In two-and-a-half hours we arrived at the great mass of granite, which rises in the form of a tower on a large base. We left this to the left and entered the Wādī Yomga through a series of hills. Before entering it, we had a fairly extensive view of the mountains surrounding us; to the north-east, we saw the chain of the Badab; to the north-west there is the Bokmaleb mountain; to the south-west in the distance we can just make out Mismar; to the south-east Rawai, and almost due east the chain of the Kokreb.

Wādī Yomga begins from a valley extending along the foot of Jabal Badad, in a north-easterly direction. We crossed the wādī in six hours, after which we came across the dry bed of a stream, which led us due west; the vegetation begins to flourish and as we stepped forward, the shrubs gave way to trees.

Here we were, then, at the bottom of the valley at Bīr Ariab. Two acacias, with trunks of amazing thickness (five metres circumference) and proportionate height, attracted our attention. The well nearby was wide and deep, and its water was the clearest that we found throughout the entire journey, but had little taste. Each day numerous caravans halt at this spot. Two government guards maintain order and security. Ariab is considered to be half-way between Sawākin and Berber. Jabal Ariab to the south, and Jabal To Nakadoi to the north, enclose this so-called wādī. Several valleys branch out from here, mostly with rich and flourishing vegetation. We kept to the south-westerly road, through hills and the Durumga valley (or Bey Deroo), which is enclosed by the mountains of the same name. Then came Wādī Baraud (or Berood), always towards the south-west. A narrow and quite difficult road wend-ing through two chains of mountains, led us to the valley of Mashuwa. After about two hours we found ourselves in the Wādī Kamoieb, we saw Jabal Ofik and Guratt to the west-south-west, whilst to the right in a corner, we could make out the isolated Shakrib, which can also be seen in the distance as one comes from Berber. Another short walk over the isolated hills, and here we were in the Wādī Laiameb. This wādī is large, and there are numerous wells to be found in it. The stream beds of the Laiameb all join, and during the rainy season pour their waters to the east of Jabal Ofik; towards the north-west, skirting the foot of Jabal Shakrib, the waters cross the great plain between Obak and Berber, and find their way into the Nile.

According to Dr. Schweinfurth, the areas of the Rawai belong hydrographically to the Nile, with their waters merging in Wādī Laiameb. The *panicum turgidum* and the selem acacia cover the ground of the wādī. Having passed the Ofik plain near Jabal Ofik and Jabal Takarireb, we arrived at a hill which is also named Takarireb, because it was here that a Takrūrī [5] died of thirst on his return from Mecca, after having vainly searched for water in the Obak wells.

Here we picked up our road to Rawai, and continued along it. The plain, which at first was barren but then well-covered in shrubs, was crossed in two-and-a-half hours. The sandhills got bigger and bigger, until they were half as high as the grass, then bigger and bigger again until the grass was entirely covered — while finally the shrubs themselves disappeared from view. The wells, which are very numerous, are found at the foot of these hills; I counted some twenty. The water is cleaner than that of Laiameb, and other wādīs, which are fed by streams. In two hours, we crossed the sandhills. There are no proper roads. Although nature has fitted camels with special feet, even they kept sinking into the sand. The height of these hills above sea-level varies between 417 and 454 metres. From these heights the isolated Jabal Eremit can be seen to the south-east.

After five hours walk through a barren plain, we passed the two Eremit hills which looked like real hermits [6] in this vast and poor plain. Another half an hour further on and to our right, we came across the granite obelisk, 35 feet high and named Abū Odfa ['Utfa]. It stands on a narrow base, and has the appearance of an upturned pear.

Always continuing to the south-west, we passed the Wādī Eremit. For twelve or fourteen hours, the country from Obak was completely barren. This is followed by the rich Wādī Abū Kolod (Koloda) which has its maximum depression between Obak and Berber. Here too the waters which meet during the rainy season form lagoons or small lakes. Already we could see the mountains of Berber, which lie on the

---

[5] Takrūrī (plural *Takārīr, Tukārna*), used by Arabic-speakers in the Sudan for any African whose origin is west of Dār Fūr. There were considerable settlements of Takārīr at al-Qallābāt, Kasala and other places.

[6] *Eremiti* (plural), Italian for hermits — a play on words.

left bank of the Nile. After three hours we crossed a small section of the
very rich Wādī Abū Salām, where, in autumn, *durra* flourishes prolifi-
cally; the fields of *durra*, and the varieties of wild acacia (*salem acacie*)
extend as far as Jabal Dogwaya to the south-east. In three hours from
there we came across the well of Abū Tagger, or Bīr Mahū Bey. [7]
Finally, after a trek of a hundred hours, the *fata morgana*, which right
from the wells of Obak, between nine in the morning and five in the
evening, conjured up visions of date palms, lakes, and rivers with shady
banks and woods, became at last a reality. Here we were, then, at the
end of our desert journey: at Berber, called by Arabs al-Mikhayrif.
It was ten o'clock in the morning on 24 February 1876.

[7] Named after an early military area commander of Berber, Mahū (short for
Muhammad) Bey Urfali (d. 1828), a Kurd, respected by the Sudanese for
his justice and benevolence.

INDEX

Abayo village, 254, 255

Abbadie, A.T.d', geographer, 80n., 107, 107n

'Abbās Pasha, viceroy of Egypt, 6, closed gold workings at Qaysān, 214-16

'Abbās Ibrāhīm Muhammad 'Alī, cited, 2n

Abialang Dinka tribe, 15, 130, 135

Abiong/Abujo Dinka tribe, 135, 150, 154, 172

Abrè, refreshing drink, 234, 234n

Abū Harāz village, 32, 252

Abū Jarīd, People of, 219-20n., 229-34

Abū Rūf tribe, raided Dinka, 130, 151n.; Beltrame among, 248

Abū Shanab, 225, 227

Abū Sinn, Shaykh, 254; village. See al-Qadārif

Abū 'Utfa, granite rock, 319

Abū Zaghulī village, 229

Abujo, Abuyo, See Abiong

Acacia, wild, Selem acacia, 251, 254, 319, 320

Adansonia tree. See Baobab

Adar, Khawr, 141

Agar Dinka tribe, 130, 134, 135

Agarian, Mgr. A., Mechitarist abbot general, 5

Agati, P., lay brother, 9

Agnarquei Dinka tribe, 130, 135

Agot Dinka tribe, 197

Agriculture, 250

Ahmad Aghā, Jabal, 63, 63n., 131, 142, 160, 162, 168

Ahmad Efendī, 49

Ahmad Pasha Abū Adhām, governor general, 1, 34, 34n

Akhū ikhwān, al-banāt, 221, 265

'Alī Aghā, 53

'Alī Efendi, government official, 49, 51

'Alī Khūrshīd Pasha, governor general, 31

'Alī, Rās, 210, 210n

Aliab Dinka tribe, 54, 61-2, 108, 134, 152, 155

Almagià, R., geographer, 74

Alok/Allok, a fruit, 134, 134n, 151, 156, 156n

Alwal Dinka tribe, 197

Ambatch tree, aeschynomene elaphroxylon, 141, 177

Andreis, A., mother superior, Dilling mission, 27

'Anqarīb/Angereeb, bed, 43, 43n, 44, 226, 291, 299

Angwara, See Nyangwara

Angwen, chief of, 54; village, 59

Antimony, cosmetic, 44

Ant-bite and preventative, 209

Arab settlements in Equatorial regions, 95, 95n, 122, 122n

Ariab, locality, 316-8

Arnaud Bey, J.P.d'., French engineer, 2, 66, 66n

Arol Dinka tribe. See Agar

Asp, dangerous, 208-9

'Assār village, 254

Association of the Good Shepherd, 19

Aswan/Assouan, 262, 263

'Atash, Jabal, 253

Atwot Dinka tribe, 134, 172

Aurelin, chief of the (?) Chioko tribe, 94

Awliyā, Jabal, 129, 129n

Azande/Niam — Niam, tribe, 113, 121-3, 283n; reputation for cannibalism, 120, 120n

Bāba, Khawr, 243

Bahnholzer, Fr. L., 28

Bahr al-Ghazāl, 133, 141

Bahr al-Zarāf, 132-3, 141-2, 151

Baker Pasha, Sir S.W., vi, cited, 17, 18

Bāmyā/okra, hibiscus esculentus, 124

Banī Shanqūl, district, 11, 207, 237, 240, 245

Bano, Fr. L., cited, 109
Baobab tree, *adansonia digitata*, 226, 258, 285, 293
Baqqāra tribes, 21, 21n., 56, 57, 133, 151; buy horses at al-Qallābāt, 256; Humr, 284-5
Barābra, tribe, 159n., 261-2, 264-6
Bari tribe, 12, 61-73, 80n, 178-81; customs, 100-5; dances, 185-8; famine, 110, 110n; huts, 191-2; inheritance, 191; language, 136; mountains, 142; occupations, 182-3; origin, 112-13; ornaments, 66; religion, 99; war, 181-2, 189; weather, 143-5
Barīs, village. *See* al-Buraysh
Barnabò, Cardinal A., 14, 14n, 15
Bartoli, P., lay brother, 19
Beads, varieties, 90, 113, 121, 121n, 125
Beer Dinka tribe, 135, 137n
Beir/Beri/Böri, tribe, 85, 85n, 103, 112, 113
Beltrame, Fr. G., 8, 11, 12, 14, 15, 26; biographical note, 35, 129; Blue Nile, 219-48; Dinka grammar 35; Khartoum in 1853, 35-38; Nubia, 261-79; White Nile, 129-39
Beny Dit, title of Nuer chief, 148
Berber, 21, 22, 261, 262; Carcereri at, 308-9; Kuruskū road, 303-8; Massaia at, 308-9; Sawākin road, 313-20
Beri. *See* Beir
Berta, language, 242, 336; Mts., 237, 242-3
Bibi R., 117
Bilād al-Jarīd, Lands of the Date Palm, 267
Bilinyang/Belinian/Belinyan village, 67, 69, 74-105 *passim,* 110, 112, 137, 145, 181
al-Birka, 284, 285n
Bisaysa, biscuit, 269, 269n
Bishārīn/Bishāriyīn, tribe, 262-4, 314, 317
Blondeel van Cuelebroeck, E., Belgian consul general, 1, 31

Blue Nile, *See* Nile
Blumenbach, J.F., cited, 265
Bonaventura, Fr., 19
Bonomi, Fr. L. 21, 25, 27
Bor Dinka tribe, 55, 62, 133, 135, 140, 152, 155, 168
Bosco, Fr. A. Dal, 12, 19, 26, 263; biographical note, 38; Khartoum in 1858, 38-41
Brinowitzer, stimulant, 118, 118n
Brown, R., cited, 18
Brun-Rollet, J.A., 6, 195; biographical note, 131n
Buckwheat, *fagopyrum esculentum,* 198
Bullrush millet, *pennisetum typhoideum,* 120n
Bunit/Bonit/Punit, diviner, 99, 100, 115, 117, 122
al-Buraysh village, 229
Burgotschi, Bari chief, 110n
Burial customs, 125, 195, 201-2, 223-4, 228
Burma, basin, a measure of grain, 299
Buwayda al-Qalʻa village, 32, 252-3

Camel, description and kinds, 272-9,
Camillian missionaries, 19   [305
Caprini, M., Sister, 27
Carcereri, Fr. P.S., biographical note, 283; in Blue Nile valley, 207-18; in Kurdufān, 19, 21, 21n, 25n, 280-92; Sawākin-Berber road, 313-20
Casolani, Mgr. A., 2-4, 10
Casoria, Fr. L. da, 19
Castagnaro, Fr. A., 8
Castelbolognesi, A., 15
Cattle, disease, 115, 115n; love of Dinka for, 159-60
Chibuk, *çubuk,* pipe, 36, 230, 263, 277
Children, abandoned, 190-191; breast feeding, 165
Chincarini, Sister C., 27
Choko tribe, 94, 95
Cic/Kich, Dinka tribe, 15, 58-61; 133, 135, 162, 167, 169-70; de-

scription, 152-3; welcome Vinco, 76, 108

Cicatrization, tattooing, 44, 125, 149, 153, 180, 201, 227, 265

Circumcision, female, 265; male, 201, 201n, 221, 234

Climate, 142-3

Clot Bey, A.B., 215, 215n

Colquhoun, Sir R.G., consul general, 15

Comboni, Bp. D., 4, 14, 15, 18, 28, 287n; arrival in Sudan, 12, 130n; Berber, 21, 22; death, 25-6; enthusiasm for geography, vi; health precautions, vii; Kurdufān, 25n, 20-1, 23-5, 283; White Nile, 14, 133

Comets, herald disaster among Dinka, 169

Copper, 108, 124

Corsi, Sister, 27

Cream fruit, 3

Crocodiles, 303, 309-10

Cuaka, Bari chief, 110n

Cubuk/Chibuk, 36, 263. *See also* Pipe

Custard apple/qishta, *annona reticulata,* 3, 253

Dafafung/Tafafan. *See* Ahmad Aghā, Jabal

al-Damazīn village, 229

Darabukka, kind of drum, 222

Date palm juice, 268

Dates, culture, 266-72

Delen. *See* Dilling

Delī Mehmed, Egyptian officer, 235, 237

Dellagiacoma, Fr. V., cited, 109

Denab, Arab and European name for Shilluk capital, 132n, 147

Den Did, Dinka deity, 170

Dhahab, Khawr al-, 243

Dhanab, al-Kalb, Jabal, 255

Dichtl, Fr. J., cited, 3, 28

Didinga tribe, 89n

Dihn, fat, oil, 292

Dilling/Delen, Jabal, 294; mission station, 20-2, 27; Carcereri at,

286-90; description, 293-4

Dilong, Bari dish, 81

Dindir R., 220, 246

Dinka, Jabal. *See* Jabalayn

Dinka tribe, customs, 153-75, 198-203; description, 135, 150-1, 197-8; fishing, 175-6; marriage, 200-1; Nuer, Shilluk and Arabs harrass, 130-1; on Blue Nile, 208; on source of Sobat, 243; slaves 251

Dissibil, well, 315

Doka, Bari chief, 79, 83; village, 254, 255

Dōm palm, 119, 134

Dovjak, Fr. M., 6-8, 26

Dragoman, interpreter, 57, 57n, 62, 73

Dropsy, 98

Dukhn, *pennisetum americanum,* bullrush millet, 120, 120n, 278; pastry, 288

Dulayb/Dolieb, palm, 198, 255, 285, 299, 299n

Dungjo/Dungiol, Dinka tribe; 135, 136, 150

Durra (for *dhura*), millet, 10, 114, 114n, 120, 120n, 156, 178, 250; Egyptians introduced white variety, 103

Earthquakes in Bari country, 138, 139, 144-5

Efendī in charge of camel transport, 304-5, 308

Elephant, harm crops, 115; hunting, 104-5, 117, 119, 121, 168, 210; man descended from, 120; village of elephants, 120

Elephantiasis, filarial, 120n

Emin (i.e. Muhammad Amīn) Pasha, 27, 220

Erba, Jabal, 315

Ethiopians at al-Qallābāt, 255-6

Euphorbia abyssinica, Arabic *shajarat al-samm,* tree, 134, 316

Euphorbia officinalis, 179, 316

Fadasi, 216, 235

al-Fadlī, Shaykh, 241
Famaka village, 208, 209, 235, 246, 257, 258
Faqīh/Feki, teacher of Islam, 37, 37n, 227, 224, 228, 237, 224n, 310n
Faqīr, Fakir, 297
Fashoda, town, 132n
Fath Allāh, servant, 229
Fāzūghlī, 209, 210, 216, 235, 237, 257
Feki, see *Faqīh*
Fertīt, Dār, 251
Fishermen despised, 185
Fishing, Cic, 60; Dinka, 175-6
Flags on Nile ships, 49n
Franceschini, Fr. G., 19, 20, 287, 287n
Franciscan Order, 16-18, 263
Franz-Joseph, Emperor, aid to missions, 5, 54
Fu'ād I, King of Egypt, 249

Galla, country, 90, 207-218 *passim;* merchants, 239-40
Gessi Pasha, R., 24-5
Gew Kwathker wad Akwat, Shilluk King, 147
Geyer, Bp. F.X., 196
Ghulfān, Jabal, 25, 293
Gienghe. *See* Dinka
Giovanni, lay brother, 19
Giusto da Urbino, Fr. G.I., 311, 311n
Ghiel. *See* Nyiel
Gok Dinka tribe. *See* Ngok
Gold, dust for exchange, 134; tax, 237; workings at Qaysān, *see* Qaysān
Gondokoro Mission, 7, 113, 128, 142-3; abandonment, 15-17; foundation, 11; fracas between Bari and traders, 8-9
Good Mothers of Negroland, 21
Gordon Pasha, C.G., governor general, 23, 24, 26, 315-16
Gostner, Fr. J., 14, 36
Grancelli, Prof. G. cited, 26
Grant, Lt.-Col. J.A., explorer, v,

32n, 48, 106
Gray, Prof. R., cited, 8n
Gregory XVI, Pope, 1
Ground nuts, Arabic *fūl sūdānī,* 121, 198
Guinea worm, *farendit,* 98
Gugo, granary, 103, 183, 192
Gumberi, interpreter, 53
Gumuz tribe, 227
Gwandoka, Bari chief, 96
Gwara-Kolmion, Beri chief, 88

Hadrian, Fr. P.G., 20
Hamad Asūsa, shaykh, 285n
Hamilton, J., cited, 12
Hansal, M.L., mission teacher, then Austrian consul, Khartoum, 6, 8, 11
Hareitri, Wadi, 315-16
Harnier, W. von, German sportsman, 14
Hasan, Prof. Y.F., cited, 129n
Hawāzma tribe, 285
Heglig (Arabic *hajlīja*), *balanites aegyptiaca,* tree, 198, 251, 252, 254
Henriot, Fr. L., 25, 27
Herodotus, 265
Heuglin, T. von, Austrian consul, Khartoum, 6
Hicks Pasha, Gen. W., 27
Hill, R.L., cited, 151n, 251n
Hillelson, S., cited, 219, 220, 220n
Holy Cross mission, 13, 133, 135, 143, 173; abandoned, 15, 178; description, 17; founded, 8, 12
Honkong, chief, 240
Huber, Fr. O., cited, 109
Hufrat al-Nahas, copper mine, 108
Humr. *See* Baqqāra tribes

Iban, Loudo chief, 97
Ibrāhīm Pasha, viceroy of Egypt, 2, 49, 210n
Ibrāhīm wad Ibrāhīm al-Qandalāwī, Takrūrī chief of al-Qallābāt, 31n
Ibrāhīm Khayr, 34
Ichneumon, waral, 186, 317

Igushok/Yugosuk, chief, 111, 128
Illiberi, *See* Libo
Imatong Mts., 90, 90n
Ingassana tribe, 208, 211-12, 218, 227
Iron, deposits near Yei, 124; extraction and smelting, 63, 65-6, 69-70, 93-4, 192-3; for exchange; 184; rings for adornment, 103, 115, 298; ironsmiths despised, 94, 185, 193; immunity from attack, 84
Ismā'īl Haqqī Pasha, governor general, 198
Ismā'īl Pasha, son of Muhammad 'Alī Pasha, 240-41

Jabalayn/Jebelein/Jabal Dinka, 63, 108, 108n, 130, 140, 142
Jallāba (Arabic, sing. *Jallāb*), itinerant traders, 38; armed raiders, 197, 197n; buy gold dust, 243
Jallābīya, long skirt, 298
Jāmūs, Khawr al-, 243
Janna, Khawr al-, 235, 243
Jār al-Nabī, religious teacher, 129, 129n
Jazīra, description, 249, 252
Jieng. *See* Dinka
John IV, Emperor of Ethiopia, 215
Johnston, Sir. H.H., vi
Jok, Dinka divinity, 172, 173
Jubek, Shobek, Bari rain chief, 51, 65, 67, 77-79, 82, 83
Judda/Jeddah, 254, 313, 314
Jummayza, *ficus sycomorus*, tree, 254, 258, 285
Juoc, Bari divinity, 99

Kaka village, 16, 131
Kākamūt, *acacia polyacantha*, subsp. *campylacantha*, tree, 134
Kakum, *kojur* of Dilling, 287
Kan, Nuer chief, 75
Karīm Khān, 268
Karkadè. See Laka
Karkūj/Kerkog, village, 225, 228
Karoka/Karakra, tribe, 89, 89n, 91
Kaufmann, Fr. A., 7, 8, 11, 16, 26;

biographical note, 140; the White Nile and its people, 133, 140-95
Kerabombi, chief of the Kwenda tribe, 94, 95
Kereki Mts., 69
Khālid Pasha Khusrū, governor general, 5, 53, 53n, 56
Khartoum, canal proposed on southern perimeter, 33, 33n; fever; 24, 310-12; in 1843, 31-5; in 1853, 35-8; in 1858, 38-41; in 1881, 41-44; mission, 9, 10, 18, 26, 34-36, 39-42
Khayr al-Dīn Pasha, 6
Kich. *See* Cic
Kinyeti Mt., 90n, river, 88n
Kirchner, Mgr. M., 13, 15, 16, 26, 263
Kiri village, 209-10, 217, 218, 235, 246
Kisra, a kind of bread, 222, 251, 286, 286n
Kleinheinz, G., lay brother, 15
Knoblecher/Knoblehar, Mgr. I., pro-vicar, 2-13, 26, 28, 36, 107; biographical note, 47-8; on White Nile, 47-54, 55-73; 137, 142
Koch, L., lay brother, 10
Kocijancic, Fr. J., 6, 8
Kohl, Fr. I., 8, 9
Kojur, diviner, 59, 287, 294-297
Kokrayb/Kokreb, well, 316-18
Kovalevski, Col. E.P., 207, 213n
Krurulung, tree and oil, 179
Kurdufān/Kordofan, province, P.S. Carcereri in, 284-92; missions, 19, 20-2; slave trade, 25
Kuruskū, 303-305; desert, 305-308
Kwenda tribe. *See* Quenda

Lado, chief of the Irye, 97
Lado, Jabal/Nyarkanyi Mt., 63, 69, 97, 136, 136n, 137, 137n
Laka, *hibiscus sabdariffa*, Karkadè, refreshing drink from, 114, 114n
Lakoya tribe, 83, 97, 100, 103
Lanz, Fr. J., 11, 13, 14, 16; biographical note, 133n

Laot/Leot, grain, 103, 114, 114n

Leghe/Lege, Bari chief, 51, 112

Leghr (?Lugor), Lirya chief, 97

Lejean, G., French traveller, cited, 7

Le Moyne, A., consul general of France, Egypt, 7n, 106, 106n

Lenchok, Marju chief, 97

Leot, *elusine coracana,* 103, 114, 114n

Leri/Lori, drum, not dance, 15

Libo/Illibari, village, 7, 137

Lips, perforation, 125

Lirya/Liria, Mts., 87, 112, 113; tribe, 90, 111-13

Locatelli, lay brother, 27

Locusts, 251

Lodovico, lay brother, 19

Logopi tribe, 96

Lokusek/Logushek, Bari chief, 52

Logwaya Mts., 70; tribe

Logwek, Mt. and village, 51, 69, 142, 178

Logwit-lo-Lado, F., 10

Lokidi, Bari chief, 79

Lokoya. *See* Logwaya

Losi, Fr. G., 27

Lotus seeds, *helumbium,* 178

Loudo tribe, 83, 87, 98

Luac Dinka tribe, 153n

Lungasuk/Longashu, Bari traveller, 122

Luqma (Arabic = titbit) sweetmeat, 226, 226n; date palm juice, 268

Lutweri, Bari chief, 7

Makedo/Machedo, rapids and town, 96

Madanī Shanbūl, shaykh, 251

Madi tribe, 96-7

Mahdist movement, 26-8

Mahrāra, hors d'oeuvre, 247, 247n

Mahū Bey, well, 320, 320n

Makaraka/Makarayang tribe. *See* Azande

Makhāda, ford: Makhādat Abū Zayd, 141; Makhādat al-'Anza, 141; Makhādat al-Kalb, 141

Makk, title of certain tribal chiefs, 257, 257n

Malaria, 42, 42n, 309, 309n

Malbes. *See* Mulbas

Malwal Dinka tribe, 137n, 201n

Mandara, Jabal, 129

Marayq, a kind of millet, 288, 290

Mardrūs, Fath Allāh, 311, 312

Maremo, village, 96

Mariani, G., lay brother, 27

Marien-Verein, Austrian missionary society, 5, 10, 11

*Marīsa/*Merissa, millet beer, 57, 77, 79, 88, 89, 295, 299

Marju/Margiù, village, 76, 97

Marno Bey, E., 283, 283n

Marriage, among Bari, 104, 188-9; among Dinka, 200-1; in Sinnar, 221-3; in Yeī valley, 121

Martini, Fr. G., 24; biographical note, 249; Nuba Mts., 293-9; al-Qallābāt and Fāzūghlī, 22, 242-58

Marzano, Fr. V.P., 25

al-Masallamīya, town, 249- 251-252

Masherbon, Beri chief, 88

Massaia, Cardinal L.G., 6, 7, 240; biographical note, 106; Khartoum to Fāzūghlī, 207-18; Kuruskū to Khartoum, 303-12; White Nile basin, 106-8

al-Matamma, frontier post, 31, 211, 215, 255, 257

Matat, chief, 112, 117

Matteucci, P., cited, 24

Mazza, Fr. N., 3, 38

Mede/Medi, Bari chief, 110n, 111, 186

Mege, clay used for toilet preparations, 101

Melly, G., English traveller, 3, 3n, 4

Melotto, Fr. A., 12, 14, 15, 130, 130n, 135

Menelik II, Emperor of Ethiopia, 310

Meroe, ruins, 308

Metempsychosis, 224-225

Miani, G. explorer, vi, vii

Milharcic, Fr. M., 6, 8

Millet. *See Durra*

Mimosa

Mislat/Misslad, R., 97

Mitterrutzner, Prof. J.C., 10, 10n, 35

Molot, hoe, 125, 198

Montuori, Fr. L., biographical note, 31; Khartoum in 1843, 1, 31-5, 210n

Monye, tribal elder, 111, 113-28

Morlang, Fr. F., vi, 11, 16, 17, 26; biographical note, 109; east and west of Gondokoro, 14, 14n, 109-28, 137

Moru, locality, 126

Mountains of the Moon, 95, 95n

Mozgan, Fr. B., vii, 6-8, 10, 12, 142, 143, 160

Mudīr, governor of a province, 254n, 257, 309, 312

Muhammad Aghā, 53-4

— Ahmad al-Mahdī, 26-8

— 'Alī Pasha, viceroy of Egypt and dependencies, 2, 12, 34, 38, 47; built Kiri, 209-10; established gold workings at Qaysān, 213, 214, 216, 240

— Asūsa. *See* Hamad Asūsa

— Bey Urfali, 320n

— Efendī, director of mining operations, Qaysān, 213

— Muhammadayn, 314

— al-Nūr b. Dayfullāh, biographer, cited, 219, 219n

— Ra'ūf Pasha, governor general, 25

— Sa'īd Pasha, viceroy of Egypt, 263

Mulāh, stew, 222, 251

Mulbas/Malbes, agricultural station, 22, 27

Murhāka, millstone, 299

Murrāt wells, 308, 308n

Mūsā, Jabal, 129

Musā'id, Fekī, 224, 240, 241, 246

Nabak (Arabic *nabaq*), *ziziphus spina-christi,* tree, 134, 151, 251, 252, 252, 256

Natterer, J., Austrian consul, Khar-toum, 6

Na'ūm Bey Shuqayyir, cited, 220n

Nebel, Fr. A., cited, 109

Ngok Dinka tribe, 134, 136, 153n, 201n, 256

Niam-Niam tribe. *See* Azande

Nile, Blue, travels of G. Beltrame, 219-48; G. Martini, 249-58; L.G. Massaia, 207-18

— White, 112, 126, 136, 137; annual trading expedition, 49, 56, 56n; cataract, 68-9, 125; fords, 141; levels, 138, 143, 144; source, 94-97

Nimr Muhammad Nimr, *makk* of Shandi, 241

Nuba, customs, 290-2, 298-9; mountains, 25, 283-99

Nubia in 1861, 261-279

Nubian desert, Massaia's account of, 303-9; language, 262

Nuer tribe, 58; description, 135, 148-50; welcomed Vinco, 75-6

Nun, Bari divinity, 99

Nuqud, trader's agent, 122

Nyagi tribe, 90

Nyangwara/Jangbara, etc., tribe, 97, 115, 123-5, 153; language, 14

Nyarkanyi Mt., *See* Lado, Jabal

Nydhok, Shilluk king, 132

Nyiel/Gniel, Dinka tribe, 135

Nyigilò, Bari notable, 8-10, 51, 52, 181, 191; death, 111n, 194-5; relations with missionaries, 64-70 *passim,* 76-92 *passim*

Nymati Mt. *See* Jabalayn

Obak well, 317, 319, 320

Obeid. *See* al-Ubayyid

Ohrwalder, Fr. J., 24, 27, 28

Oliboni, Fr. F., 11, 12, 18

Olive, wild, *olea hochstetteri,* 179n

'Osman Multāzim, 314, 314n

Otao well, 315

Owen, Col. R.C.R., cited, 10n

Panicum turgidum, 317, 319

Panyamok, chief of Tambura, 128

Papyrus, *Cyperus papyrus,* 58n

Pedemonte, Fr. E., 2, 5; biographical note, 55; on White Nile, 51, 52, 55-73, 107, 108

Penazzi, Count L., cited, 13, 26

Peney, A., principal medical officer, 11, 224-5

Pesavento, Sr. E., 27

Petherick, J. British trader, vice-consul, Khartoum, 4, 113, 113n

Pfeifer, Fr. F., 16, 18

Piaggia, C., hunter, explorer, 283, 283n

Pie Madri di Nigrizia, 21

Pipe, tobacco, 36, 36n, 225, 263

Pircher, Fr. L., 11

Pitia, Pitah, Bari chief, 80n, 96

Pius IX, Pope, 6

Polinari, D., lay brother, 19, 27

Poncet, A. and J., traders, 9

Prostitution, 189

Prout, Bey, H.G., map, 313

Punok, diviner, 193-4

Pygmies, 266

al-Qadārif/Gedaref/Abū Sinn, village, 22, 24, 31, 253-5, 312

Qa'im maqām, assistant to a *kāshif,* 31

al-Qallābāt, village, 31, 254; description, 255-6

Quasce/Kwashe, Sr., 27

al-Qamr, Jabal, 95, 95n

Qashsh, reeds, 252, 255

Qaysān, gold workings, 211, 213-16, 235-46; Khawr, 243

Qishta. See Custard apple

Quinine, 42n, 211, 309-11

Qurūd, Jabal. *See* Ummat Qardūd

Qwenda tribe, 94-6, 103

al-Rāhad, R., 252

Rahat, girl's loin fringe, 44, 147, 154, 180

Ra'īs, ship's navigator, 68, 68n, 304

Rajjāf/Regaf, rapids, 68-69; village, 69

Rakūba, straw shade, lean-to, 120, 234, 234n, 235

Ramla, Khawr al-, 243

Ra's al-Fīl, Jabal, 255

Rats, delicacy among Bari, 102

Regnotto, O., lay brother, 25, 27

Regong, Mt., 127-8

Reinthaler, Mgr. J., Pro-Vicar, 15, 16

Reitz, C., Austrian Consul, Khartoum, 6, 310, 310n

Rek Dinka tribe, 201n

Repetti, Fr. G., 4

Reth, title of king of Shilluk, 146; monopoly of ivory and giraffe tails, 147

Richarn *(sic),* exemplary boy, 17

Ritter, C., cited, 4

Rolleri, Fr. B., biographical note, 41; Khartoum in 1881, 41-4

Rosignoli, Fr. P., 22, 27

al-Rusayris/Roseires, village, 208, 209, 225-9, 258

Russegger, J. von., Austrian mineralogist, 213n

Ryllo, Mgr. M., Pro-Vicar, 2, 3, 6, 35-40

Saat, impeccable lad, 17

Sa'īd Aghā, chief of Dilling, 20

Salāma, Coptic Archbp. of Ethiopia, 210

Salīm Qapūdān, naval officer, explorer, 2, 33n., 66n, 106

Sand, effect on transport, 307, 307n

Sandstorm on Berber - Kuruskū road, 306-7

Sant/sunt, tree, 229; timber for boat building, 50

Santandrea, Fr. S., cited, v

Santoni, L., postal official, cited, 23

Sape, clay pot, 119

Sāqiya, water wheel, 33, 253

Sawākin/Suakim, port, 313-14; Berber road, 313-20; school opened, 27-8

Scalabrini, G.B., Bp. of Piacenza, 41

Schlatter, Fr. H., 18

Schreiner, G.F., Baron von, 263, 263n

Schweinfurth, G., explorer, cited, 266, 319

Sembiante, Fr. G., cited, 74
Serao, Fr. G., 1
Serut fly, 108
Sesame, *sesamum indicum,* oil seed, 103, 116, 178
al-Shallāl, mission house, 15-19
Shambe village, 142, 142n
Shandaloba, Shaykh, 224-5
Shandi/Shendi, village, 240, 241, 309
Shea butter tree, 156n
Shenuda, Coptic trader, 122n
al-Sharīf, village, 229
al-Sharīf Hasan, trader, 2, 3
Shilluk tribe, 50, 56-8, 131- 6; description, 146-8; slaves, 251
Shindiru, locality, 96
Shir/Chir/Zhier, tribe, 51-4, 62-4, 76, 108, 136, 140, 178
Shobek. *See* Jubek
Shukkāba, wall of straw, 234, 235
Singe village, 238-9, 242, 244, 246
Sinkat, town, 315
Sinnār, province, description, 220- 5; history, 312, 312n; town, 198
Sisters of the Apparition of S. Joseph, 19, 22-3
Slatin Bey, R.C., governor of Dār Fūr, 25
Slave trade, 25, 26; slavery 17, 18, 26, 54, 298; slaves in Khartoum, 2, 2n
Sleeping sickness, 115
Snakes, asp dangerous, boa constrictor less dangerous, 208-9; python a quiet neighbour, 202
Soba, ancient Christian site, 33, 303; finds, 311-12
Sobat, Nile tributary, 88n, 132, 140, 243, 243n; river rising in Imateng Mts., 88, 88n 90-1
Sogaro, Mgr. F., Bp., 27
Sollok (Arabic *Shulaq*) ring, 115
Sorur, Fr. D.D.F., 23; biographical note, 196; on the Dinka, 197- 203
Spaccapietra, V., Archbp. of Smyrna, 31, 31n

Spada, L., Italian engineer, 23
Specke, Fr. J.E., 27
Speke, Capt. J.H., explorer, v, 17, 17n, 32n, 48, 106
Stadel-Meyer, Fr. D., 18, 20
Stanley, H.M. explorer, vi
Stella Matutina, iron-hulled sailing dhahabiyya, 6, 9, 150
Stool, used by Bari chiefs, 64
Subek/Shobek/Shoba, Bari chief, 51, 65, 67
Sulayman Abu Zayd, *ra'is,* 68
Sunt. *See Sant*
Surayfa village, 235, 246
Surtuq, hollowed-out canoe, 114
Syphilis, 189

Tabi Mts. *See* Ingassana
Tafafan, Jabal. *See* Ahmad Aghā, Jabal
Tager (? Tāhir), saint, 315
Takrūrī, death, 31n, 319, 319n; shaykh of al-Qallābāt
Tamarind, *tamarindus indica,* tree, 198, 285; decoction of seeds, 211, 309
Tambura/Tombur village, 116, 126, 128
Tarciam channel, 131-2
Tattooing. *See* Cicatrization
Taylor, B., American traveller, cited, 13
Teeth, incisor, removal, 201
Telabūn, eleusine coracana, kind of millet, 114n
Theodore II, Emperor of Ethiopia, 210n
Tobacco, 36, 36n, 90, 103, 111, 114, 134, 136, 156, 162, 164, 164n, 178, 180, 183, 186, 225, 263
Tōkar, 28, 307n
Tokiman village, 9, 51, 68, 114, 128
Tome, Dinka musical instrument, 159
Tongun, Bari notable, 79
Trabant, Fr. O., 6-8
Trémaux, P., French traveller, 207
Trypanosomiasis, sleeping sickness, 115

Tuic Dinka tribe, 135, 151, 153, 155, 167
Tukul/tukl, kind of hut, 110n, 114, 288
Tumat, R., 213-15, 236-7, 243
Tūra al-Khadrā, locality, 20, 50
Tusicvien, Cic chief, 76
Tyet, Dinka medicine man, 172
Typhus dangerous at Khartoum, 310

al-Ubayyid/Obeid, mission, 22; town, 284, 287, 293
Ueberbacher, Fr. A., 10, 13, 190
Ulivi, N., Tuscan trader, 100, 107, 107n
Umba/Weri Benetit, elephant hunter, 117, 119, 123, 126
Umm sūf, echinochloa pyramidalis and *vassia cuspidata*, water plant, 58n
Ummat Qardūd/Qurūd, Jabal, 31, 32n, 253n
Urine as a substitute for salt, 174
'Ushar, *eusclapia*, Sodom apple, 315

Vaissière, Caterina, 34, 34n
Vantini, Fr. G., cited, 109
Vaudey, A., Sardinian vice-consul, Khartoum, trader, 9, 9n, 182
Vayssière, J.A. French trader, 219, 219n
Venereal disease, 189
Venturini, Sr. E., 27
Viehweider, Fr. F., 14
Vincentian/Lazarist, Order, 51, 52
Vinco, Fr. A. (Don Angelo), v, vi, 2, 3, 5-7, 51, 52, 55, 66, 71, 73; biographical note, 74; accompanied trading expedition to Bari country, 51; death, 74, 74n, 137; travels in Bari country and beyond, 74-106

Volcanoes, extinct, near Gondokoro, 145

Wad Dayfullāh, Biography, 129, 129n, 219, 219n
Wad al-Gharbī, shaykh of Banī Shanqūl, 237-45
Wad al-Shalā'ī, shipyard, 49, 50; southernmost Egyptian post, 107n
Wad al-Turābī village, 250, 258
Wakīl (Arabic), agent, deputy, 288
Wari, Beri chief, 88, 89
Waw, Shilluk village, 58; village on Jur R., 58n
Weyi village, 122
White Nile. *See* Nile
Winds, 139
Wischnewsky, A., lay brother, 20
Women, clothing, 244, 247; cosmetics, 44; dance, 296; in war, 181-2; inferior status, 164-6; village of, 120-1
Wurnitsch, Fr. M., 11

Yal, R., 141
Yangbara, *See* Nyangwara
Yawa, beer 77, 121, 145, 186
Yei, R., 14, 117, 124, 126, 153
Yirrol village, 119n
Yom Dinka tribe, 135

al-Zabala'āt, opprobrious term for People of Abū Jarīd, 231n
Zaghi, C., cited, 109
Zamzamīya, porous water container, 277, 277n
Zara, Fr. G., 4, 5, 56
Zarība, thorn fence or enclosure, 118, 123, 203, 251, 155
Zibet, civet cat, 186
Zilli, I., lay brother, 12
Zucchinetti, P.V., cited, 18